Is There a Sabbath for Thought?

John D. Caputo, *series editor*

PERSPECTIVES IN
CONTINENTAL
PHILOSOPHY

WILLIAM DESMOND

Is There a Sabbath for Thought?
Between Religion and Philosophy

FORDHAM UNIVERSITY PRESS
New York ■ 2005

Perspectives in Continental Philosophy Series, no. 45
ISSN 1089-3938

Library of Congress Cataloging-in-Publication Data

Desmond, William, 1951–
    Is there a sabbath for thought? : between religion and philosophy / William Desmond. — 1st ed.
        p.   cm. — (Perspectives in continental philosophy; no. 45)
    Includes bibliographical references and index.
    ISBN 0-8232-2372-8 (hardcover) — ISBN 0-8232-2373-6 (pbk.)
    1. Philosophy and religion.   I. Title.   II. Series.
    B56.D47   2005
    210—dc22   2005003801

Printed in the United States of America
07 06 05   5 4 3 2 1
First edition

To Carl Vaught, in admiration and friendship

By reason of the multitude of their oppressions, they make *the oppressed* to cry:
They cry out by reason of the arm of the mighty.
But none saith, Where *is* God my maker, who giveth songs in the night.

—Job 35:9–10

One more
Sunday in Savannah
Hear the whole creation shoutin'
Praise the Lord
See them flinging out the banner
While the congregation says amen

Young folk
Tendin' Sunday School
They sing merrilly 'bout the golden rule
Horse sense preaching all the day
They all hollar in the righteous way

It's time for me to call on Mother Hannah
While she sits there wishing for her last reward
One more Sunday in Savannah
One more Sunday in Atlanta
It's the same thing
Same feeling

Don't ya dare
go fishin' son

Amen

—Hugh MacKay, "Sunday in Savannah,"
as sung by Nina Simone

You can refute Hegel but not the Saint or the Song of Sixpence.

—W. B. Yeats

Contents

Preface and Acknowledgments

I remember a time when to mention God or religion in the company of advanced intellectuals was like mentioning sex in a prudish Victorian drawing room. An icy silence would descend, and the silence communicated more than overt argument possibly could: *we* do not now talk of these things. I have an acute memory of this—for it is within my living memory. And now? There are those I remember who danced in Dionysian sandals but who now wear the penitential rags of ethics. I know dancers who have become sandwich-board ad men for capitalist greed—handsomely waged for their conversion to what the times require. Times change. Yesterday's necessary truth becomes today's old hat; and neglected constancies of yesteryear are whirled around in the gyre, facing us once again, and everyone who's who must have his or her say. I am content. If the talk is about the most worthy things, who can carp. I dare to hope that perplexities about God and religion, as well as talk that has finesse, will again have their worthy time.

The chapters of this book reflect that hope. They are in the main ruminative essays that try to engage the reader in a style more meditative than allowed by the speedreading to which too many, if they read at all, aspire. The essays may be read independently. But they are ordered in a certain sequence that, I hope, calls forth resonances across the whole work, and in virtue of which none of the meditations is entirely self-standing. There is something musical to this, in that themes are stated and developed, only to go into recess, then to reemerge in a different form, and recall an earlier variation of the theme. More systematic philosophical resources are reserved but where I thought it helpful I have called them out of their recess. As a philosopher I have sought that hard and simple thing—to speak in a human voice—and not without some touch of *sprezzatura*.

Some of the chapters have appeared in earlier versions, versions significantly revised for their present publication. I am happy to acknowledge that a version of Chapter 2 appeared in *Hegel on the Modern World*, ed. Ardis Collins (Albany: State University of New York Press, 1995), 1–28; of Chapter 5 in *Vladimir Solov'ëv: Reconciler and Polemicist*, ed. Wil van den Bercken et al. (Leuven: Peeters, 2000), 185–210; of Chapter 6 in *Tijdschrift voor Filosofie* 61 (1999): 27–61; of Chapter 7 in *Courage*, ed. Barbara Darling-Smith (South Bend, Ind.: University of Notre Dame Press, 2002), 11–29; of Chapter 8 in *Irish Theological Quarterly* 3 (2000): 211–30; and of Chapter 9 in *Tijdschrift voor Filosofie* 63 (2001): 127–51.

I want to thank Merold Westphal who first suggested I collect some essays on philosophy and religion. I want to extend my thanks to Jack Caputo for his encouragement to publish them in the series he edits. I also want to thank Cyril O'Regan for the continuing generosity of his comments on my work. I am very grateful for the warm welcome that Helen Tartar, editorial director of Fordham University Press, has extended to my work. Finally, I dedicate this book to Carl Vaught from whom, as my teacher, I learned much about what it means to philosophize on the boundary between religion and philosophy.

Is There a Sabbath for Thought?

By Way of Introduction:
The Intimate Universal—Between Religion and Philosophy

The Intimate Universal

How speak of the space between religion and philosophy, how speak in that space? What are some of the questions, disconcertments, disquiets occasioned by that space between? What release or confinement—of thought itself, of reverence—is possible there? What enabling or endowing there? What provocation of one by the other? What agon between religion and philosophy, and what affinity or bond? What sleep and peace there, what poverty, or courage or enmity there? Is there a Sabbath for thought there?

These are some of the perplexities addressed in this book. They ask for thorough consideration, and they might be pursued in different ways. One way might be a more systematic exploration of the philosophy of religion, or of God. Such an exploration has its rights but this is not the occasion to undertake that exploration in its proper amplitude. Another way would be more meditative, dwelling on certain elemental experiences or happenings, or exposures that keep the soul alive to the enigma of the divine. The chapters of this book are written more in the spirit of this second way. They are meditative reflections on themes at the limit of systematic comprehension, reflections not devoid of systematic resources though these resources are not here put too much in the foreground.[1] A complex interweaving of systematic and nonsystematic considerations is entirely appropriate to that space between being religious and being philosophical. By way of introduction, I want to say something about this, as well as something about the different chapters themselves.

It is not easy to speak philosophically about religion or God, to find the right tone or register. One might claim that being religious, as ultimately the ultimate relation to God, makes seemingly contradictory demands on us: to remain true at once to what is *most intimate* in us, and what is *most universal*. Most intimate: for if the relation to God is not in the heart, is not the heart itself, do we not then deal with sounding brass and tinkling cymbal? Most universal: for if this singular relation is constitutive for, offered for all humans, it makes the most extreme demands on the promise of community. If that seemingly impossible togetherness of intimacy and universality is not enough, there are further complications. For philosophers have a tendency to shun what is intimate, as supposedly merely "subjective." This, in turn, is matched by a desire for a universality whose neutral homogeneity also spells difficulty for living community. Such a neutral or impersonal universal spells trouble for both the intimacy and community of being religious. Can one speak in such a way, speak in a *philosophical* way, that will neither betray the intimate nor desert the universal?

Consonant with this double solicitation of intimacy and universality, one might venture that when it comes to being religious the contrast of the "lover" and the "theorist" is important. "Lovers" participate in a way of being, "theorists" make of this way a theme for analysis. Lovers are passionate in their search and speech, theorists dispassionate and sober. Lovers esteem singularity and show it themselves; theorists value universality and selfless understanding. Among the lovers one might number Plato, Augustine, Bonaventure, Pascal, Kierkegaard, Nietzsche; among theorists, Aristotle, Aquinas, Descartes, Kant, and Hegel. Of course, this distinction needs qualification: thinkers without love are sterile, lovers without thought mindless. Philosophy is both: *philia* and *sophia*. Plato was a great thinker yet a philosopher of eros; Hegel, great champion of systematic reason, was not devoid of a kind of reverence. The "lovers" tend to be moved by (in Pascal's terms) the *esprit de finesse*, the "theorists"

---

[1] I hope to amplify on these resources more fully in a work in progress, entitled *God and the Between*.

are often tempted by the *esprit de géométrie*. There is something to be said for both. Many philosophers are a mixture here. Some are more like "theorists" who dissimulate a secret love, others more like "lovers" who keep in the background more theoretical considerations. Is there a position somewhere between these two? If so, I am somewhere there.

And yet there can be a tilt in this middle, and the tilt has to be toward the lover, necessarily so, I think, when it comes to being religious. Being philosophical in that middle space makes one mindful of the fragile ambiguity of being religious, and concerned about the possible sterility of "theory." If being religious is more intimate than philosophy with the sources of living that charge our lives with worth, perhaps it will take care of itself, or be taken care of, more fruitfully than philosophy. Maybe it is the fruitfulness of philosophy as a form of life that should worry us more—and especially if it has fractured its affiliation with being religious. But maybe this is to be of little faith—in regard to philosophy itself. For, of course, there is an older, premodern meaning of *theōria*, namely, a kind of delight in seeing, in knowing, and this is more like a "love" than the more modern sense of "theory," as a kind of instrumental hypothesis that gives us a "handle" on reality. Some practices of philosophy, like being religious, partake of that delight; some dissolve it.

When I was in love with my beloved, I sang my beloved. Now that I am not sure about my beloved, or my love, I begin to analyze my love, and I no longer sing. And what then do I love? So it is too often with philosophy. It is gray at its birth, and the green of life is already strange to it.

I note that philosophy of religion, as a distinct scholarly discipline, is a fairly recent invention, dating from around the end of the eighteenth century. An analogous invention might be "aesthetics," considered as a distinct philosophical specialty (commonly attributed to Baumgarten, 1714–1762). Not that philosophers were previously silent about art and beauty, or about the divine or God. Quite to the contrary, there are hardly any philosophers who did not in some way talk about God, even though none would have thought of themselves as "specialists" in the philosophy of religion. Similarly there is no aesthetics, say, in Plato, though he is deeply concerned with image and art and things aesthetic, and all in light of the pedagogic, psychological, metaphysical, and political implications of art. Yet there is something striking about the invention of philosophy of religion as a specialized field of studies: this seems to have occurred around the time that religion itself was coming under unprecedented assault by some of the leading "avant-garde" intellectuals of the West. As intellectuals stake their claim for autonomy from theological supervision, and, on a scale hitherto unknown, take atheism as a respectable, indeed necessary position, philosophy of religion is born among the intellectuals. We fall out of love with the divine and our loss was reborn as theory about what we have lost, and perhaps its impossibility in the first place. Out of this is born a diversity of academic approaches toward religion. Plenty of "theory," it seems, but where is the "love"? From where then will "theory" derive its own finesse? And what then does the philosopher love? The beloved? Or his intellectual specialization, perhaps really his own superior cleverness?

I do understand that many factors have influenced changes in attitudes to religion, especially in Western societies, some factors themselves religious. My brief here is not to give a genealogy of modernity in its sometimes equivocal, sometimes hostile relation to being religious, though I will offer a few remarks in the next section. In my own case, I cannot conceive how I might have become a philosopher *at all*, if my life, the life I shared with my family and native country, had not been permeated with religious seriousness, before ever questions of a philosophical nature emerged for me.

I grew up in an Irish Catholic family, in which, as was often the case, the piety of my mother was more expressed than my father's, which is not to say that this was not communicated in its quiet way. Religious life embraced the whole ethos of life. I spent some ten months as a Dominican novice, and that time is now another life to me, but it attests to concerns that have never left me. Some people now hate this past ethos of religious life, and especially hate it because of the position of ascendancy previously occupied so ostentatiously by the ecclesiastical powers. No doubt, there were hypocrisies and sly exploitations of will-to-power, and mindless adherence to external observances and the like. The reverence in which religion was held was abused as power by some priests. None must deny misdeeds done. But to reduce it to that alone would be a lie, however reprehensible this crime or that now being brought to light. If that earlier time were as contemptible as some now say, its people would be no less contemptible, and these contemptible people would be, for instance, my parents and their generation. Were they contemptible? They were not.

Not least, there was the cultivation of a certain reverence, a certain porosity to the elusive mystery of things, and most especially the enigma of the human being, and the *nec plus ultra* of mystery, God. So also there were sacramental rituals keeping open a space of porosity between the human soul and what ultimately exceeds it, even if also in intimate communication with it. This offered a way of dwelling in the world, with a nonliteralistic mindfulness, a poetry of the divine. As is to be expected on this score, some people had more delicatesse; there were always the aggressively wooden-headed; and, as with everything ambiguous, there were doors leading to madness here and there. And why not? Why does intelligence so quickly desert us when it comes to thinking about religion? Religion shows something great, but with all great things, there is great promise and great danger, if the finesse of the ultimate porosity to the divine is coarsened or corrupted.

To be in the happening of being religious is very hard to render in objective terms, and such a rendering may well contribute to the evaporation of being religious. If being religious is closer to a being in love than to any form of analytical thinking, it thrives on the chiaroscuro of life, not on the geometrical clarities on which more scientific thinking prides itself. If you entirely destroy the chiaroscuro of living, or seek to do so, you are attacking the roots out of which religion grows, and indeed many other peculiarly human happenings, such as, for instance, the making of art. There can be a clarity that is the enemy of human life in its univocalizing assault on the ambiguous matrix of creative life.

This is not to say that being religious is *only* something "existential." It is this most intimately, but as I have already suggested it may be that only in religion, nowhere else, is this intimacy of being brought into an obscure consonance with a sense of community that extends to the whole, even beyond the whole of immanence. Being religious is participation in what I would call the *intimate universal*.

Being religious is also undoubtedly something historically mediated, and in that respect inseparable from the gift of time, and not only with regard to the promise of the future and its generations, but also the manner in which our ancestors vanish, with their death, into the chiaroscuro of life. We are the beneficiaries of what they have passed on—or the victims, as the case may be. I suppose in modernity the more dominant feeling is of being the victim of history, over which one has had no say or control. More important, I would say, is the feeling of a certain receptiveness, of having been given something before doing something for oneself. This can seed a sense of our being grateful beneficiaries, and especially in relation to religion.

This orientation has become more and more difficult to sustain as the sweep of time is reduced to the immediacy of the televised sound bite; as the sense of individuality is contracted to the human being as a machine of appetite that adapts itself and seeks to maximize efficiently its options in the present; and as extraordinarily complex systems of the media, economics, and politics exploit all the cybernetic resources of our superior geometries to serve this contraction of time and the human being.

Religious people are sometimes said to be the enemies of time, and this is not without some element of truth, but I would offer a reverse view. A feel for time is very important, because it can help relativize us. It places us in relation to what exceeds our self-determination in the universal impermanence, and so chastens insolent hubris. Existential memory, historical memory, are each in an intimate relation to life itself as an intimacy of being lived from within. Both are at an angle to objectifying thinking, an angle hinting of what is greater than ourselves, and requiring finesse, not geometry. I am grateful that nameless sources of communication in my own life kept alive in me some glimmer of openness to these secret sources of finesse, though so many forces in our contemporary life drive relentlessly toward the stopping up of these sources. Philosophy purely as an argumentative technique that tries to stand alone can do almost nothing to help with this. Something prior has to be attended to, for the soul, as Plato reminded us long ago, needs its *periagoge*.

This is not to deny that there are systematic considerations also, but in terms of the historical memory of philosophy itself it is worth recalling that the originating occasion of philosophy is religious. I think of Socrates' response to the Delphic oracle. The oracle pronounces who is wisest, Socrates himself; Socrates accepts the oracle, but is perplexed as to its equivocity, for he knows he knows nothing; his philosophical seeking is born in this acceptance and perplexity. Without the acceptance, no perplexity; without the religious occasion, no searching. Though the search is both other to and continuous with what occasions it, the occasion is not merely occasional, but intimately enters the definition of what it precipitates. I think my own philosophical relation to being religious is something like that. The religious occasion precipitating philosophical perplexity enters immanently into the reflective unfolding of that perplexity. While there is a difference between being religious and being philosophical, there is an intimacy between them, and one is older than the other and a more nurturing source of an openness to ultimacy.

Life is before reflection, as "love" is before "theory," as religion is before philosophy. If the theorists are in love (yes, love) with a homogeneous, neutralizing universal, the lovers, even when open to the universal, never forget the singularity of particular loves in which something more is anchored and fleshed. Being religious is more like that love, and its language is more intimate than the neutral universal. If there is a universality here, it is one which has to love the intimacy of the singular. Philosophy has never been very comfortable with the latter, and perhaps less comfortable in much of modern philosophy than in ancient philosophy, which was never just a "theory" but turned on the practice of a life. We may speak of the "turn to self" in modern philosophy but much depends on what this turn serves. The intimate universal? Or more powerful scientific theory? More powerful autonomy? More and more will-to-power? The post-Hegelian existential strain resurrects this stress on the singular. It is very important for philosophy and religion. And a turn *away* from self in a postmodern manner? There are here more turns than one, but not many of them seem turned to the intimate universal.

Speaking More Objectively

Let me offer some more "objective" remarks on what I take to be important philosophical landmarks shaping the place of religion in Western modernity. I do this in no Eurocentric spirit. The modern West, in some respects, is anomalous relative to the rest of the human family, and indeed relative to its own traditions. But the arm of its influence extends globally, and it is an open question to what extent the exportation of the characteristic ethos of science and technology, and the attitudes that go along with these, will not create difficulties elsewhere, certainly discomforts for religious orientations to being. The objectivizing projects patented in the West have universal pretensions, but how they respect the intimacies of being, whether in the West or elsewhere, or relative to the more universal human family, is in serious question. I see an attenuation of finesse for the intimate universal, at best its moralization, at worst its oblivious reduction. Nevertheless, there is hope in the fact that, as we shall see, the relation of "lovers" and "theorists" continues to come up—even within theories that are reductive or moralizing.

One might say that Western modernity, just in its powerful objectivizing projects, shows a progressive process of stripping the world of the signs of the divine and its ambiguous communication. As being becomes more objectified, the less it provides the nurturing matrix for religious reverence. In tandem with this, we find increasing recourse to our own powers to deal with this world in its now qualitative poverty. We understand ourselves as seeking to be masters who can overcome its equivocal thereness. Yet this our claimed ascendancy seems to issue in a stifling of the communications of the divine. Whichever way we turn, the world seems to mirror back to us our own face. We "love" ourselves as we "theorize" about what is other. Thus results what might be termed an ethos of humanistic autonomy, itself resulting in deep difficulties in our being open to any transcendence as other to us.

In an earlier time, Augustine described his own itinerary to God in terms of a double movement: *ab exterioribus ad interiora, ab inferioribus ad superiora*. The soul journeys from the exterior to the interior, thence from the inferior to the superior. I have always found Augustine's description very suggestive, not only for my own ruminations, but in helping orient one to other thinkers, religious or not. We might improvise on the thought. Suppose our first movement toward ourselves is made in order to move beyond the lack of univocal evidences in the outer world. Yet the inner to which we turn is *itself equivocal*. This turn to ourselves, or the soul's innerness, is one of the major recourses of religions. The religious way says: in its deepest intimacy, the soul finds itself before the height of a radical other: God. God is the superior. There is an ultimate other to be beloved. The turn above to the superior is toward community with transcendence as other which sustains the universal without annihilation of the intimate.

But now note: this return to self might also seem to be the turn to *our own power*. We are such beings as can feel intimately irritated with the acknowledgment of anything superior to ourselves. And so in the turn to self the seeds of a kind of usurpation can be sowed—even let the usurpation call itself the final release of our genuine freedom and creativity. We make the claim to be both autonomous and transcending: we are autonomous transcendence itself. No God above me, and no man either, to vary a Nietzschean exclamation. We move from externality to ourselves, and then from ourselves to ourselves. But who is now the superior one, if we project ourselves above ourselves? Who now or what is the ultimate beloved?

The redirection of our loves is, of course, equivocal. I illustrate this way. Descartes is considered to be the father of modern philosophy, renowned for his turn to self in the famous argument: *cogito ergo sum*.

The argument was already formulated by Augustine relative to the skeptics: *dubito ergo sum*. At one level, Descartes looks similar to Augustine, for on the basis of the self so proved, he proceeds to prove God. Is not this the movement from the inferior to the superior? But then we ask: which is the real foundation, or ultimate: self or God?

Our suspicions are aroused when Descartes seems to use God as a means to certify our cognitive confidence in a new mathematical science of nature as external. When Augustine interrogated himself as to what he sought to know, he replied: God and the soul. He further asks: *Nihilne plus*, nothing more? He answers, no further: *Nihil omnino*, nothing at all. The knowing of God was the *nec plus ultra*. For Descartes, by contrast, with God on our side as knowers, we are emboldened to make ourselves "masters and possessors of nature," secure in a foundation that grounds the new science as a project to be completed through a myriad of experiments, and to yield tremendous practical benefits. We today are the beneficiaries of the success of that project. But one still asks: Can God be used thus? Have we taken a fateful or fatal step outside fitting reverence, when God is thus used? Is the self-perfection of our own power not then the superiority we project? Not God as the superior, but ourselves as creating ourselves at a higher level as superior being. Voilà the apparition of a kind of *Übermensch*! The pious Descartes and the impious Nietzsche take on the look of blood brothers — notwithstanding the differences of a scientistic *Übermensch* and a rhapsodic.

Misgivings about the redirection of our secret loves were felt from the start. I cite the witness of a great mathematician and scientist, also an intrepid explorer of the labyrinth of the human heart: Pascal. If Descartes embodies the *esprit de géométrie*, and Nietzsche the *esprit de finesse*, Pascal embodies a certain unity of *géométrie* and *finesse*. This is his demurral: I cannot forgive Descartes; all he wanted from God was to give a little fillip to the world, and then he had no more need of God. Pascal should know. He suspected sleep coming on, sleep coming over us to communication of the divine. Religious finesse wanes as geometrical construction waxes. The outcome? Is it the hollow earth on which we have constructed a variety of crystal palaces, as Dostoevski might suggest? Our hollow earth, in whose hollowness Nietzsche's shout about the death of God echoes and re-echoes, until it becomes mere white noise, humming in the background of our postmodern chatter?

To step back again: something of what is at stake in the double movement from exterior to interior, and from inferior to superior, is reflected in philosophical attitudes to the traditional proofs of God. Here too philosophical reason cannot avoid coming to the question of what it ultimately loves. I speak now of a tradition referred to as natural theology. At work here is the contrast of the natural and the supernatural. While our access to the supernatural was primarily said to be through revelation, human beings might also make use of natural reason without any reference to revelation. Unaided reason is called upon to establish, through its own immanent powers, God's existence, regardless of our specific religious affiliation, or lack thereof. Reason is understood to speak for a neutral universality free of the particularities of religious traditions. Aquinas's five ways are perhaps the most well-known. These consist of the arguments: from change in the world to the first unchanged mover; from causality to the first uncaused cause; from possibility or contingency in finite being to God as necessary being; from gradations of perfection in the world to absolute perfection; from the teleology of things in nature to God as ultimate governance. Among the proofs Anselm's ontological way has also been of great interest. It has supposedly been refuted again and again, and yet also defended again and again by strong thinkers, and indeed reinvented in new guises, by Hegel for one.

Generally the first set of proofs is *a posteriori* and dependent on evidences from the external world. By contrast, the second is *a priori*, at least in seeming not to be beholden to an evidentiary source external to reason itself. The first set looks to the evidences of externality for signs that communicate some sense of a divine source. The second claims that the way is through what is most intensive in inwardness itself. Here we find what I would call the *hyperbolic thought* of God — the being greater than which none can be conceived. The claim is something like this: we come upon this hyperbolic thought in our immanent exploration of thought, and at its limit of self-knowing. The ontological proof is a way that, having turned toward interiority, seeks to make a transition from the inferior to the superior. We are the inferior, even in the inward infinity of our thinking. Within that interiority there is an inescapable reference to what is more than us, infinitely more than us: God.

I am putting the point in a manner that might not always be granted about the ontological way. I mean the argument is treated as a kind of logical puzzle: in question is the logical validity of the deduction from the concept of God to God's existence, purely on the basis of the concept of God alone. This is more the neutral universality of reason than the living intimacy of the soul. In fact, when Anselm first formulates the proof, very clearly it is situated in an ethos of religious meditation. Logic is embedded in a milieu of prayer. Anselm is a lover first and a theorist second. Without the ethos of the intimate universal, we are only juggling abstractions.

This ethos does not quite figure in the modern reformulation, say, in Descartes and Kant. The ethos of thought now is more geometrical, mathematical, rather than meditative prayer. Not surprisingly, the concept of God is considered on the analogy with the concept of a *triangle*. Inherent in the definition of a triangle is the necessary truth that its three angles together constitute 180 degrees; considering the concept alone, it cannot be otherwise. So with the concept of God: it cannot be other than that God must exist; for the concept of the most perfect being must necessarily include existence. Once we understand the concept either of a triangle or of God, we know what is necessarily implied by this. God as the necessary being or the perfect being is similar: once we understand the concept of absolute necessity or perfection, it follows it must exist. We might have the neutral universality of geometrical reason, but where is the intimate finesse that being religious nurtures?

Kant is an interesting figure in being halfway between the supposedly neutral universality of theoretical reason and the intimate finesse of being religious. Halfway: he tries to move beyond theory, but stops with moral duty, not love. Wearing the hat of the critical theorist of pure reason, Kant claims that *all* we have in the ontological way is the analysis of a concept. Such an analysis will always deal with possibility; it will not get you to existence; there is a gap between concept and existence that cannot be bridged by conceptual analysis alone. The ontological proof provides us with a conceptual analysis of the idea of God. If God exists then he is necessary; but the proof gives us no rationally necessary evidence that he does exist. Indeed in the world we cannot find such evidence, for God is not a finite and determinate object. God transcends possible experience, and we are not allowed so to transcend it, at least not transcend and claim rational cognitive certainty about God. A hundred possible thalers and a hundred real thalers do not differ in concept; but there is a world of difference between the two, which cannot be bridged by concepts alone. Kant claims that since all the other proofs, seemingly *a posteriori*, reduce to the ontological, they too lack the rational cogency claimed. See Kant thus as engaged in a critique of the poverty of "theory," revealed in the unsustainable pretensions of speculative reason.

Kant is often seen as a destroyer, but mainly he seems intent on destroying the self-certainty of rationalist metaphysicians and with instruments he learned to perfection in the school of the rationalists. He offers us a different way to God—through our moral being. Do we here find Kant the "lover"? The version of the ontological proof he attacks can be seen as a version of a kind of logicist inner way. But might one take the moral argument as a variant of the "inner" way? It too suggests an effort to move from the inferior to the superior—on the basis of what is implied by our moral being. Something unconditional comes to emergence in our moral being, something unconditional not to be found in the evidences of externality. On the basis of this moral unconditional, a way is found to affirm God as a postulate demanded by our moral being.

Undoubtedly, this suggests a noncognitive approach to God. "Dare to know [*sapere aude*]!" exclaims the enlightener Kant. But then it turns out we cannot know very much! Does the bang then become a whimper? And it is not quite that Kant finally becomes a "lover" rather than a "theorist." For moral duty surpasses theory and love, and Kant resists the abandon of love as too equivocal, too off-limits to the rationalistic superego in his intellectual blood. "Dare to know!" dares not become "Dare to love!" It is content with: "Do your duty!" "Do your duty regardless of God, even without God." Remember Augustine's *nihilne plus*? Duty finally, not God, seems to be Kant's *nec plus ultra*. This is not the intimate universal of being religious.

Kant's critique of the traditional proofs has been taken as definitive, but is this so? Not quite. As formulated in the ethos of modernity, it conceives of nature in terms of Newtonian mechanism, where at most we might make a plausible inference from the machine to the machine maker. In his *Third Critique* Kant moves in a somewhat different direction to rethink nature in qualified teleological terms. But as I said, the ethos of his thought lies quite far from Anselm, far also from the ethos of thought of Aquinas. I will confine myself to one major point. Nature here is not a machine. The scholastic philosophers often argued like forensic lawyers, but beneath the surface of disputatious univocity, there is more at work. Aquinas's attunement to the being of the world is redolent, if hesitantly named so, of the glory of creation. The world is a creation, and communicates the glorious, albeit initially ambiguous, signs of the creator. His third way, the way from possible being, later called the proof from contingency, hangs on the fact that the world is a happening that carries no self-explanation. It is, but it might possibly not be; there is no inherent necessity that it must be. It is a happening that happens to be, but the happening as happening points to being beyond contingency that is the source or ground of happening. This he names as God.

I would suggest that if this way has any power, it is not just as a logical argument, but only insofar as it presupposes deep openness to the ontological enigma of the "that it is" of beings. This is the elemental wonder of metaphysical astonishment: astonishment at the sheer being there of the world, its givenness as given into being, not the "what" of beings, but "the that of being at all." This is at the edge of determinate science and more akin to religious reverence or aesthetic appreciation. Perhaps it is even a kind of unknowing love. There is a taste of the intimate universal in it. What can we say about Aquinas the theorist? His theories might seem as thin as the arguments of forensic lawyers if we lack finesse for the living concern at stake, but this concern has to do with secret loves. Pascal suggests something like this: when we are reflecting on the arguments we might be intellectually engaged, but a few minutes later they are out of mind and we forget them. But this is also to forget the love that remains shy in the arguments.

And are not the proofs, or better "ways," sourced in a variety of different forms of metaphysical astonishment or perplexity? These sources are as much intimate to us, as intimating something universal. The argument from design: does it not grow out of metaphysical astonishment at the aesthetic marvel of the happening of the world? Remarks in Kant's *Critique of Judgment* border on this, but in either an aesthetic or a moral way, not in a more robustly religious way. Or consider the anomalous *excess* of human transcending. We are self-surpassing beings: but is this an excess overreaching into emptiness or into something other? Nietzsche will claim we are creatively exceeding ourselves—to ourselves. Is this excess enough for us—or for what exceeds us? Consider how Kant tried to canonize our moral being: is not this seeded in the great wonder of our sense of unconditional good? All of this suggests to me what I would call *hyperboles* of being: happenings in finitude excessive to complete finite determination, beyond objectification and subjectification; and yet about which we must think as philosophers, both as intimate and as intimating something universal; and in whose excess our unknowing love of being—and perhaps God—already blindly moves.

All this has a bearing on what a philosophy of finitude might mean, and what we love, whether in immanence or beyond. Kant, the moralizer of being religious, tends to vacillate equivocally somewhere between immanence and something "beyond." He wanted to avoid both materialism and pantheism. Hence his desire to retain the gap between God and the world. Inevitably, the "theoretical" ways to God were conceived as a bridging inference or deduction that would get one from the immanent world to a transcendent deity. The ontological proof claimed to do this by deduction; the other proofs by evidential inference from being as here given, or from significant aspects of the world. The gap remains on both approaches: the first cannot move from concept to existence by means of concepts alone; the second might establish some persuasive case, but no necessarily compelling proof—at most we might establish that God is the architect of the world (physico-theological proof) but this falls short of the full reality attributed to the absolute God of monotheism, including of course God's goodness. The moral way, as not "theoretical," offers us, by contrast, the immanence of something unconditional: the moral law. It is on this basis that a move to the divine as "beyond" is charted. But if we must and can do our duty regardless of God, can we not do without God? And if this divine "beyond" is postulatory, why approach the world in terms of a "postulatory moral deism" rather than a different "postulatory finitism" in which immanence is given a different weight? This is a question to which I will return in terms other than "postulatory moral deism" and "postulatory finitism."

And suppose in the spirit rather than the letter of the matter, one were to propose: Maybe there are "gaps" that are falsely rendered when we fix them into dualistic oppositions. Maybe these "gaps" are spaces of communication and intermediation—betweens of porosity in which what is more than us, the superior, communicates most intimately to what is given in finite immanence. This is not Kant's way of speaking but it suggests a doubleness that is not a dualism, a rich equivocity that affords a milieu of being that calls forth finesse, and, who knows, secret love.

Already in Kant's time, reaction to the mechanical worldview was strong enough to demand a way of immanence that was more than moral. We find the upsurgence of pantheism, and also engagement with the sublime. This engagement is also a very postmodern one, though its earlier religious resonances are now too aestheticized, hence weakened, relative to the spiritual brunt it previously bore. Does this engagement reflect a crossing of the divide between lovers and theorists? Does pantheism, and its more current variant panentheism, try to unite both? Think of Spinoza as reflecting the doubleness. He claimed to philosophize *more geometrico*, and initially in the seventeenth century he was excoriated as an atheist or materialist, though he spoke of the one substance as God or nature. And then in the revival of Spinozism in the eighteenth century he was baptized anew by Novalis as the God-intoxicated man. But can you hang on to the geometry when the intoxication takes over? Or if geometry remains in the dominant, does not its universality turn its back on the intimacy? How find or keep the balance?

Pan(en)theism, and philosophies of the sublime, reject the merely quantitative world of mechanism for a more qualitative world, whether of organism, or something more unmastered. If we consider the organism as the design of the divine, we see it shows signs of *immanent* life and vitality and becoming. Think of God thus and we seem freed of the anorexic transcendence of mechanism and deism. We seem to have a more immanent vitalizing principle. (Something reminiscent of this is resurgent today, say, in the Gaia hypothesis.) And if the world seems less a mechanism than an organism, a living totality, we do not need "proofs," for there seems to be no gulf of immanence and transcendence to be negotiated by inference or deduction. We need the exploration of the divine in immanence itself. Hence we find the re-emergence of the ontological proof but now transformed from merely rational deduction from a concept into an exemplification of what is said to be most fundamental in thinking and being.

Thus we come to Hegel: against the mechanical sign that points to an external machine maker, we are to think the God of the whole. The sign of God is the absolute organism as a living totality, which contains its own principle of becoming within itself. Beyond external dualism, we are asked to see the immanence of God in the whole. But pantheism is often associated with a nature that is outside history. Hegel incorporates the emphasis on time and history we find in the biblical religions: the story has a beginning and an end, and it is in the end that we will find is the fullness. Hegel gives us a kind of historicist panentheism (not any simple pantheism). Is Hegel's claim to balance religion and philosophy dialectically the answer to the intimate universal?

My answer is no, but the reasons for this are too complex to give now.[2] I will only say that Hegel's claim to offer a higher speculative universal generates a dialectical counterfeit double of the intimate universal. Hegel's God was a changeling. His "sublationary infinitism," as I call it, ballooned into inflationary speculative claims about God. Human reason lived beyond its resources on much counterfeit wealth not truly invested in the reserves of God. The bubble burst and the recovery has taken a long time. In the post-Hegelian deflation, "postulatory finitism" has tended to take over from "sublationary infinitism." We are paying for the speculative bubble with a long atheism, an atheism given, on and off, to generating its own bubbles.

Something of this was sensed by some of Hegel's successors, though their critique was not necessarily directed toward fidelity to religion as embodying the intimate universal. Nevertheless, a more general panentheism continues to be popular in postevolutionary times, as in, say, process philosophy (shorn of Hegel's grander vision). After the chastening of Kantian critique, philosophical thought is emboldened to reach out to the whole; and why not, if we can determine the meaning of what is other to ourselves? Of course, the sublime fits uneasily with this as seeming to breach the self-containment of immanent totality. And is it not true that the overreaching of reason, overreaching even the sublime, such as we find in Hegel, seems to have produced by reaction a different chastening,that leads all the way from Kierkegaard to different forms of postmodernism? There is something exceeding our self-determination, and there is something other than an immanent self-contained totality.

In the contrast of Hegel and Kierkegaard, do we come again to the tension of theorist and lover? Yes and no. Hegel will affirm the ontological argument, and generalize it by saying that thinking and being cannot be sundered. Kierkegaard will demur, most passionately relative to God: to think God philosophically, and to be religious, are not one and the same. To be religious requires more than thought: it requires the singularity of an adventure that takes us to the limits of thought, and indeed beyond, insofar as God is more than the measure of human intelligibility. There is a space between us and God but it cannot be speculatively rendered in terms of the self-mediation of an immanent totality beyond which there is nothing. In the terms I am here using: There are "gaps" that are betweens, and they

---

[2] See my *Hegel's God: A Counterfeit Double?* (Aldershot: Ashgate, 2003).

are porous to communication from the superior other, but this porosity is opened most ultimately in the intimacy of the singular soul.

Of course these chastenings, after the overreaching of idealism, also produced other forms of nonrational overreaching. If we find an anti-idealist but religious chastening in Kierkegaard, we find an anti-idealist and, in certain respects, antireligious chastening in Nietzsche. We also find a different overreaching, which veers in the direction of a more rhapsodic amoral pantheism. If Nietzsche seems to be the progenitor of the postmodern self, the old God may be said to be dead, but a new god dances toward the empty throne—or slouches. Again I ask: What then of the intimate universal, and what do we love as ultimate?

Speaking More Intimately

To speak more intimately again, if the influences shaping me as a young person were those of a strong Irish Catholicism, this was one in which something like a pagan appreciation of the earth was not absent, and no absolute incompatibility between these two was felt. This reflects a feel for nonhuman nature as a creation in which traces of the enigmatic God are not absent. While the sense of the unconditional goes beyond this, it does not necessarily negate it, and one can live with finitude in which both are duly respected, and revered. It might be that the practice of religion is at its best when it moves us to this ontological reverence, overflowing into the ethical practice of agapeic service. Perhaps if I had been brought up as a northern European Protestant I would have felt their duality differently, and felt forced to opt for one or the other, either as a Kierkegaard or as a Nietzsche. A God who is the enemy of nature makes no sense to me, just as the glory of nature betokens a glory greater than itself.

The atheism that has been common among intellectuals since the Enlightenment is something I could not, do not share, even if my perplexity about this was, and is, intense. Some intellectuals are so asleep in taking this phenomenon for granted that its anomalous, indeed freakish character is hardly noted, relative to the longer history of the human family and indeed to most other human beings today. When intellectuals affect to have no interest in religion, I think of Pascal, who found it incomprehensible, even monstrous, that humans should speak as if these issues of ultimate moment mattered not a jot. It is quite easy to become an intellectual always looking over one's shoulder at other intellectuals. This looking can well turn into a defection from perplexity about what is the most worthy of thought, namely, the question of God. It is not quite that the atheism of many Western intellectuals scandalizes me—though if I am honest with myself my heart of hearts is stupefied by this scandal—but that they seem so *undisturbed* in their atheism, so smug. I will be rapped on the knuckles for saying this, but I also notice how tender these atheists become when someone does not sing from the same hymn sheet. *Mea culpa*: try as I might, I am the crow in the choir.

This is not to say I lack appreciation of atheism. The responsibility of the philosopher is to understand, even what he or she will not finally endorse. I sometimes think of the philosopher as a poison taster. We are imbibers of toxins. Some of these intoxicate and overwhelm us. Some are lethal to weaker constitutions. To some toxins one develops resistance, even immunity. Others might weaken one, and one might not even know one is a carrier. Some transmutate into harmless ailments. Others harbor monstrous mutations, even if they are right now more or less in recess. The immediate effect of what one takes in is not always what is most decisive. The effects of atheism might be in remission for quite a while. Health is a longer constancy, sustained by a taste for the trustworthy. Philosophy too requires this taste, this finesse.

If I were to name some thinkers who shadow me I would include Plato, Augustine, Hegel, Nietzsche. Love and theory mingle differently in each. I have struggled with the second pair, Hegel with reference to the systematics of the divine, Nietzsche with reference to the poetics. With the first pair, there is a different intimacy between systematics and poetics; there is a sense of transcendence beyond human self-transcendence—with Plato the Good beyond being, with Augustine the personal God of the Bible. With the second pair, there is a sense of immanence in which transcendence as other is compromised. Again I cannot now give all the complex reasons. But Hegel's holistic god, I argue, is a counterfeit double of the God of the biblical tradition. Nietzsche gives us a hyperbole of human self-transcending that is ambiguously religious but that, I fear, rhapsodically counterfeits the divine on its musical heights.[3] There are other figures religiously important for me, and they will be recalled again in this book: Shakespeare, Dostoevski, Pascal, Shestov (Kierkegaard, less so).

---

[3] See my *Hegel's God*; in addition to Chapter 6 below on Nietzsche, see also my *Art, Origins, Otherness: Between Art and Philosophy* (Albany: State University of New York Press, 2003), chapter 6.

Deeper than these I have wondered at the poverty of philosophy when it faces figures like Jesus or Francis of Assisi, or the Buddha. Do we here meet the wisdom of the simple—the idiot wisdom that keeps intimacy with the porosity of being and lets itself be a passage or passing of communication from the divine? Or Job: exposure at the extremities or on the heights. Nakedness: this is the porosity: helpless and yet the place asking of us the absolute trust. Naked I came, naked I go. Can philosophy follow Job and say: Blessed be the name of the Lord? It would have to be blessed to be able to say this blessing. It would have to be gifted with that different poverty I mentioned, and be philosophy other than itself, be a philosophy beside itself. The "theorist" would again have to become a "lover" or be graced with love.

I think here of the philosopher as being in an in-between position: not any longer quite a spontaneous "lover," but not necessarily a "theorist" so lost in concepts that he or she is lost to love. Being true to thought entails a fidelity that can take thought beyond itself, and hence qualify, in multiple ways, one's inhabitation of the middle space between being religious and philosophical. I have explained my position of "being between," and with regard to the metaxological sense of being, in many ways and on more than one occasion. The between can also be a place of purgatory. The desert is a noplace we all find ourselves in at some time of life. The desert may destroy us, make us despair; it may make us stronger, more patient, more fecund. The standard form of "being between" religion and philosophy is the one inherited from a long tradition and expressed in this quest: *fides quaerens intellectum*. While not denying this, I would ask about the less evident quest of *intellectus quaerens fides*. I do not just mean the converse of the first. There is a more radical "between," as it were, "beyond" the satisfactions of determinate cognition concerning finite things and processes, and the excellences of self-determining knowing at home with itself. Something more than the warrants of science and the self-determinations of moral autonomy is solicited from us.

I mean something like this. We find ourselves, "objectively" speaking, in an "information age." We know more and more about this and about that, and the intellect is glutted. With this seems to go, "subjectively" speaking, a loss of faith: enlightenment produces a dying of the light. Is there a fidelity beyond this glut of the intellect, and this loss? I connect this with a need for the resurrection of astonishment and perplexity in a *second* sense, in a second dimension beyond determinate cognition, no matter how comprehensive. Excess of light produces a blindness.

My question: How would one learn to find one's way again if, so to say, one had gone blind? Everything would be the same, and everything would be different, and one would stumble. *What one well knows would become dark.* It is as if the face with which knowledge made one familiar is suddenly returned to its mystery, and one's hands grope over its newly strange lineaments. Its mystery is renewed by one's intimacy with its strangeness, and one does not know what is there before one, though one knows all these things about what is there before one.

If there is this second astonishment and resurrected perplexity,[4] it does not seek for some new *information* about this face. For it is not some withheld fact about it that one lacks. It is rather the light in which it is seen that is perplexing, or the darkness in which it is felt. What is this light, in which the same thing, previously known, still known in its exquisite determinacy, takes on again the aspect of darkness? The same is the same and yet newly other. What is this light, or darkness, and how do we come to be in it anew? Could we gain the measure of it entirely through our own self-determining powers? I think we need what I would call a new *poverty of philosophy.*

In such a new poverty, philosophical thinking is in the position all but exactly the opposite to Hegel's absolute knowing, which he describes as that point when knowing no longer feels the need to go beyond itself. In this new poverty, it is just this absolute need to go beyond itself that overcomes it. That need is lifted up into a new dimension of desire and longing—longing for a knowing that is not an objective or determinate cognition, nor a matter of self-determining self-knowing, but other again. It is more than determinate cognition and more than self-knowledge. This is a poverty of philosophy in which it empties itself of its conceptual hubris and seeks out the guidance of the great poets and religious figures, those touched by the exceeding simplicity of the holy, as if by an idiot wisdom. All this makes the "intellect" newly seeking: seeking to be faithful, with a new *"fides"* or fidelity but in a darkness on the heights. This is not a matter of any finite determinate cognition such as we find in the objectifying sciences, nor is it a self-knowing immanently satisfied with itself. It is thinking struggling in the dimension of the hyperbolic.

---

[4] On this, see my *Being and the Between* (Albany: State University of New York Press, 1995), chapter 1.

Nihilism brings us to nothing, but this poverty of philosophy entails a kind of return to zero in which a new interface with creation may be possible. Job exclaimed his nakedness in coming forth from the womb, his nakedness in going hence, but proclaimed in the coming forth and going hence that the Lord was blessed. There is a nakedness in the middle that remembers the beginning and the end. This poverty awakens in us something of the urgency of ultimacy.

The Urgency of Ultimacy, the Porosity of Being Religious

"The urgency of ultimacy": elsewhere I have spoken of religion as marked by this.[5] Different possibilities are suggested, none devoid of ambiguity, and as I will shortly indicate I would now modify this language. We can name the ultimate in different ways, and some names will name what is less than ultimate, and so the name will tag an idol. One of our names is: nothing. Nihilism too sings its *Te Deum*: nothing is ultimate. We cannot, it seems, escape some relation to what we take as ultimate. Is it not very significant that we humans are capable of idolatry *at all*? Is this not indirect confirmation that our being is religious? Our being is to be in relation to ultimacy, even when we deny ultimacy, as in nihilism. Of course, what the relation is, what the ultimate is, what the idols are, remain to be understood more.

Why the *urgency*? We do not create the relation to ultimacy; we are in the relation, are what we are in it. An urgent happening is not first the result of some deliberate choice. It may communicate from within or from without, or both; its source may be immanent or transcendent, or both. An obscure passion is precipitated and we are importuned. This importunity may be our opportunity. More settled forms of domesticated life are disturbed: something more absolute importunes us, as does a gap of difference, through which we are coaxed closer to a deeper rapport with that something more. Such urgency can be ecstatic, in that it catapults us *beyond* ourselves. Often it can communicate—from within out—secret intensities of being, for it surges from abysmal sources beyond secure self-consciousness. At the same time, this urgency can *open inward*: its outbreak startles us with dawnings of obscure intimation. Urgency has the bite of the unbidden that breaks up our more standard self-satisfactions. Even if it

---

[5] *Philosophy and Its Others: Ways of Being and Mind* (Albany: State University of New York Press, 1990), chapter 3.

does not shatter us, it makes our claimed autonomy unquiet, or puts it under stress.

What of the reference to *ultimacy*? The word seems to have an indeterminacy, even as it also seems to name a finality. Urgency of ultimacy: the "of" is ambiguous. Is the ultimacy of our urgency, thus revealing only our desire or transcending? Or is it *of us* only because more fundamentally the urgency is *of ultimacy*? I think the latter first of all, and only the first because of the latter. "Ultimacy" seems to refer us to an end, but here in fact it is a beginning: it is at the start, though also at the end, if in a different sense. Ultimacy makes our being urgent, but could we be urgent about ultimacy *at all*, were not the urging of ultimacy somehow already leavening our being? The urgency brings the urging of the ultimate to desire, to mindfulness. Urging points us toward a goal because urging itself is a source in us that disquiets, rouses, moves, and quickens. We are moved by, we strive toward, the ultimate out of the urgency of ultimacy. Our seeking for God is our struggle to find the right words for what is ultimate.

Admittedly again, we frequently try to determine the ultimate, wrongly reduce it to this or that thing, and then, once again, we secrete idols. We are caught up in an equivocal process through which we have to pass. The equivocity is not just due to us, but to our ontological situation in the middle. Its character is constrained by necessities conducive to multiple ambivalences, obfuscations, impertinences, refusals. We always risk vainly reading *our own face* into any initial intimation of the ultimate. We have to undergo a transformation of mindfulness to release us to understand the otherness of the ultimate. This allowing other is not to be mistaken for the mirror of our self-reflection, or merely the medium of autonomous self-determining.

Poverty here may mean the stripping of false selves. It may be extremely difficult for us to come again to this nakedness. A life of certain counterfeits of being may cling to us like a *false skin*. One *is* that false skin, and to strip it away may seem like being flayed. The discipline of an asceticism may be needed: an *askēsis* that is a "no" seeking to waken again a "yes," like the blessing of Job in his exposure. Any violence here, of course, is very dangerous, fraught with ambiguity. The stripping that seems to purify may actually flow from an indeterminate negation rather than the elemental "yes." Great discernment is needed to sift the mingled opposites. There is an asceticism of hatred; there is a purging of love; and hatred may speak the language of love. We need love to see the difference, but love may be what now we most lack.

I would now give more weight to what I call the *passio essendi*. "Urgency of ultimacy" can be taken too much as *our* urge: *our* will to be in relation to the ultimate. This is not wrong, but there is something more primal at the root of this urgency of ultimacy. Before the *conatus essendi*, the *passio essendi*: before the seeking in which we are put in question and put ourselves at risk, there is a porosity of being which is always already presupposed by all our acts of self-transcending. The primal porosity of being, I believe, is most intimately expressed in our being religious. Being religious is the primal porosity of being, since it is the living middle between the soul in its most abyssal intimacy and the divine.

In this porosity the communication of what we later call prayer happens. When we place ourselves, or find ourselves placed, in the space of praying, the opening of this porosity is brought to mindfulness again. Thinking itself is a later formation of the self-transcending of mind that is rooted in the primal porosity: the self-transcending power of thinking is derivative from this primal porosity. Hence there is a sense in which the roots of philosophy are not contingently in a religious occasion, but essentially so. This is our being, what we are: porosity to the divine that gifts us with the power to be beyond ourselves, for already the beyond is beside us before we are with ourselves, with ourselves in a more self-knowing manner. This is why I have written below (Chapter 8) about a reverence in which religion, philosophy, and science participate, albeit differently stressing it. And being religious is closer to the root of this reverence.

Is the love of being religious a form of eros? It depends on what one means by eros. I myself think eros refers us to a more primal affirmative power of being that cannot be fully described in the language of lack. But this is not now the occasion to speak more fully of other forms of love, such as the agapeic. I make this one remark relative to eros and the porosity. Just as the poverty of philosophy is not a mere deficiency, so eros is more than lacking. The myth of Diotima in Plato's *Symposium* tells us of the *double* parentage of eros in *poros* and *penia*. The lack is usually associated with *penia*, and less often is the "resource" of *poros* foregrounded. My question: Is *poros* related to porosity? Is there a resource of *poros* intimately related to the porosity that I believe is at the root of being religious? Is there a resource in lacking itself that is not just a simple expression of power but intimately connected with porosity?

Poros also has some connotation of a "way across." Porosity enables a passage between or through or across: something that is not any one thing, something more an energy, an energy that seems like nothing, that passes or is communicated from one to another. *Poros* names the making of a way: a transition that is no transition; since in making a way, it makes way and hence there is a withdrawal in the very opening of the way. The passage, or passing through, cannot be fixed as this or that: so it seems nothing, but in another sense it is not nothing, it is a way being made; a making way; an original coming to be that yet makes way. In some such wise, I think of the between to be constituted as a space of primal porosity, and every being within it as marked by this porosity in different manners. (One might also put this in a somewhat different idiom: being created out of nothing, but as something, and as good, by the agapeic origin.) Porosity would itself be a kind of poverty, but a gifted poverty of being that is always rich beyond itself.

Here one must be particularly concerned philosophically with the claims made for autonomous reason. Is there such a thing? Is philosophical reason ever defined by and through itself alone? Is anything so defined? Is not philosophical thought always defined, overtly or in a hidden way, by relation to its significant others, be these said to be science, or religion, or art, or everyday life? It will be said that autonomous reason gives us a sense of control over the subject under discussion, reducing disturbing equivocities to satisfying univocities. But what of the promiscuous ambiguity of human existence? Is the will for such a clarity appropriate to religion? If religion has to do with our primal porosity—which is prior even to our self-transcending, be it in science, or art, or philosophy, or everyday practice—then it makes sense that mystery, ambiguity, and enigma should be essential to it, *positively essential* and not as mere defects of univocity.

With this porosity we are dealing with something overdeterminate, something hyperbolic, something that is no thing, that makes determinations possible but that is not itself just a determination. Defining such "things" in the wrong determinate way may well distort the pivotal point at issue. We cannot thus make determinate the primal porosity, and hence also the originating source of being religious. I do not at all argue for giving up thinking philosophically, but if what I say has any truth, thinking needs a renewed access to "love" beyond every success of "theory." What if the "success" of determinate "theory" was a function of the contraction of the primal porosity? We need another kind of thinking in the space between religion and philosophy.

Outline of the Work

Let me outline the reflections that are to come. Chapter 1 begins with what I call the sleep of finitude, addressing the unease of philosophy and religion, the unease each exhibits and the unease each has with the other. I connect this reflection to what I above called "postulatory finitism," which I think marks much contemporary Continental thought. "Postulatory finitism" is a kind of atheistic inversion of Kant's "postulatory moral deism." It proposes something like this: if we want to think of life as finite and nothing but finite, then we must think nothing beyond. The question of God, for instance, not only becomes difficult but may not even emerge for consideration. For the postulatory finitism goes underground, so to say, and influences what will be allowed to emerge as a genuine perplexity. When the impasses or aporiai of finitude then emerge, as they do, we tend to swerve back to finitude and not fully consider anything other than what the terms of postulatory finitism allow.

This is my question: Philosophy claims to wake us up from the sleep of common sense, sometimes treating religion as but another sleep, but what if philosophy falls into a new sleep, from which only a different sense of religious sleeplessness can wake us? I look at different kinds of sleep and sleeplessness, in Plotinus, in Pascal, and in Shakespeare's *Macbeth*. I argue that these reveal a hyperbolic sleeplessness that exceeds the terms of postulatory finitism. Perhaps it is from the sleep of postulatory finitism that we must wake. Our supposed awakening may have sent us to sleep about God, but from this second sleep there must be a different awakening, requiring an openness to the religious that most standard practices of philosophy seem to lack.

My view is not a repudiation of philosophy as addressing finitude, but it is a question to philosophies of radical immanence that immerse themselves in immanence such as to close finitude off from what is other to it. This does not mean we need endorse Hegel's speculative *Aufhebung* of finitude into infinity. Chapter 2 explores the relation between finitude and infinitude, by way of a study in contrast between Hegelian reason and the Pascalian heart. There are different ways of understanding our intermediate condition, and here I explore some different senses of "being between."

The Pascalian way troubles us with the abysses of the heart, while the Hegelian invites us onto the heights of speculative reason. Hegel is more the "theorist," Pascal the "lover," and yet both unavoidably think from the *metaxu*, the between where religion and philosophy cross, meet, and also separate. The relation of finite and infinite is differently defined by both, as is the relation of philosophical thought and religion. What is at issue is the fidelity of Hegel's dialectical-speculative middle, and of Pascal's fragmented, equivocal middle. Fidelity to what? Certainly to our metaxological condition, but also to the signs of transcendence ambiguously communicated in that middle condition. We are asked for finesse, dialectical and more than dialectical, with reference to that *metaxu*, but also to the God of the *metaxu*.

In Chapter 3 I turn to the relation between religion and the poverty of philosophy. Poverty here is meant in both a negative and an affirmative sense. I argue more fully for a practice of philosophy, undertaken at an angle to Hegel's claim about absolute knowing where, supposedly, knowing no longer feels the need to go beyond itself. This is not quite Pascal's so-called fideism, but more a kind of finesse in philosophical practice itself. Hegel to the contrary, there is another kind of "absolved knowing" where this is just what is most radically needed. This has everything to do with a renewal of the relation of philosophy and religion, and not just faith seeking understanding, but understanding seeking a fidelity beyond the self-satisfactions of traditional philosophical knowing. In this poverty of philosophy, new porosities of thinking open up for us, some of them tokens of a richer thinking beyond thought thinking itself, and calling for a different communication between religion and philosophy.

In all of this, we are moving in a space of mindfulness full of equivocity, all the more making a call on our powers of finesse, both religious and philosophical. In Chapter 4 I turn to the religious imagination and the counterfeit doubles of God. I discuss the meaning of imagination as a threshold power of articulation which has intimate religious significance. I try to make sense of how human beings secrete counterfeit doubles of God, most especially when the original power emergent with imagination becomes intoxicated with itself and circles round itself, closing off the gift of the more original divine power. I will not now anticipate a statement of the problem of the counterfeit doubles of God, except to say that we are dealing with "doubles" that claim to be the same as the "original," but their sameness dissimulates a difference that turns them into idols. And this turn can take different forms, among which I include the aesthetic, fideistic, moralistic, and rationalistic. The closure of human self-transcendence to divine transcendence as other to us, the clogging of the porosity of being in terms of diverse claims to autonomous self-determination, make it difficult for us to think of a God other than radical immanence, a God beyond the whole of immanence. Such an other God is just what we need to wake up from the enchantments of the counterfeit gods of immanence.

In Chapter 5 I turn to this question of the God beyond the whole, taking my bearings by means of the divergence between the Russian philosophers and religious thinkers Lev Shestov and Vladimir Solov'ëv. Both are "lovers" and not mere "theorists," but Shestov is more suspicious of philosophical theory than is Solov'ëv, who is more under the spell of some inheritances from Spinoza and idealism. I do not quite identify with either, yet I find both instructive and worth listening to. What can one say about the idea of God beyond the whole, both as a fundamental theme, and as reflected in the pan(en)-theistic tendencies of a philosopher like Solov'ëv? I study his view of the "all-unity," in contrast with Shestov's existential protest on behalf of the God of biblical religion. I think we must think of a God beyond the whole, whether we understand the whole in Hegelian or pan(en)theistic terms, or indeed in terms of the dis-composed "whole" such as we find in the philosophies of finitude after Hegel. For these, even with their de-totalization of Hegel, are still philosophies of radical immanence, just as Hegel's is.

Here too we have to face the difficulty of philosophical-religious discernment with respect to the problem of the counterfeit doubles of God. In the contrast between Solov'ëv and Shestov this issue comes to focus in the question of the anti-Christ: the double who seems the same as Christ, and yet for whom the directionality of spiritual energy is absolutely opposite. How discern the absolute difference in the seeming of absolute sameness? The problem is here not only between religion and philosophy, it is between religion and religion, it is between philosophy and philosophy. None escape the need of discernment and finesse. There is no purely "objective" response, since our perplexity here returns us to the *intimacy* of the intimate universal, and the fidelity to porosity solicited from each of us in his or her singularity.

Chapter 6 continues such concerns with specific attention to their expression in the writings of Nietzsche. Deleuze calls Spinoza the "Christ of the philosophers," but, in turn, I am inclined to call Nietzsche "the anti-Christ of the post-philosophers." Yet the figure of Christ is of immense significance for how Nietzsche seeks to determine a higher sovereignty beyond all servile submission to a transcendent God. His phrase "a Roman Caesar with the Soul of Christ" is a striking description of the highest creators, other times called *Übermenschen*. So Nietzsche seems to name his highest possibility. I argue it is his highest impossibility, if we properly understand the meaning of Caesar and Christ in terms of erotic sovereignty and agapeic service. I explore the different senses of will-to-power in Nietzsche, higher and lower. I look at an absolutely crucial issue, namely, the agon for spiritual superiority between Nietzsche and Jesus.

The postmodernization of Nietzsche, if I am not mistaken, seems to have consigned to silence this agon for spiritual superiority, maybe because the work of postulatory finitism has been so effective, and the difference of higher and lower deconstructed by those strange mutants: the democratic Nietzschean, the left-wing Nietzschean. But this agon is in the dimension of the hyperbolic and calls the finite terms of postulatory finitism to account. I discuss the issue in terms of the meaning of the anti-Christ as a hyperbolic instance of the problem of counterfeit doubles. In this instance, I show how Nietzsche's understanding of "giving" ("the gift-giving virtue," *die schenkende Tugend*) seems to be very close to agapeic giving, and yet one must wonder if it is rather its counterfeit double, in that no service of the other as other seems to be possible. Among themes to be discussed are Nietzsche's view of the neighbor, and of solitude. There is no "outside" (*Es giebt kein Aussen!*), Zarathustra will exclaim, but can one show Nietzsche the way out? And not with curses on his head, but blessings?

Just as in earlier chapters I dealt with elemental themes such as sleep, or poverty, or the heart, so in the chapters now to follow I turn again to very elemental things, such as courage, reverence, hatred and love, war and peace. Each of these is immensely rich in terms of ontological consequences for philosophy, alive with importances for being religious, and resonant with significance for the communication between religion and philosophy.

Chapter 7 is a reflection on courage with respect to the secret sources of strengthening. Nietzsche called for courage, but is there too much of the *conatus essendi* in this call, as if one could just will it through oneself alone? I find courage to be far more enigmatic, with its roots in what I have called the *passio essendi*, the patience of being that is more primordial than the *conatus essendi*, the endeavor to be.

There is no "being courageous" without a first "being en-couraged." Philosophers have not been at their best in understanding the secret sources of strengthening. An understanding of our being as religious, marked by a certain primal porosity to the divine, brings us more intimately into communication with the secret sources of strengthening. While different forms of courage are explored, the chapter culminates in a discussion of the courage of the witness, most crucially the witness of the philosopher and the religious martyr.

Chapter 8 is a philosophical meditation on reverence and its betrayals. What is the significance of reverence, and how do developments in modernity make it difficult for us to understand its ontological and religious meaning? Developments of objectifying science, as well as the pervasiveness of certain forms of humanistic autonomy, often either contract, or misunderstand, or distort, or refuse what true reverence entails. A rethinking of reverence is inseparable from addressing the nihilistic consequences that follow from the devaluation of being in modernity. I argue that there is a reverence prior to science and philosophy that makes their quest of knowing possible, and with which our being religious can be in more faithful rapport. The porosity of being, and our first being given as *passio essendi*, are crucial. Without reverence we become monsters.

Chapter 9 directs itself to the nature of enemies. Often we make things too easy for ourselves when we speak facilely about love, as if we were all too familiar with its nature while being all too asleep to its intimate mystery. Less often do we consider the nature of enmity. Hatred has the smiting power to wake us up—wake us up also to love. Enmity too has ontological, metaphysical, and religious significance. Approached in terms of the *passio essendi* and the *conatus essendi*, I think important light can be thrown on the different forms of love. It is as if hatred were the "reverse negative" of love. In the reverse negative we see something of the original, which indeed it doubles, but as it were from behind, and with the aim of undoing its enabling energy. How does the sense of the enemy arise? By a certain mutation in the love of being as good, in which a counterfeit double of that love comes to be apparent. Does evil "arise" as an apparent counterfeit double of good? An apparent shadow, not quite nothing, not quite something, but battening on the power of being as good, to nihilate that good; being effective in defection; being the shadow that seeks to usurp the light it doubles in a counterfeit way? More particularly, I look at four forms of love and their corresponding senses of the enemy: self-affirming love, eros, philia, and agape.

In considering the extreme malignity of the enemy, I ask if something is communicated about God and the ultimate in agapeic love?

In the final chapter I come to the question: Is there a Sabbath for thought? I pursue a response in terms of the light that being religious and being philosophical throw on peace. Is there a sense of peace that has ontological significance as prior to war? What does "sabbatical being" mean? Is it possible to address this without serious engagement with being religious? What would it mean to say that there is a Sabbath for philosophical thought? I especially consider the contrast between those who think that war is the father of all things, such as Heraclitus, Nietzsche, and the (at least) earlier Heidegger, and those for whom inspiration comes from the Sabbath of being, witnessed to by the divine blessing on creation in the "It is very good" of Genesis. There is, for instance, Augustine's great meditation on peace in the *City of God*. How do we participate in that great "yes," and how is it reflected in being religious, and in philosophical thought? Is it possible to produce a counterfeit "Amen" to being? —a question I ponder with reference to Nietzsche's claim to offer the great "yes." But can there be *any* Sabbath of being, if war is the father of all things? How get from original *polemos* to peace?

If being is sabbatical, must not thinking rather wake up to its own sabbatical promise? And would not this require a different practice of philosophy itself, in which something like an agapeic mindfulness would be asked? Would openness to a Sabbath for thought ask philosophy to come again into a poverty where its thinking finds itself losing one peace, as it is beckoned toward another? It loses its satisfied peace with itself, but finds itself also unsettled by a new porosity in which it is solicited, beyond its self-insistence, that it must only be self-determining. From where does this "must" come? Must we bow down before this "must"? Or does its immanent imperiousness, seemingly spellbinding, dissolve like a dream in this new porosity of being? Is there a release toward a peace no philosophical understanding can grant to itself? What then could grant it, if it is granted?

Love and Theory and Again the Intimate Universal

To round off: Nothing in what I have said intends to lay a charge against philosophy as such. Rather it is to ask if philosophy is charged with an openness to being religious it does not always deliver, especially in our time. I see the opportunity to recharge an old affiliation of the two, weakened, diminished, abandoned, or refused in the dominant practices of philosophy in modernity, whether in terms of reason's infatuation with scientistic temptations, or philosophy's claim to autonomous knowing, or so-called post-philosophy's postulatory option for radical immanence. Is there a freedom of mindfulness beyond such infatuations, or claims, or options? Is there a new, yet old, modus vivendi asked, in which, returning to my opening reflections, the "theorist" and the "lover" can join hands?

More than anything else, I think this middle space between being religious and being philosophical puts us in question today, and the questions it charges us with bear on the idolatries of our cherished forms of knowing and being, be they determinate scientific cognitions that answer our curiosity, or self-determining knowing that claims to give us self-knowledge, or our bind to immanence that deputizes for our love of the good of creation. For we may have unfittingly reconfigured the porosity of being, and defected from what is communicated of transcendence to our being as *passio essendi*. Can there be renewed communication with the intimate universal? Can philosophy witness to the charge of a universality not objectifying and an intimacy of being not subjectifying?

Again suppose I am in love. Must analysis risk killing the passion? We seek a universality but we betray the intimacy. Is the passion already dying or dead, if and when such analysis rears its head? When I am in love I sing the beloved. When I analyze and ask if I am in love, I am no longer in love. Worse, I may be deluded into thinking that I am in the superior position, for after all, I am in charge now, putting the question. I am no longer intoxicated with my love, but am I in a better situation? Perhaps when I loved—loved God—then I was home—at home with the intimate universal. Maybe now I am wretched, but I think I am in a better place. What source this delusion? This is my worry about some practices of philosophy. We search for clarity against ambiguity, but the search for clarity is itself ambiguous, so it drags its own lack of clarity with itself, lack of clarity about itself. We fool ourselves into thinking we are enlightened, when we have only conspired with the dying of the light.

But there are other deaths, and one wonders if philosophical thinking must, so to say, again learn to sing. When we come to dying, or practicing death, we might consider with Socrates whether we ought to try to make music. I am inspired and sing a stirring poem of love. No longer inspired, I get my own back with a theory that singing songs is impossible, not in accord with logic (Socrates toys with this in the *Apology*). I am in love and in my love something is generated. I am not in love, and I make a theory to show that love is a misstep or delusion. I become the eunuch in the harem preaching about the impossibility of eros. Is it not so with some kinds of philosophers? I would hate to be that kind of philosopher. Eunuch for theory, eunuch of theory, I generate nothing, my concept sterile.

If being religious is not unlike a love song, a kind of intoxication with the divine, I do not forget that some festivities can descend into debauch. But I do remember that the divinely drunken *poros* fathers eros. The feast is in full swing. The thought police knock on the door. What happens? Either the feast envelops them and they cease to be police or their police presence induces a sobriety in which the festivity vanishes. Was the vanished festivity unreal? Or was it truer to the reality: the agape of being: hyperbolic being: being as full; and we ourselves porous to it?

The feast vanished, we are tempted in the vacancy to spin new post-religious "theories." Our compensation for losing the intimacy of being is to conceive of ourselves as "creators": we bypass the glory of creation and then we think we are making it all up. We secrete new gods: in aesthetics, "genius" or "creativity"; in ethics "autonomy" is god. Nor do I forget either that there can be a music that is forced and not intimate with the primal porosity. It is more disenchanted with the loss of face it suffered when "idealism" or "system" or "theory" jilted it, and it sings to get them out of its own system. Its post-philosophical disenchantment is disappointed love on the rebound and liable to infatuations with any counterfeit come-on. It has not yet become fully free to woo anew the sourcing muse.

And philosophy? Without something like a new poverty of philosophy, in communication with the porosity of being religious, I fear we will remain enchanted with some new counterfeit double of God. Our thought, thoughtless, because bereft of the fullness of being. Our love, loveless, because without the beloved. Our god, false, because without God.

How avoid such counterfeit doubles? How think otherwise? How is a love resurrected? Can philosophy do it, do it alone? What kind of philosophizing could come to our aid in undoing our bewitchment with the counterfeit doubles? Does philosophy have its own sleep from which it cannot quite rouse itself? Will its dialogue with religion call it to the intimate universal and a further awakening? To such questions we must turn.

1

The Sleep of Finitude: On the Unease of Philosophy and Religion

The Weight and Sleep of Finitude: On Measure and More

Shortly before his death, Ludwig Heyde published *The Measure of the Human* (*De Maat van de Mens*), and the following reflections are occasioned by a memorial dialogue with his concerns.[1] Heyde's book deeply engages the finitude of our condition, but it is marked by a philosophical courage to think laterally to the currents of thought, seemingly inexorable, that flow from the claims of modernity, and now postmodernity, to embrace finitude and nothing but finitude. Most notably, the book refuses to be silent about religion and the affiliation and unease between it and philosophy. In this regard, *The Measure of the Human* is complementary to Heyde's earlier book, *The Weight of Finitude*, which sets out in quest of the traces of God in fini-

---

[1] Ludwig Heyde, *De Maat van de Mens* (Amsterdam: Boom, 2000); Ludwig Heyde, *The Weight of Finitude: Concerning the Philosophical Question of God*, trans. W. Desmond and A. Harmsen, introduction W. Desmond (Albany: State University of New York Press, 1999). A version of some of these reflections was originally presented at a conference given in honor of the work of Ludwig Heyde, held at Katholieke Universiteit Nijmegen, December 8, 2000. These reflections are sympathetic to the spirit of his thinking, even if the letter is not, need not, be exactly the same, and even if my disagreement with Hegel is much sharper than his. In a posthumous conversation the absence of the interlocutor alerts us to presences of the other that we cannot measure in an entirely determinate manner.

tude. There is a somewhat reversed movement in the second book: we seem to come back from God to the human instead of going from the human to God. Nevertheless, the overall trajectory of both books brings us to a boundary where this question can be posed: Is the measure of the human itself the human?

Let it be granted: the human being seems the measure of all things. But is the human being the measure of itself? Is there something about the human being that exceeds measure? Insofar as measure seems to call for finite delimitation, is there something about the human being that exceeds limit and finitude? But then if there is something about the human being in excess of this measure, what is the measure of that excess? Can this excess of finite self-transcending be the measure of itself? Questionably so, if to measure is to introduce a determinate limit. Were this excess to measure itself it would be limiting itself, hence in a way be untrue to itself, and know itself as thus untrue. Does this then leave us in the essentially equivocal position: knowing we need measure but knowing that every measure we determine is untrue to what we are?

Would this then mean: for us to be true to ourselves, we must be untrue to ourselves? And that being untrue to ourselves is just what is demanded by the truth of our excessive transcending? If so, there seems to be something radically equivocal about us. It seems to mean that in being true to ourselves, we cannot be completely the answer to our own dilemma, since every answer we pose on our own terms reintroduces the equivocity: our being true to ourselves becomes our untruth to ourselves. The only answer that seems possible is that the human being is radically questionable to itself. But if we are thus so radically questionable, it seems our own being cannot be the answer. We are the question to itself that cannot answer for itself completely. But what could the answer then be? Must it transcend human being?

We exceed finite measure, but the measure of our excess exceeds even our excess, and hence not only exceeds finite measure, but exceeds any claim on our part to be the measure of either things or ourselves. Is there then a measure that exceeds finite measure, not only of finite things, but of the human being as exceeding the measure of finite things? How find measure in the exceeding of finite measure, if we humans are not the measure of our own exceeding of measure? Is not God a name for this doubly exceeding measure, a measure that cannot, in fact, be measured, an immeasurable measure? And so we come to the exorbitant, or hyperbolic thought of God.

The measure of man returns us to the quest of *The Weight of Finitude*, which is to seek the spoors of God in finitude itself. Here what "finitude" is becomes itself newly questionable, and not necessarily in the terms customarily thrown up by that tide of finitism coming down to us, coming down on us, from post-Kantian philosophy. I will say more below on this in terms of "postulatory finitism." I want first to say something about the *sleep of finitude* as well as its weight. Why speak about this sleep? Is the difference between the sleep and the weight significant? What is it? What is this weight?

The theme of "weight" is inseparable from the notion of measure, but we might say that weight is something *double*. On the one hand, weight is oppressive, it drags us down, it keeps us from flying up, keeps us tied down or in bondage. Weight is heavy. Think of Nietzsche's spirit of gravity (*Geist der Schwere*), said to keep us from the dance of life. On the other hand, weight is stabilizing: it gives us ballast and steadiness, it confers seriousness and gravitas (we speak of a "weighty" issue). Weight also holds us in a field of attraction or relation, just as gravity itself does. This efficacy of weight in a field of attraction can have a religious resonance. Augustine: *pondus meus amor meum*; my love is my weight. I love in a field of attraction that draws me, weights me toward what I love—God. My being as love tilts me to God. I have to go against the ingrained balance of my being to upset this tilt, or to tilt away from God, or against the inherent field of ontological attraction.

These two senses of weight are brought together in what Wordsworth, for instance, refers to as the "burden of the mystery." This burden is something that weighs on us, and yet as mystery it is something that solicits us into deeper rumination and rapport with being. I think also of Keats who, like Hamlet, knew the weight, but also sought the "negative capability" to abide with mystery, and the released mindfulness that is beyond this or that determinate fact or reason.

What of a philosophical reflection on this weight? Must it lack that "negative capability," or what Wordsworth called a "wise passiveness"? Reflection might address itself to the *oppressiveness* of finite existence. And this address itself might be plural: we might seek to transcend the oppressiveness by transcending finitude; or we might so emphasize the weight of finitude that we collapse under the load of its seemingly overbearing burden. Death communicates something of this overbearing burden. Think of the beautiful, shocking, rough and unfinished *Pietà* of Michelangelo in Florence, sculpted for his own tomb: we behold the hooded Joseph of Arimathea—with the face of Michelangelo himself—trying to bear up the weight of the limp body of Jesus, but the lifeless weight is unbearable and seems to press all down, Jesus, his mother Mary, Joseph of Arimathea, Mary Magdalene, living and dead, all inexorably down, down into the earth, down into death.

There is yet another side: weight here allows us to stress the affirmative nature of our being *native to finitude*. Finitude would be the "rough ground" back to which Wittgenstein essays to call us. It would be the immanence that makes a claim on us, in upending the dove of Kant that seeks to fly in an empty, resistanceless "beyond." This weight might mean we are to become mindful of the inescapability of finitude, as the milieu, the between, within which *bonds of being* are shaped for us and by us. This weighty between would be the very network of relativity that keeps our feet on the ground, and keeps us from false flight into counterfeit beyonds with "our heads in the clouds." (One recalls philosophers who did not always keep their feet on the ground: Thales jeered at by the Thracian maid; Socrates mocked by Aristophanes in the *Clouds*.)

Suppose further it is so that in all the above possibilities, and just in that weightiness, something *other* is being insinuated or intimated? A reflection on the weight of finitude could not resist asking what keeps that weight itself in place.[2] We are grounded, given ground in a milieu of being that places us in a field of relativity, an intermediated ethos that relatively fixes us, ballasts us, and yet releases us dynamically to be in relation to what is beyond ourselves. What holds that intermediated between in place? That there is this weight of finitude seems undeniable, and it is plurivocally articulated, and extends from the most life-sapping oppressiveness to the exhilaration of being native to the earth. But now one asks whether in these extremes, or in the many possibilities in-between, something other might be intimated that one cannot quite pin down as this or that finite being or item. And this "something other" (as I very indefi-

---

[2] Think of Newton's worries about gravity, though the analogy is not quite correct: That the systematic network of finite things holds together at all, that too is astonishing. Not just the fact of the internal intelligibility of the system itself, but the network of finitude's holding things in place or being held in place at all, this can arouse astonishment; and this, regardless of how much we know in determinate terms about the internal processes that govern this astonishing network. I make the point not in the direction of scientific theory but of metaphysical perplexity.

nitely call it now) is intimated in the plurivocal weight of finitude itself.

An illustration of this weight as both oppressive and lightening: think of the way *boredom* can transmute into something other. I think of the weight of empty Sunday afternoons I knew as a child—nothing seemed to stir—loaded quiet—a heaviness in the air, especially in summer—human noises retreating to nowhere—and yet in the heaviness of thereness, a different shimmering of presence in absence, of absence in presence. And one was strangely at home in this heaviness, strangely contented with a mystery one could not quite identify—it passed into one, and one hardly noticed, till a mild hint of gentle surprise made one lift up one's face and wonder: *what was that?* A godsend in the heavy silence; boredom yielding to nameless greeting; and the soul porous to a sabbatical communication for thought.

The weight of finitude, expressed from one side or the other, makes our being in the between open to question. There is more than this, of course, if there are such greetings or communications or godsends. But as making us open to question, making us questionable, it also helps to make us wake up: we *start up*, as if from sleep, surprised by noticing now what was there all along, but not at all noticed all along. (We start up like this too when someone we love dies; though we soon fall into sleep again.) Whether weight is oppressive or giving ground, we can wake up to that, and, startled, wonder about the sleep of finitude. What might this sleep be?

The Sleep of Finitude and Postulatory Finitism

Consider what goes under the name of a *philosophy of finitude*. I am not at all certain what is meant by a philosophy of finitude, and especially not completely clear about its meaning in the wake of Nietzsche. At the core of many rejections of "philosophies of infinitude" (as we might crudely name the opposite) seems to me to be some form of cartoonish Platonism: a simplistic dualistic vision of here and there, time and eternity, immanence and transcendence, finitude and infinity. A cartoon is not necessarily untrue, but it is not necessarily true either. Like a caricature, the exaggeration of a true element may risk untruth to the whole, and even untruth to the true element caricatured. A true caricature is true only because it is false, though its very being false hits sharply on a kernel of truth. In a word, a cartoon or caricature is *equivocal* through and through. Can one say the same about "philosophies of finitude"?

There seems to be a long line of inheritance since Kant allegedly drew the bounds of finitude and the limits of metaphysics, reinforced massively through the vehemence of Nietzsche's "announcement" (how one winces at that overused word) of the so-called "death of God." Kant first suggested that his so-called Copernican revolution was something like an experiment (*Versuch*). But as the experiment continued, more often than not it was overlooked that it was an experiment at all. Its programmatic character faded from view, we forgot it was a program, we forgot too that, at its inception, we were asked to *suppose* that we try to look at things in this hitherto untried way, namely, not from the ordinary perspective of objects known, but from the point of view of the knowing subject itself. Why *suppose* thus? No doubt, many significant influences and reasons motivated the supposition (see, for instance, *Being and the Between*, 23–29). But why not suppose otherwise? My query: Is much of so-called philosophy of finitude "programmatic" in an analogous respect — a program, a project laid down in advance, raising for us the question whether this philosophy is quite the free exploration of finitude it claims to be. There might be an analogous postulatory structure in different philosophies, even if the results might well be different. For instance, instead of Kant's "finitism" leading to the postulate of God, we come across a kind of "postulatory finitism" that will fasten on its version of finitude and nothing else besides. And then a new "god" postulated: this version of finitude as the being greater than which none can be thought?

I find an instructive example of this in Nietzsche's *Zarathustra* ("On the Blissful Islands"). Zarathustra declaims:[3]

---

[3] Friedrich Nietzsche, *Also sprach Zarathustra*, in vol. 6 of *Werke*, edited by G. Colli and M. Montinari (Berlin: De Gruyter, 1980). The German word Nietzsche uses is *Muthmaassung*, which W. Kaufmann translates as "conjecture" (*The Portable Nietzsche* [New York: Viking Penguin, 1982], 197), and R. J. Hollingdale as "supposition," (*Thus Spoke Zarathustra* [Harmondsworth: Penguin, 1961], 110), though it might also be rendered as something like "guess," or "surmise." Interestingly, the word brings courage (*Mut*) to mind, but as we shall see in a later chapter there are different kinds of courage. I might also mention Kant's "Conjectural Beginning of Human History" (*Mutmaßlicher Anfang der Menschengeschichte*, 1786). Kant's title — *Mutmaßlicher Anfang* — uses the same word as Zarathustra. Kant's "postulatory deism" and "postulatory finitism" are in the same family. Kant's conjecture wants to substitute a secular "likely story" or *muthos* for the religious *muthos*. I mention this

God is a supposition; but I want your supposing to reach no further than your creating will. Could you *create* a god? —so be silent about all gods! But you could surely create the superman . . . God is a supposition: but I want your supposing to be bounded by conceivability. Could you conceive a god? —but may the will to truth mean this to you: that everything shall be transformed into the humanly conceivable, the humanly evident, the humanly palpable! You should follow your senses to the end. And you yourself should create what you have hitherto called the World: the World should be formed in your image, by your reason, your will, and your love!

In an outburst of confession, Zarathustra announces: "But let me reveal my heart to you entirely, my friends: *if* there were gods, how could I endure not to be a god! *Hence* there are no gods. Though I drew this conclusion, now it draws me." This is very revealing, for it not only speaks to friends, it also betrays the heart, the deepest intimacy of the soul. The high importance for Nietzsche of the passages I am discussing is evident in the fact that in *Ecce Homo*, § 8, he significantly cites from them, endorsing them in relation to Zarathustra's task, a task he here identifies with his own. The crucial point: the postulatory character of what is at stake is very evident: "*If* there were gods, how could I endure not to be a god! *Hence*, there are no gods." The entire declamation urges a putatively new project: the turning away from gods and the turning to the human. Not quite so new: this is rhapsodic homiletics, a lyrical version of Feuerbach's reduction of theology to anthropology.

I underscore that this is not an argument; it is an exhortation on the basis of a different supposition; it is preaching that urges an orientation, said to follow from the rejection of a supposition now deemed impossible, or unacceptable—namely, the supposition of gods or God beyond humanity. "Rejection" is maybe too lightheaded a word, since Nietzsche himself uses a bloodier word: murder. And after the murder of God? "Must we ourselves not become gods simply to appear worthy of it?"[4] And then, in a strange summersault from the funereal to the almost dizzy, Zarathustra urges a different

---

again in Chapter 5 (see also note 6 there) when discussing religious imagination and the moralized "making up" of a counterfeit double of God.

[4] *The Gay Science*, trans. Walter Kaufmann (New York: Vintage Books, Random House, 1974), § 125.

supposition, full of atheistic faith in a new project for liberated humanity, namely, "being true to the earth." This is the repeated refrain of this philosophy of finitude, but again it is postulatory: it proposes a project on the basis of a certain understanding of the human being from which God and gods have been excluded. The postulation: If you want to think of man in such and such a wise, and if you want to remain true to the earth, the following project is then to be followed.

The details of that project are not what is right now at issue, but the fact that at this point something very important happens. *The supposition goes underground.* Once granted, it is taken for granted, and falls asleep to its own suppositional character. And then it is as if a kind of sleepwalking can take over. Zarathustra is either extraordinarily naive or candid on this point when he confesses: "Though I drew this conclusion, now it draws me." What first I proposed, now proposes for me; the supposing, as it were, disposes me, or disposes of me, in becoming a later hidden pre-supposing. It begins, it seems, to think my thoughts, to live my life—it draws me, in the sense also of drawing out what is implicit in the postulate and project. The project is indicated thus: "Willing liberates: this is the true doctrine of will and freedom. . . . This will lured me away from God and gods; for what would there be to create if gods—existed!" One sees clearly the *als ob*, the "as if" structure: If you would have man as creative, then no god(s). Decades later, Sartre offered the bargain-basement version of this.

Zarathustra's project: "Again and again it drives me to mankind, my ardent, creative will; thus it drives the hammer to the stone." Zarathustra sees an image "sleeping in the stone, the image of my visions." What then would it be to be woken from the sleep of finitude? It would not be a gentle knocking on the door. It would be a very violent hammering on the stone: "Ah, you men, I see the image sleeping in the stone, the image of my visions! Ah, that it must sleep in the hardest, ugliest stone! Now my hammer rages fiercely against its prison. Fragments fly from the stone: what is that to me? I will complete it. . . ." Pity the stone that has to be so smashed to be completed. Pity the sleeper that has to be so thrashed to be made to wake up. Pity the prison that has to be so demolished to rouse the feeling of the freedom of willing.

Suppose further the postulatory finitism goes underground in a more widespread sense, namely, with respect to *an era* in general, not just one or two particular thinkers. The supposition then turns into something like a kind of absolute pre-supposition, and the "as if," the *als ob*, is entirely lost from sight in a wider sense. A sign of this, for instance, is the continuity between Kant and Nietzsche, despite the surface impression of great discontinuity. Nietzsche was more a son of Kant than he knew or acknowledged, except the *als ob* of a postulatory moral deism mutates into the *als ob* of a postulatory amoral atheism.

And what of the sons of Nietzsche, the philosophers of finitude? What if they too are being drawn by a similar "as if"? To what extent then is their philosophy really being true to finitude? As with Nietzsche, is their project not also motivated by its own "suppose," its own *Muthmaassung*: the supposition of finitude and nothing but finitude? To what extent has the mindfulness of its postulatory character been erased? For if this supposition has become a presupposition about the whole of being, almost inevitably its suppositional character falls from foreground view the more busy we become with the project as such. If you are smashing the stone, it is very easy to forget that the slender motivation for the destruction, excuse me, the creation, is but a surmise.

No matter. "What is that to me," spake Zarathustra. We proceed to construct for ourselves a space within which our transcending energies circulate, and since they circulate we have the feeling there is the utmost of freedom, the more so since these energies also seem most intimately to circulate around themselves. What then when some stray horrors arise that this circling, and even more this circling around ourselves, is the *counterfeit* form of infinitude? Perhaps we have created this self-encirclement as the "false infinity."

By this I do not mean Hegel's "bad infinite." In fact, Hegel's so-called "true infinite" would itself be a form of this "false infinity," as self-encircling immanence. By contrast with "postulatory finitism" Hegel offers a "sublationary infinitism": the finite is sublated in the infinite. A dualistic opposition of finite and infinite is false for Hegel. To assert one in opposition to the other is one-sided. Hence Hegel says: "The infinite is . . . the self-sublation of [the one-sided] *infinite* and *finite*, as a *single* process—this the *true* or *genuine infinite*."[5] It is because of opposition to Hegel's "sublationary infinitism" as untrue to finitude, or not true enough, that "postulatory finitism" derives quite a bit of the plumage of its contemporary persuasiveness. In

---

[5] G. W. F. Hegel, *Science of Logic*, trans. A. V. Miller (New York: Humanities Press, 1969), 137. On what I call the reserve of the infinite, see my *Hegel's God*, 203–4.

truth, both "sublationary infinitism" and "postulatory finitism" have something in common: both are philosophies of unremitting *immanence*. Both emerge from an elemental decision not to consider, or a refusal to consider, transcendence as irreducibly other to immanence. Do we need a philosophy other to each: a philosophy of finitude not postulatory, a philosophy of infinitude not sublationary; a philosophy in which we are not closed off from rethinking transcendence in a sense that neither of these positions can, or will, contemplate?

I put sublationary infinitism aside for the moment and concentrate on postulatory finitism. Do we find ourselves, with postulatory finitism, counterfeiting infinitude, because the very truth of finitude is just that it cannot be for itself alone? And suppose (I am now supposing otherwise), suppose then we wake up in this circle with alarm that we are in a prison, and it seems to oppress us massively. It grounds us, but the weight of finitude grinds us down, for the space between earth and heaven has collapsed, and the ether of true porosity in which our spirit might soar is squeezed empty to the point of suffocation. For in coming to ourselves in this circle, we might now have the foreboding that we are not only in bondage, but in this form of being *we are bondage itself.*

Or otherwise: we grant this new waking up, but we still want to be fatally consistent and cleave to the terms of the "postulatory finitism," and hence we need to wreck this prison, hoping thereby to gain at least the feeling of being free. But we are the prison and hence this self-encircling degenerates into self-laceration. We tear strips from ourselves, cannibalize ourselves to ingest energies that impel the circle into one more turn. But having a riot in a prison, burning everything within it, though we might even claim this riot and inferno as a kind of ontological potlatch, does not change the prison into free space. It is now merely a desolated, devastated prison. I think of Bataille—thrashing the prison house of utility. Free at last, one feels, free at last—but this feeling does not last. Can one think of others? But has Zarathustra above, again either in extreme candor or extreme naïveté, betrayed the need to thrash the prison to rouse the feel of free willing? Hammering the stone can feel like a really smashing freedom.

Alternatively, one might say: Maybe I was wrong, and wrong at the start, I go back to the start, in fact, I am now at point zero, and I must begin again. Maybe a truer philosophy of finitude always allows this return to zero? But how allow? And what if the false start is the "postulatory finitism"? Would it not be an odd thing if this all started in a so-called Copernican revolution that counterfeited Copernicus? After all, Copernicus's revolution was toward *heliocentrism*. One might say: Copernicans are a little like the despised Plato—they look to the *Sun* as their point of reference; they look beyond the earth to remain true to the earth; they do not chant spellbinding incantations about remaining true to the earth and forget the sun; they wonder if the truth of the earth must look to the sun, since it can only be seen by the light of the sun. If these reflections have any truth, Kant's Copernican revolution, if taken as a turn to the human self only, would be a counterfeit double of the heliocentrism of Copernicus's revolution. We would be, or have to make ourselves to be, the sun. How could we remain true to the earth at all, were we to blot out the sun or obliterate the heavens? For philosophies of finitude that follow the turn to ourselves, and to ourselves only, be we self-glorifying or self-lacerating, would also be in danger of producing counterfeit doubles of finitude.

Aporiai of Finitude?

I agree: philosophy must honestly acknowledge finitude, and search its significance. But how are we to respond if our searching leads us to what might be called *aporiai of finitude*: impasses that arrest us but that we cannot pass beyond simply in finite terms? There are aporiai we cannot even determine in finite terms, since in the immanence of finitude something comes before us for consideration that exceeds the terms of finite determination. I have already indicated one such aporetic situation with reference to the human being as "measure": a measure that while on a par with other finite beings is yet not the measure of itself qua measure of finitude. Toward the end of my reflections below, I will come back to four other major considerations bearing on this aporetic situation, namely the idiocy of being, the aesthetics of finite happening, the erotics of selving, and the agapeics of community. For now I make a more general point in connection with postulatory finitism.

All in all we search what is immanent to finitude, but come upon, or are overcome by what is excessive to finitization. We are in the between—between finitude and infinitude. How dwell in the between, if the sublation of finitude into infinitude seems not right, nor the rebound back into finitude from the boundary? How dwell in the between if that boundary becomes porous to what is hyperbolic to finitude qua finitude? The aporiai of finitude might be said to demand honesty about perplexity that exceeds finite terms. Addressed as such, they call into question any closure into finitude of philosophical thought about finitude. This seems the most honest thing: to wonder about what might be *other* to finitude. For already we have been brought to encounter something of such exceeding otherness.

I think of Kant's recognition of the knotted situation of metaphysics itself: reason is burdened with questions it cannot either answer or dismiss (*Critique of Pure Reason*, A viii). This betokens both what weighs on reason as well as an aporia of finitude. We are to wake from our dogmatic slumbers. Maybe we also need to be woken from the slumber of postulatory finitism? Maybe we need a second dimension of thought beyond determinate (scientific) cognition. Maybe we need a reborn astonishment and perplexity in the dimension of the overdeterminate that is hyperbolic to determinate finitude. Kant's moral philosophy is his answer to this aporia. Hegel's speculative dialectic might be seen as a rejoinder also, though giving us sublationary infinitism, not second-born astonishment in the overdeterminate. Interestingly, there may have been a second birth at a certain point in Kant's own life,[6] bringing to the fore the Kant we have come to know, and intimately connected with the moral direction of his philosophy. Kant strove for the autonomy of moral self-determination beyond the aporia of finitude constitutive of metaphysical thought. Moral justification will deliver reason from the burden of being finite. This is not the awakening beyond the sleep of finitude about which I will shortly talk and that is more religious than moral. Kant turned from this and moralized it, maximized it. It may well turn out that this maximization of autonomy becomes a new sleep of moralized finitude.

Nietzsche, we know, scorned this moralized finitude as a contemptible slumber. What seems to happen with certain post-Nietzschean philosophies of finitude? Instead of facing toward something other that might address the impasse, I suspect a tendency to *swerve off the aporiai*, or to accentuate them further in the light of a particular configuration of finitude, say, in terms of will-to-power, or *Angst*, or groundless freedom, or a reiterated insistence on radical immanence.

---

[6] If Manfred Kuehn in his biography of Kant is correct (see *Kant: A Biography* [Cambridge and New York: Cambridge University Press, 2001], 248). Regarding Kant and the moralization of the sublime, see my *Art, Origins, Otherness*, especially 80–86.

Let me cite a passage in Heidegger's *Sein und Zeit* §58 that I find perplexing on this score.[7] I do not have space to quote in full these tortured passages of Heidegger. I will cite enough to give their flavor. In this section, §58, Heidegger is discussing how to understand the call of conscience and guilt. He says: "Dasein exists as thrown, brought into its there *not* of its own accord. It exists as a potentiality-of-being [*Seinkönnen*] which belongs to itself, and yet has *not* given itself to itself." One might say: There is a fundamental givenness of our finitude which we do not originate but within which we find ourselves. Heidegger speaks of Dasein as "being delivered over" to this, and "because it has not laid the ground itself, it rests in the weight of it [*in seiner Schwere*]." Mood, *Stimmung*, reveals this weight to it as a burden (*als Last*).

We are dealing with the weight of finitude and being "thrown," but how relate to this? If I am not mistaken Heidegger wants to say Dasein is not its own ground, and yet would be a ground: since thrown, it does not ground itself, but as thrown, it is determined to be the ground (*Grund-sein*). It is as a thrown ground. "And how *is* Dasein this thrown ground [*geworfene Grund*]? Only by projecting itself upon the possibilities into which it is thrown. The self, which as such has to lay the ground of itself, can *never* gain power over that ground, and yet it has to take over [*übernehmen*] the ground in existing. Being its own thrown ground is the potentiality-of-being about which care [*Sorge*] is concerned."

In my view, the great difficulty here lies in the meaning of this "taking over." What can this mean? Originally groundless and given, how can one, how does one, "take over" this groundlessness and givenness, and "take it over" in such a wise that one, with all due guilt-wracked qualifications, "lays the ground of oneself"? Thus: "Dasein is not itself the ground of its being, because the ground first arises from its own project, but as a self, it is the *being* of its ground. The ground is always ground only for a being whose being has to take over [*übernehmen*] being-the-ground [*Grund-sein*]." There is no being a ground without Dasein, and yet Dasein is both not its own ground and yet has to "take over" being-the-ground.

But what then can this "taking over" mean, if there is no ground without Dasein and Dasein is not its own ground? There seems to

⁷ Martin Heidegger, *Sein und Zeit*, 7th ed. (Tübingen: Niemeyer Verlag, 1953), 284–85. Translated by Joan Stambaugh as *Being and Time* (Albany: State University of New York Press, 1996), 262. I insert the German where I think it helps.

me something fundamentally aporetic about this situation, but that is not what Heidegger stresses. I wonder if the convoluted manner of describing what seems to be at issue betrays a "swerve" back into the aporia, dictated by a postulatory finitism whose secret workings remain out of focus. I get the distinct impression Dasein is getting its knickers in a twist, as it tries to acknowledge its own groundlessness, while trying to be the ground, and all this without reference to any ground other than itself that might take it outside the bounding terms of a postulatory finitism.

There is an original groundlessness to this Heideggerian self— "being the (null) ground of a nullity [*Das (nichtige) Grund-sein einer Nichtigkeit*]"—yet it is determined to lay its own ground, even though this determination to be the ground is itself groundless: groundless and self-grounding; given to be, not giving itself to be, yet determined to give itself to be, through its own projection of its potentiality-to-be. This is not entirely wrong—but it is not entirely right either. I would say: we come to be between an original being given to be and the promise of our own being that, in finite form, can give to itself its own determinations of being. But the promise of the second (self-)becoming is always qualified by the original givenness of the first coming to be. We are given to be before we give ourselves to ourselves; but the issue hangs on the nature of the first being given to be, the character of the second giving of self to itself, and the relation of these two.

In the language I use, there is a *passio essendi* that is prior to the *conatus essendi*, and the second cannot "take over" the first absolutely into "being-the-ground," or, for that matter, any form of self-determination through itself alone. This is not to deny that the second can seek to "take over" the first and, as it were, even try to ingest the first givenness of being into its own resolve to "be the ground." But we can also consent differently to our being given to be. A different understanding of the *passio essendi* releases us differently toward the original givenness of being, as it does to the question of grounding, which now itself is released from the secret constraint of postulatory finitism. Finitude, our finitude, can be looked at otherwise. Not least, we must hesitate to use any language that speaks of our being as one that "has to take over being-the-ground."[8]

---

[8] More generally, one detects in modernity what I call an antinomy of autonomy and transcendence which calls attention to a particular aporia of finitude: if we absolutize our autonomy, we must relativize transcendence as other to us; if transcen-

I have to confess I find something strained, even forced in the way Heidegger speaks. Suppose one said: We must "take up," assume one's finitude. Very well, but why not simply say: We must consent to finitude. Heidegger would not dream of saying anything so simple. Yes, there are different kinds of consent. I know that. But consent of itself is not a "taking up," or an assuming, or a "taking over." One can consent to taking up a burden, but the consent is not the taking up, but rather the taking up presupposes the consent. As the nature of the "taking up" is in question, even more is the consent. I would say there is a "yes" that is released to an other, or otherness, a "yes" that has nothing to do with "being-the-ground." There is a consent that releases—something is transmitted in released surrender that passes across a boundary and we are reconciled to what we are. The consent and release happen in a more primal porosity of being in which we say "yes" to what is beyond us. Is the strain we find in Heidegger's tortured language a reflection of a will to "take up" the weight of finitude—within a finitude not open to its own beyond, or any beyond, but circling back on itself as the absolute last enclosing horizon of being, beyond which or behind which one cannot step?

Responding to the burden of being thrown, one wills no longer to be thrown down, but wills to lift oneself up. Very well. I do admire those who lift themselves up. But can we lift ourselves up—here in this ontological situation? Did not Michelangelo show us—without strain, and with profound simplicity—the shocking elemental truth in the Florence *Pietà* I mentioned above? Mary cannot lift, Joseph of Arimathea cannot lift, Mary Magdalene cannot lift up the dead

---

dence as other to us is absolute, we must relativize our autonomy. See *Hegel's God*, 4–7. Much of modernity has chosen for the former. Heidegger does not choose for it, rather he sees its limit; but that does not mean he chooses the latter—he vacillates somewhere in between these two, always constrained, I believe, by the effects of a postulatory finitism. Dasein is transcendence but not absolutely autonomous, since thrown, yet it is resolute to be its own, in a swerve of self-transcending to itself and its ownmost possibility. But one can take oneself over and yet one's owning oneself is one's usurping oneself—instead of one's being released—and perhaps released beyond finitude. Time is the horizon of finitude, but time seems to be both as giving and as given. Is there a swerve here in which time is made to do the work of both time and eternity, as the latter might be understood outside the frame of postulatory finitism? There is more release in the later Heidegger, but the thought does occur to one that there might be a dissimulating release, a quasi-move beyond, an *als ob Gelassenheit* (see *Art, Origins, Otherness*, 209–63) And *Sein zum Tode*? "No man liveth unto himself alone, and no man dieth unto himself alone."

Jesus. Jesus cannot lift himself up. Even the stones cry out: We cannot do it! Nothing of this is heard in Heidegger.

To return to the general point: there are boundaries of finitude where we find ourselves punctured by an impotence that cries out for something beyond itself. Yet this "impotence" is paradoxically releasing. Postulatory finitism must stifle that outcry, for there can be no "outside" into which it might cry. It must swerve back into the same finitude that just now brought it to the point of aporia.[9] The aporia does not give birth to a new porosity. Pushed to an extreme — and remember we are at an extreme — this swerve back means turning finitude against itself, making it dig into itself, as a rider's spurs violently dig into a horse before a ditch that stalls it. And, of course, new energies are released in that violence. But in what direction are they going? And the direction does make a huge difference, for extraordinary energies can be expended on *evading the aporiai* — even in the very act of loudly calling attention to them. Then the attention is a counterfeit double of the mindfulness of finitude that would allow the energy of self-transcending to call into question, at the very least, the postulatory character of the "postulatory finitism." If as philosophers we are free enough, courageous enough to ponder this possibility, then in trying to be mindful of the other of finitude, we might not only have to return to zero, but we might also have to *give up* this entire way of thinking of postulatory finitism, give it up as a *project*. For this return to zero might open up new access to the primal porosity of our being, and passage to rebirth beyond the impasse of self-enclosed finitude.

Why shy off that most hyperbolic of perplexities: the question of God? Why not face the music? If it were the case that some philosophies risk producing a counterfeit double of finitude, would not these counterfeits also produce a *different weight of finitude*, also indeed a particular form of what I am calling the sleep of finitude? I now come to

---

[9] Something like a recurrence of this swerve in contemporary Continental thought was one lesson I gleaned from the thought-provoking analyses in Rudi Visker's *Truth and Singularity* (Dordrecht: Kluwer, 1999), though perhaps he would not see this as a lesson he was giving. For a sense of the unease of the human being not unrelated to what I am suggesting, and to the porosity of finitude, see Ignace Verhack's fine book, *De mens en zijn unrust: Over het 'raadsel' van de beweging* (Leuven: Acco, 2000), especially 394ff., "Het aporetisch wezen van ons in-de-wereld-zijn." Verhack makes use of some Heideggerian resources but moves in a direction that is not quite Heidegger's, and that sympathetically overlaps with some of my concerns.

that theme, for sleep can be variously slept; and just as a "philosophy of infinitude" like Hegel's may finally sleep to finitude, so a "philosophy of finitude" may produce its own reversed somnolence. Nothing is univocal or straightforward. My own surmise, as will become clearer, is that contemporary philosophies of immanence risk falling into this second kind of sleep, rather than the first, and indeed falling into it just insofar as they accuse the first of sleep, and they fall into this second sleep even as they claim to wake up from the sleep of infinitude. I must say something more.

The Sleep of Philosophy?

Sleep is a happening and a metaphor, and it is, of course, plurivocal. This plurivocity will engage us, since it reflects something of the equivocities of the weight of finitude above discussed. I will draw attention to a number of different senses of "sleep" with relation to finitude. "Sleep" is also relevant to the notion of measure, and especially to exceeding the measure, in that there may be forms of sleeplessness that bring us to the limit of finite measure. How we wake to this limit, awake at this limit, concerns the unease of philosophy and the unease of religion. In that regard, it concerns our address to certain aporiai of finitude.

There is first what seems to be the sleep of *common sense* that takes its own being for granted, that is neither astonished at being at all, nor alert to its own being open to question. This is a *first* sense of the sleep of finitude, and against it traditional philosophy has often railed. Witness the inhabitants of the Platonic Cave. Do not they seem to be kinds of sleepwalkers? A *second* sense bears on the claim of philosophy: namely, to awaken us from that first sleep of finitude. Now, however, the question arises as to whether philosophy itself, in seeming to awake us, falls into *its own* form of sleep—a more intractable form of sleep, since it has rationally convinced itself it is awake!

Is there a *further* sleeplessness that now might descend on us? Is there an awakening from the sleep of philosophy? Has philosophy not only to become uneasy about the first sleep of finitude but also about the possibility of *its own second sleep*? And what does the unease of philosophy have to do with the religious? Is there a third paradoxical sleep of religion bound up with such a further sleeplessness? For instance, in the Mandukya Upanishad of Hinduism, beyond the everyday waking state (*jāgarita-sthāna*), beyond the dream state (*svapna-sthāna*), there is a deep sleep (*susupta-sthāna*) suggesting less a sacred soporific as proximity to ultimate peace in Brahman. There is a fourth state (*turīya*) beyond this sleep. One wonders about something both slumbering and waking at once: peace beyond the normal dualities of everyday waking, sleep in one sense idiotic, in another sense divine; sleeplessness patient and energetic at once, effortless and at work, absolutely resting and intensively alert. Is the religious that other of philosophy that *can* startle philosophical thought into the awakening that it too slept, and lift up its face? And is not this unease something hard to accommodate to the traditional terms in which philosophy thinks of itself in relation to religion: say, faith seeking understanding? What if now *understanding* qua philosophical understanding seems to be asleep? Is it a kind of *religious unease* that might then wake it up *from itself*?

Religions, of course, have claimed to wake the human from the first sleep of everyday life. What if that first sleep is now softly bound in the cybernetic cocoon created by advances in science and technology over the last four centuries? How will the watchfulness, wakefulness of being religious strike us in this cocoon of comfort? As something we welcome, something that irritates us, or something that makes us yawn? As we yawn, we seem to say: it, being religious, is what is asleep, not us. And suppose modern practices of philosophy sometimes were intellectual versions of this yawn? Has the passionate desolation of Nietzsche's madman become the blasé all-knowingness, all-knowing nothingness, of postmodern kitsch?

The issue is further complicated in that *religion itself* has sometimes served as another form of the sleep of finitude—a sacred soporific that less bears, as denies, the "burden of the mystery." This can be so, yes, and it might be that the philosophies of finitude stemming from Nietzsche dominantly stress this possibility. What if these philosophies are themselves in danger of being forms of the sleep of philosophical finitude—sophomorifics of finitude that cannot comprehend, much less grant as a possibility, that religion, understood as a different unease, is what just might wake such philosophies from their sleep of finitude? How could they consider this as a possibility, since religion has been stylized as the soporific of finitude, beyond which they have claimed to wake to finitude? Their claims to be awake may well be soporific in a far more insidious sense! What if, so to say, this has been the bewitching power of the *vis dormitiva* of Nietzscheanism? Its wakefulness will also be a slumber, though troubled by episodes of night terror and bouts of cold sweat that periodically disturb it. Such night terror might bring before us a brief suspicion of God, but that will now seem to us more nightmare than dream.

The soporifics of the sacred are only the counterfeit doubles of what is the deepest issue here, namely, true peace. This is a concern often unacknowledged if we are paralyzed in the face of different aporiai of finitude, even though true peace may well be highest wakefulness. Being at peace, far from being evasive, is deeply connected to how we face death, and how we consent to being, in exposure to this extremity. In Greek mythology sleep and death, *hypnos* and *thanatos*, were twin brothers. (Here one must be thankful for Ludwig Heyde's profound meditation on death in the last chapter of *De Maat van de Mens*.) The meaning of "sleep" is bound up with the meaning of "being at peace." It is also connected with evil. Think of Macbeth and what ensues on his horrible crime: he murders sleep and cannot pronounce "Amen," when he has most need of blessing. What does it mean to murder sleep? Is there a peace more ultimate than that murder? And what could prevent us from saying "Amen" at all, since like Nietzsche and Lady Macbeth we might claim to be "beyond good and evil." Why, is "Amen" not a mere word, in their "beyond"?

With such questions in mind, let me now explore a number of extremities of sleeplessness beyond determinate, finite measure. Can postulatory finitism be true to the full measure, a "measure" that exceeds finite measure, of what is at stake at these extremities? I will look at the image of "sleep" in three forms: with regard to a great philosopher, a religious thinker, and a great dramatic artist. In addition to Shakespeare's *Macbeth*, I will refer to Plotinus when he says that the soul is in the body as in a deep sleep; and to the prayer of Pascal when he says that Christ, in Gethsemane Garden, will be in agony till the end of the world—till then, we must not sleep. There is a *double edge* to "sleep": it can be a rich metaphor of a genuine being at peace with being; it can be its counterfeit double, a false being at peace in which the extreme perplexities of life are evaded rather than faced. If philosophers too can end up sleeping in this counterfeit double of peace, can philosophy also seek to awaken us from that sleep which is the evasive tranquillization of life? Is this not something it shares in common with the religious? And can both seek to wake us, if one can thus put it, to the paradoxical "sleep" of true peace? We must sleep deep to wake well refreshed.

Sleeplessness and the Unease of Philosophy: Plotinus above *Nous* and *Epistēmē*

There is something in Plotinus that puts us in mind of the *unease of philosophy*, though this is not at first evident. He is not a philosopher we associate immediately with finitude but with the mystic; and most famously with the claims that there is to be a union with the One, a flight of the alone to the Alone. Philosophies of finitude seem to abjure the One, as they claim to shatter too high a confidence in reason, and perhaps also the world's reasonableness and goodness. Where then is the unease? Has not it been said that Plotinus offers something like a culmination of the great Greek tradition of philosophy, marked by its seemingly unshakable confidence in reason and the ideal, a tradition that in the figure of Plato seemed to have inaugurated the quest of philosophical wisdom with a turn from the dark equivocity of finitude, symbolized by existence in the Cave. Think here of Nietzsche's polemos with Socrates, with respect to the tragic vision and philosophy. What then of the sleep of finitude?

Plotinus remarks that the soul is, as it were, asleep in the body (see *Ennead*, III, vi, 6). This seems very Platonic: the body seems the prison of the soul, and from this prison we must fly to the ideal. But what if we see Plotinus as coming to the limit of a certain kind of idealism? Plotinus speaks about philosophy and "the most worthy" — *to timiotaton*; but our engagement with the most worthy emerges at the point where *nous* and *epistēmē* reach what seems like an insurmountable limit. There is a flight or ecstasis of the soul about *nous* and *epistēmē*. It is a flight into the night of a divine darkness. Can one know that the darkness is divine when one begins that flight, or feels impelled to go further? *Daring* seems needed, an audacity, a courage, beyond the measure of secure rational justification, to undertake this last exitus. (The question of daring beyond the rational measure comes back in a different form with Macbeth.)

This is where the sleep of the soul is at issue, and the unease. Recall the point above: there are different sleeps; the soul may sleep differently. There is the everyday sleep — the standard Platonic sense — the sleep of underground men from which philosophy seeks to wake us. Does Plotinus open up the possibility of a further sleep, the sleep of philosophy itself? Only if there is a further awakening. There is the sleep of reason in which it lacks the inkling that it sleeps, since it claims a great awakening from the sleep of common sense. Waking from one sleep it falls into another sleep it names as rational enlightenment. This second sleep is strangely a deeper sleep, since it thinks it is wide awake. Rational enlightenment takes itself as having woken up from the sleep of ordinary consciousness and to be full lucid wakefulness. How could it possibly be asleep, how possibly need a new and further and more radical awakening? For is it not already awake?

My suggestion: As there is a god higher than thought thinking itself, so there is a wisdom more ultimate that this rational enlightenment. Truer philosophy begins to wake up at this extreme: in its unease, it begins to suspect that it has slept in its rational self-certainty, and now is made sleepless by a quest that takes it even more radically beyond itself and its previous sleep of rational enlightenment. This new sleeplessness is hyperbolic, beyond finite measure, and determinate reason, and what initiates it is not entirely clear. But if we see it in a certain light, or darkness, it implies the defect of those rationalistic philosophies that cannot shake off their own idealistic self-satisfaction.

One might say: Plotinus's thought of the most worthy makes one sleepless with the worthlessness of one's previously claimed wisdom. This "most worthy" is other to thought thinking itself. Plotinus explicitly offers us an argument that Aristotle's god—*noēsis noēsis noēseōs*—is not ultimate ("On the Good or the One," *Ennead*, VI, 9.2, 33ff.). There is a higher One above thought thinking thought. And most philosophers have bowed down and adored Aristotle's God. Hegel is an outstanding example of this: he sees Plotinus through the eyes of this god, and has no time for the last exitus of our soul above itself and thought thinking itself. What if Hegel's adoration is paradigmatic of the "higher" sleep of the philosophers? What if perhaps it is also the self-satisfied worship of a counterfeit double of God (see my *Hegel's God*)? Hegel's "true infinite" would be, in fact, a false infinite, and not in the sense he means by his so-called "bad infinite"? (Ludwig Heyde did not put this question to Hegel, certainly not in this form. If I am not mistaken, something of this other sleeplessness was overtaking him, even in relation to his much admired Hegel.)

One could ask: What would the peace of a diviner sleep be, beyond the sleep of everyday understanding and rational enlightenment? Has it something to do with the way being religious might make philosophy newly uneasy, not about religion, but *about itself*. One thing one can say: of this sleeplessness and peace, there is no system. The going out of the soul, the going above *nous* and *epistēmē* is beyond rational system. It is idiotic—most intimate to the disturbance of the soul at its most extreme point of entrance into itself where it now sees it has to be lifted up or driven above itself, and this lifting up or lashing is an extreme sleeplessness, or better put, an extreme vigilance or watchfulness. Philosophy, uneasy about how to take the measure of the loss of its own self-certitude, now asks for this *hyperbolic watchfulness*.

Sleeplessness and the Unease of Religion: Pascal and Hyperbolic Vigilance

Pascal draws our attention to a religious form of this hyperbolic watchfulness. Pascal looks very heterogenous to Plotinus: instead of mystical ecstasis above philosophy, we meet torment before a universe where the signs of God seem either to have evaporated or become shrouded in a thick equivocity. The ecstasis of the soul seems choked in that stifling equivocity. The rational powers of Pascal were of the highest order, his achievements in mathematics and science could rival the best minds in history, and yet he was tortured by the straw of all that, and most deeply tormented by our ultimate destiny and relation to God. History seems like the still-unended night of vigil in Gethsemane Garden. This night puts us at the opposite extreme to any Hegelian or idealistic progress toward a dialectically guaranteed completion, or to satisfactions delivered by materialistic or cybernetic progress (though ironically Pascal was the inventor of the first calculating machine). In the dark equivocities of time, we need finesse, not geometry, to find some stumbling way. And maybe we need even more than finesse in order to keep vigil when time itself strikes us as a seemingly unending wait in Gethsemane Garden.

Thus Pascal's critique of the sleeping self-satisfaction of the philosophers. Descartes: useless and uncertain, Pascal says. Descartes who, for all his self-proclaimed commitment to the ordeal of doubt, strikes one always as strangely self-conceited, strangely self-satisfied. It is Pascal who lived the ordeal more deeply in a hyperbolic doubt, but doubt also *against* that dormant self-satisfaction of the scientific mind. What spurred him to wake? There was the undergoing of a certain suffering: a *passio essendi* rather than a *conatus essendi*; a suffering of spirit in the agony of perplexity, before the equivocal signs of a God both withdrawn and intimate; an almost unremitting suffering of body in the invalidity that afflicted Pascal from a very young age, and about which one must wonder if it was as much due to spiritual affliction as to physical; suffering also in the sense of experience of

the passion of the divine — I refer to what is recorded in the stammer-
ings of Pascal's *Memorial* — the experience of conversion and grace,
given without premeditation and given in the burning of fire, divine
interruption of our satisfied powers of being and the reawakening of
the *passio essendi*, when we anticipate it not, and which ruptures the
satisfactions of finite life evermore.

But this is the nub of the issue — Pascal's remark in his meditation
on Gethsemane night: Christ will be in agony until the end of the
world; we must not sleep during that time. The drowsy apostles show
"ordinary sleep": they find it impossible to stay awake. "Watch and
pray with me": the appeal does not seem to ask much. But what if
the appeal goes out for the hyperbolic watchfulness? Does it ask too
much? And does not the appeal for hyperbolic watchfulness match
the extreme ordeal of evil that impends for Jesus, and the prayer for
access of extreme strength to face it? From where in the secrecy of
this black night would come that source of strengthening? Is there
not something monstrous about Pascal's suggestion that *we* must not
sleep until the end of the world? Is this monstrousness proportionate
to the disproportionate agony of Christ himself? To be proportionate
to the disproportionate itself asks something disproportionate of us.
What then of this monstrous sleeplessness?

I would say: there is a "sleep" that is our falling into the unconsciousness of finitude, because we cannot bear to be exposed to evil
and suffering, beyond a certain measure. What if the evil and the
suffering are *beyond finitude*, and *beyond finite measure*? Sleep is the
ruse, even the necessity of finitude by which we can continue to be.
We cannot bear to be as awake; we must sleep, else we die. It is
amazing how a good night's rest can make life bearable again! Yet
what if, sometimes for reasons mysterious, one cannot fall asleep?
Then one has lost this consolation of escape, not only from ourselves,
but from the evil and the suffering. Who could bear to be so endlessly
awake? Is this what God is: endless wakefulness, not only to the
good of being, but to the evil? We speak in theology of God's omni-
science: but were we to take seriously the hyperbolic character of
this wakefulness, we might recoil in horror. Such wakefulness would
also be the most intimate knowing of horror and evil and suffering.

In passing: Nietzsche claimed superiority for the tragic vision
(say, over against theistic religions) because of its ability to endure
some such dark knowing, or some such knowing of darkness: honesty about the abyss, which almost all of us shun — God, he implies,
is our escape from this dark knowing. *Sed contra*: follow the above

line of thinking, and the divine knowing could not be the simplistic anodyne Nietzsche suggests. Looked at in terms of the hyperbolic character of the sleeplessness, this knowing is either madness pure and simple, or its own unique divine madness. The latter means: divine in its madness, not mad in its divineness. And maybe this madness can only be seen as mad madness, by that knowing that sleeps in the contentment of finite life.

For Pascal one thing seems to be true: if sleep must await the end of time, so also must true peace. Before then, all forms of peace participate in evasion of the dark play between good and evil that finds its site of strife in the Gethsemane night of every soul, and every time. The agon(y) in Gethsemane garden is hyperbolic enough to make one wonder if any trace remains of the "It is good" in the garden of Eden. Is there a Sabbath after the night in Gethsemane garden, as there might be a Sabbath that recalls the garden of Eden? Does Golgotha roll an immovable stone before the grave entrance of Easter Sunday? For it is the *lack* of peace Pascal wants to accentuate. Every interim peace also counterfeits the truth of peace. That hyperbolic lack of peace entails the provocation of the sane rationalities of philosophy into a religious and metaphysical insomnia from which it cannot wake *just to itself alone*. Philosophy must be woken up to *being beyond itself*. (Hear an echo of what I said about Plotinus.)

I recall Nietzsche's admiration for Pascal, yet his horror at what he took to be the *sacrificium intellectus* Pascal's religion demanded. What then of Pascalian watchfulness? It shows something like Nietzsche's extremism, but the directionalities of their spiritual energies seem quite opposed. We have to consider this: If the thought of God makes us radically sleepless, Nietzsche's godlessness must be the deepest slumber, and not the sleep of highest peace either. Nietzsche calls for war, not peace. But if the sleeplessness of his godlessness is such a deeper sleep, then he may have woken from the peace of mediocre contentment but woken to nothing. And waking from nothing to nothing is not waking. It is an even worse kind of sleep. It is a counterfeit double of being awake.

Pascal desires to disturb our "sleep" in a God-forgetting world. This "sleep" of forgetting, as a counterfeit double of peace, is something monstrous for him. I recall his pained bewilderment at those who affect to care not a jot about questions of God, of immortality, of our fragile finitude. He cannot fathom this blithe disregard: it strikes him as monstrous. The hyperbolic watchfulness that wakes us up also *postpones* the peace it seems to promise. We must wait. And what would true peace be at the extreme level, the dimension of the hyperbolic? This is not entirely clear. Despite the diffidence of philosophies of finitude with respect to the consolation of something "affirmative," we must press the question: What could peace be, in the dimension of the hyperbolic, and beyond finitude? Could such hyperbolic peace be thought of, or be possible, apart from what religious persons call redemption? Is there a sabbatical for thought?

Murdering Sleep and the Unease of Evil: Macbeth Beyond Good and Evil

My third instance of sleeplessness, from *Macbeth*, has to do with the lack of peace in the dimension of the hyperbolic—peacelessness now in consequence of an evil deed which unlooses its inexorable karma. This third instance is not entirely heterogenous to the other two: it has to do with the *excess of evil to finite measure*, excess that precipitates hard questions for all philosophies of finitude.

Macbeth the warrior is described as fighting as if he would "memorize another Golgotha" (1.1.41). This memorizing of Golgotha is not the memorizing of Pascal's *Memorial* or his meditation on Gethsemane night. It is the reversed negative of the saving Golgotha: it is a Golgotha that damns. The theme of "sleep" is foregrounded in this play from the beginning, when the Weird Sisters, the Sisters of Fate, portend the curse that is to descend on this man: "Sleep shall neither night nor day / Hang upon his penthouse lid. / He shall live a man forbid" (1.1.3, 19). Sleeplessness comes in the shape of a *curse*, nor is it evident if there is any *blessing* to serve as its redress.

Macbeth is a play of daring, of *daring in excess of measure*. I would stress not only the dangers in daring beyond finite measure, but that there are *different* darings. Here the daring is one that dares evil. At the outset Macbeth draws back from the murder of Duncan, the sacred king: "I dare do all that may become a man, who dares do more is none" (1.7. 46–47). Then his daring, or lack of it, is put to the dare by Lady Macbeth, who speaks to him, not without contempt, about being hard. *Daring is redoubled.* When Lady Macbeth speaks to him thus—"but screw your courage to the sticking-place, and we'll not fail" (1.7.60–61)—I think of how Nietzsche sometimes talked to himself. Macbeth resolves to dare then, in the excess of evil: he does dare do more, more than becomes a man, but in daring so, he becomes no man, he becomes a monster. This monster of daring must finally "dare fate into the list."

Having committed the murder, Macbeth in disarray immediately cries out: "But wherefore could not I pronounce 'Amen'" / I had most need of blessing, and 'Amen' / stuck in my throat" (2.2.31–33). "Methought I heard a voice cry, 'Sleep no more! / Macbeth doth murder sleep,' the innocent sleep, / Sleep that knits up the ravell'd sleave of care, / The death of each day's life, sore labour's bath, / Balm of hurt minds, great nature's second course, / Chief nourisher in life's feast" (2.2.36ff.). The sleeplessness here is one that shuts one out from the great Amen, the "yes" in "It is good." Quite the opposite: life is a brief candle that must be outed; a tale told by an idiot, full of sound and fury, signifying nothing (5.5.23–28). There is no idiot wisdom in this signifying of nothing. This sleeplessness, whose torment comes from the doing of evil, knows no rest, save utter annihilation in "dusty death."

Macbeth's excessive daring entails a refusal of finitude, in his will to overreach the equivocity of time. He insists on having time's ambiguity resolved now in the action, in the deed. His hyperbolic daring wants to have the future in the instant. He will not wait, he will not watch and wait. So he enters into temptation. Indeed, he tempts the darker powers, even as he is himself tempted by them. But he is betrayed by their temptation, as by his own tempting of them. Unlike Pascal, he will not allow the final judgment to be postponed according to the proper ordinance of time. The last judgment will be now. "Shake off this downy sleep, death's counterfeit / And look on death itself! Up, up and see / The great doom's image" (2.3.83ff.).

We are neither in the Garden of Eden with the "It is good," nor the Garden of Gethsemane where the prayer is "It will be good, thy will be done." We are brought into the waste of the Kingdom where finally the outcry is "Better not to be" — "Out, out brief candle, out I say." In Macbeth's daring to demand that future and that judgment now, he is condemned by his metaphysical *impatience*. This is a treason to the *passio essendi* of a usurping *conatus essendi*. Macbeth cannot be, though he would be, the measure of the equivocal powers, through his own daring will; and not least because his own daring incarnates the evil equivocity he claims to conquer.

We need to be attentive to the qualitative difference between evil daring and divine daring. (Might we think of Plotinus's last audacity as a *good* daring?) For *Macbeth* is a play about the *false overreaching of finitude* in which the loss of metaphysical patience turns divine daring into evil daring. There is a deep equivocity when it comes to courage, and the secret sources of strengthening. There is a counterfeit of strengthening that comes from evil. Macbeth is strengthened from evil sources—his wife's evil promptings, the wicked sisters. His courage does not dip into deeper and higher sources; his strength does not sleep in the divine. And yet the strengthening he achieves is a counterfeit, for its final issue is weakness and impotence and death. Instead of sleep as "death's counterfeit," we end with death, just death.

Macbeth is *the* play of Shakespeare about the *equivocity* of being. Radical equivocity attaches to time, to daring, to trust, to power, to the elementals, to the nefarious powers, to sleep, to life itself and to death. "Fair is foul and foul is fair." In this equivocal world, is the hurly-burly ever done? Is the battle ever lost and won? The question seems beyond final settlement here and now. And so in *Macbeth* the images of sleep and sleeplessness are redolent of a radical equivocity. The sacred king, Duncan, is murdered in his sleep; but sleep here is also an image of trust in hospitality. The king, perhaps innocently, perhaps unwisely, trusts Macbeth. He comes without suspicion to sleep in Macbeth's castle; but from this sleep he will not be allowed to wake. Faces are also equivocal: "There's no art to find the mind's construction in the face," Duncan says (1.4.12–13). And yet art is most needed, finesse is wanted most. And Duncan says this just on the entrance before him of Macbeth, his future murderer now warmly embraced.

The crime of Macbeth is a crime to heaven, against heaven. Shakespeare leaves us in no doubt of that. Macbeth is in no doubt. Immediately after the murder, horror makes him long for a resurrection to life: "Wake Duncan with thy knocking! I would thou couldst" (2.3.74). But he comes to be "supped full with horrors" (5.5.13), and longing for resurrected life dies. The loss of sleep, the murdering of sleep with the murder of the sacred king, is not any wakening up to a higher wisdom, some sense of which was implied by the hyperbolic watchfulness of Plotinus and Pascal. This sleeplessness is the karma of evil that destroys the ontological peace of the human being at its deepest roots. For it is the peace of Macbeth's *being*, or any promise of peace, that is destroyed in and through his evil deed. He knows that for peace to be restored he must repent, but he will not, for his daring is such that it cannot retract itself: "Things without all remedy / should be without regard: what's done is done" (3.2.11–12). The evil is a sticky evil. Lady Macbeth: "A little water clears us of this deed: How easy is it then!" (2.3.66–67) But the stain·cannot be washed out, as Lady Macbeth came to know: "Out damned spot, out

I say" (5.1.38). And what then happens with her? She cannot sleep. She "lack(s) the season of all natures, sleep" (3.4.141). She cannot sleep but she is waking to madness. Macbeth's daring knows no repentance: "I am in blood / Stepped in so far that, should I wade no more, / Returning were as tedious as go o'er" (3.5.137–39). His evil daring is ensnared in its inability to say "Amen" or to turn to forgiveness. It can only will itself, incite itself further into darkness, but this is not divine, but hellish.

The meaning of "sleep" here then is more than merely equivocal: it is plurivocal. This we see in its connection with peace. Peace is something more healing, maybe divine. So sleep "that knits up the ravell'd sleeve of care" is wedded to its darker twin, sleep as "death's counterfeit" (2.3.83). The same point holds for sleeplessness. Sleeplessness for Macbeth himself is rather the counterfeit of wakening: the wakening that cannot wake up. It can only go down, as it were, for all it knows of itself is the weary tiredness that would rather escape itself into oblivion: it is a life in death, a death in life that finally wills death *as* death. *Hypnos* is utterly overthrown by his darker twin *Thanatos*.

What about *watchfulness*? Again we find something hyperbolic, but it is the *reverse negative* of the watchfulness of metaphysical mindfulness, or *thaumazein*, or the vigilance of saving prayer. Hyperbolic watchfulness is corrupted into the *unrestrained spirit of suspicion* that can only look on everything other as its potential enemy. It is consumed by the evil it has itself dared to commit. Qua sleeplessness it looks like Pascal's or Jesus's, but it is its counterfeit double; and the counterfeit is the result of its own effort to redouble reality in the image of its own counterfeit power—divine power that is not divine but rather diabolical. The power here is *daimonic* as between human powers and more ultimate powers. We might think of the daimonic power of the eros of the Platonic philosopher, and perhaps too the last exitus of Plotinus; but in Macbeth, the daimonic daring of eros becomes downwardly directed on darkness and evil and not upwardly ecstatic, as in Plotinus. There is now another ecstasy, but it is the restless ecstasy of the tortured mind that lies on itself sleepless, as on its own rack. "Better be with the dead," says Macbeth, "whom we, to gain our peace, have sent to peace, / Than on the torture of the mind to lie / In restless ecstasy" (3.3.19–22).

Much more might be said about, for instance, the connection between the innocence of sleep and pity, the pity that Macbeth and Lady Macbeth stifle in themselves; about the Amen, about cruelty and hardness, about being beyond good and evil; about lack of sleep and madness; about the equivocations of temptation and of the non-human powers; about sleep and God, and waking to good beyond good and evil. All of these bring on sleepless thought about the limits of finitude within finitude itself. The excess of evil daring, and the equivocal karma it lets loose, make us wonder whether, finally, finite being reveals a *smeared world* unredeemable through itself alone. Or whether, to the contrary, there are healing waters, and a peace more than the quiescence of death, and beyond the sticky evil.[10]

One might argue, and rightly, that the play encourages one to remain true to finitude, not to insist willfully on what is other, and against Macbeth's metaphysical impatience. Yet that alone is not fully to the point. There is more to finitude than can be contained in it: the earth itself has bubbles, as the water has, into which the Weird Sisters vanish. This is a world that seems bewitched as well as besmirched. Its quintessential equivocity is such that it cannot be so univocally determined to finite terms. Our perplexity is concerned not only that the other of finitude be not consigned to silence. It has to do with *our relation to that other*, that other as itself good or evil, our relation to it as good or evil, and whether in our audacity to be beyond good and evil we step not into our superior freedom, but into the hyperbolic evil of a witches' Sabbath.

Sabbath is the seventh day of creation, but also the first day, the day of rest and joy in being, the day of peace, when the Creator saw that "It was good." What is a witches' *Sabbath*? There is no day of the week in which it falls, and it can fall in every day. It is the day without peace, when fair is foul and foul is fair, when the hurly-burly's never done, and when the battle won is always lost. It is sleeplessness as the reversed negative of the "It is good": sleeplessness not only cursed, but sleeplessness cursing.

Unease with Postulatory Finitism

Let us take stock. There is the sleep of common sense, and an awakening beyond it; there is the sleep of rationalistic philosophy, and the wakening beyond it; then there are more extreme forms of sleeplessness, evident with Plotinus, Pascal, and Macbeth, that make one

---

[10] I have more to say on this and other themes in "Sticky Evil: On *Macbeth* and the Karma of the Equivocal," in *God, Literature and Process Philosophy*, ed. Darren Middleton (Aldershot: Ashgate, 2002), 133–55.

wonder if philosophy has its own sleep, not only with rationalistic philosophy, but with other ways of thinking that seem to dare beyond the safety of reason. Is there a peace beyond that safety? Or is there only the daring, such as Macbeth's, that seems to take us beyond good and evil, but that enmeshes us more stickily in seemingly indelible evil? The struggle for a higher vigilance beyond the first two sleeps must also be a struggle for vigilance beyond the equivocations of the sleeplessness of evil. Putting aside for further meditation the issue of a more ultimate peace (see Chapter 10), it seems to be that there is an unease of religion that makes philosophy most uneasy, and uneasy in both good and bad senses. Bad: in that something too hyperbolic to safer reason is suggested. Good: in that the sanity of a safer reason may turn out, without this religious unease, to be mind asleep on the contented lowlands of finitude redoubling itself and nothing more.

Contemporary philosophies of finitude may well be attentive to what they deem to be the sleep of reason, whether in Hegelian, idealistic, or more classical forms. In opposition to the supposedly false peace of the latter, they make us face something of the insomnia of unreason. What is this insomnia? Is it like Macbeth's? Certainly, if you take Nietzsche's claim to be beyond good and evil, Nietzsche had a Shakespearean precursor: Lady Macbeth. Lady Macbeth: Why, our crime against the sacred king is nothing—"A little water clears us of the deed: How easy is it then!" (2.3.66–67). Nietzsche, refusing remorse, denying forgiveness, writes it thus: "A rage, a reach, a knife thrust: what of personality is in that? . . . a single deed, whatever it may be, is, in comparison with everything one has done, a zero, and may be deducted without falsifying the account."[11] Macbeth—warrior, murderer, usurper—is superior to both: if you kill the sacred king, you murder sleep, that is, peace, and you must live the karma of the equivocal: you must become the counterfeit double of sleeplessness. Not longing any more for God but at best for "some-

---

[11] Friedrich Nietzsche, *The Will to Power*, trans. W. Kaufmann (New York: Vintage, 1968), 136. This is from a section entitled *"Against remorse"*: "I do not like this kind of cowardice toward one's own deeds; one should not leave oneself in the lurch at the onset of unanticipated shame and embarrassment. An extreme pride, rather, is in order. After all, what is the good of it! No deed can be undone by being regretted; no more than by being 'forgiven' or 'atoned for.' One would have to be a theologian to believe in a power that annuls guilt: we immoralists prefer not to believe in 'guilt.' We hold instead that every action is of identical value at root."

thing"—often secretly for "nothing," for death. But is man a being toward death or a being toward peace, being toward God? And this last peace inseparable from a sleeplessness of finitude that cannot find its measure in the immanences of finitude itself?

We come back to a question broached earlier: If we sedate our-selves against the hyperbolic sleeplessness that bears on finitude as such, has the sleep of philosophy now assumed the form of a "postu-latory finitism"? I remind you of the likeness between this and Kant's "postulatory deism," though their postulates and effects go in oppo-site directions. In Kant something is unconditional, namely, moral obligation; in postulatory finitism, nothing seems unconditional. Clearly, considering the just cited passage from Nietzsche, even mur-der could be reinterpreted as nothing. Between Kant and Nietzsche, nevertheless, there are certain structural likenesses. Kant: To think of human life as moral, and moral thus and thus, namely, as uncondi-tional, we must think *as if* there is a God. God is a postulate said to be necessitated by this way of looking at life. But if we look at life otherwise, say "beyond good and evil," to take a famous slogan, then the "as if" will begin to take shape very differently. Nietzsche: If we would think of life thus and thus, that is, as in itself void of moral value, indeed of any intrinsic value, then our "as if" cannot lead to a "postulatory deism"; quite the opposite, it dictates a "postulatory atheism." This is obviously so in the crude arguments that Sartre of-fers us about God—if you can call them arguments: either God or freedom; but freedom, therefore no God. And this performed with the sleight of hand of a crude theological determinism, counterposed by a hyperbolically self-creating human—this last as absurd as the absurd *en-soi* from out of which it inexplicably, miraculously, springs forth as "nothingness."

There are less crude forms of postulatory finitism, of course, but the crucial point is its *als ob* structure: if you want to think of finitude thus and thus—say human freedom as absolutely autonomous—then no God. What if there is a sleep of finitude at work in this *als ob*? What then is the force of the "then"? Why accept it, and why accept the first phase of the thought: if you want to think of finitude "thus and thus . . ."? What is the "thus and thus . . ."? The above "thus and thus" of freedom as autonomy may now, in postmodern times, lacerate itself with self-uncertainty, but there are many other more masked forms of "thus and thus." All of them name "finitude" as the unsurpassable horizon of life and thought, beyond which we cannot, must not go, beyond which there is nothing.

A postmodern philosophy of finitude tends to think of itself as awakening from the sleep of traditional philosophy, and awakening from Enlightenment reason that previously thought of itself as awakening from the sleep of religion and common sense. If this postmodern sleeplessness is, in truth, a deeper sleep of finitude, it will be extremely difficult to realize this as such, since this sleep takes itself as the *nec plus ultra* of wakefulness to finitude. Why accept its "thus and thus," which might not even have been made explicit? Even more, why acquiesce in its "thus and thus," if we have been visited with a hyperbolic sleeplessness recalling either the philosophical, religious, and poetic forms we have explored in Plotinus, Pascal, Shakespeare? That hyperbolic sleeplessness must seem absurd on the terms of the self-enclosing immanence of a finitude not to be surpassed. Nevertheless, if this hyperbolic sleeplessness shows the ultimate porosity of finitude as such, why continue, how continue to circulate within self-enclosing immanence? This self-enclosing immanence makes of finitude a false whole that in the hyperbolic sleeplessness is fissured by that ultimate porosity.

One is struck with the thought that the postmodern sleeplessness might even be a kind of sleepwalking, induced according to the secret suggestions of the postulatory finitism. Are we such philosophical nightwalkers when, as I put it before, we swerve off the aporiai of finitude, veering back, as if led on by a fatality, into the self-enclosing immanence? The other hyperbolic sleeplessness makes one ask if truer thinking is no falsifier of finitude but comes to mindfulness in a porosity of being relative to which any such self-enclosing immanence must seem rather as the falser to finitude? Truer philosophizing opens to the happening of being as it comes to show itself; it does not dictate to it that it must be thus and thus finite. This entire matter is, as the idiom has it, "up for grabs." This is even more so, if the sleeplessness of finitude has been undergone in the hyperbolic registers witnessed by Plotinus, Pascal, Shakespeare, none of which can be made sense of without honest openness to the unease of the religious. Of course, we should grab nothing.

"If you want to think of life this way, then you must . . ." What then is the status of this "must"? If it is the somnambulant effect of the postulatory finitism, how wake from this sleepwalking? Suppose the misgiving has been growing on one that this *als ob* of postulatory finitism shows, in fact, a *lack of imagination*? If you find you cannot (then must not) think of life that way, then what? Suppose life shows itself as other to one? Suppose one's metaphysical imagination finds itself in rebellion against the insinuation of the secret suggestion that is secreted by the postulatory finitism? One has the presentiment that one is being overcome by something, and it is not at all out in the open, and one mutinies against the spiritual tyranny of the secret suggestion. Far from being free, one has the suspicion one is being drawn by the nose.

One might then, so to say, break against the bars. Or one might well begin to wonder if the bar of Kant, the bar of Nietzsche, other barring orders, are no bars. One's sleeplessness is already invaded by intimations of what is beyond these holds of the imagination. One even wonders if these bars are *spells* cast by a kind of *subterranean will* not to think of what might lie beyond. There is the deeper trouble, in that since the "postulate" itself has gone *underground* there is a kind of *invisible limit*, limiting one, holding one back, all the time. One does not determine that limit, it determines one. One is as if ensnared in a kind of spell. How does one wake from a spell, especially when one does not know one is spellbound but rather feels oneself to be fully awakened? To shake one, something must strike one from outside or from beyond. We might well be hit by the salutary unease of a hyperbolic sleeplessness. But these invisible limits lull one to sleep, and this is just what one is now coming to suspect, perhaps even coming to hate. One tosses to and fro and cannot sleep, but sleeplessness might be like the fever that rises to decisive intensity when a toxin or a virus is coming to a crisis.

Let us dream we have passed through this crisis. On coming round to mindfulness, how might one see the finite? Otherwise — something like this: Finite being is a happening; it happens to be; it might not have been; it might well not be; but it is, and is without absolute necessity; what happens comes to be, it passes out of being. We too happen, in that sense, and can know it: there is no necessity we must be, and once given to be, no denying that we will cease to be. All turns on the interpretation of this happening qua happening. "Postulatory finitism" finally seeks to turn the happening into a closed totality, albeit now said to be devoid of intrinsic necessity, even when this philosophy officially rejects any appeal to "totality" and "closure." By contrast, I would say, this very happening of finitude shows its *porosity*, and its excess to this closure. In its porosity, it is the medium of communications in excess of its own determinacy and self-determination, and these communications just as communications it cannot claim as its own absolutely. Nothing finite can claim to own anything absolutely. In a primal sense, nothing is its *own* simpliciter.

Every being is, qua happening, a *being given to be*. It is not self-originating, not just self-becoming, but is in a *coming to be* before it becomes this or that (this "before" is not a "temporal" before). Qua happening, it intimates its source as other, in excess of what happens to be, by reference to a more radical ontological origin than itself. Is this reference a referral of finitude to nothing? If you say that a philosophy of finitude entails *nothing but* finitude, how then speak as if this nothing were an other of finitude, for certainly it is no finite being? Why go on about it as if it were a kind of ultimate? You say: finitude comes from nothing and overreaches itself into nothing. Then all this too comes to nothing, and hence all is nothing but nihilism — as in the beginning, so in the end. But how could this be, if finite beings *come to be*, even if it is out of nothing? There must be more than nothing, not only with reference to the being of finite beings, not only with reference to their coming to be at all, but in that the very being at all of finite beings is in communication, is finite in an ontological referral to an origin that is other to nothing, and other as ultimately originative. Otherwise there would be no finite being, there would be simply nothing.

Beings are, and so we must think otherwise. The porosity looks like nothing but it is not nothing; it is, so to say, on the interface between nothing and the coming to be of finite being; it is the origin that creates on this interface, and communicates beings to be as more than nothing. The referral of beings to an origin that is not finitely determinable, and is not nothing, transcends the terms of the "postulatory finitism," as indeed it does of finitude qua happening.[12] In my view, metaphysics, whether traditional or more contemporary, is at its best when mindful of the porosity of the milieu of finite being, and attuned to this ontological referral beyond itself. But being religious, more deeply, constitutes, in finitude itself, the *awakening* to the call of this referral. Cut loose from religion as hearing and trying to answer the call of this referral, philosophy tends to sink back into its own self-satisfied sleep. Religious unease makes philosophy more truly uneasy.

---

[12] On the issues of origin, nothing, creation, coming to be, see my *Being and the Between*, chapters 6 and 7, as well as my "Hyperbolic Thoughts: On Creation and Nothing," in *Framing a Vision of the World: Essays in Philosophy, Science and Religion*, eds. Santiago Sia and André Cloots (Leuven: University Press Leuven, 1999), 23–43.

Aporiai of Finitude Revisited

It is opportune to make good on a promise I made earlier to say something about four crucial considerations significant for the aporiai of finitude. *First*, there is what I call *the idiocy of being*: the sheer "that it is" of given finite being. This is a given that happens to be without inherent necessity; we wake up in astonishment to its being given to be; but this being given to be as finite exceeds the terms of finitude itself, since this original "being given to be" makes possible the intelligibility of these terms. There is an intimate strangeness to the idiocy: the "that it is" is not determined by a homogeneous general category, nor is it self-explanatory or self-determining. It arouses a more intimate mindfulness before finitude in a metaphysical astonishment that exceeds exhaustion in finite determinations. A certain postulatory finitism might be tempted to see this idiocy as a surd that is a mere absurdity, not astonishing givenness that stuns mindfulness and rouses thought hyperbolic to finite determinacy or our own self-determination. In the stunning of mindfulness, there is no reason why thinking cannot become porous to what exceeds finite determination, instead of veering from this porosity into a programmatic insistence on finitude and nothing but finitude.

Second, there is the givenness of *the aesthetics of happening*. The incarnate glory of aesthetic happening also rouses astonishment and appreciation before finite being, yet it seems to exceed finitization. This aesthetic glory of finitude is impossible to characterize exhaustively in finite terms, as like a great work of art that is richly determinate and yet exceeds fixation in any one determination, or set of finite determinations. Something more is communicated in the beauty and sublimity of finitude that incarnates an otherness exceeding all finitization. The beauty of creation: integral being lovely for self, splendid immanence as a whole, but not a closed rather an open whole. The sublimity of creation: the beyond of aesthetic finitude shattering finitude in finitude and elevating it above itself. There is an astonishing determinacy of finite being(s) but something overdeterminate also, and this aesthetic overdeterminacy of finitude may make us porous on the boundary of finitude, transporting us, like a music, into a mindfulness hyperbolic to any self-enclosing immanence.

A somewhat similar consideration might be applied to the intelligibility of finite being and process: itself astonishing, one might wonder what makes finite intelligibility itself intelligible. This cannot be just another finite intelligibility, since this is in question, but rather we are pointed to an intelligibility hyperbolic to finite intelligibility. The aporia of finitude: the intelligibility that allows us to render the finite intelligible, is not itself intelligible in fully finitizable terms. We are pointed to the hyperintelligible.

Third, we might turn to human being and what I call *the erotics of selving*. We are finite beings yet infinitely self-surpassing. This is evident above in our being the measure that exceeds itself as its own measure: beyond measure in terms of itself as measure, it points to a measure exceeding itself. It is also evident in the very dynamism of philosophical thinking. The measure of the self-transcending of mindfulness that measures and makes the finite determinable is beyond the determination of finite measure. We are marked as both finite and infinitely restless, the incarnate conjunction and tension of these two. This doubleness is not reducible to univocal terms that insist on finitude and nothing but finitude. There is always more than finitude in our finitude. This "more" is not just our "more." Finite and more than finitude, the erotics of human selving makes us a living incarnation of an aporia of finitude: a living impasse in finite being that cannot pass beyond itself as impasse through its own power alone, even when it seems to surpass itself infinitely. This aporetic situation provides the basis of Hegel's dialectic of limit, though in my view the opening to the other of finitude is also subverted when rendered in the terms of a speculative sublationary infinitism. A different account of the relation of finitude and infinitude is necessary: neither the sublation of finitude in a self-enclosing infinitude, nor the erasure of infinitude in a self-encircling finitude. The erotics of selving is more than a *conatus* driven to its own most complete self-determination in immanence, but is marked by a primal porosity to what exceeds its own determination and self-transcending.

Fourth, we might consider what I call *the agapeics of community*. Here our relation to others is at issue. Our being is in receiving and in giving. We are receptive to the gift of the other, and we are free to give beyond ourselves to others, and in some instances, simply for the good of the other as other. In the finiteness of human life, there is the promise of a generosity beyond finite reckoning. There is a sign of this in the ontological situation of our finitude itself: we are given to be before we can give ourselves to be; finitude as such is given, but not given from itself alone. Nothing is alone, hence the idea of finitude as for itself alone, and nothing other, is hard to take as the last word, or the first. Our being freed into ethical responsibility is difficult to render on purely finite terms, since the call of something ethically *unconditional* emerges. In our ethical relation to the other, this unconditional is given before one's freedom to determine oneself. Certainly, Kant makes use of this unconditionality in his postulatory deism, but suppose there is an agapeics of generosity beyond even moral reckoning? This would be a religious agape, more unconditional than the moral unconditional, a hyper-unconditional generosity toward finitude exceeding finitization. The agapeics of community intimate a surplus source of good that makes itself available in an absolute porosity, an absolved porosity of the *passio essendi* that ethically lives itself as a *compassio essendi*. This is a sign of something more than the ethical, since it incarnates the holy.

These are four considerations that I think put severe strain on the terms of any postulatory finitism. Yet when a philosopher comes to one or other of such considerations, the spell of the postulatory finitism can be so strong that he or she *will turn back*. The (under)grounding presuppositions of postulatory finitism work on mindfulness, but out of mind, and hence are not exposed for reflective consideration. The spell continues its enchantment. We might even talk ourselves out of a cure, and call the cure a worse sickness. The birds of paradise are said to be extinct, but one wonders *whose* future will be that of the dodo? The metaphysicians or the post-metaphysicians? Too convinced that the doves of metaphysics, or the dodos, lie dead behind us in the tradition, we preach to new birds of the air, to convince them they cannot fly—nor should they want to, for we are where we should be, now at last supposedly earthbound. After all, the weight of finitude keeps our feet firmly on the ground. And yet the urge to fly still stirs. There is a daring to know that is not reactive to threat but manifests the energy of a courage that is the life of mindfulness. There is a courage to try that is not downed by difficulty, for after all one could well stay on the ground *very contentedly*. Just to know and try—for its own sake: this is an unknowing love of otherness—and it rises up, rouses us, from the sleep of finitude.

Bad Dreams, Religious Sleeplessness, Released Porosity

Time to call time. It was because they could not fly that the dodos died out. Were they able to rise into the air above, they might have lived. But we are creatures of the between; we are between creatures, double beings: native to the earth, yet looking above it as we move on it. Why should we be surprised if those in the spell of postulatory finitism might want to give those tempted to fly a bad conscience? The thought alone can be enough to enervate our native energies. Perhaps this is why we find that the philosopher after Kant has more than once assumed the robes of the *preacher*—to make sure we do not fly. Hegel is a good example of a preacher of his brand of speculative infinitism—though interestingly, he too wanted to prevent us flying, from thinking of any "beyond." At the opposite extreme to inflationary infinitism there is deflationory finitism, and verging on the paradoxical apotheosis of banality, I find the preaching of Richard Rorty. Nietzsche is a good example of an inspired preacher of finitude—you must will it, o my brothers—remain true to the earth, o my brothers. A fine exhortation—but why exhort? I thought preaching was behind us, suitable only for priests and Platonists.

Hamlet: "I smell a rat." The future becomes a this-worldly otherworld. Postulatory finitism mimics in finitude the opening to something other to finitude, but within finitude. Like the regulative ideal of Kant's *als ob*, the future here becomes a kind of *focus imaginarius*. Like all things imaginary, much depends on the visionary power of the seer. What if, as I said, postulatory finitism *lacks imagination*? What if this lack of imagination is another form of the sleep of finitude? If you have suffered the unease of being religious, beyond the unease and sleep of philosophy, maybe one can only stand by with charitable astonishment and watch the passing of the banner carriers of banality, masquerading as (post)philosophers, or the visionaries of immanence who prophesy the coming god, or the last, intrigued by how they well betray the uneasy fevers of their own post-metaphysical divinations.

"Remain true to the earth!" Yes, yes. But our destiny is not to be cave dwellers sunk in a hole in the ground, but to find our way to the surface of the earth where, standing upright, we exist above ground *between* the earth and the sky. Is not fidelity to the earth just this upright standing between earth and heaven? Standing thus, why should we not *look up*? Being true to the earth is standing upright looking up. Is this not also a kind of *looking away*? Maybe we must resist the temptation of Orpheus: to bring the beloved above to the surface of the earth, we must look away, have the patience and trust to look away, to make a way in making way, and in this bring our love to life on the earth.

There is the inner underground, the immanent grave within whose earth or humus we must be buried, maybe to be reborn as posthumous mindfulness. Hamlet again, Hamlet who embodied unease, who sought, seemed to find too, a kind of peace: "Denmark's a prison." And not only Denmark. Hamlet: "O God, I could be bounded in a nutshell, and count myself a king of infinite space, were it not that I have bad dreams" (2.2.258–60). Would it be impertinent to call postulatory finitism such a bounded nutshell? What kind of king would be the sovereign of this immanent nut? What philosopher buried here could consider himself king? Hamlet yet again: "To die, to sleep— / To sleep—perchance to dream: ay, there's the rub, / For in that sleep of death what dreams may come / When we have shuffled off this mortal coil, / Must give us pause" (3.1.64ff.). What might those bad dreams be, for Hamlet, the philosopher of uncertain finitude, sleepless, "sicklied o'er with the pale cast of thought"? Bound in his nutshell of finitude, he might count *himself* the king of infinite space. Can he *only* count himself as *that* kind of king? And count himself as king of infinite space only in *imagination*? But *those* infinite spaces are empty. What bad dreams visit us in the emptiness? Could we count among them postulatory finitism, or is it rather a rejoinder to bad dreams? But we all know that one of our most loved protections against bad dreams is to sink deeper into sleep, and to be lost in utter unconsciousness.

Is there any waking, then, from the sleep of finitude? I think any awakening must seek the measure of our essential equivocity, such as we saw earlier, for instance, with Macbeth. In a nutshell, sometimes the dreams of angels beckon us, but just as frequently finitude awakens itself to monstrousness. Even in finitely postulated boundedness, the seed of imagination will stir in us, and imagination will dream, for it is our being to surpass ourselves into the space of the infinite, or to be made porous to its threshold or breach. Infinite space: in a nutshell the hyperbolic arrives. And yet the monstrous, like the holy, is in the dimension of the hyperbolic. We are riveted to our own excess, exceeding measure, even if we are the measure of all things and all immanent space. We exceed measure in the measureless space of our self-exceeding; but still we need a measure of finesse to dwell as delivered in this space of passage.

It is here, I believe, that we are visited with the saving promise of religious sleeplessness. Beyond the sleep of finitude, religious sleeplessness is released porosity in the dimension of the hyperbolic. Everything here is exposed to great danger, great terror, fired by great passion and the grandeur of endeavor, and soliciting a great largesse of soul, for there is nothing safe and we cannot save ourselves. Great strength is needed to live this hyperbolic sleeplessness, great finesse to dwell with discernment in this porosity to the hyperbolic. Religion is the wise instructress of human, that is to say, metaphysical imagination in the dimension of the hyperbolic. True religion is the great mother of reverent finesse in the dimension of the hyperbolic. Religious sleeplessness wakes the child of time to prophetic imagination and endows its exceeding suffering with the promise of fulfilled finesse.

2

Between Finitude and Infinity: Hegelian Reason and the Pascalian Heart

Popular Philosophy and Philosophy Proper

Pascal is a religious-philosophical thinker of finitude, though not at all marked by any postulatory finitism. A hyperbolic sleeplessness visits our finitude, and then we wonder if we can ever be at home with finitude. In Hegel, the speculative philosopher, there is a kind of sleeplessness of finitude but this is said to awaken us to a sublationary infinitude that includes finitude as a moment of the totality's own self-mediation, and then we wonder if we have fallen asleep to finitude. Finitude and infinity, and the relation between them, take on significantly different characters if our response to the exceeding of finitude is Pascal's religious heart or Hegel's speculative reason.

Hegel makes scant reference to Pascal. He does refer to Pascal in the conclusion to *Faith and Knowledge*, an early work. Here Hegel endorses in a qualified way and criticizes in a revealing way the metaphysics of subjectivity he attributes to Kant, Jacobi, Fichte. He endorses: This metaphysics sets forth and completes the formative process that is the necessary condition for the appearance of true philosophy, philosophy proper, namely, Hegel's own. He criticizes: It continues to erect a fixed antithesis between finitude and infinity which makes of infinity all but a vanishing nullity. Hegel tersely hints at what for him is the real truth of this nullity, namely, the negativity that is one side of the "positive Idea that being is strictly nothing outside of the infinite, or apart from the Ego or thought." This sense of negation, he says, "must signify the infinite grief [of the finite] purely as a moment of the supreme Idea, and no more than a moment."[1]

Formerly, Hegel claims, this infinite grief existed only in the formative process of culture, expressed in the feeling "God Himself is dead." Upon this feeling recent religion rests, he says. It is now that Pascal is invoked. Pascal gives expression, but only "in sheerly empirical form," to the infinite grief and the sense of a lost God, within the human being and without. Hegel concludes significantly by reiterating that this feeling is but a moment of the Idea. What previously was historical must be re-established on a proper philosophical plane. The speculative Good Friday must be established in place of the historic Good Friday. In Hegel's well-known words: "Good Friday must be re-established in the whole truth and harshness of its God-forsakenness . . . the highest totality can and must achieve its resurrection solely from this harsh consciousness of loss, encompassing everything, and ascending in all its earnestness and out of its deepest ground to the most serene freedom of its shape."[2]

Much is suggested by this passage, not least the notion of Hegel's view of the whole as a single dialectically self-mediating totality, wherein the finite and the infinite mediate with each other. While the issue is not here explicitly addressed, we can also detect traces of Hegel's later *Aufhebung* of religion into the speculative concept, an *Aufhebung* carried by a dialectical-speculative appropriation of thinking as negativity. For Hegel himself there will be a properly philosophical passion and resurrection. Pascal remains outside of this, in so far as he remains empirical and historical. Here he remains with all previous philosophers who contribute to the *Bildungsprozess* that makes true speculative philosophy possible but who do not really enter into this inner *sanctus santorum* of proper philosophizing.

But maybe it is rather Pascal who really dwells more radically with the harsh consciousness of loss, such that resurrection rendered conceptually as dialectical-speculative *Aufhebung* must be contested.

---

[1] G. W. F. Hegel, *Glauben und Wissen* (Hamburg: Felix Meiner, 1962), 123. Translated by Walter Cerf and H. S. Harris as *Faith and Knowledge* (Albany: State University of New York Press, 1977), 189. I will refer to these as *GW* and *FK*. This chapter is a somewhat revised version of what was originally a Presidential Address to the Hegel Society of America, meeting at Pennsylvania State University, October 1992.

[2] *GW*, 123–24; *FK*, 191.

This matter interlocks with a number of fundamental issues: the nature of finitude and infinity and their interplay; the recalcitrance of historic singularity to Hegel's version of philosophical universalization; the scope of reason, especially regarding the limits of its philosophical form; the appropriate form of philosophical discourse itself, whether it must take shape as system and nothing but system, or whether there is something philosophically considerable about the fragmentary as such. I will touch on these issues.

Hegel makes another brief, but significant, reference to Pascal in the *Lectures on the History of Philosophy*. Consistent with the remark above about Pascal and the "sheerly empirical," Hegel distinguishes "philosophy proper" from "popular philosophy." "Yet this philosophy [popular philosophy] must also be cast aside," he pronounces. What Hegel means by "popular philosophy" is suggested by his invocation of Cicero's cultured concern for the affairs of life most important to human beings. Pascal himself is mentioned in relation to the "fanatics and mystics," also included in the category of popular philosophizing. "They give expression to a deep sense of devotion, and have had experiences in the higher regions. They are able to express the highest content, and the result is attractive. We thus find the brightest gleams of thought in the writings of a Pascal—as we do in his *Pensées*."[3]

There is a trace of praise here, but it is the praise that withholds its cut. Hegel elevates Pascal only to cast him down from the heights of "philosophy proper." The deficiencies of "popular philosophizing" are briskly spelled out by Hegel. It relies on human existence in its naturalness, appeals to the *consensus gentium*, resorts to feeling in religion and moral instinct. "The source of popular philosophy is in the

---

[3] G. W. F. Hegel, *Vorlesungen über die Geschichte der Philosophie* 1, vol. 18 of *Werke*, edited by E. Moldenhauer and K. M. Michel (Frankfurt a. M.: Suhrkamp, 1971), 114; *Lectures on the History of Philosophy*, trans. E. S. Haldane and F. H. Simson (London: Kegan Paul, Trench, Trubner and Co., 1892), 1: 93. I will cite these as *VGP*, and *LHP*. Hegel distinguishes *die Philosophie* from *die Populärphilosophie*. I retain the phrase "philosophy proper" since it captures the sense of contrast that, I think, is intended by Hegel. Hegel says of Pascal: "in seinen Pensées finden sich die tiefsten Blicke." Knox and Miller in their translation put it: "Pascal . . . in his *Pensées* has given us a look into the depths." I find this flat, and not as properly suggestive, philosophically speaking, as the older translation. Their *Introduction to the Lectures on the History of Philosophy* (Oxford: Clarendon Press, 1986), 162, translates *Einleitung in die Geschichte der Philosophie*, ed. J. Hoffmeister (Hamburg: Felix Meiner, 1940), 222.

heart, impulses, and capacities, my impression of what is right and of
God; the content is in a form which is of nature only." Since the
source of its content is nature, an externality is attached to its mode
of thought. Thought is tied to immediacy and the given, to externality
and feeling. Hence, for Hegel, it is still infected with arbitrary caprice. It does not advance to the full freedom and independence of
thought that relies on and draws from itself alone.[4]

So says Hegel in dismissal. Unlike "popular philosophy," "philosophy proper" will be generated by thought from the free inherent
resources of thought alone. Much is hidden in this dismissal, as we
will understand as we proceed further. I am reminded of Hegel's dismissal of Diogenes the Cynic. There is nothing here of any interest to
systematic speculation, and hence nothing of interest to "philosophy
proper." The dismissal is of a piece with a particular view of what it
means to philosophize, reflecting, in turn, an approach to the activity
of thought and its object. Thought, for Hegel, is telos-bound to system, and the telos of autonomous system is attained when thinking
makes itself its own object and becomes thought thinking itself. This
is the highest thought, when it is freed from dependence on externality and anything given, when it also purifies and overcomes the ambiguous caprice of its own less developed forms in feeling. The
presupposition of system as the self-determination of thought thinking itself in its own dialectical-speculative determination provides the
implicit standard of what it means to "philosophize properly." This
too provides the standard by which Pascal's "gleams" are com-
mended and then condemned to inferiority. "Popular philosophy," in
whatever form, is an abortion of the Hegelian embryo. Even if it sur-
vives beyond the womb of immediacy and lives a little, it remains an
arrested growth. It may be an infant for whom we have affection and
pat condescendingly on the head, but we would not dream of putting
this infant on a par with philosophy for grown-up reason.

To my knowledge the mature Hegel did not spare much thought
on Pascal. This is not surprising, since there is something antithetical
about their entire ways of being and mind. Pascal was the younger
contemporary of Descartes, eminently familiar with the ascendant
Cartesianism of the time, a youthful prodigy of mathematics and science whom the older Descartes visited, warily and perhaps with a
touch of jealousy. Pascal might have surpassed the great Descartes
as a Cartesian had the bent of his soul been consumed entirely by the

---

[4] *VGP*, 1: 114–15; *LHP*, 1: 93–94.

esprit de géométrie. Pascal was an obsessive but not a monolinear thinker. He was a discordant thinker, who inhabited the middle space between the *esprit de géométrie* and the *esprit de finesse.* The older Pascal's mind of *finesse* made him reject the certitudes of Descartes as pseudocertainties. Even more extremely, he would eventually judge Descartes: "Descartes useless and uncertain." From the standpoint of the *esprit de finesse* the mathematical certainties of Descartes are uncertain and useless.

Would Pascal have dismissed Hegel thus? Can we imagine Hegel thus dismissing Descartes? Hegel is not a monolinear thinker. And, though opposition plays a crucial role, he is not finally a discordant thinker, but a mediating one. Yet undoubtedly for him Descartes is a hero of thought, and more to the point a hero of thought that recovers its independence in the autonomy that recourses to itself alone. Descartes restores "philosophy proper." He returns it to its autonomy vis-à-vis the given and externality and all heteronomy, and hence renews the project of systematic science. Hegel himself is directly an heir of Descartes in that sense.

I am well aware that Hegel's claim to complete the project of philosophy as systematic science includes much that cannot be handled under the rubric of Cartesianism. This is a measure of Hegel's multifaceted system. His dialectical-speculative mode of thinking cannot be assimilated to the *esprit de géométrie.* Nevertheless, even if Hegel can claim some dialectical finesse, he subscribes to the same Cartesian emphasis on the self-certainty of true philosophical knowledge. Granted all needed qualification, Hegel is still an heir of transcendental philosophy in its turn to the self as offering the true pathway toward the self-certainty of knowing, the knowing that determines itself and its own validity out of itself, and that hence realizes the highest autonomy of thought at home with itself.

Hegel may significantly transcend Descartes, but there is no way we can envisage him saying: "Descartes useless and uncertain." Descartes is eminently useful for Hegel's purposes. Descartes's limitation is not his uncertainty, but his failure to exploit radically the breakthrough into the true realm of certainty in the *cogito me cogitare.* Descartes too is a Hegelian of arrested growth, though from the retrospective view of Hegel's own consummation, Descartes is not philosophically infantile like Pascal. Descartes is a "philosopher proper," not a mere popular dilettante.

I offer this contrast: Hegel's *Wissenschaft der Logik* is a monumental work, a colossus of sustained continuous thinking that flows on and on, from an alpha to an omega wherein the alpha rises again, like a resurrected phoenix. Hegel writes a masterwork, an epic of triumphal reason. Think now of Pascal: the sickly genius, the weary prodigy, wearing himself out until an early death; then after his death, the little piles of papers, scraps and shreds of paper, bundles and bits and torn slips. These were the fragments for his putative apology for Christianity, fragments whose posthumous arrangement compose the *Pensées*: Not the Science of Logic, not God's thought before the creation of nature and finite spirit, but raw drafts of thoughts, the unfinished building blocks, the straw and mud, or perhaps the ruins of a never finished apology. Not triumphal thought, but shards of thought. Perhaps not the infantilism of philosophy but the invalidism of thinking that sporadically surges up in "gleams."

Had Pascal lived longer he might have composed a work of continuous development, smoothing the jagged edges of broken inspiration. He might have been more "Hegelian." Instead we have a crippled system. Hegel *contra* Pascal: The validity of triumphal logicism against the validity of invalid thinking? And the "gleams" of thought in the crippled system? Do some of these "gleams" shine with a light in excess of the successful system?

Being Between

I chose the theme of being between because it is essential to Pascal and Hegel. It also reflects perhaps the central theme of my own thought.[5] I will not make direct reference to my own reflection on what I call the metaxological here (though in reserve, it will not be completely out of play).

Some of the most striking passages in Pascal reveal his acute sense of the intermediate condition of the human being. Numerous citations might be adduced, but one of the most famous is the following.[6] It is worth citing for its power to provoke rumination. I do not know if it can be surpassed. What is the human being in nature? Pascal answers:

---

[5] See, inter alia, *Desire, Dialectic, and Otherness: An Essay on Origins* (New Haven: Yale University Press, 1987); *Philosophy and its Others* and *Being and the Between*; see also my essay in the edition of *CLIO* that discusses my work, "Being Between," *CLIO* 20, no. 4 (Summer 1991): 305–31.

[6] Blaise Pascal, *Pensées*, trans., with an introduction by, A. J. Krailsheimer (Baltimore: Penguin, 1966), 90. See also p. 157: "I do not know who put me into the world. . . ."

A nothing compared to the infinite, a whole compared to the nothing, a middle point between all and nothing, infinitely remote from an understanding of the extremes; the end of things and their principles are unattainably hidden from him in impenetrable secrecy.

Equally incapable of seeing the nothing from which he emerges and the infinity in which he is engulfed.

What else can he do, then, but perceive some semblance of the middle of things, eternally hopeless of knowing either their principles or their end? All things come out of nothingness and are carried onwards to infinity. Who can follow these astonishing processes? The author of these wonders understands them: no one else can.

This is not just an example of "Pascalian thought," but an honest naming of the perplexed predicament wherein the human being finds himself. In the middle between an enigmatic origin and an uncertain end, the mindful human being is enveloped by a perplexity that thinking seems unable entirely to dispel.

Hegel is not devoid of his own attunement to the intermediate condition. He says: "In thinking, I raise myself above all that is finite to the absolute and am *infinite self-consciousness*, while at the same time I am *finite self-consciousness*, indeed to the full extent of my empirical condition." He adds:

I am the relation of these two sides; these two extremes are each just me, who connects them. The holding together, the connecting, is itself this conflict of self within the unity, this uniting of self in conflict. In other words, *I am the conflict*, for the conflict is precisely this clash, which is not an indifference of the two <as> distinct but is their bonding together. I am not *one* of the parties caught up in the conflict but am both of the combatants and the conflict itself. I am the fire and the water that touch each other, the contact (<now separated and ruptured, now reconciled and united>) and union of what utterly flies apart; and it is just this contact that is itself double clashing relation as relation.[7]

---

[7] G. W. F. Hegel, *Vorlesungen über die Philosophie der Religion*, vol. 1, ed. Walter Jaeschke (Hamburg: Felix Meiner, 1983–85), 120–21; *Lectures on the Philosophy of Religion*, ed. Peter C. Hodgson, trans. R. F. Brown, P. C. Hodgson, and J. M. Stewart, with the assistance of H. S. Harris (Berkeley: University of California Press, 1984–87), 1821, 212–13; I will cite these as *VPR* and *LPR*.

These citations from Pascal and Hegel might seem to indicate a shared sense of our intermediate condition, but there are radical differences in the way they articulate the between. For Pascal, the finite self is caught between the extremes of nothing and infinity: there are extremes other to the self and they define its mode of being between. For Hegel, certainly in the above citation, the self *is* the between: it is both finite and infinite, both the war of the two and their mediation into unity. For Pascal, the infinite is irreducibly other to the finite self. For Hegel, the infinite is not thus other but is the self-mediation of the finite self who, in this dialectical self-mediation, comes to know the finite and infinite as within one encompassing whole or process. For Hegel finitude is nothing apart from its dialectical relativity to infinitude and vice versa. The between is simply the dialectical relativity, the dynamic self-mediation of these two. Finitude, negation, infinitude are ingredient in the self-mediation of the Hegelian between; but we are not *in* this between, we *are* this between. The Pascalian between is rent differently.

Perplexity Between Faith and Reason

For both Hegel and Pascal thought involves a radical perplexity in the middle. The question then is: How do we further make response to this perplexity? Hegelian reason and the Pascalian heart move in directions that ultimately repel each other. Yet in both we find acute attention to the condition of antithesis: the thinking self is sundered in the space between opposites. This is not the end of the matter, for in the between we are driven beyond our own finitude, or rather discover finitude to be a movement of self-surpassing. This is most evident with thinking itself. We plot a limit and the act of laying down a limit is already the deconstruction of the limit and hence its surpassing. We are already on the *other* side of the limit that we would plot from this side. In the middle we are at once on both sides of the limit. Instead of being frozen in a paralysis between extremes, we inhabit the middle doubly, multiply.

With suitable qualification the middle can be made alternatively to take on a Hegelian or Pascalian face. We stress the self-surpassing of limits in thinking, and Hegel will smile. We stress the tense doubling of being in the middle, and Pascal will nod his approval. With the first we are asked not to forget the mediated unity of opposites; with the second we are not allowed to forget that the opposites frequently engender a struggle for ascendancy in the doubled self. The Hegelian self thinks but embraces contradiction; the Pascalian self lives contradiction but is wounded by it.

There is an agitation of spirit that makes it impossible for us, in thought, in existence, to remain in any stasis of fixed antithesis. The between is the site of self-transcending, hence also the locus of human restlessness and distress and distraction. We stress the middle, walled by extremities, up to which we march, or sidle, and to which we offer challenge or capitulation. We try to match the extremities. We are the stress of the middle.

On this score both Pascal and Hegel are extremists in the middle. The middle as stressed is not the space that offers the comfort of the mediocre response, we being middling, in the sense of being lukewarm, tepid, insipid. There is an extremism of thinking in both Pascal and Hegel. They push to the limit and beyond the limit. There is no fixed limit. This is not to say there is no limit. But in matters of mind and spirit and existence the limit cannot be spatialized in any completely determinate or univocal sense. The middle is a kind of field of energy wherein mind and spirit seek and perhaps find; it is not a determinate entity or space that univocally allays philosophical perplexity and existential restlessness. Finding has to be commensurate with the unconditionality of the seeking itself. Absolute restlessness for truth seeks a finding from truth as itself absolute out of itself. Such a truth could not be completely determined or univocally fixed. The "answer" of this finding is always a "mystery" from the standpoint of univocal mind, and constitutively enigmatic in another quite different sense that I must leave for now without comment.

If Pascal and Hegel both evidence this restlessness in the milieu of being between finitude and infinity, neither is immune from the metaphysical malaise that may go with this middle condition. I mean that the restlessness that drives to the extreme is not the mere surge of naive energy that would joyfully embrace the all. I mean that the agitation is often driven by despair in the middle.

Consider. In the middle we do not immediately or directly meet anything absolute. Everything is relative. Everything finite is defined in a network of relations with other finite beings or processes. The milieu of finite being is a between of radical relativity. Hence to become agitated about the thought of the unconditional or absolute is to look initially with dismay at what is there, what is not there. One cannot find the answer there. The agitation is a restlessness for the absolute but that restlessness cannot be pacified by anything in the finite milieu.

Can one look elsewhere? But there is no elsewhere in the sense of another domain of determinate beings outside the milieu of the middle. One must look in and through the finite middle. If one finds nothing, one fears that there is nothing to find. One is nagged by metaphysical suspicion. The nagging unease grows to dimensions that match the surrounding middle. The unease becomes metaphysical despair of any finding that answers the seeking with commensurate absoluteness.

Healthy common sense will recoil from this malaise, but in a different respect, known to both Hegel and Pascal, common sense is often already in metaphysical despair. It will not dwell with the answer that there is no univocal answer, and that our transcending might be an anomalous excess that reaches, overreaches itself into nothing. Common sense will chastise this reaching and say: Let that overreaching contract itself. It will so dictate. The order will be ineffectual, perhaps not with some, but certainly with extremists like Pascal and Hegel. Pascal and Hegel are thinkers who claim, albeit differently, that we cannot renege on this excess of self-transcending that overreaches the milieu of finite being. There is an audacity of spirit that searches out whether we overreach into nothing merely, or into something other to nothing and to finite being.

The point might be more soberly put by remembering that skepticism is indispensable in all philosophical endeavor. One is not a philosopher if one's voice does not include the disturbing voice of the skeptic. This is clear with Hegel, who transforms the skeptical mode into the negativity of dynamic thinking itself, always and ever dismantling its partial and provisional efforts. Thinking, in this mode, is a negativity, a negativity that tests the grounds of itself, tests itself radically. Pascal is also a severe skeptic. This is not all, not the complete position, of either Pascal or Hegel.

Pascal was deeply aware of the generally precarious grounds on which much of human knowing is based, on the flimsy foundations on which customary morality rests. "It is a funny sort of justice whose limits are marked by a river; true on this side of the Pyrenees, false on the other."[8] Skepticism goes with an acknowledgment of the diversity in human opinions. It grows with a suspicion of the human all-too-human underside of our ideals. Pascal is hardly surpassed by Nietzsche in his sharpness, indeed cruelty toward the sheer silliness, the self-deluding cowardice, the comfortable laziness nesting in our

---

[8] *Pensées*, 46.

declaimed nobilities. To be a skeptic in the sense intended demands an extraordinary spiritual freedom, a distance from mindless immersion in the taken-for-granted phantasmagoria. Skeptical mindfulness is a kind of death. Much of what is called life makes recourse to lies and hypocrisy. The death of skeptical mind frees one from insistence on consolation in looking at this. One looks at this and does not rush to judgment. The patient mind would see it as it is. One would be vigilant for wretchedness, and yet not destroy the promise of human greatness. Such balanced skepticism in the middle is one of Pascal's great virtues.

Skepticism may destroy mind and spirit; it may free them. It visits a violence on self; it may release a more free selving. It can take on a number of different forms. Though skepticism and despair agitate us in the middle, neither is the end; both may induce an opening, a new initiative. Here we note differences between Hegel and Pascal. Pascal came to hold that despair can only be overcome in faith: One despairs of oneself, and there is no remedy in oneself or nature; one must throw one's despair into the hands of the living God. This will be a different death, and in faith a new life.

Hegel will not quite deny faith, but he will insist that there is a salvation from despair in reason itself. Reason is the seeking, reason the finding. Thought may come to itself, find itself in an autonomy of reason that has passed through the valley of bones and reconstituted the meaning of being purely out of itself. Skepticism here serves the reversion of thought on itself, the release of a more radical thinking that insists on thinking purely from itself. Every heterogeneity will let reason down; hence its despair of itself is really its misunderstanding of the more radical power of thinking to effect an answer purely through itself. There is no saving from the despair of thought that is rent by radical skepticism, no remedy except in thought itself. As Hegel insists: the hand that wounds is also the hand that heals. In Pascal's faith, the hand that heals is not the hand that wounds, for the wound, though self-inflicted, is ultimately beyond self-healing.

Pascal is sometimes characterized as fideistic. Indeed we do find utterances indicating a will to humiliate reason. Pascal is extraordinarily complex, however. There is little doubt that he was one of the great rational minds in history. As a mathematician he had the endowment of genius; he also showed the power of engineering genius, as inventor of the calculating machine, the *machine d'arithmétique*; he knew the connection of *ratio* and power; toward the end of his life he showed himself capable of being an effective administrator of a profitable bus company, the first in Paris. In all his writing there is a perspicuity and intensive attention to the matter at issue. We find a mind whose powers of concentration on determinate thoughts were extraordinary.

Man is a thinking reed, the famous saying has it. Against any simplistic fideism, for Pascal human dignity is vested in man as thought. Again, Pascal is a thinker of the between: between the wretchedness of thought and the greatness of thought. In my view, any Hegelianism that identifies our being with thought would be wrong not to acknowledge an equally strong stress on the human being as thought in Pascal. The sense of thought is qualified differently, and this is where the quarrel lies.

The human being is thought, the form of being that is the possibility, the promise of being mindful. Our wretchedness comes from the gift of mindfulness that awakens us to our difference in the cosmic immensity. Sometimes this sense of difference takes on the shape of alienation and estrangement. Like Pascal we feel abandoned in the cosmic immensities, alone and forsaken in a cold and indifferent universe. Thought and mind are essential to the differentiation of the human from immediate absorption in any totality. Without that rupture we would not be what we are. Yet we also come to wonder if there is anymore a totality wherein we will again be at home. Hegel is not a stranger to this—he sees thought as rupturing the immediacy of immersion in nature, and indeed as at the source of our sense of evil and estrangement from being. Hegel's interpretation of the Fall is instructive here.

Thought is also a condition of greatness for Pascal. Our awareness of our anomalous condition as mind makes us superior to the universe that finally will crush us. Things in the exteriority of nature do not know their wretchedness. We know, and in our knowing are great, are more than the indifferent universe, in principle more than being merely wretched. Scotch any caricature of Pascal as a simpleminded fideist. When faith intervenes it is in relation to an extraordinarily complex sense of the human self as mindful being in the between.

Hegel might be tempted to see in Pascal an embodiment of that figure so central to Hegel's *Phenomenology of Spirit*: the unhappy consciousness. There is some basis for seeing resemblances here. As Pascal said to his sister: illness is the natural state of the Christian. Illness was his unrelieved state for much of his adult life; he ended walking with a cane. There are reports of ascetical practices, and the hairshirt and belt found on his body after his death. In 1659 he was very sick, and did no real intellectual work for a year. He wrote the moving "Prayer asking God for the right use of illness" ("Prière pour demander à Dieu le bon usage des maladies").

Pascal's thought is not musical, as Hegel says of the thinking of the unhappy consciousness. There is laughter in Pascal but it is tinged with cruelty: sarcasm, satire, irony. There is a laughing at, not always a festive laughing with. There is perhaps too little of the festivity of thought in Pascal. There is energy, yes, but there is much of coldness to the fire. Is there too much of cold geometry in the finesse? Is there the violence of the self-assured intellect taking apart the idolatries of the self-assured intellect?

I do not doubt there was a tyrannical side to Pascal, but neither do I doubt that he fought it fiercely. It is relevant to Hegel to mention Pascal's first theological controversy (1647) with Jacques Forton, sieur de Saint-Ange. Forton believed, in a manner reminiscent of Hegel, that we could reason out the dogmas of Christianity, suggesting that we might even demonstrate the truth of the Trinity. Pascal hounded him for his alleged heterodoxy. He took the case to the ecclesiastical authorities and persisted until finally forcing the hapless Forton to recant. This says something about a tyrannical streak in Pascal's nature. Hegel certainly would have been hounded for the claims he made on behalf of reason and the Trinity. Pascal had a zeal for certitude, and yet all certitude is ever elusive. Pascal himself came to know the ambivalent power of ecclesiastical authority. He himself heard the baying of the hounds and beheld his beloved truths the prey of their hounding. How sweet to humble another, and in the name of divine truth; how galling, how bitter to be humbled oneself, by that same claim of divine truth!

I sense a side of Pascal that hated to be in the wrong; hence at times there is a certain cruelty to opponents, the great power of his mind mingling with a *libido dominandi*. For instance, in 1658 there was the contest he proposed regarding the famous problem of the roulette. Pascal already had worked out the solution, and this, as his sister tells the story, while assaulted by a terrible toothache, from which he sought relief in mathematics. In judging the contestants, Pascal pulled no punches; he aroused bad blood by his wounding criticism of others and his attitude of ascendant incontrovertability.

Pascal certainly is an unusual case, and undoubtedly does show a profile at times not entirely unlike Hegel's unhappy consciousness. So, for instance, going with this lordly side, there is an extraordi-

narily strong emphasis on *submission*. Who is being forced into submission, and who is in revolt? Sometimes it is Pascal's opponent;
sometimes it is Pascal himself as his own opponent, revolting and
submissive at once. (His *Mémorial* speaks of: Total and sweet renun-
ciation [*renonciation totale et douce* / Complete submission (*soumission*)]
to Jesus Christ and to my director.[9]) We remember that the unhappy
consciousness in Hegel comes to *mix* the master and the slave. Not
irrelevantly, Pascal was deeply imbued with the skepticism of Montaigne. Among philosophers he retained some reverence for Epic-
tetus the Stoic. As we know for Hegel, the Skeptic and the Stoic sage
produce their spiritual descendant in the unhappy consciousness. In
religion the erstwhile slave may later become the master, just as the
erstwhile master may become the subsequent victim. Both the master
and the slave can wear the mask of the inquisitor. This is especially
so when religious truth is made to serve as a vehicle for a secret will-
to-power, the sweet power that sanctions itself in God's own sanc-
tuary.

The broadcast of festive laughter is a transmission of the celebrating energy of the "to be" that forces no one into submission. As a
Christian, Pascal enjoins compassion and forgiveness. Is there
enough of a forgiving laughter in Pascal—outbreak of free release at
home with itself and being, freed either to ask for forgiveness or to
forgive, freed even to forgive itself? If we wait for a last judgment,
there is to be no glee in condemnation and revenge, no complaint.

When Pascal points to our condition as a double one—both
wretched and great—we recall Hegel's explicit description of the unhappy consciousness as the epitome of the double consciousness. It
is caught in a middle that allows no affirmative mediation of the extremes. It seeks an absolute answer but seeks it elsewhere; it sees in
itself nothing but wretchedness, to assuage which it looks away to
something absolutely other. But this other does not alleviate the despair. It deepens it, precisely to the extent that it continues to remain
other. In addition to Pascal's asceticism, already mentioned, there is
a tendency to look upon the world as a degraded creation: an indigence of fallen being, not the very good creation of God. Pascal's
sense of the results of original sin darkens not only his idea of humanity but of the world, as a vale of tears.

Pascal will suggest that God respects the middle condition in giving us enough evidence to believe, but not so much that we have ab-

---

[9] See *Pensées*, 309–10.

solute transparency. Yet overall it is the *absence* of the traces of God that seems to receive the primary emphasis. Pascal was intent that we not sleep too easily in this life. It was as if his own restless agitation were the condition necessary to bring us all to a saving despair over ourselves and the world. A danger here is that we are offered a slander of creation in the interests of restoring us to the Creator. But slander the creation, slander the Creator.

One senses a violence in Pascal, an absence of release, a lack of serenity. He struggled to say "Amen," and yet the prayer sometimes either sticks in his throat or seems somewhat forced. Even his final words seem less releasing as trembling — 19 August, 1662: "May God never abandon me [*Que Dieu ne m'abandonne jamais*]!" These words echo the same words found in the *Mémorial*. It is as if Pascal was riven by fear of loss, the ultimate loss. The *Mémorial* itself can be seen as a talisman against loss again, like a sacred object one places between oneself and the abyss toward which one still rushes. I do not want to overstate the point. But where there is unresolved struggle for faith, there is not quite faith yet. Pascal was not unequivocally safe in faith. Perhaps this is too much to ask. Perhaps it is fairer to say that he struggled between despair and faith.

For Hegel the doubleness of the unhappy consciousness is really a *failure to be at one with oneself*. It is double because it does not recognize that the other is really itself, and has been projected into a beyond, where the face it returns is that of a radical stranger; there is no "pure self-recognition in absolute otherness," in Hegel's telling phrase. To overcome the unhappy consciousness for Hegel is dialectically to pass through the double of opposition of self and other, to see the double as two sides of a single self-mediating totality. The double is dialectically superseded by a one. Finally the stress for Hegel is not at all on the so-called absolute otherness, but on the pure self-recognition.[10]

I do not find that this is entirely true to the sublime wretchedness of Pascal. Pascal's doubleness is genuinely a double in that God will

---

[10] *Das Reine Selbsterkennen im absoluten Anderssein*, in *Phänomenologie des Geistes* (Hamburg: Felix Meiner, 1952), 24; *Phenomenology of Spirit*, trans. A. V. Miller (Oxford: Clarendon Press, 1977), 14. This phrase is sometimes cited by those among Hegel's admirers who want to make him a philosopher of radical otherness. I take the absolute otherness precisely to be an "absolved" otherness that is a passing or medial otherness through which the self passes to "*pure self*-recognition." Hegel himself emphasizes the *pure* nature of the self-recognition: the absolute otherness is its own otherness, that is, of the self itself.

never be reduced to sameness with the self, not even to a mediated identity. There is a difference that is not a moment of dialectical-speculative identity. There is transcendence to God, before which we always finally fall silent. There may be *self*-recognition in the face of this absolute otherness but not at all because the other is the self in the form of otherness. It is because the human self meets the limit in which it finally sees its own face in its double aspect of wretchedness and greatness. But there is nothing pure about this self-recognition and there is nothing dialectically necessitated about it. If it takes place it does so at the Last Judgment, though we already are before this Judge even now. Contra Hegel, *die Weltgeschichte* is not *das Weltgericht*.

Pascal and Kierkegaard here have much in common. Some of Pascal's characteristic responses to Descartes anticipate Kierkegaard's responses to Hegel with an uncanny likeness. For Hegel being between serves to define two extremities that are mediated opposites; moreover in this process of mediation, the double is seen as penultimate to the one reconciled with itself in its own otherness. Being between for Pascal is constitutively double; the double is ultimate relative to the resources of human thought and its will to effect its at-onement with God as its radical other. Even this at-onement is not a dialectical oneness, but a community of grace and forgiveness in which the doubleness is not done away with or dialectically *aufgehoben* but transfigured.[11]

The self as doubled can fall into a condition of duplicitous being. We experience the middle as an impasse: between our passion for truth and our impotent knowing; between our longing for justice and our flawed will; between our desire for happiness and our repeated frustration; between our aspiring for peace and the grim rebuff of coercive power. Life in time is a trial between two eternities, but how are we to overcome the impasse? What will provide victory, and what or who will judge the outcome? Will reason and philosophy serve? Pascal loudly says "no": reason and philosophy articulate our

---

[11] I know forgiveness has an important place for Hegel in the *Phenomenology*, but I find Hegel systematically equivocal in a way few of his admiring commentators seem willing to grant, or even see. See my *Hegel's God*, 62–65, 194–95. See *Beyond Hegel and Dialectic: Speculation, Cult and Comedy* (Albany: State University of New York Press, 1992), especially 104–17, on the unhappy consciousness and doubleness, in Hegelian and other senses; on evil and forgiveness and the double, see chapter 4; this chapter also discusses Hegel's view of the Fall, to which I referred above.

fallen condition, and in part sprout from our deformed powers. Only a God can save us. If there is an answer to the extremity of our impasse in the middle, it can only be faith. This is not our answer. It is a gift to which we must answer.

Hegelian Reason and the Pascalian Heart

What are some of the options for *thought* in the between? One will say, naturally, that reason must go to work on the problems, quandaries, and confusions of the middle. Pascal and Hegel would agree. Reason in Pascal is different than *Vernunft* in Hegel. It is closer to *Verstand*, the analytical understanding. Pascal, in this matter, is more like an heir of Cartesian mathematics. Reason is related to the *esprit de géométrie*. Such a mathematical *ratio* is marked by the precision and exactness of the univocal mind. A is A is A: all equivocation and ambiguity is to be done away with, analytically overcome. Pascal was a master of univocal mind in this sense. Univocal mind corresponds again to *Verstand* in Hegel in that *Verstand* insists that the terms of knowing have determinate meanings that allow no contamination from their opposites or what is other. A category of *Verstand* is itself and nothing but itself and refuses trespass from any other category. Hegelian *Vernunft* is not *ratio* or the *esprit de géométrie* or *Verstand*. *Vernunft* is open to the passage between opposites, or the mediation of differences or antitheses that are merely distinguished and set apart by *Verstand*.

Vernunft might be interpreted as a dynamic way of thinking the between as the becoming of a process of othering; for nothing simply is itself, but is itself in an open network of relatings. *Vernunft* does not seek to impose a grid of static concepts or categories on the between, in the way analytical geometry allows us to impose a frame of precisely determined coordinates on a space that in itself is neutral and homogeneous and static. The latter homogeneous milieu is not the between of either Pascal or Hegel. Nor is the thinking of *ratio* ever adequate to dynamic being in the between or to the becoming of entities that pass toward their others in the universal relativity. Relativity here implies a "being related" in an entirely dynamic sense. Thus Hegelian reason is not amenable to inclusion under what Pascal designates as *raison*.

Hegel himself is very disparaging of reason as *räsonnement*. At this level no Pascalian hit can be made on Hegel. Hegelian reason, one might suggest, tries to unify the spirit of geometry and a dialectical

Se + that he got fran schelling

finesse in its own way. *Vernunft* has a finesse that *Verstand* lacks. Whether this finesse is finesse enough is the real question, not whether we simply have a juxtaposition of reason with this *esprit de finesse*. If the finesse of dialectical reason is not altogether nuanced enough for the middle, this is not because it is reducible to the *esprit de géométrie*, but because it fails to reach the discernment of metaxological mindfulness.

Is there another sense of thought in Pascal that is neither univocal nor equivocal nor dialectical in Hegel's sense? Sometimes, sporadically. Pascal is not essentially a systematic thinker when he steps outside mathematics, and even then his sense of system is strongly determined by the sense of mathematical *ordo*. Hegelian system cannot be included in this sense. Yet quandaries surface in Pascal's unsystematic discourse that put hard questions to Hegel's sense of system.

In Pascal, however, there is present the temptation to oscillate back and forth between univocity and equivocity. While Hegel's dialectical finesse is not available to him, Pascal is a dialectical thinker in many ways (though not in any systematic manner). This dialectical power is evident in his understanding of opposites and, as we have seen, their coinciding in the equivocal being of humans. Is there another sense of thought that goes beyond univocity, equivocity, and dialectic, and that answers to being between in a manner that is continuous and discordant with Hegel's dialectical way?

Suppose we pursue this question in terms of the disparity between systematic science and the outcries of the heart. We are between nothing and infinitude, the abyss on one side, excess on the other. The abyss of nothing and the excess of infinity both are indeterminacies that initially at least we struggle to pin down, to make determinate. Nothing floats free of thought into the nebulous and the indefinite. Infinitude escapes beyond thinking as impossible of exact determination. One is an indetermination, the other an overdetermination. We are between these two.

Hegel responds to this between by harnessing the self-surpassing power of thinking thus: thought is a negativity that can negate the indeterminacy of the indefinite nothing; thought is negation that is also determination; thought as negation of the negation is also affirmation, and not in any merely indefinite sense either. The dynamism of thought in the middle hence negates and overcomes affirmatively the negative indetermination. In the process it also determines itself. That is to say—and this comes from the side of the other extreme—the self-surpassing dynamism of thought is both a self-determination and a transcendence to infinitude. In fact, the radical self-determination of thought in the middle is the very movement by which the finitude of the self determines the infinitude, that is, overcomes the indeterminacy said to be initially characteristic of infinitude; infinitude is determinately concretized by this self-surpassing of finite thinking in the middle. The self-determining, in Hegel's words, this "self-sublating" infinite is the dialectical play between finitude and infinitude; hence the middle between finitude and infinitude is this infinitude that determines itself in finitude and this finitude that becomes itself in its self-surpassing to its own infinity.

In sum: The space between the abyss of nothing and the excess of infinitude becomes the medium in which the finite self as speculative philosopher mediates the extremes as merely two sides of a total process of self-mediation. Systematic science dialectically-speculatively mediates the between and redefines both abyss and excess as merely abstract moments of the inclusive process of the whole that in developing itself conquers abyss and excess as beyond determination by thinking.

This is Hegel in the between. Pascal is very different. The abyss remains unconquered; the exceeding infinite provokes terror. This is not all, but the response is an existential outcry rather than the pursuit of systematic science. There is a story that Pascal lived with the perception that the abyss was there right next to him, literally to his left side, and that he always placed a chair to that side to buffer himself against it: a chair between, an inconsequential, derisory distraction which obviously Pascal himself knew was a distraction. So he says: We rush toward the precipice, and throw an object before us, between us and it, to shield ourselves from this abyss.

This response might well be dismissed as pathological. Yes, there is something pathological here, but this is double-edged. For there is a suffering, an undergoing, the pathos of an other, beyond our power of self-mediation. I suggest that Pascal's sense of the between makes him blanch before the ontological fragility of finite being. A thin membrane of life separates us from nothingness. We are the crown of creation but a vapor or a little drop of water will kill us. A surge of the terror of contingency assails us. This terror induces what we might call a kind of *blackout* of mind, especially mind as the *esprit de géométrie*. The frailty of contingency produces a liquefaction of our being in the middle. We dissolve and flow away at the thought that we are as nothing. We necessarily must divert ourselves from this thought, otherwise we could not continue to live. When the thought does strike home—home here means striking to the heart of selving—the self dissolves, is liquefied in its own metaphysical insecurity.

Hegel will famously speak of staring the negative in the face, of tarrying with death and seeking truth in utter dismemberment; he will celebrate the magic power that turns the negative into the positive. I find none of this magic power in Pascal. There is dismemberment without human solution. Behold the human self, lovely in beauty and being. In the flick of a finger, deformity or death replace this beauty. There are indescribable horrors. The legs go from under one; one is buckled, one goes down in a liquefaction of self. Why did Pascal need a cane to walk?

The heart cries out in anguish before a condition of being which reveals its helplessness. Our helplessness is our very being. Reason cannot grant this helplessness, for reason will immediately seek the pretext or means to make determinate this formless helplessness. It will turn the pervading agony into a problem with a specific or determinate solution; reason will seek its reiterated salvation in its own powers of self-determination. Descartes's project of the self-certainty of knowledge is only the formulation of this salvation in philosophical terms; a self-certainty that wants the self-determination of thought to lead even to the mastery and possession of nature. Hegel's systematic science continues, some would say completes, this project of self-certainty. But the outcry of the heart cannot evade its own helplessness, and in its dissolution this project strikes it as insolent hubris. Every project of self-certainty is rejected; the terror of the abyss is the ontological deconstruction of every such project; the self undergoing the liquefaction of its own ontological certitude cannot countenance this insolence of self-certainty and the project of mastery that follows from it.

Hence Pascal will say against Descartes: the self is hateful, *le moi est haïssable*. (I know Pascal was addressing Damien Mitton when he said this.) Self-determination is derivative, not absolute; it derives from the gift of our power of determining, but this determining power as given is never amenable to its own self-absolutization as radically self-determining. For the human self there is no radical self-determination. This is a metaphysical lie and a falsification of our being between. Break down this lie, and our being as a *passio essendi*, as a kind of ontological patience, will come back to haunt us, to make us sleepless. And perhaps too in our knowing ourselves to be as nothing, there is also a new, or renewed, porosity to the divine.

We might run from the abyss of nothing toward the excess of exteriority, and nature will rise before us in its overflowing thereness. Before this infinitude of nature Pascal does not experience the exultant release of power that Giordano Bruno expresses before the open universe. The infinite space makes him afraid. Fear, not systematic science; but fear is the beginning of wisdom, even Hegel will agree. Such reasons of the heart are at the origin of reason's reasons. The world of nature as infinite space is for Pascal a God-forsaken world; it is the world of modern mechanistic science; the God of creation has all but vanished from his creation. In fact, nature seems not to be experienced by Pascal as a creation in a proper sense at all, with all the rich dimensions of its gifted glory. The chill of abandonment wherein he shudders before the cold cosmos carries little echo of the almighty "It is good" that we hear in the book of Genesis.

Without endorsing Pascal's cold silent nature, I simply stress that his outcry of the heart arises on an entirely different plane to the mechanistic calculation of nature's mathematical intelligibility. As a good scientist and mathematician Pascal could well have offered us, and did offer, a fine account of this homogeneous space in terms of prevailing scientific views. Such an account is removed from his interest here: the between as lived evokes an other response, even when its extended spatiality is reduced to a homogeneous medium. God is not there in that indifferent space, and the heart cries out in anguish. Where then is the communication of the intimate universal?

The indigence of this world is another abyss, the pit of God-forsakenness out of which Pascal cries to be heard. Recall my citation at the outset of Hegel's reference to Pascal in regard to grief at the lost God: Hegel claimed to know this pit, indeed it is the religious condition of modernity; but Hegelian reason will lift itself out of this pit through its own self-determining thought. Pascal denies that reason has this power. Certainly his outcry reveals an appeal that is entirely antagonistic to the Cartesian will to be master and possessor of nature.

Nature as forsaken by God turns into a metaphysical prison. One may take the bars out of the window, one may turn one's confinement into a technological paradise, but that still does not change the prison. The prison is still a prison. Scientistic and technological mastery may still be a penitentiary for the spirit. The project of this mastery may become, as it were, a world-historical *divertissement*. We become so busy in the space of our confinement that we forget that it is a detention. We violently turn on thinkers like Pascal who try to remind us we remain unfree. In Plato's terms, the technological paradise is still the Cave, and man manacled. The thought of this confinement crucifies mind.

There is in Pascal another sense of infinitude, a specifically religious sense referring to God as infinite transcendence, unmasterable in His mystery, unmasterable in His involvement with finitude. Once again the traces of this infinitude in the middle are hard to read; the heart must read them, but the traces and the heart are both equivocal, wrapped in ambiguity. Pascal does not think that the world is absolutely God-forsaken: it is a middle, between too little and too much. God reveals Himself sufficiently to those who seek, He does not reveal Himself in any mode that is completely transparent to a univocalizing rationality. We have to divine the traces, interpret the equivocal images.

The heart is the power of divination. The heart is hence an epistemological, as well as existential reality. We cannot know unless we are or have become certain kinds of selves: persons whose selving lives a particular porosity to the truth. The truth of God as infinite transcendence, transcendence not reducible to human self-transcendence, is not available as a neutral impersonal truth. As a truth it speaks the truth of God as selving, as person, as communicating; and it communicates to the human as person, not as abstracted mind. An entire transfiguration of selving is necessary for one to be open to any communication from the otherness of God. Only thus comes renewed porosity to the communication of the intimate universal.

Nevertheless, a gap remains in this middle, even with this more affirmative sense of infinitude. Human self-transcendence is potentially infinite; Hegel and Pascal would agree. Hence Pascal: Man infinitely transcends man. Man is beyond himself, even when he is himself. His meaning is beyond him, his being is beyond him, the dynamism of his becoming is beyond him, even when its vector pursues its own self-becoming. The human being is self-transcendence in quest of, in the middle of, transcendence as other, as more ultimate than even human self-transcendence. The difference between human self-transcendence and divine transcendence cannot be reduced; the two remain other. They are not, as I see it in Hegel, two sides of a single process of self-sublation, or a total process of inclusive self-mediation in and through its own other. Being between retains its ineradicable existential tension in Pascal. No speculative science will completely integrate the extremes to the middle in terms of one absolute self-sublating, self-mediating totality.

And, of course, Hegel is not incognizant of what Pascal calls the heart. It is not that we have here a simple "either/or": either Hegel or Pascal, either reason or the heart. But Hegel's admission of the heart is finally very un-Pascalian. Heart is essentially assimilated to the immediacy of feeling.[12] Recall Hegel's reference to Pascal that connects his "popular philosophy" with natural feeling. In Hegel's philosophy of religion the importance of feeling is not denied. Yet the heart here is mere subjective immediacy, with all of the indefiniteness of immediacy and self-particularity. Hegel says the heart is only a source or "seed," again in the bare sense of implicit immediacy. Hence the danger of subjective caprice: the contingency of selfhood is potentially antithetical to rational universality. Hegel interprets the heart in terms of his logic of dialectical-speculative self-mediation; the immediate must be mediated, and the full mediation of the immediate is a process of explicit self-mediation through its own otherness; the heart as an indefinite origin must be mediated and cannot make any claim in itself to ultimacy. The heart is hence not an opening to transcendence as other to the self in intimate selving itself. It is the moment of equivocal, subjective immediacy within a dialectical logic of a self-completing mediation of reason. Of course it is, at the very least, also equivocal if the dialectical-speculative universal of Hegelian reason remains entirely true to the intimate universal of being religious.

Pascal would not deny that the heart can be mediated in the sense of being interpreted and brought out in the light of reason, so far as this is possible. After all, he does say that the heart has reasons. If so, there is an implicit intelligibility to the heart that is not that of the *ratio*, and presumably one can be more or less explicit about such reasons. There is also an equivocity about the heart that comes out in Pascal's utterance: "What sort of freak then is man? How novel, how monstrous, how chaotic, how paradoxical, how prodigious! Judge of all things, feeble earthworm, repository of truth, sink of doubt and error, glory and refuse of the universe!"[13] Whether the heart can be made completely explicit is another question. For Pascal the equivocity of the heart will never yield a complete univocal self-transparency to the human knower. The human being cannot know the heart; yet the human heart can be known. There is no Cartesian or idealistic self-transparency here, for this would be an illicit geo-

---

[12] See *VPR*, 1: 285–91.

[13] *Pensées*, 64.

metrical claim, here where, properly speaking, the mind of finesse must live with ineradicable nuance. Only God has the mind of finesse faithful to this nuance.

Certainly any explication of the heart must see it as much more than a mere immediacy. What does the mediation of the heart bring out? It brings home to us a core of enigma within human selving itself; it brings home to us a sense that ultimate truth is not self-created, nor completely self-mediated. There is a mediation in the immediacy of the heart from a source of truth beyond our own selving. This is an Augustinian rather than Hegelian idea. The light of God shines in the heart; the heart is the self at its deepest, as this gift of the shining truth. The heart is not simply a moment of feeling in a process that leads from feeling's indefiniteness to the express self-mediation of determinate thought. The heart is a source, but the source is not an indefiniteness, but an excess of transcendence in the self itself, a reserve of immanent otherness in selving, the inward otherness of self that carries the trace of God as the absolutely other. We live in and out of touch with the heart in this sense: we are the heart, yet we are not the heart; the shine gleams but also has been tarnished or blurred or dimmed or snuffed out. We are cleft selves, heart and heartless, godly and godless, flesh and stone, between the hateful self exclusively for itself and the selving that is for God as the other.

The heart is what I call the elemental.[14] There are depths to our selving that exceed dialectical self-mediation. The heart is an inward abyss and excess that will never be made completely transparent to itself in a purely conceptual way. The heart is the metaphor for what we are in the intimacy of our being, the idiocy of our being. It names the marvel of inward singularity, the mystery of the "this" of personhood.

Memorial Mind and Speculative *Erinnerung*

Consider further, relative to personhood and singularity, the difference between the elemental and system. As we all know, Pascal is said to have gone through two "conversions," conversions not in the sense of turning from non-Christianity to Christianity but in the sense of a rupture in life and the renewal of a Christianity previously

---

[14] See *Philosophy and its Others*, chapter 6; on the idiotic and intimate, especially with regard to Hegel's view of evil, see *Beyond Hegel and Dialectic*, chapter 4.

held in a perfunctory, nominal manner. The first conversion was at the age of twenty-four. Subsequently, after the death of his father, he is said to have had a somewhat worldly period. At the end of this the second conversion occurred. Incidentally, throughout most of this time Pascal did not forsake his mathematical and scientific interests, and indeed solved the famous problem of the roulette only a few years before his death. Nevertheless, this second conversion was a turning around of the entire self. How do we understand this in relation to Hegelian system?

I say there is something elemental in it. The self seems to reach a bedrock or an abyss, a bottom or a nothing, and a choice between them; and if there is a turn about, this is a redirection of the whole of self-being out of this porosity to the ground or the abyss. The elemental in Pascal's case is revealed in what has come to be called the *Mémorial*. After his death there was found, stitched into his clothes, a parchment describing a profound breakthrough that occurred on November 23, 1654. It had been stitched, unstitched, restitched into new clothing for eight years, from the moment of breakthrough until his death.

As written, the *Mémorial* communicates a great outcry of release. Something breaks through—FIRE is the image used—in this moment of crisis and renewal that is ineradicably particular and that yet bears on the whole of an existence. The *Mémorial* exclaims the famous contrast of the God of Abraham, Isaac, and Jacob with the God of the philosophers and savants. The proper names of particular persons name the God who is person rather than principle. The exact times are recorded by Pascal: between 10:30 p.m. and almost half past midnight. The singularity of the occasion of breakthrough is constitutive of its significance. Singularity is not a mere arational contingency, but a momentous this-here-now of time that is potentially fateful for all eternity for this-here-now human self.

Consider the sense of memorializing mind involved here by contrast with Hegel's sense of speculative *Erinnerung*. The question: Can the momentousness and singularity be completely comprehended by speculative *Erinnerung*? There appears to be more at stake in the *Mémorial* than can be completely encapsulated in the concepts of the system. This more or excess is related to the idiocy of singularity. There is an intimacy of selfhood that is radically singular and that would be significantly falsified if we tried to yoke it completely to, for instance, Hegel's dialectic of sense-certainty, as the proper way to deal philosophically with the this-here-now. There is something about this this-here-now that is richer than a speculative universal, and that yet in its singularity is not devoid of a significance that extends beyond this one momentous occasion itself. There is a surplus immediacy to this singular occasion.[15]

That Pascal secretly carried this parchment with him all through the rest of his life is indicative that the breakthrough in that moment had for him an absolute significance for all subsequent moments. One surmises he knew he could well betray this significance; hence the imperative to carry the *Mémorial* about his intimate person; it was his self as other that was broken by an otherness of the divine. We are pointed to a mode of memorializing mindfulness that offers testament to a decisive breakthrough, always calling for renewal, always harboring a possibility of betrayal. Is there anything analogous to this breakthrough, this possibility of renewal or betrayal in the speculative *Erinnerung*? But this momentous moment is not a moment of a speculative universal.

My point is not quite any simple rejection of Hegel or the elevation of Pascal. Yet there is something to the Pascalian heart that exceeds the terms of Hegelian reason. Memorial mind has an existential singularity and might well seek some speculative universality, though perhaps not quite in Hegel's sense. Both are necessary to the between, and a sense of both is at stake in the intimate universal of our being religious. While Pascal tends to disparage the second, Hegel does not always do justice to the first. We need both to be true to the between. This is relevant to their different attitudes to faith and reason. In Pascal we find a hierarchical notion of different orders. If Pascal does have any tendency to scholastic pigeonholing, not uninfluenced by a Cartesian separation of the orders of faith and reason, it is here put under severe strain by Pascal's deeper experiences and insights. In the hierarchy of orders, faith and reason can be made so distinct that it seems easy to keep each off the other's territory. This is Descartes's strategy: they are so other as to have nothing to do with each other.

This will not work, and Hegel knew this. We can plot a border between territories and insist that faith and reason only travel to the other's country under proper visa. Then they will enter illegally,

---

[15] See my "Surplus Immediacy and the Defect(ion) of Hegel's Concept," in *Philosophy and Culture: Essays in Honor of Donald Phillip Verene*, ed. Glenn Alexander Magee (Charlottesville, Va.: Philosophy Documentation Center, 2002), 107–27.

without certification or passport. There are no univocal borders in mind and spirit which bar trespass or illegal entry; there is a porosity more elemental than all passports and academic policing. Man's being is thought, faith will be thought about, thinking may corrode faith; in the between their mutual confrontation and possible concord cannot be indefinitely evaded. The between is a porosity, hence also a border of trespass and passage, or freedom to cross or be crossed. Travel to and fro is always at work in some way, even when we insist that the two are dualistic opposites. Where is the pure faith relative to which thought is excluded? Where is there pure reason that entirely excludes all trust? Does Pascal have pure faith? Pascal's way of thinking is undoubtedly closer to a Kierkegaardian "either/or," rather than a Hegelian "both/and." But Pascal is no simpleminded antirationalist. Certainly he is an enemy of human reason absolutizing itself. Does he always do justice to the passing between of the two, their crossing and even interpenetration in the duplex middle?

Here we find a radical difference with Hegel. Pascal will reject any absolutization of autonomous thought. Absolutely autonomous thought is idolatrous. This is the idolatry of Descartes that Pascal could not forgive. This is the idolatry of Hegel that Kierkegaard could not absolve and that I think Pascal would not either. Thought ultimately is heteronomous. The law of the other is written into thinking. Faith is what brings home to thought the final heteronomy, which is theonomy. Thought itself is solicited by faith to think the other, as other to thought itself. Man transcends man infinitely; man is thought; thought infinitely transcends itself, but not toward itself as thought, rather toward the divine other that, even when thought, is beyond thought. One might say: The *credo* overtakes the *cogito*. Pascal will then exact a submission of reason. This too is not without ambiguity and hence Pascal says: "To have no time for philosophy is to be a true philosopher."[16]

Truth and the Fragment

In Hegel we find the speculative apotheosis of thought thinking itself in its other. In Pascal we find the finesse of the heart, but often it is a heart torn in two, a heart that in its cleft condition is tempted to humiliate reason. Then there is the double of metaxological mindfulness, beyond this apotheosis and this humiliation: thought must both

---

[16] *Pensées*, 212.

think itself, remain true to its own inherent exigence, and thought must think the thought of the other to thought, remain open to the promise of the truth of what remains beyond its concepts. How differently is truth understood here? Suppose we now situate the fragmentary character of Pascal's most important writing, his *Pensées*, relative to Hegel's claim that the true is the whole. Hegel would surely say that Pascal fell short, and this not merely in the sense implied above, relative to the unhappy consciousness. He fell short relative to the *form* in which Hegel claims the truth must be expressed.

The question now is: Is there any truth to the fragment? Is there an ontological truth here, and not merely one of aesthetic or rhetorical genre? Granted, if Pascal had lived longer it is not likely he would have published a set of fragments. The *Pensées* were working notes for a book that might well have been marked by its own facade of completeness. Life and illness robbed Pascal of the fulfillment of his ambition, or made him abandon it. Pascal did not deliberately choose to be a fragmentary thinker or a thinker in fragments. We ought not to assimilate his *Pensées* to the Romantic genre of the fragment, à la Schlegel, or to the self-consciously detotalized writings of some postmoderns. Pascal's modernity, and perhaps postmodernity, need not be denied. But he is modern and postmodern by being tortured about modernity, and perhaps by modernity, and by hearkening back to Christian history and its theological articulation in an Augustinian, Jansenist vein. He is an advocate of a return to the origin; his attacks on the accommodating casuistry of the Jesuits reveals his hatred of any compromise of what he sees as the original purity of pristine Christianity.

Nevertheless, the fortuitousness of his final fragments does suggest a happy chance. Their very brokenness is intimate to their appeal; their impotence is their power. I am tempted to call this: invalid thinking. The fragment expresses the thinking of an invalid. (Nietzsche was another famous invalid; suffering made him the thinker he was.) But there is a strange validity to this invalidity, when we take account of our condition suspended between finitude and infinity. The ontological truth of the fragment is most appropriate if the world itself is denied its own totality, or entirely immanent self-completion. The world for Pascal is an equivocal creation. It is a fallen world, a world broken into fragments, and very few traces of its original integrity remain.

This affects the very form of the fitting discourse of truth. Hegel insists that philosophy must be systematic, not out of arbitrary assertiveness, but because the presupposition of totality governs his ontological preview. Being as such, even when experienced in alienation and in divided consciousness, is implicitly whole; the truth of division is the articulation of its own meaning as the division of the whole. The meaning of any fragment is not the fragment itself but the whole of which it is a broken part. A fragment is symbolical of the whole; Hegel cannot countenance it as perhaps the tormented stammering of the hyperbolic. Philosophical discourse will follow the unfolding of fragmentation toward the wholeness that is necessarily inscribed in the fragment itself. There is no other intelligible answer for Hegel.

I am tempted to say that Pascalian thinking detotalizes the fragment, in that the fragment lacks the traces of its own implicit wholeness. There are no univocal signs in the fragment allowing us to be led back or forward to its presupposed whole. The fragment stammers of what it cannot speak, by speaking of the impossibility of any whole claiming to be entirely and immanently self-constituted. This impossibility stems from the given character of our being in the between. Does Pascal then imply the logically impossible idea of a part without a whole? Hegel will rightly say a part is a part of a whole; there is no part without its whole. Case closed.

I think Pascal, while perhaps even granting the impeccable logic, would still remain equivocal, and not without right. His view of the benighted condition of fallen humanity makes him insist that we lack an image of the whole. Or we have images but the images are equivocal and hence make it impossible to univocally read off their original. We are mired in the condition of the equivocality of being, and no dialectical mediation of part and whole will by necessity lead us from image to original. The images of the original are themselves fragmented; hence fragments of fragments; hence double in themselves as equivocal, and as fragments of fragments doubly removed from the original. Even if the heart is a metaphor for the self as whole, the human heart is cleft, doubled, equivocal. The fragment as discourse is thus an image of our equivocal condition in an equivocal, not to say broken, world. All knowledge is fragmented in the middle, mired in equivocity.

Even the *esprit de géométrie*, which insists on univocity and precision, becomes itself a form of equivocation if it absolutizes itself. The same is true once we begin to raise the question about the whole human, and our place within the whole. For then the *esprit de géométrie* must be balanced by the *esprit de finesse*. This means that we cannot ask in an entirely homogeneous way about the truth of the whole, in a manner that yields absolute univocal precision. Geometry and finesse may be a complementary double; yet because this double is never reducible to a unified self or subsumable in a more comprehensive mindfulness, our best asking of the truth of the whole, and our best effort to answer it, will always be marked by an ineradicable equivocity, ineradicable because constitutive of the cleft being of the seeker.

Is there a mind of finesse that goes further than this equivocity? Hegel's dialectical-speculative reason certainly will *claim* to go further. How justified is this claim? That is the question. What I call metaxological mindfulness does hesitate before that tendency in Pascal to insist on a kind of radical equivocity without any mediation. I would say there is an *esprit de finesse* in the mindful power of reading the equivocations of being, the unavoidable ambivalences. This reading is not univocal in reducing the ambiguities to exactly calculated precisions. Nor is it entirely dialectical in Hegel's sense, which speculatively incorporates otherness as a moment of the same, or domesticates its perplexing enigma in the inexorable logical circle of thought's own self-determination. In that dialectical-speculative circle we lose the middle, because the middle is then only the medium of thought's own self-mediation, all the way to absolute knowing. The human being's intermediacy between the abyss of nothing and the excess of transcendence is whited out.

There is, I believe, a metaxological dwelling in the equivocity that witnesses to an essential difference between God and the idea of the whole. This dwelling may image—in our not being on a par with transcendence—and in our knowing that we do not know—the God beyond the whole. For if all were absolutely equivocal, as Pascal at times comes close to suggesting, we would also lose the middle. Hegel saw this, at least in one respect. An irredeemable excess of the equivocal deserts the intermediate condition. To be intermediate is to be a particular singular someone, standing somewhere in particular, even if hemmed in by enigma on every side. Absolute equivocity would deconstruct this singularity of existence and the particularity of being placed somewhere, for we could not know who or where we were in a world of complete equivocity. This excess is perhaps a defect that deconstructive thinking does not always do enough to avoid. The middle is not absolutely clear, univocal, not absolutely obscure, equivocal. It is shaped by a play of clarity and obscurity, univocity and equivocity. We might call this a dialectical play, but I think we need not take this in Hegel's sense. The play remains open. Pascal is a kind of existential dialectician who is not systematically self-conscious of what is at play here. He does not transcend Hegel's dialectic in self-reflective awareness of the plurality of modes of interplay. On occasion, he is metaxological in practice, but tends toward the dualistic and equivocal in avowal or theory.

That said, the ontological truth of the fragment, namely our impotence to grasp clearly the ultimate truth, is ultimately religious. God is to be glimpsed, divined in the fragmented image. Hence our dwelling in the fractures of being is absolutely essential. We would not break through did we not suffer breakdown. Breakdown fractures the smoothness of self-assured being. Something breaks through in the fracture—an other porosity, a different energy, another faith, a different asking. Against the systematic continuity of pure self-determining thought, the broken bits give off sparks, like shards of flint struck by a rock. We are the shard, we are the flint. We are not the rock.

Time is out of joint, for Pascal. Time is not the self-unfolding of the concept. Time is fractured, ruptured, time is essentially discontinuous, a middle between itself and eternity. The ruptures of time are the interruptions of eternity. Here Hegel and Pascal are antithetical, though both are concerned with Providence in history. For Hegel historical development is governed by *Geist* as the world-historical universal. There is a necessary progress toward freedom in history, and each epoch is governed by a different manifestation of freedom. Against this macrohistorical view, Pascal stubbornly recalls us to recalcitrant contingencies and intimate singularities. In one sense, this recalls us to the caprice of history, and the accidental. More importantly, it recalls us to the momentous significance of intimate triviality. "Cleopatra's nose: if it had been shorter the whole face of the earth would have been different."[17] Cleopatra's nose: a slight chagrin to the world-historical universal—as if *Geist* will always find its way around such trivialities. But Cleopatra's nose is to the world-historical universal what Krug's pen is to the logical universal of Hegel: a minor embarrassment that is a major irritant.

And is there not unmined meaning in this folly, this comedy of the trivial, so irritating to the world-historical universal? Montaigne said somewhere: sit we on the highest throne in the world, still sit we only on our own tail. Is the folly of the accidental another sign of the sig-

---

[17] *Pensées*, 148.

nificance of the fragment? Or of the comedy of the intimate universal? The face of the earth might be *essentially* different because of some such triviality. Think of Spinoza's desire to know *facies totius Universi*. How might Cleopatra's nose mar this face? Are we philosophers able to face the momentous significance of the trivial? Might the powerful powerlessness of the intimate universal open here in the high comedy of the divinely low? Do we scent a God who providentially ordains the meaning of caprice, without a by-your-leave to human reason? The cunning of reason this? The cunning of the trivial? Is there such a second cunning. Might it con even the first cunning? What is confided even in all the conning? Is Hegel able to face it?

Metaphysical Insomnia and Consent

I close by recalling our beginning with Hegel's reference to Good Friday, historic and speculative. I close with a question generated by two different images of Jesus. Hegel: the death of Jesus is the moment penultimate to his resurrection, not as a singular but as dialectically *aufgehoben* into the universal, the universal community of reconciliation. Pascal: there is no dialectical *Aufhebung* of this singularity; it resists inclusion in any speculative concept and in any world-historical universal. Again *die Weltgeschichte* is not *das Weltgericht*. Remember Pascal's meditation on the night in Gethsemane: Christ will be in agony until the end of the world; we must not sleep during this time.

The two images offer us two senses of being between, relative to the extremes of death and not just life, but what, if anything, outlives death. Jesus reconciling; Jesus making us sleepless. Jesus bringing peace beyond finite measure, acceptance even in death; Jesus agitating infinitely, disturbing immeasurably. History as the dialectical progress of *Geist*; history as the prolonged Gethsemane night of time. Is one the universal without the intimate, the other the intimate without the universal? Are these two absolutely repellant? Can we think the togetherness of the universal and the intimate, of metaphysical consent and insomnia, of being-at-home and not-being-at-home in the between? Must we not think their togetherness in the metaphysical stress of the between? Is Pascal's equivocal togetherness, is Hegel's dialectical togetherness, enough? Beyond speculative satisfactions and fractured gleams, can sleeplessness wake to sabbatical seeing?

3

Religion and the Poverty of Philosophy

Between Philosophy and Religion

Often we come across references to the richness of religion, relative to which the more analytical and conceptual approaches of philosophy appear to be impoverished. This is one sense of the poverty of philosophy. There is some truth to this view, but it is not rich enough a view, and indeed not rich enough in its view of philosophical poverty. Interestingly enough, poverty and richness are notions that here easily convert into each other. I mean that the richness of religion is not separable from its sense of its own poverty. I mean also the hesitation of religion, no matter how rich in significance, to claim for itself an appropriation of the fullness of the divine. Religion is richest when it confesses its poverty, just in relation to what exceeds all human efforts, religious or other. Richness is poverty, poverty is richness.

An analogous point could be made about philosophy: the forms of articulate reflection that a good philosophy offers may seem poor relative to the ontological richness of the happening of being that these forms of thought essay to determine. Or contrariwise, the sheer thereness of that happening may seem poor in articulation by contrast with the rich reflective determinations wrought by sound philosophical thought. The poverty of philosophy is now richness, the richness of philosophy is now poverty.

What I propose here is in the nature of an exploration rather than a set of incontrovertible assertions. I am searching along a line of probing, even halting inquiry, in which one must hesitate to be too assertoric. My remarks are searching, especially since what I propose goes, in many ways, against a dominant self-understanding of philosophy in relation to religion, namely that religion is to be interpreted, understood, and judged, whether negatively or not, before the tribunal of philosophical reason. But how does it stand with philosophy, if we are open to the ultimate claim that being religious may make on us?

I am not countering philosophical reason with an opposing irrationalistic fideism. My purpose is to pose a question to philosophical thinking at certain limits. While I will make suggestions and even assertions about the direction in which the question points us, the main difficulty is to *hear* this question, for some of our characteristic ways of thinking deafen us to it. How deafen? We philosophers think we *have already heard and answered* the question. My argument will be that there is another question that has not been heard, or only rarely or sporadically so, and that this further question solicits a new origination of philosophy: a post-philosophical reverence that yet is philosophical through and through; a reverence that some philosophers once knew, maybe sometimes in a taken-for-granted way, when religious reverence was also perhaps too taken as granted.

For suppose there is a *two-way* intermediation or communication between religion and philosophy, not just a singular direction from religion to reason. I can accept something of the truth that being religious seeks to be understood or to understand itself, and that philosophy is absolutely indispensable in this, and indeed can bring its own richness of thought to bear on that task. But suppose having done this, either well or meanly, there still are further perplexities to face. And suppose we reach even a measure of philosophical fulfillment, when we claim to do conceptual justice to the richness of religion — suppose that then, even then, a new bafflement comes over one, and a new searching and probing makes its call on us. The two-way intermediation of philosophy and religion may make other demands on us *as philosophers*. We might have thought we had conceptually consummate(d) religion, even the consummate religion, but instead of finding ourselves within the whole that finally has closed a self-completing circle around itself, we are drawn on into a new outside, a new desert even, indeed a new poverty beyond the play of the first poverty and richness.

Suppose we are led to wonder if we must set out again in quest of a different richness of spirit, by comparison with which the richness of seemingly consummated philosophy now seems poor. We seem to know everything, and come to know in everything we know nothing. What do we know when we know that nothing? Has it to do with a different poverty of philosophy, and indeed a new seeking for the religious that is less a reversing of any ascent from religion to philosophy as one that finds itself called to a new affiliation of religion and philosophy? Has it to be a new *being between* the religious and the philosophical, in which philosophy would not even dream of claiming to comprehend the religious, though all its resurrected energies are devoted to just some such comprehension? I am open to correction, but having studied Hegel on just this point for more than twenty-five years, I am minded to think that this matter is beyond Hegel's absolute knowing. I will later indicate why.

What recommends undertaking an inquiry of this sort? The philosopher may indeed be a perpetual beginner, but there is, so to say, an age in that perpetual beginning when, though determinate cognition may be relatively matured, metaphysical perplexity seems darker and more intractable than ever. Then the unavoidability of some such quest grows on one, even as one seems to come into the competent mastery of fundamental philosophical possibilities. Standard possibilities of relating the religious and the philosophical seem also less and less satisfying, though this is not to deny their pertinent nourishing qualities. But they can seem to provide inadequate fare at the limit of religious wondering and philosophical perplexity. And some of these standard models are deeply at work in certain practices of philosophy, as I will below try to illustrate.

There is also the fact that we live in an epoch that is, so to say, saturated with determinate cognitions. That saturation seems to go along with a defect of reverence (see below, Chapter 8). Defect of reverence not only makes us defective humans, potentially it makes us monsters. We are saturated with knowings that, so to say, do not save; knowings that seem to make us more and more lost, even though they illuminate many a dark spot in the mysterious cosmos we inhabit. The more light we throw on things, the more things as a whole seem to become dark. The more we know, the more we sink into absurdity. Must not philosophers also be willing to risk thinking about this strange light and darkness, willing to explore other knowings that may address, even counteract, the defect of reverence?

To be ready to enter into that perplexity is not simply a matter of the further expansion of that cognitive saturation. It calls for a discerning of the kinds of knowing, with special alertness to the danger of the false doubles of saving knowing. Could we not think of philosophy thus: as mindful care for the counterfeits of saving knowing? And what if it were the case that these counterfeits more often than not baptize themselves with names like "absolute knowing"? Would such a discerning of the false doubles of saving knowing be more "absolute" than "absolute knowing"? Would it be more absolute, more absolved, just because it comes into a new poverty that gives it no place to lay its head, no place to consecrate, with an idol of philosophy, any claim to self-certainty. Such absolved discerning would seem to belong nowhere, and yet it might be devoted to the care of the most intimate ontological promise of all places. It comes to be more at home by entering into homelessness.

I stress that my point here is not directed against knowing, but concerns knowing at certain limits, where one comes to know that one does not know, where yet also one may know in not knowing that something of ultimate moment is being communicated. In that sense, I speak about something that cannot be quite stylized as faith seeking understanding. Rather it might be likened to understanding seeking an other knowing, that may indeed resurrect its mindfulness of what was most energetically intimate to faith. The couplet faith and understanding may not be enough, nor a dialectical unity of this doublet. Beyond dualistic doubling, and dialectical unity, a different One is to be acknowledged and a different redoubling of mind fostered.

As I say, saturated with knowings, we may be malnourished in reverence, and that saturation and hunger may feed in us the dragon's teeth of the monstrous. Discerning the knowings means also facing the monstrous. What would the nature of monstrous knowing be? In our time, one might claim that monstrous knowing is evident in the devouring will-to-power of instrumental reason. This seems a far cry from idealistic *Vernunft*, but as I have tried to indicate elsewhere,[1] both are modes of mind in which knowing is finally concerned with its mediating with itself. Again ask: Beyond the knowing of the monstrous, and monstrous knowings, is there a saving knowing that is more than concerned with mediating with itself? And does this have anything to do with becoming "poor in spirit"? Can philos-

---

[1] See *Art, Origin, Otherness*, 129–30.

ophy also become poor in spirit? Is this, for example, what Hegel's spirit occupies itself with or what it too studiously skirts? Is the self-completing spirit too puffed up with itself? Could we make sense of poverty of spirit in terms of Hegel's *Geist*? I doubt it.[2]

Discernment of knowings is itself a knowing, though not knowing simply as self-activity. It is a knowing in act, not a known product, and more than just self-activity. For discernment is not self-concerned; it is concerned with the nuance of happening; and if with itself, with itself as nuanced happening also. Philosophy asks for this discernment. A philosopher without reverence is a thinker defective in *delicatesse*.

Philosophy Emergent and Autonomous

We are familiar with the *emergence of philosophy itself* from religious sources. You might say, philosophy enters into a double relation to those sources: at once open to their communcation, and yet questioning of them. This double relation can be developed in different directions. One direction: Openness to the communication of the religious source may mean a continual devotion of philosophy to reverence, and hence a community, even friendship, between source and off-spring. A somewhat different direction: Though philosophical questioning may be done with the aim of searching the truth of religion, it may also call that truth into question as not the truth it claims to be. Such questioning may put a strain on the community between them, if the philosophical questioner simply insists that the religious

---

[2] Considering what Hegel says about the *religious vows of poverty*, clearly he had little appreciation of what is at stake. Hegel shows a too, too solid bourgeois prudence, perhaps even smugness, by contrast with the joy in destitution of Francis of Assisi. One could see Hegel sympathizing with Bernard, Francis's father and a wealthy merchant, as he tried to beat some worldly sense and sense of responsibility into the *Poverello*—Get a job! But could you say the same about the deeper spirit of philosophy? It has no job, and is always being told to get a job; and it is always getting a job to mask and hide its deeper impulses from those wiser in worldly ways—and this more and more in modernity. The search for "success" of modern philosophy—does it grow out of shame at its uselessness? Consult Descartes's repudiation of the useless ancients. And now, after centuries of trying to be of some use? Does philosophy end up useless in quite another sense, when the monster of instrumental reason tries to devour everything, including philosophy? Vico was prescient when he looked to a turn of the gyre, when in would come the barbarism of reflection, and reason go mad and waste its substance. Beyond that waste, a new poverty?

other answer in the terms philosophy proposes. The enactment of philosophy is often carried through with a mixed formation of the double relation. I think that, generally, premodern philosophy maintained a more flexible, even fluid balance of openness and questioning, of affiliation and searching. Modern philosophy, on the whole, accents the side of questioning in a manner that alters that affiliation into a potential opposition, thus tempting philosophy to stake a claim to dominance. Here are some reasons why this happens.

There is the obvious reason that in modernity questioning itself is such that *doubt* has wormed its way to the heart of thinking. Then there is philosophy's insistence on its own autonomy, in the face of the seemingly all-inclusive character of the religious or theological horizon. Philosophy reinvents its own ideal in terms of the paradigm of autonomous, or self-determining knowing. Result: all others are summoned into the openness between themselves and philosophy, to answer philosophy's questioning of them, relative to their conformation to the ideal of rational self-determining knowing. It is hardly surprising that these others, and not least religion, fail to conform to this ideal. But is this *religion's* failure, or a different failure, or defection, of philosophical thinking?

There is also this reason. Religion, like the givenness of being, seems to show a face that is *equivocal*: it seems constitutively ambiguous. This equivocity calls for interpretation, you say. Of course. But everything turns on what kind of interpretation. One kind of interpretation will insist that in itself the equivocity cannot be allowed to have the final word, because it does not deliver to us its intelligibility in a univocally determinable way. In face of this equivocity, philosophy will intensify its own demand for univocal determinability, especially when new forms of determinative cognition, such as the mathematical, seem to show increased power to dispel the ambiguity of initial conditions. Univocal determinability goes in tandem with increase of power over the obscure and threatening conditions of existence. What if among those conditions we find the darkness of being overcome, the darkness of the divine, as eluding our grasp in mystery impenetrable. Rational enlightenment, it seems, must say "no" to all that. If this is how we look, how can religion look but defective?

Think of it this way: I love the other, and when I do, I trust the other. When I begin to question the other, I am already on the verge of falling out of love with the other. My questioning risks disrupting my trust. Can philosophy be a form of questioning in which that love is not slain? There can be an aggressiveness to questioning that is counterproductive: killing the welcome of the other, which must be allowed if the desire to know that other is to meet that other on the terms of its own self-manifestation. Questioning that insists that the other answer to it seems to deny this welcoming way, and hence proves false from the outset to that self-manifestation. I prove more myself than anything else; the other serves my will to be self-determining, as well as my claim to self-determining knowing. Have I not already fallen into falsehood, just in thus laying claim to knowing?

I loved the other, then fell out of love, and now I am tempted to hate the other I loved before so intimately. I expel the intimate other, but is my knowing, no longer loving, now a hating? Knowing that hates—maybe this happens more often than we are wont to acknowledge. If questioning breaks faith with the endowment of given trust, what prevents it from passing from a knowing that loves to a knowing that hates? Can philosophy be a questioning in which that basic trust is not destroyed; or a way of mindfully recovering that trust, again and again lost in our ontological and cognitional aggressions against being? If this is possible, is it so on condition that the philosopher find again a way to a condition of mindfulness alike to being religious, or being reverent?

The Need of Philosophy

One will immediately meet the rejoinder: philosophy is needed by religion. The meaning of religion is ambiguous, and so even if it does embody truth, that truth must be clarified rationally. This is an immanent demand of the religious itself. And hence faith seeks understanding. It is faith that seeks: *fides quaerens intellectum*. You must not caricature the philosopher as the dog of disenchantment. He is an agent of extending the religious into the rational: faith itself seeks reason, because faith itself is rational.

There are multiple branchings here. Question: Is faith then acceptable because, after all, it is rational; and is it qua rational that it is to be accepted? Voilà: then the philosopher represents the higher ideal, since not only can he or she be religious, they can be more, both religious and more explicitly rational. Religion is more fully completed in the explicit rational comprehension of its intelligible truth. Religion for the masses who believe, philosophy for the masters who know. But—and this is the point now—the masters of those who know can also be friends of the masses. Examples: consult the

Platonic guardians and their *eleos*, compassion for the many; consult the *Earliest System Program* of German idealism on a certain dream of the affiliation between philosophy, religion, and the *Volk*; consult even Marx's inverted, that is, atheistic version: those with the political wisdom of communist science will supply the head to the body of the proletariat, otherwise indigent in knowing.

By contrast, now consider the matter from this angle: suppose reason is derivative from a kind of faith. Then perhaps it is a thinking transformation of a basic faith. At the more elemental level is a kind of "faith," which finds a mindful form in reason; reason itself is grounded in a more fundamental *fides*, or con-fidence. The confidence reason has in truth is *given* with and to reason, not just produced by reason through itself. This fundamental (*con-*)*fides* is a primal gift. Philosophy is an attempt to understand and make intelligible its truth.

Of course, one must distinguish different senses of *fides*. There is, as I am suggesting, an elemental, but also what seems like a relatively indeterminate sense of fidelity; to what, one is not exactly clear; and the question "Fidelity to what?" is crucial. It may turn out, as I will try to indicate, that this seeming indeterminacy should more truly be called an overdeterminacy. There is another, second sense that concerns a more determinate faith: commitment of trust to a more particular set of views or propositions or a specific religious tradition, sometimes with determinate dogmas and so on. I will be more concerned with the first, but it is inseparable from some confidence in the second determinacies also. Or: My interest is not with sheer indefiniteness, nor fixed determinacy, but with something of the play *between* the indeterminate and determinacy; and again not an interplay that leads to the determination or self-determination of the indeterminacy as indefinite. I am concerned with an awakening to the overdeterminacy of the indeterminate in the surplus of its transcendence as other. Is this the primal faith: not the faith that we have in it; but that it has in us, in that what we are given to be is as such, just in the communication of being as determinate and self-determining from the original surplus overdeterminacy of transcendence as other? God in religious language?

What further can we say of faith as confidence, whether elemental or derived? Confidence is a *con-fides*, a *fides* "*with*," that is, it is already in fidelity with and to an other. The "con" is a "cum" or "with" that already announces a basic community: this bases faith, con-fidence. And that other to reason *confides to reason*, unknown to it at the start, a grounding confidence, or trust, that there is truth and intelligibility to be attained, were it further to seek. This means of course, that reason is never simply self-determining; for this confiding, this *fides* *"with,"* this confidence, is what energizes all its processes of determining, including its own confidence in its self-determining powers. The reason of the philosopher is first given to us, before we can even dream of insisting that reason accept only what it gives to itself. In fact, this second insistence means that the grounding *con-fides*, or confidence, has already been reconfigured, and not to mince words, corrupted. The gift of thinking to itself is betrayed by a thinking that insists only on thinking itself. True thinking asks of us a spiritual fidelity.

Again if I am not mistaken, almost all philosophical discussion takes the directionality that follows faith seeking understanding, whether this leads to a new fraternity between philosophy and religion or to a war of enlightenment debunking. As agent of reason, philosophy sets the terms. If my above proposal has truth, is the matter not the other way round? It makes us newly ask: How does *philosophy* stand, if it is the derivative? What does *intellectus* seek? Understanding also, hence *itself*? Or does it seek what is *other* to itself? If so, would not philosophy have to be a thinking that is other to thought thinking itself? (Think here of Plotinus's One, above thought thinking itself, by contrast with Aristotle's *noēsis noēsis noēseōs*; think of Hegel's post-Kantian re-echoing of Aristotle, and his not really knowing what to do with Plotinus's One above.) What is at stake is our reconfiguration of the above double relation of openness and question. If I am right, the dominant philosophical reconfiguration insists that the openness be rethought in terms of the questioning of philosophy as finally determining the terms of the relation. What I am suggesting is that, beyond *fides quaerens intellectum*, we must ask if there is an *intellectus quaerens X*?

Why ask this? Again, in an age in which all reverences are under onslaught, in which scientific understanding seems more and more to assert a hegemony over all things, human and nonhuman, maybe it is not more understanding *of that sort* we need, but more than anything else a new reverence, and perhaps a kind of saving knowing. If so, this would amount to a significant qualification of how we define the quest of philosophy. Certainly, the ideal of self-determining knowing would have to be reformed. If we think the religious is always behind us, then we will look to the future with our faces turned away from reverence. But what if proper reverence is what we need now more than anything else? We would have to turn our faces again. And the point cannot be to give up thought, but to think in that turn more truly. But the poverty of philosophy may have to be relearned to think more truly in that turn.

What kind of a saving knowing could here be at issue? A knowing saving not only the appearances, but saving the appearance for community, and more, saving the community of being, as endowed to be what it is with a grounding trust or con-fides. There is, for instance, a knowing of love that saves, keeps safe, a community—a knowing at the heart of the intimate universal of religion.

Kantian Cautions

The strategies we find in German idealism are continuous with the dominant possibility outlined above that puts the primary stress on philosophical reason as autonomous. I will remark on Kant and Hegel. First Kant: he is comfortable only with religion within the bounds of reason. What are those bounds? Those set by reason. Reason questions, reason defines itself as the form and act of openness; reason also is the standard and judge. But what then of the relation and openness *between* reason and religion. It seems to be defined by one side. Do philosophers gives *themselves* too much confidence here, go too easy on *themselves*? (I say: *We are obscure to ourselves, yes.* But you say: *No, I am not obscure to myself.* Reply: *Very well, your clarity obscures your obscurity, and therefore doubles the obscurity to yourself.*)

Must the philosopher here confess to the danger of being a critical judge, namely, being caught in a "conflict of interests"? Does the suspicion of "special pleading" apply as much to (a-theist) philosophy as to (theist) religion? Suppose we ask again: What if reason is derivative of a source that is enigmatic to reason itself? Suppose its mother is closer to the condition of reverence. Well then, here we witness the offspring placing constraints on the elder source. The offspring is embarrassed by the excess of its original source. It will plead or demand: please mother be moderate! You will make a show of yourself, in this higher age of rational enlightenment! You will make a show of me! And how much of shame and embarrassment is at work in all this? More than we are comfortable confessing.

In passing: Is it not so that shame is a very important cause of people turning from religion? We are made to feel ashamed of what we believe; we are not undermined by arguments but by silent strategies of embarrassment. Silence that shames silences many people.

Nothing has to be said, then. Or in another image: the intellectual might believe that thought must be rationally purified, that is, *detoxified*. Religion is the intoxicant that must be purged. But what if the detoxicant is itself a toxin, a toxin that now has circulated in the blood line of many intellectuals, especially since the eighteenth century? Well then, these toxins may now even seem like nutrients in that bloodstream. Were we to be weaned from addiction to them, we might have a different delirium tremens, a secular delirium, so to say. And suppose, in any case, that these nutrients are really debilitants. What then would a healthy philosopher need? A purge, a new therapy and a new immunity to toxins, secular and religious. The philosopher would have to become, in an image I used before, like a strong *taster of poisons* (like those who once served the sovereign). Being such a taster, the philosopher might find that some of the poisons do debilitate; hence, counterpowers must be energized to empower the body human to continue to be and thrive; and among those counterpowers must be a religious reverence.

Maybe Kant tried something like this when he suggested: God impossible to prove, theoretically, God necessary, morally. So we get in Kant the double vision: dare to know, you cannot really know. Kant seems like a transcendental equivocator, vacillator: cautious and bold; fearful and certain; skeptic and dogmatic in one. Nevertheless, his moralization of the religious amounts to a sentencing of religion to clean up its act, to wash itself of its excesses. Strip it of its nonmoral accretion; make it rich in morality, but poor in everything else. And when it is stripped of these other things, but clean in moral message, let it then come before the tribunal of reason, now with its case properly prepared. As a character witness for the defendant, I cannot but see this as an extraordinarily condescending, patronizing attitude. In *Die Religion innerhalb der Grenzen der bloßen Vernunft*, Kant excoriated the spiritual despotism of *Pfaffentum*, and the *pappas*, but one wonders if there is not a streak of philosophical despotism in his denunciation. I wonder how his own pious mother might have liked this inquisition of the *pappas*.

Yes, yes, of course, we philosophers will be reasonable about religion; but that means religion must be reasonable for us: and so, more than anything else, it must present itself to us in the terms we recognize as valid; this is our openness to its self-manifestation. But where is the openness to *its* self-manifestation? Surely this has been reconfigured into something like: Show yourself but as I can see you, and then I will grasp you to my bosom. That is to say, the appearance of religion before the tribunal of philosophy is the appearance of philosophy as the judge that will endorse only itself, and so religion does not appear to philosophy, but philosophy once again appears before itself. I fear this is a tribunal of tyranny.

What then is the new critical philosophy? The new autonomy for itself, but the old heteronomy for the others? The new skepticism against the others, but the old dogmatism for itself—even though it arrives at this new disguised dogmatism by a detour through the ruins of the old open dogmatism, plumed in the Emperor's new clothes of transcendental philosophy? Is this why one gets the impression: the more I can criticize the others, the more I am content with myself? You object: look, I criticize myself! You do, you do. But is it so only to expel what is other in you; what you have come to hate in yourself, that is to say, (intoxicating) religion?

I would say that this expulsion of the other in philosophy itself has had a significant succession, with many afterlives, in German philosophy notably. And then the attitude goes around: Let philosophy hate itself because it is secret theology; and this hated other in the inner soul of philosophy must be purged. Marx will use this toxin of self-hatred against the residues of theology in Hegel; Schopenhauer against the residues of Christianity in Kant's morality; Nietzsche against almost everyone else, including those before Kant; and then a somewhat similar strategy seems newly resurrected in Heidegger, or perhaps in some of his deconstructive progeny, who plot the overcoming of ontotheology—the whole logocentric tradition is the old "other" in the self of thought that must be purged in the name of an "other" thinking.

I beg to differ. My sixth sense warns me that here lurks the danger of the secret tyranny of philosophical critique. The tyranny is sometimes aroused and virulent, other times indifferently sleepy. One wonders what is up, especially when new preachers of hatred emerge to scourge the older preachers of hatred, so-called; the antireligious preachers who preach their own hatred, oddly fiery with a passion that puts one more in mind of mutant religion rather than religion deconstructed. If this clerisy were alive and held power in a previous inquisitorial age, what books might be burned. I have an image of even the genial Hume looking on approvingly, with fire-reflecting eyes, as the tomes of theology and metaphysics are, in his immortal words of philosophical toleration, "consigned to the flames."

Consider this. Suppose that, in this expulsion of the other, philosophy suffers a wound at its own hand, though it seems to wound religion; for it is its intimate other that it has thus wounded, and so itself. It thinks its hemorrhage is its true freedom. As a medicine, it has resorted to bleeding itself, and toxins seem to leach away, leaving it purer and whiter. But it is in fact dying, though it seems to have adjusted well to the spiritual feebleness in all this, and it will say it is doing just fine, thank you, never felt better. Why then does it seem such a pale wraith of its former self? I do not quite blame Kant for this. But was he a great witch-doctor who insisted that more bleeding of the patient would hurry up the recovery? If so, there is too much of snake oil in the therapeutic promises of transcendental philosophy, and too precious little of the tonic of saving knowing.

Hegelian Confidences

I turn to Hegel who, you say, is surely more complex and rich. I have studied Hegel extensively in relation to the point at issue.[3] One of the great attractions of Hegel is just the seriousness with which he appears to take religion. By comparison, on this point at least, there is something callow in the rationalism of Kant. Openness to the rich diversity of the religious, without loss of desire for speculative comprehension; extensiveness of range and intensiveness of understanding — Hegel sought to embody these excellences. Philosophy itself, he knew, was nourished on religious sources. In Hegel's case, we find the speculative transformation of trinitarian motifs. The speculative transformation has to be nourished on what it transforms, even if the results of the transformation may not please the devotees of the source transformed. Hegel's passion for the religious does not seem to be false. It was more open in the younger Hegel, you suggest? But this is not so easy to say, since one finds here also a philosophical gene that, though it later becomes more recessive in Hegel, will later again no longer be latent in thinkers like Marx and Nietzsche. I refer to the less restrained critique of religion. (This I take as *one* lesson from that gene bank called the *Earliest System Program.*) There was always something more to Hegel, which is why I object to the contemporary taste for what I will call Hegel Lite. Hegel Lite is a watered-down version of Hegel, suitably drained of the headier religious and metaphysical intoxicants, just about palatable to the middling tastes of the last professors. (There are also versions of

---

[3] For instance, in *Beyond Hegel and Dialectic*, and more recently in *Hegel's God*.

Kant Lite, and Nietzsche Lite, to name two of the most obvious of the new intoxicant-free brands.)[4]

The more I dwell with the issue, the matter itself, the more discontented I become with Hegel, especially in relation to religion.[5] Ask again: What would saving knowledge be? One might claim that this is the special care of religion. If so, such a saving knowledge would not only be a knowledge in the theoretical or propositional sense, since it would be enacted in ritual and sacred dramatics, and "proved," in the sense of "put to the test," in its ethical incarnation. Saving knowing, answering the urgency of ultimacy, would be shown in its imagistic dramatics, and in its being ethically "lived out." Saving knowing would be neither theoretical nor practical, though clearly there would be elements that answer to both of these: theoretical since it would enact a fidelity to its understanding of what the ultimate is; practical in that the ethical "living out" would be what is called for as enactment by the knowing itself. Knowing the truth is doing the truth, and thus being true to it. This is not just knowing but saving, and if a knowing, more like a loving knowing, as I put it above.

What is saving, what is being lost? The ultimate good of being for the human being. Hegel tends to favor a more "theoretical" tilt with respect to the mission of philosophy. This reflects too strong a commitment to the typically modern bias toward philosophy as science. The premoderns were often more aware of philosophy as a way of life. When Hegel makes claims about absolute knowing, does he trade in the innuendos of offering a kind of saving gnosis? What kind? Certainly there is his famous claim in the *Phenomenology* to have overcome the ancient love of wisdom and to have achieved science itself. Hegel seems excessively guarded about philosophy as a way of life that seeks a saving knowing for the fundamental existential perplexities of life. He stresses the *what* known more than the *way of knowing*, the way of being, the way. In this respect, Kierkegaard was right to worry about the lack of a genuine ethics in the system, as

---

[4] We say *in vino veritas*, but perhaps neither Hegel Lite, nor Kant Lite, nor Nietzsche Lite have enough of the real stuff to loosen the tongue of truth. What would Plato's *Symposium* have been like if the drink were some form of vino Lite. Would we have the divine *parrhessia* we so love about eros: both in its poverty and in its festivity? Perhaps instead we would have the domestic sobriety of a seminar on a passionless puzzle, pleasing to technical tinkering or professorial excogitation.

[5] On this more fully, see *Hegel's God*.

were those unhappy with the "intellectualism" or "rationalism" of Hegel.

Does speculative gnosis, in fact, turn out to *mimic* a saving knowing? Saving knowing, relative to religion, is not ritualism, not fideism, not rationalism, not traditionalism, though there are elements of each. It names an understood and affirmed intermediation, binding the singular self, the communal and the divine. It is enacted dramatically in the religious mimetics that are the rituals or sacraments of a community. And it lives its "being true" in the configurations of ethical life that embody our willingness to participate in saving, and this by keeping and properly realizing the promise of our being. Saving knowing is fidelity to the promise of the intimate universal.

What of Hegel's version of *fides quaerens intellectum*? Religious *Vorstellung* seeks, or spirit seeks in the *Vorstellung*, though an immanent transformation, to be articulated as *Begriff*. The truth of the same immanent spirit is an immanent God. And the truth of the immanent God is also the truth of the religious *Vorstellung*. *Vorstellung* has the content, but its form is such as to separate the content into an elsewhere. There is the residue of an as-yet-not-overcome transcendence. The *Vorstellung* is an immanent sign of transcendence, but this immanence, in principle complete, is also the sign of incompleteness for Hegel. *Begriff* completes what this sign means, namely that the immanence is not total; the completion will be with this total immanence; only the concept has both form and content, each immanent to the other, hence both as moments of a total process of immanent self-determination, the immanent self-determination of *Geist* itself. God is self-determining in the knowing of philosophy itself as absolutely self-determining knowing. God's otherness as other is transcended. Transcendence is transcended and now is dwelling with full immanence. In philosophy, faith has found what it sought: understanding. In completing itself thus, it also abolishes itself qua faith.

But does it? That is one crucial question. Does the *Begriff* save the *Vorstellung*? What if the *fides* is not just an implicit form of the understanding this philosophy here privileges, namely self-determining knowing? What if the sign of transcendence is the communication of the otherness of the divine that cannot be comprehended in terms of any forms of self-determining knowing: a different communication to our middle condition; a different intermediation of transcendence as other to our self-transcendence; and a different community of the human and divine in the intimate universal that is not exhausted by Hegel's holistic immanence or speculative universal? The immanence of transcendence in the religious sign is at once a way to name a pointing to transcendence, to confess the failure of the name, and in that confession to give a richer sign of success. The poverty of the sign is just its richness.

In Hegel's approach, we find a dialectical variation on the theme of the One and the double. For him *Vorstellung* remains burdened with an as-yet-not-overcome doubleness. The content is the One, but the form separates the One into a here and a there, a now and a yonder, an immanent God and a transcendent. The form points to what is other to what is immanent in the form, but does so by making immanent that other, and hence the otherness signaled is also undercut by the immanence necessary. But because it is the otherness that is signaled, the representational immanence wavers about its own absolute character. And this wavering, this being in two minds, this double seeing, this being cross-eyed between the here and the beyond is what must be overcome in the return of the double to the all-including, indeed self-appropriating, self-including One. The One in which all is immanent, and which itself is the absolute of immanence, is more absolute than what for Hegel is the potentially false double of the transcendent other and One. Transcendence is appropriated as self-transcendence, which, as absolute, is absolutely immanent. But only the *Begriff* is able to comprehend and do justice to this absolutely immanent self-transcendence: it is the One at home with itself, beyond the double vision, and this being "beyond" is not beyond but is the death of all beyonds. Religious *Vorstellung* is, from this point of view, conducive to the false double of transcendence: an other transcendence, not an immanent self-transcendence.

On this schema, Hegel's philosophy *must* claim more than religion, even if it also claims that its "more" is the same "more" as that of religion. It is not quite that religion is poor and philosophy rich. Both as absolute are rich; but philosophy is richer, if that can be said, in having the form of richness; religion is poorer in lacking the form that is true to the richness of immanent content. You cannot say that Hegel will want to impoverish religion in any straightforward way. Still, in the relativity of religion and philosophy, it is clear that philosophy consummates even the consummate religion, and so is religion's richness exceeded.

Hegel will claim that the religious is "preserved" by and in the philosophical concept. What this means is controversial, and indeed not easy to comprehend. Why would not the religious be preserved, if it is closest to the origin, and the origin continues to work in all?

But there are preservations and there are preservations. Some preservations effect a transmutation of the original; and hence what they preserve may well turn out to be a false double of the origin. Hegel's dialectical *Aufhebung* claims to redouble the religious original in conceptual form. And it does so, because the claim is made that the religious original risks being a false double—a false double of the absolute, only to be grasped in its Oneness by the *Begriff*.

But what if religious reverence lives more intimately with the primal confidence, more faithful to the origin, even if in the temptations of idolatry it must also struggle with the counterfeit doubles of God? And what if philosophy has preserved a false double of religion? Then philosophy would be the one that is trading in conceptual counterfeits. I mean that if philosophy gives us a concept of the religious that is false to the religious, its sublation of this false double may itself produce a false double of the One. Certain ways of philosophizing might then be seen as ways of succumbing to the temptings of an idol.

How would you decide this issue, apart from seeking a discerning knowing that tries to discriminate the difference of the true One and the counterfeit doubles? You could not decide in terms of reading Hegel alone. For his thought is in question just in terms of this issue. One could only judge Hegel to be right or wrong in terms of a radical discernment that returns mindfully to what is at play in the deepest intimacy of religious reverence. But if you are deficient in reverence, how could you do that? Once again, reading Hegel alone will not be enough to meet that deficit. Indeed philosophy alone can never address that deficit, since any philosophy *insisting on itself alone* either instantiates that deficit or gives rise to it.

One might well argue, in Hegelian fashion, that religion may be the potentially false double of the truer One of the *Begriff*. But what if the One of the *Begriff* is itself a counterfeit double of the One, the true living One? And thus so, because the *Begriff* has not properly comprehended the doubleness of the *Vorstellung*? And this, despite the fact that the counterfeit double *mimics almost exactly* the true original? The religious double as *Vorstellung* may be the truer image of the living, true One. Philosophy may have erected its own surrogate idol in place of the One; and by that erection demoted the imagistic richness of the religious sign into the form of a potentially false double.

Again, what if the so-called false double—false, that is, for the dialectical sublation—may, in fact, be the truer double, just in keeping open our referral to transcendence as other? Its power to keep open may be the *essential poverty* of the religious image, which, just as poor, is the rich power to open up a way to transcendence, or for transcendence to come into the between, with no reduction of the otherness of transcendence. The constitutive ambiguity of the religious image would not be a *defective poverty*, so to say, but an *effective poverty*, a rich poverty.[6] It might be the truer way to say what cannot be absolutely

---

[6] One might here ask: Why did Hegel so despise Schleiermacher? Different reasons, as we know, some more personal and professional, some intellectual. We recall the contempt in his remark on Schleiermacher's view of religion as bound up with the feeling of *dependence*: and so, mocks Hegel, the dog would be the best Christian. There are a number of somewhat snide hints of this in Hegel's *Lectures on the Philosophy of Religion*—see part I of the 1824 series, 279–80. Here he speaks of animals (*Tiere*) as having religion if dependence defines it. In the introduction to the 1821 lecture series Hegel talks about bringing spirit into a dog (*Hund*). Hegel wrote the preface for Hermann Friedrich Wilhelm Hinrichs's book, *Die Religion im inneren Verhältnisse zur Wissenschaft* (Heidelberg, 1822), in which Hegel says: "Gründet sich die Religion im Menschen nur auf ein Gefühl, so hat solches richtig keine weitere Bestimmung, als das *Gefühl seiner Abhängigkeit* zu sein, und so wäre der Hund der beste Christ." See *Hegel, Hinrichs, and Schleiermacher on Feeling and Reason in Religion: The Texts of Their 1821–22 Debate*, ed., trans., and with introductions by Eric von der Luft (Lewiston, N.Y.: Edwin Mellen Press, 1987).

Hegel disdains dependence. Even if there is some element of truth to his remarks, nevertheless there are dogs and there are dogs. My point is not a defense of Schleiermacher, or an attack. But maybe there is a poverty of philosophy that has some family relation to a kind of new cynicism. This will seem like "going to the dogs." It will be so, in a way. I mean it will strip off the unnecessary and rediscover the elemental, just like the *dog philosophers*. Hegel had little time for Cynicism as merely "popular philosophy," like Pascal's, not "philosophy proper." There is nothing here for his system, he says in his *Lectures on the History of Philosophy*. But this—there being nothing there—may well be the whole point. The dog philosophers deal not with philosophy as system but as a way of life, and with the saving knowledge of finding finite equilibrium in the fragility of the universal impermanence. Philosophy is a therapy of life in the widest sense, an *askēsis* of life that superficially seems to just say "no," but more deeply is a "yes" to life in poverty itself. This is what a new cynicism would be: love of the elemental, even in destitution itself. Think here of the reverence for the sun. Alexander, the world-historical conqueror, had enough finesse to suspect a free sovereignty to Diogenes that made him wonder if there was something here that his bestriding the world had somehow missed. World-conqueror to the dog-philosophy: Ask of me, and I will give you what you want. Answer from the dog: Get out of the way between me and the sun! Hegel admired Alexander the more: the world-historical world conqueror is rich in significance; the poverty of the dog-philosophy is a blank; and Hegel cannot quite see the sun that shines in and

said. Or rather, the absolute saying for us is just a saying that, in being said, immediately confesses its own poverty as a saying, and thus converts its temptation to false success into a silence, a silence more successful than the concept that crows about its own intellectual glory on the speculative apex. What crows on the apex has already fallen into the pit. Its ascending crowing is falling. It seems to know itself as the intoxication of moving vertically, but its intoxication with itself is as the descending movement that merely mimics ascent as its reversed double.

But you object: Surely, Hegel's dialectical "preservation" of the religious involves both a "yes" and a "no." Yes, I agree. But the character of the "yes" and the "no," and *how we balance them*, is all important. If the balance is finally a "no" to the surplus of transcendence as other, then, in my view, its "yes" shows itself already to have lost the passion of the religious—regardless of its claim to say "yes" to it. And have you not noticed how a "yes" on page one in Hegel, having passed through various dialectical qualifications, by as early as page three, begins to look a bit more like a kind of "no"; or more precisely a kind of dialectical "yes/no"—though where the precise stress falls we do not precisely know, but it certainly does not seem to be quite the "yes" we thought was affirmed on page one.

Post-Hegelian Poverties

The equivocal passion for the religious, and its loss, brings to mind a further, related reversal in which poverty and richness get differently

---

through and on the blank; or the absolute point of keeping open the space between this sun and our elemental being. Of course, Diogenes is hardly an attractive model for professors who perhaps have more of the pampered poodle in them than something of the wilder hounds. Yet for this cynic, being a dog was closer to being divine. Homeless and at home with self, homeless and at home with being in its otherness: needing nothing, in destitution itself, rich in the given. Hegel notes only the shamelessness, in a bad sense. The cynics deserved their name as dogs, for "the dog is a shameless animal," Hegel says. Does this not also mean that the (dog-)Christian of Schleiermacher is also a shameless animal? But is there not a reverence of the cynic, as when Diogenes calls himself the watchdog of Zeus? It's a dog's life, but there is a genuine line of inheritance from Socrates to this dog's life, even though Plato is said to have dubbed Diogenes as "a Socrates gone mad." But perhaps Diogenes masked less a madness that was kept more intimate, more idiotic in Socrates and his poverty? And perhaps there is an elemental reverence also with the (dog-)Christian, and this reverence is inseparable from the poverty of radical ontological dependency.

defined. I think now of the left-Hegelian line of thought. Suppose this line inherits from Hegel an equivocal counterfeit of the religious, counterfeit in dialectically reducing transcendence to immanence, equivocal in thus claiming to be true to the religious itself. I mean now especially a counterfeit version of the "unity" of the human and the divine. This line of thought then proceeds to "deconstruct" this counterfeit, but in a manner that wills to abort, even kill more effectively the passion of the religious. Thus Marx can be seen as genuinely an heir of the dialectical equivocity of Hegel's "yes" to religion. He univocalizes this equivocity, itself richer by far than the univocalization. He gives us a humanistic reduction of the religious, which more forcefully thrusts humanity to the forefront as the original, and the religious image, in its reference to God as other, as the counterfeit double. To get to the richness of this true original, this counterfeit double must be all the more killed in the womb: radically, in the roots. For at the true root will be humanity as the original.

It was Marx after all who wrote a book entitled *Das Elend der Philosophie* (*The Poverty of Philosophy*) responding to Proudhon's *Philosophie de la misère* (*Philosophie des Elends*). This book deals mainly with money, economics, workers and machines, competition and monopolies, interest rates, strikes and so forth. But even here our question comes again, like a catastrophe in the old tragedy: Are we once more dealing with a counterfeit double of the true condition of philosophical poverty? What is meant by this talk about the poverty of philosophy? A number of things for sure, but one of the recurrent claims is that philosophy, and Hegel's is no exception, is secretly theology. This is put down as a defect, as an *accusation*. A philosopher who remains a secret theologian is one whose blood still runs with residues of obscurantist toxins. One recognizes what will become standard slogans. The philosopher emerges under the cloak of the priest, and the cloak was both disguise and protection. Now we need courage to throw off the cloak. We no longer need to be in the guise of another, no longer need protection. Now autonomous, we can go on the attack against the others that kept us in submission hitherto.

Schopenhauer used this strategy against Kant; as Feuerbach and Marx use it differently against Hegel; as Marx uses it against others who have not "overcome" theology fully. And did not Zarathustra, with a little more delicatesse, at least confess, and not totally without admiration: the blood of the priest still runs in my veins? Heidegger, with a perhaps grimmer Germanic tonality, offers us the program of overcoming ontotheology, overcoming philosophy as metaphysics, itself cartooned too easily, with a little help from Nietzsche, as the caricature of Platonism, the philosophy of the yonder world, now inverted into the cybernetic world here, where, as Heidegger *rightly* says, with all due genuflections to the piety of thinking, only a god can save us now. But what god? And what God can save us truly and not betray us with another counterfeit of saving?[7]

Do I have to mention certain kinds of deconstructive thinkers who, it sometimes seems, need to accuse and exorcise ghosts, the ghosts of ontotheologians past that, Banquo-like, rise again and again from their graves? Is this an ontotheologian that I see before me? What power conjures up this apparition? Macbeth, killer of a sacred king, had a guilty conscience, a mind full of scorpions, but what of the conjuring power of the post-metaphysicians? What saving power will exorcise these apparitions of ontotheology that oddly seem to spook us? Or is it that we only pretend they spook us, as if some other secret need is really served by our exorcism of what is not really there?

But enough of that. The refrain returns, now loudly, now muffled: The poverty of (old) philosophy is that it is disguised theology. This is a defect of (old) philosophy. Ergo: empty philosophy of theology and traces of nostalgia for religious reverence. Then it will assert its full autonomy. Even more: by emptying itself of the religious, it will be what religion previously claimed to be, namely, absolute. The poverty of philosophy will thus be reversed into infinite richness, as now at last it can truly fulfill itself as philosophy. No god above it, no religion either. Itself absolute, *ab-solo*, on the height it itself is, or creates itself to be, determines itself to be. To empty philosophy of religion is to empty it of its emptiness, and positively to appropriate the absolute of religion, and free it from this form of being the false double.

This means: the process of emptying is an appropriating that also makes philosophy a kind of religion, in the transformed sense, or mutant or corrupted form we have seen, for instance, in the philosophy-inspired totalitarian project of the Marxists. This is a topsy-turvy world. But who now knows how to distinguish what is up and what is down, what is on the heights and what is in the pits? For fair seems foul and foul seems fair in a topsy-turvy world wherein religion is the false double of man, masquerading as God. The new philosophy sees God as the false double of man, hence man as the true One, re-

---

[7] On, for instance, *der letzte Gott* in Heidegger, see *Art, Origins, Otherness*, 260.

deemed from God as the false double. *The saving knowing of philosophy* now comes to this: *being redeemed from God*. But what if philosophy here is merely recreating itself as the false double of God? Is philosophy here a poverty qua lack that believes its own lack will redeem itself by its intensification, which surely follows when it asserts itself *ab-solo*, autonomously? The negative asserts its absoluteness in the process of negating first the divine other, then itself. But in this topsy-turvy world in which up is down, and down is up, in which poverty is richness and richness poverty, we may well be dragged into a devouring vortex of destitution, as all are dragged into the hollow pit of our spirit's own emptiness.

A New Poverty of Philosophy

What of a different sense of the poverty of philosophy? This is a large question, demanding more elaboration than here can be given. I can only make a few suggestions, focusing on reverence as something crucial for philosophy, as well as religion. We might think of religion as rich, rich in reverence. We might also think that this is closer to the primal reverence for the origin out of which determinate religions, and philosophies, take more definite form. This primal reverence witnesses to our *passio essendi* that is before the *conatus essendi*: a patience of being that comes before our endeavor to be.[8] To be is to be given to be, primally. To think is also to be given to think, primally. No human being understands the primal sources of mindfulness; and the more one advances in knowing, it seems to me, the more one knows this baffling happening. It is not that there is always more to be known, though this is true; it is that the very upsurge of mindfulness, from the origin, shows itself in excess of what we determinately manage to thematize or bring to articulate expression. There is an inward otherness to thinking itself that is not completely self-mediated in determinate mindfulness itself; and yet this "more" can come to be minded more and more, the more mind mediates with itself. Nevertheless, what also comes to mind is this: *The immanence of thought intimates what is other to thought as immanent to itself.*

My point now: Religions are often closer to acknowledging this more primal "more." Artists as well often have a finer sense of it than those philosophers who fixate on what can be fixed in determinate

---

[8] See my *Ethics and the Between* (Albany: State University of New York Press, 2001), chapter 12.

propositions. We are closer to the source of determining, prior to and in excess of determined products. A consequence of this is that "autonomous" knowing is always indebted to secret others. Knowing is heteronomous. Perhaps knowing must be "poor in spirit" to inherit the earth; though it does not think about what it will inherit, for in its intimate porosity to what is other it is as if it were nothing, and hence less and less thinks about itself alone. Philosophers often interpret this in terms of the impersonal universal, but I think it is more complex. There is an intimate universal where inheritance is a divestiture.

Were *intellectus* to quest now for *fides*, what would it seek? Among other things a new confidence, in the face of the loss of confidence and the advent of "being as nothing" we find with nihilism. This return to zero would concern a new openness to a confiding that was always at work, though not always noted. It is granted, but was taken for granted; and so we did not grant it as granted. If so, philosophy could not be described as a self-determining knowing, or the quest of it. Philosophy would have to include openness to other knowings, beyond self-determining thinking and qualifying this and its claims. It would not only open to these knowings, such as we find in art and religion. It itself would have to *embody something* of such other knowings. Thus it could not be that philosophy redeems dialectically, as self-determining, what remains determined by an other source, as in art and religion. This would be to be blind, not only to the truth of this other knowing they differently communicate, but also to philosophy's own vocation to be true to this other knowing in itself. Philosophy would have to recover its roots in the primal reverence for the origin, and seek to say again, however poorly, what is communicated in the granting of the primal origin. The One is communicated, or communicates being, and in the primal reverence we participate in the love of that origin and communication. Its character is always too much for us.

This poverty is clearly as much redolent of richness as of destitution. It also refers to the potentially radical character of the openness of thinking. I am as nothing; but strangely as nothing I am potentially open in an unrestricted way to what is other, and also to a recreation of what I am, beyond the fixation on the currently sedimented determination of self. Poverty may mean a return to a kind of formlessness—a dissolving of the potentially false forms, or counterfeit doubles that fix the energy of coming to be—a return to the more overdeterminate energies of coming to be that is not a matter of a determinate process of becoming this or that, or a process of self-determining becoming of self (though these latter are not precluded). Coming to be is more primal than becoming or self-becoming. Likewise, there is also a "being as nothing" more primal than determinate negation, which already presupposes something has been given to be, or as having already become thus and thus. Philosophy as "poor" might lay mind open to this "being as nothing."[9] There is nothing nihilistic in this porosity.

One of the reasons philosophers can be defective in reverence has something to do with the feeling of power that comes with the power to question, and the way questioning can aggressively smother the openness to what is other, even though it loudly proclaims its interest in the other. Certain modes of questioning subject the other to interrogations that grant no "inter," and so risk refusing our being given over to the other as other. There can be different ways of questioning; some more indirect and coaxing, hence less lacking in reverence; others more hectoring, and intrusive, and indeed shameless. The very same question can be posed in hatred or in love. And the *how* of the question-posing can corrupt the spirit of truthfulness the question rightly asks. There are questions posed in silence that willingly wait for an answer, that do not force the answer. This waiting for an answer is closer to a devotion to questioning, where questioning remains faithful to the wonder of original astonishment. This is not the condition of a sponge, but an alertness of mindfulness that is sharp with intense vigilance. But it is the question, it is not the answer. And it knows it cannot be the answer, because of its poverty.

Philosophy claiming to be science can lose this expectancy: the determined content, as determined by intelligent thought, is articulated into a defined intelligibility; and its definition may seem to have nothing to do with the waiting or keeping watch, but just with the *determination of thinking itself* to mark as its own the intelligibility of what seems other. We move from the overdeterminacy of the original astonishment to the determination of intelligible thought.

One is put in mind of a more archaic ideal in which sapiential love is more basic than scientific conceptualization. Wisdom is bound up

---

[9] Return to zero is related to the sense of philosophy as a form of what I call *posthumous mind*, which is always open to being reborn, out of the nothing. What is posthumous mind? I have made some remarks in *Philosophy and its Others*, 278ff., 300, 368–69, and in *Being and the Between*, 36ff., 192ff. Certainly there is a seeing things new, as if anew, for the first time. Philosophy, as Socrates said, is the practice of death: but there are different deaths. As there are also different lives.

with our loves, and philosophy is not just concerned with *scientia*. Consider how St. Bonaventure, a sapiential thinker, speaks of the "poor man" in his *Itinerarium Mentis in Deum*. The poor man for Bonaventure was St. Francis. Is there a poor man of philosophy? (Do not worry, I heard that jeer.) For such a philosopher of poverty, knowing is a loving. Signs of this are evident in premodern philosophy, where the self-image of philosophy as science is offset by a variety of other forms of knowing that have more to do with the mind of finesse. These forms are also more steeped in the ethos of religious reverence than disciplined by the methods of geometry to love only what is clear and distinct. The ethos of reverence makes one patient to ultimate obscurity, and hence to obscure thought about the ultimate and its intelligibility.

One might ask: Can one really love what is only clear and distinct? Does univocal clarity and distinctness arouse desire? But I speak of more than the obscure. This arousal is true of a certain strike of the light itself. Do we not love the sunlight just because it strikes us and moves us, and so is always more than us? Its power to move is enigmatically in excess of thematization as clear and distinct. The light makes the heart leap. Its communication produces an effect that is more than any clear and distinct idea. How could such an idea leap? It has already settled into its own fixation, and to be more than its fixed form it will have to become less again, become as nothing, hence poor. So will be made young again our taste for the elemental communication of the light. Becoming poor is becoming youthful in that taste, even as one inexorably ages. It does not matter, it does not count, we say—but we are dismissing nothing. We are going toward everything anew and with a new abandon. Love loves the chiaroscuro of mystery, which is more lightsome than the clarities fixed forever down to the last determination.

If we remember that philosophy names a *philia*, hence an affiliation, we may be less likely to lose the expectancy of a fitting poverty. It is true we grow familiar with our friends, but genuine friendship never loses the essential *admiration* for the excellence and worthiness of the other. Such admiration is not an indefiniteness to be made determinate. It is in a different dimension to determination, and hence cannot be made the object of a scientific objectification. Admiration is a poverty: it is the worthy other that counts; I am as nothing, in the admiration; I am there, but my self-insistence is put out of play. Admiration is a cousin of reverence, even adoration.

And friendship here is of *sophia*, and not just *scientia*. Sophia as *sapientia* includes the essential element of "tasting," something more akin to the art of the connoisseur. I do not mean this in a merely aestheticist sense: philosophy is not quite just a matter of "taste," and yet a kind of taste, or discerning savoring, is needed. I mean again the mind of finesse. Can finesse be made systematic? Not quite, since it is addressed to a singular happening. It is idiotic, as is the happening that opens up the admiration. The friend is idiotic: this friend, not friends in general.[10]

Consider this too. Tasting is a kind of *porosity*: the soul or mind that tastes is as a passage way. Could one say that thinking that "tastes" is not unlike a prayer? I mean it finds itself awakening to a process already in play, in which it participated, though it did not know it before, and now it wakes to what makes it possible, and awakes to an admiration and love for what is given as good in this process. Prayer is waking up to the already effective communication of the divine in passage: not just our communication with the divine, but our being already in that divine communication, within which we participate, now in sleep, now more mindfully awake. Prayer is awakening to the passing communication of the divine in the finite *metaxu*. We do not produce it; it is not the result of our determination or self-determination; we are "determined," or better, released into the middle where we can sink deeper into ontological sleep, or begin to awake more fully to what communicates us to be at all.

The *philia* of *sophia* is a friendship of thought that loves what is most worthy to be thought.[11] One might recall Plato and the friends of the forms, but I am more talking about an ontological trust. The communication of friends is a confiding of one in the other, the other in one. Confiding is also an intimate communication. If faith is a confidence, something is confided to thought, and out of this confiding, thinking has confidence that its being is to be in relation to being as true. Being true is just the reliability of the trustworthy. Suppose *so-*

---

[10] On the idiotic, see chapter 3 of *Perplexity and Ultimacy* (Albany: State University of New York Press, 1995).

[11] Think also of the poverty of philosophy, in terms of the *penia* of *eros*, about which Socrates speaks: the Socratic seeker seems lacking, a beggar, shoeless. Socratic destitution is related to that of some of the cynical figures—but without their shamelessness, perhaps. Of course, there are different kinds of shamelessness— innocence is shameless, evil can be shameless, but there is a being good that is also shameless—as there are different kinds of poverty.

phia were a woman, then one would have to say: I am not confident first, but first she confides in me; her confidence endows me with trust; and I am confident, having been endowed with trust. Philosophia is the friendship of being true, a fidelity itself seeking the utmost in the reliability of trustworthiness, not only in itself but in being as other to self.

Once again, there can be no self-determining of this reliability or being true, or being trustworthy. Self-determining in a reliable sense is itself grounded on this more primal reliability. If it is religious reverence that more intensively places us into attunement with this more primal reliability, there can be no *Aufhebung* of this; the confidence of dialectical thinking is itself grounded in it; for every effort of thought is itself grounded on it, endowed by it. There is here a kind of *ananke* that frees: indeed the endowment allows the freedom to question and criticize the *ananke* itself; but the questioning itself is a participation in primal reliability. Questioning, one might venture, is only possible on the condition of this more primal reliability, mostly incognito and taken for granted in the questing of thinking. Were the questioning to refuse it, or become absolutely ruptured from it, it would descend into absurdity and madness. If there can be no *Aufhebung* of this, philosophical thinking in a post-idealistic mode must relate to it differently.

Absolute Knowing and the Poverty of Philosophy

Let me conclude by putting this poverty of philosophy in terms that contrast it with Hegel's absolute knowing. How does Hegel put it? In the *Phenomenology*, he speaks of the goal (of absolute knowing) to be achieved as the point where knowing no longer feels the need to go beyond itself. Must we not propose what looks like exactly the contrary? We come precisely to the point where knowing knows that this is just what it must now do: namely, exceed itself into what is beyond it, and not only now at the end, but because what originates it is always beyond it; and so in coming to itself, there is no sense in saying it has reached the point where it need no longer go beyond; and it is only coming to itself in a derivative sense, because more fundamentally it is coming to wakefulness of its original endowment and the primal reliability. If it goes beyond itself, it is not only from need, but from an enigmatic surplus or plenitude of being, always at work, though not always known. It is the original endowment that allows it to go further and be beyond itself, even as it allows it also to be freely self-determining.

To know this would entail a non-Hegelian kind of "absolved knowing." "Absolute knowing" would be a poverty of mindfulness where it is driven out beyond itself into a divine darkness that draws it forth with the promise of truth that ultimately is more reliable than all the systems of determined truths our knowing seems to have determined for itself. The poverty of this nonknowing is a richness of transcending porosity that wakes to itself as a love of transcendence as other. It is no longer an erotic self-transcending that wakes to itself only; in waking to itself, it is an agapeic transcendence that finds itself shaken up beyond itself. The point would be not Hegelian knowing's reaching the point where it no longer needs to go beyond itself, but rather a turning point when knowing is nothing, nothing but the knowing of love and the desire to be with the beyond of itself. Its poverty is a return to zero, but also is infinitely in excess of itself, excess all the way to God. This I call an agapeic mindfulness.[12]

This knowing of nonknowing, at the extremity of determinate and self-determining cognition, is the point of exodus where *intellectus* must seek a new faith, a new fidelity, or rather renew a fidelity that its previous efforts to know seem to have betrayed. The betrayal calls itself disenchantment, but this disenchantment is falling out of love;

---

[12] On agapeic mindfulness, see chapter 4 of *Perplexity and Ultimacy*. My point is not the "weak thought" (*pensiero debole*) of Gianni Vattimo, which seems to somewhat enervate the artistic and somewhat mime the religious. Vattimo's "weak thought" seems to be debilitated mindfulness in the wake of the failures of the great foundationalisms of modern philosophy: deflationary finitism after a period of inflationary self-infinitizing thought. I am put in mind of the bleeding cure, instead of a more restorative catharsis. Nor would I advocate the anorexia nervosa of philosophy as a purge for the bloatings of self-infinitizing thought. I sense a different poverty of philosophy, a second poverty, which revivifies ontological perplexity, resurrects astonishment at the limit of all determinate, self-determining knowing. Metaxological metaphysics seeks to be mindfulness in an agapeic way, in the community thought has with the artistic and the religious. For that matter, I find myself demurring with regard to a kind of secular colonizing of the religious, something that worries me, for instance, about Alain Badiou's "laicized grace." I am wary also of the use of religion as a new tool of transgression against the secular pieties of liberal intellectuals, as here and there with Slavoj Žižek: it might be delicious as spectator sport to watch these intellectuals squirm, but the religious qua religious is emptied of its religious significance. Such secular uses of the religious counterfeit the religious: something essential is missing, something that invests the religious as more properly trustworthy.

enchantment is needed in a new form, as a falling back into love. Is this what we need as philosophers: a knowing love, a loving knowing? A love that knows, or a knowing that loves, is always a confides, a confiding; we are confided to, in being confiding. Could one say that prayer is what gives us this con-fidence? Con-fides is given to us; we become giving, having been given to, and in the passage of giving that gives us to be at all. As waking up to mindful praise of this passage of giving, philosophy too is a kind of piety.

All those chilled by the disenchanting effects of Enlightenment will continue to remain cold to the suggestion of this piety, even squirm at it. They will be colder than Hegel himself, who did say, after all, that philosophy too is *Gottesdienst*.[13] I repeat again that the point cannot be to take arms against thought and knowing. The poverty of philosophy names a renewed beginning, not just a full stop—a condition of mindfulness out of which more determinate thinking can emerge again. (It is a commencement that, like a graduation, is a re-commencement.) This involves a subtle displacement of philosophical concerns that can issue in and be reflected by more systematic forms of thinking, as well as in a different articulation of the fundamental philosophical perplexities, including those we find in idealism, with its diverse emphases on (the forms of) self-determining knowing. The source, forms, and telos of knowings are exceeded by what cannot fully be formed in terms of self-determining knowing. We need intermediated knowings that recall us to a space *between* philosophy and religion, *between* art and philosophy. The poverty finds itself exposed to the more original endowment of mindfulness, laying itself open anew to more primal sources of thinking in the return to zero. If it issues anew, its new forms are never the same again. This return to zero, as an effective, not defective, poverty, endows a task for philosophy beyond idealism and beyond its deconstruction.

---

[13] On this more fully, see chapter 2 of *Beyond Hegel and Dialectic*.

4

Religious Imagination and the Counterfeit Doubles of God

Imagination as Double

Imagination has often been treated with a double attitude: on one hand, the source of error; on the other, a source of higher truth. The first attitude we find endemic in the Western tradition, not least among philosophers whose rationalistic bent has made them deeply suspicious of imagination. The second we find more and more to the fore in modernity, when the new epistemological credibility of imagination was raised to unprecedented levels with the Romantic turn in European culture, itself influenced in important respects by the understanding of imagination we find in Kant's transcendental philosophy. In some ways, the affirmative orientation of the second matches the derogatory attitude of the first: the elevation of imagination in Romanticism is the twin of the elevation of pure reason in the Enlightenment. Moreover, in both we tend to find these doublets: either strong objectivity coupled with weak subjectivity; or, alternatively, strong subjectivity weakening mere objectivity. One wonders to what extent the two views are inseparable, especially in modernity.

Why the negative view of imagination? It has to do with a wider affiliation of a particular conception of reason and truth, perhaps with a sense of univocal mind as tied to an ideal of unequivocal correspondence between itself and fixed states of affairs. Imagination seems to violate this unequivocal correspondence; it seems to be too lax and loose, too equivocal by far, not only vis-à-vis univocal correspondence, but in its inventive power relative to what is already given. Imagination's "truth" seems false, because it is not already given as fixed; and what it gives it fixes as fiction—what it has just "made up."

That said, it would be wrong to denounce the Western tradition as mere univocal logocentrism, with a phobia against imagination. While the guarded attitude was there, the power of the image has been always recognized, even by that supposed arch enemy of image and imagination, Plato. Plato famously exiles the poets from his ideal city, but what is not so often granted is that this arch enemy of the image gave to philosophy its treasury of great images, such as the Cave and the Sun and the winged soul, not to mention Socrates, a dramatic figure who for not a few is *the* paradigmatic image of the philosopher. Plato was himself an artist, a philosophical artist of the order of genius. And there is the striking fact that much of the effect of reason in his dialogues is to bring us to an impasse or aporia where another way of saying is attempted, a different porosity open to mythic imaginative logos. He offers us what Vico called "imaginative universals" in philosophy itself. It is here entirely proper to recall that it is with respect to the porosity of mythic images to the divine that Platonic philosophy solicits an adventure in a further ecstasis of the soul, or mindfulness. He would purge the anthropomorphic images of the gods, yet the indispensability of the mythic image at the limits of discursive logos is granted. By contrast, thinkers like Hobbes and Spinoza in early modernity, our epoch of regnant univocity, strike one as more callow and reductive relative to imagination. Interestingly though, it is the *poet* Milton who in *Paradise Lost* (V, 95–121) has Adam attribute to "mimic fancy," unfettered from the supervision of reason, the first "uncouth dream" that the sleeping Eve has to transgress the command of God.

What of the more positive view of imagination? One might locate it philosophically in the wake of Kant, though one finds the epistemological place of imagination earlier, with Hume and others (I am speaking now of the philosophers, not the general culture of the time). This positive view has to do with claims in modernity that the human subject is actively involved in shaping its relation to what is other to itself: it is not passive before a "given" to which it stands in a univocal one-to-one correspondence. There is a freedom in this between of relation, as also a freedom in the within of the human subject. Imagination testifies to an original articulating power emergent in human being. Imagination might well be falsifying, but there is more to it than that. Perhaps all knowing of what is other to us is inseparable from an act of original imagination on our part. I will come back to this in the next section when I speak briefly of reproductive and productive imagination.

Here I ask: What has the valorization of imagination to do with the increasing power of *ratio* in modern life? *Ratio* seems to cover everything, and yet in its imperialistic desire for univocity, something of the ambiguity of our place in the world is ignored or stifled. There are equivocities, especially about the human being, of which no totalizing *ratio* can rid us. Let what Pascal calls the *esprit de géométrie* extend its cold empire as far as it may, there are equivocities in the human condition that are recalcitrant—monstrous equivocities and magnificences. What we need to address them is not geometry; we need the *esprit de finesse*. This requires something of imaginative *delicatesse* with respect to the nuances of the human condition. Without imagination, could one have finesse? Doubtful. In our time of the dominance of "geometry," we need, but often lack, the finesse to match it.

Not unexpectedly, and apart altogether from its general epistemological unavoidability, imagination comes to be seen as indispensable in our address of the equivocal human. As *ratio* becomes more calculative and narrow, and as the *mathēsis* of nature seems more and more successful, our failure of heed to nuance intensifies the need for imagination as showing finesse for the equivocities of being. Is this a compensation for our loss of feel for the truth of the equivocal? Or does it testify to a deeper malaise about *ratio* itself—perhaps what it also does is construct *its* imaginative fictions, fictions no less for the fact that they seem to work. But if *ratio* is also involved in construction, how different is it to the imagination whose "subjectivism" its "objectivism" claims to overcome? Here we have all the anxieties that haunt us in our postmodern times. What *original as other* will give ontological anchor to this constructive power of *ratio*, of imagination? (This is a modern/postmodern version of the problem of *mimēsis* and *eidos* in Plato.)

I also ask, and am not sure how to answer: Does the above change from negative to positive image, oddly, coincide with the subjection to assault of the majestic sacramental imagination of premodern religiousness? One thinks of the iconoclasm of the Reformation, of the word displacing the image and its equivocity. If images breed idols, will *sola scriptura* rectify the equivocity? Is the *sola* here a sign of the same rampant univocity, the besetting sin of modernity; sign of the search of the foundation, the fortress of religious certainty in a sea of equivocity? Is *sola ratio* twinned by *sola scriptura*? What of the danger of a counterfeit double of religion taking a scientistic or fideistic form? What if the shattering of idols generates its own idols? Does the sacramental imagination, despite being stifled, still now send out shoots from the secret root, shoots seeking light above ground though stunted by the stifling?

The new post-Kantian apotheosis of imagination might seem the antithesis of rationalistic enlightenment, but is there a seed in it that is just the same? I mean that in both Enlightenment and Romanticism we find a culture of autonomy, granting that imaginative autonomy seems more ecstatic, rational autonomy more prosaic and domestic. Nevertheless, both autonomies have to do primarily with ourselves and our powers: *auto-nomos* — self-law. This situation is itself equivocal. There can be an aesthetic will to power in Romantic imagination, as there can be a rationalistic will to power in Enlightenment reason. The two may be in collusion, as they seem to be today: cybernetics serves our subjective "comfort levels"; alternatively we invest our powers of imagination in cybernetics, the better to make ourselves masters of the given conditions of life. There is the rationalistic will to power we find in scientism and technology; there is the aesthetic will to power that tempts us with the self-apotheosis of the artist as the exemplary figure of human transcendence — indeed as transcendence itself. This aesthetic rather than scientistic will to power we find in the divine power of the genius, but what is that power except the power of imagination? The church visible of the religion of art in the nineteenth century may now have become a "church invisible" whose devotees squirm at the word "religion," but if I am not mistaken our culture still invests something of itself in some "saving power" of art. And this even though the more ardent language of previous aesthetic devotees embarrasses some of the contemporary faithful.

Freedom and Imagination: Reproductive and Productive

In the context of modern epistemology we find the following doubleness between what has been called reproductive and productive imagination. Kant's epistemology claims that without imagination we could not know, because without it the given manifold of sense impressions would not show to us the order and regularity that we find in appearances. There is much more to Kant's epistemology, but the powers of *synthesis* possessed by imagination are central. Imagination as a synthetic power is indispensable, and the contrast of reproductive and productive imagination is instructive concerning something essential.

One might argue that imagination betokens a new beginning, relative to human singularity. An animal responds to the stimuli of its environment, registering what is before it in terms of its need for protection and sustenance. Absorbed in its environment, it makes with it an unselfconscious marriage. We human beings can free ourselves from such an enveloping immediacy, distance ourselves by not immediately reacting to stimuli. Imagination, one might say, reveals that power of freedom by which we first so distance ourselves, and in that distance mediate with ourselves. It initiates our more express intermediation with *otherness*. Thus *reproductive imagination* shows the power to conjoin previously given sensory images; it works on already given material, impressions received and retained. It is more like a sensory memory that preserves and rearranges the old without bringing anything *new* into being. By contrast, *productive imagination* is not just the retention and ordering of old impressions. It suggests the generation of new images with no complete precedent in previous experience. Something is being born—something original, something not completely explicable in terms of prior impressions. It seems to originate images from the self's own immanent resources of being, free images that cannot be univocally fixed to given sense impressions. Such free, productive origination seems to be a distinctive mark of human beings.

Imagination so understood suggests the opening up of an articulated sense of *difference* by relation to which we can begin to contemplate something of the contours of otherness, both within ourselves and beyond. Imagination is there at the birth of our most elemental and primordial freedom. It contributes to the articulation of our being in the between, not simply absorbed in the midst of things, but emerging as ourselves with some freedom to range, if only in mind, over creation as other to us, and to be as not confined like other animals to their local feeding patch.

Imagination liberates both an openness and an excess of being in us: it makes of us more than organisms in bondage to the environs; it makes us receptive to what is more than ourselves. If productive imagination shows we are not just determined by external stimuli, it also shows the beginning of our power to determine ourselves through ourselves. It shows power as self-differentiating, and potentially self-determining, but also as intermediating with being that is other to itself, and hence self-articulating power that is self-transcending. Imagination emerges from the free articulation of the aesthetic body where the original energy of being becomes surplus — think of the way only human beings *adorn themselves* in a mindful way. It reveals a kind of ontological overflow, an excess of energy that is lifted, and can lift itself, above first given necessity. As such imagination might be said to be at the birth of *mindful being*, as both incipiently self-aware and as open to the other as other.

Think also of how mindfulness as imaginative need not be stopped before given facts but can surpass them, in search of a significance not immediately given. In such wise, beyond the immediacies of an environment, imagination can begin to open a *world* of intermediated meaning. There is something mediating about imagination in multiple senses. It can open for us a realm of ideality, even as it mediates between body and mind. It seems to partake of both body and mind, as it emerges from the first and concretizes the second. It can also dip down into darker recesses of the human being where it might come upon daimonic powers, as well as diviner.

Moreover, imagination is deeply connected to human *desire*. Human desire is not just animal immediacy, but is mediated through images of what is worthwhile, images shaping the very unfolding of desire's sometimes amorphous energies. (Advertisers and propagandists know well this intimate power of the image to mediate, even create desire.) Since imagination relates to the articulation of desire closest to our bodily intimacy with being, from it may also arise darker images of monstrous possibility (this has religious and ethical significance especially relative to the extremities of good and evil). It might be like an Ariadne's thread giving us a line from the labyrinth into the light: Theseus could not return through himself alone. It might be like a song of Orpheus that calls the soul out of its nocturnal caves. But it might also look back, or down, in such a way that the beloved vanishes, just on the threshold.

If imagination allows us to envisage the other, this means it is always in some way — often secretly — originary of our openness to otherness. Productive imagination is crucial for all forms of ideal activity, but it is especially important for art's transfiguring power. When Valéry called the poetic word the "golden coin" of language, maybe he was getting at something like this transfiguring power. The golden word is, so to say, the linguistic standard of intrinsic worthiness; other words are mere means, of instrumental use only. A notable power of art is that its depiction of ugliness need not be itself ugly. Artistic perfection might allow us to see imperfection with a "yes" that consents to creation. And this too, even when we recall *breaking otherness*. Remember Rilke broken open by beauty: the angel is terrible.

One last point: reproductive imagination can be coupled with a more "representational" model of mind, in that the image seems a mere reduplication of a fixed external original; while productive imagination can be coupled with a more active, less "passive" view, hence allowing a more "creative" relation to what is other, especially encouraging relative to the sources of creativity in the human being. If the first tends to emphasize imitation, the second tends to emphasize originality. "Originality"—this is a holy word in our time when, as Emerson said, "imitation is suicide." I cannot go into it here, but the relation of imitation itself is far more complex and rich than this simple doublet allows. The contrast of imitation and creation is often too overdrawn. An opposition of imitation and creation—one supposedly passive and unfree, the other supposedly active and spontaneous—cannot be upheld. To be able to imitate is to possess the power of imaginatively identifying with the other, a power far more complex than simple reproductive imagination.

For that matter, the imaginative power to "reproduce" may be far more enigmatic than we think: it shows a *passion of being*, a patience to what is other, in which what is other communicates and passes into one. (I think of the astonishing porosity of Charles Dickens, which opens up an extraordinary creativity from which pours a whole world of singular characters, so many of them deliciously named.) The passion of being, the *passio essendi*, may communicate the original gift of the other, without which there is no activity of being, no *conatus essendi*, no self-activity, and in that sense no imagination as original. Thus too an imitating being has the fundamental capacity to be *other to itself*, and other to itself in seeing the other as the exemplar who shows me the way, or something of it. The path to originality is lined with the faithful *mimēsis* of the great masters who have trod the road of honest seeking before us. It is hard to know if one could become an example of originality without starting out by imitating some already accomplished exemplars.[1] This means that originality without *gratitude* is a corruption.

---

[1] I have said more on imitation and creation in, for instance, *Philosophy and its Others*, 87–93; and on the *passio essendi* in, for instance, *Ethics and the Between*, chapter 12.

Imagination and Being Religious

What of religious imagination? If imagination is at the source of our self-transcending, we find it at the source of all culture, and so also at religion's birth. We find ourselves in an equivocal middle, only a measure of meaning is vouchsafed; we ask more questions than we are given answers, we press for more than seems presented. The gap between our reach and grasp is especially evident with religion. If sometimes we must guess at an answer, we cannot fix our guess into a univocal certainty. A gap remains between what we know to be and what we surmise might be. When we cannot directly answer our urgent perplexities, we must perforce imagine. Religious imagination is in the gap between the presently given and the intimated or divined. Of course, religious imagination is not within the control of any individual, and bears more on the mythic memory of a people, or exemplary deeds or lives or communities serving to image in time what may have significance for other times, perhaps all time. To "psychologize" religion in terms of individual subjectivity is not enough.

We come to an inherent ambiguity in religious imagination itself. The ambiguity or doubleness turns on this: with religious imagination do we deal, finally, with ourselves alone; or is there a doubleness, a more than oneself, a middle wherein opens the meeting of our original power and a more ultimate, perhaps absolute origin?

Not surprisingly, the sacred dreams of religious imagination, as implying an origin other than ourselves, are often the battle site of conflicting interpretations. These dreams will be sanctified as the acme of truth or decried as the abyss of error. This conflict reflects the double possibility with imagination itself: empty fantasy, or promise of transcendence. The image is always and essentially double.

See imagination as fantasy, and one might judge religion to be "making up" incredible images, unbelievable pictures. The doubleness of the image becomes a kind of duplicity. The univocity of Enlightenment reason will dispel the equivocity riddling religion. Fantasy projects illusions, nonexistent things, figments, nothings. In post-Enlightenment thought especially, religions have been rejected as fantasy worlds in this sense. Consult Feuerbach, Marx, Freud, Nietzsche: religion "projects" an illusory otherworld over against this

---

See also *Art, Origins, Otherness*, chapter 1, "Eros, Mania, Mimēsis: On Platonic Originals."

here-now "real" world, with a status more real than the "real." (I am tempted to say "sur-real," were this word not already preempted aesthetically—though I divine a religious riddle in this too.) Relative to this negative sense of projecting fantasy, one can also find Enlightenment reason claiming the realism of saving univocity on its side—it possesses, so it proclaims, the rational powers to exorcise the equivocal idealities of religious imagination.

Undoubtedly, it can happen that imagination of the "other" world can eclipse engagement with this one, and we evade the complex tension of our being here in the between. What if, to the contrary, religious imagination is pregnant with the promise of true transcendence, and not only the alienated form of our own self-transcending? Rather than evade that complex tension, it might engage that between more profoundly. With this second possibility, religious imagination has an indispensable ontological significance, with respect to the original energy of human selving and its self-transcending openness to what is other to it. We need finesse to dwell mindfully with the equivocities of our being, not geometry to reduce that equivocity to rationalistic univocity. There is a more originary attunement to what is other to our autonomous self-determination, and other to being configured as the neutered world of rationalistic univocity. If the religious image is not a sensory image, not a self-projection, but an articulation of original imagination as a promise of transcendence, it is a mediating spiritual representation that concentrates in itself something of extraordinary significance (recall Vico's imaginative universal).

In participating in the bodying forth of what otherwise might remain nameless, religious imagination, thus understood, would not just transpose a representation from the secular to the sacred, the immanent to the transcendent. There would be something happening more like the reverse. What is original is not exhausted by given immanence; rather what is immanently given comes to be as, and is divined to be, the image of the sacred. If so, the sacred is there for us in the image. "In" does not mean mastered, since a *promise* of transcendence guards its reserve of mystery, even when this is here and now communicated. You cannot just will original imagination, but rather have to be, as it were, "unselved," give up a false fixity and reenter a space of opening, where nothing may come, or God. (The poet may speak of wooing the muse. This is a calling of love, a willingness that is not just will power, or will to power.) In a sense, the religious imagination is divinatory of the original show of the sacred.

This is something that sounds paradoxical: *an act of patience*. In receiving something given, something originative may be enacted.

Given the doubleness of the image we must acknowledge, of course, some truth in both the negative and positive senses. Our religious imaginings can be the lax meanderings of a mindless soul, or the gifts of vision asking the utmost in discerning discipline. They can be evasions of truth, they can be shocking awakenings to a truth we could not dream ourselves alone. There is an unavoidable hazard of freedom in the happening of religious imagination, and the separation of the communication of the divine and its counterfeit double, the image and the idol, is not easy. Weeds grow on the same ground as the wheat, they grow together, and we do not always know which is which. Religious imagination may arise from divine madness or give rise to just mad madness. And maybe one has to have a touch of divine madness to tell the difference. Those who imagine they will do away with religious imagination, imagine what they themselves show to be impossible. They are the weed or wheat that thinks it will abolish the ground that grows it. They dream of putting an end to religious dreams, but this too is a dream.

How should we see the religious significance in imagination as productive? Imagination as an ontological power of our being, one that puts its roots into the inward otherness of the human self, might be said to have religious significance. In this view, we are not mere imitations of an origin other to us, but originals in our own right, and hence capable of some kind of "self-creation"; not a mere passive image of the divine, but imaging the divine in our own finite powers of creativity. Imagination as source of self-transcending makes us an image of transcendence as other to us, and indeed the gift of free original power seems given with this power that allows us newly to give creation to ourselves. We communicate imaginatively because we have been communicated with in the original image we ourselves are. No simple dualism of *mimēsis* and creativity will do, as stated above. The inward otherness points to an immanent source in us, but as other to our own complete self-mastery, and hence as much a power endowed as one empowering our own self-activity.

Is this our immanent self-transcendence simply our own? To say "yes" would be to reduce the power of imagination to the univocity of the human alone with itself, albeit enacting the project of being its own self-creator. Or is there a plurivocity in this immanence such that it becomes also a "between" where we find the point of meeting of the finite "I" and the divine. One thinks here of Coleridge's famous remarks in *Biographia Literaria* in which the finite "I am" is an echo of the infinite "I am." The space of their resonance in humans is in the power of the creative imagination.

We are on dangerous ground here, not surprisingly. One great risk, religiously speaking, is that we do away with the doubleness between ourselves and the divine, and resolve the equivocity in favor of an apotheosis of the human: not the apotheosis in which the human gives itself over to elevation to the divine, but the self-apotheosis of the human in which it claims to elevate itself, to make itself what it is, to be self-creating, and without any reference to its own being given to be (remember the *passio essendi*) or transcendence as other to it. Our *conatus essendi* strives to overtake completely, or take over, the *passio essendi*. And this it justifies in terms of this power vested in its own most intimate immanence.[2] An extreme temptation here is for the human being to claim dominion over what is other, even its own otherness, and to claim for itself a self-sufficient being that finally becomes closed to otherness beyond it.

One might claim, contrariwise, that our finite creativity is to be true to our openness to otherness, whether immanent in us, or transcendent. To redeem the promise of human self-becoming is to struggle against the forces of dissolution while avoiding the seduction of closure. Creation is more than merely asserting one's originality, but it pays homage to the original possibilities of an open wholeness. It asks honesty about recalcitrant otherness, discernment of the fluid original power of our being, and works to transform its ambiguous energy into communicative form that reaches beyond itself. Is not a subtle closure to otherness often insinuated by the way we chant the word "creativity," like some sacred mantra that yet has nothing much to do with the sacred? Self-absorption overtakes self-knowledge; we fail the creative tension by slackening the communicative exigence. If originative power is not a private possession but something given to us, precisely as gift, our link is preserved with what is other as other. Creative power is more than swaggering self-affirmation that sets itself above the rest of creation. It is not "creative," it cooperates in creation.

---

[2] I have discussed the equivocation between different senses of transcendence in "Art and the Impossible Burden of Transcendence: On the End of Art and the Task of Metaphysics," in *Art, Origins, Otherness*, chapter 8.

The Plurivocity of Being Religious

Let us return to the question of why it seems that the tie between religion and imagination is now popular. There is the recognition of the symbolic and metaphorical dimensions of being religious, certainly neglected if not depreciated in more rationalistic interpretations. The univocal sense of literal truth that seems to be the domain of the sciences cannot do justice to the more plurivocal truth of being religious. I am not advocating here a fideism over against a rationalism. Indeed the more extensive role of imagination is now evident in that many philosophers of science have recognized the role of models and metaphors—that is, the imagination—in the construction of scientific theories. The imagination cannot be avoided, even in the so-called hard sciences.

Query: Has *religiou4* imagination paradoxically suffered a diminution in this elevation in the shadow of hegemonic univocity? One remembers, for instance, older senses of symbol, analogy, sacrament: these were not tied to an escape from univocity of the more modern type, nor tied to a sort of subjective compensation for the many, tolerated by the hard taskmasters of the sciences. The issue is not a matter of something more "subjectivist" as opposed to something more "objectivist." I know that much of reflection today is seeking ways beyond such contrasts, especially as too exclusively formulated. But one wonders to what extent the context is still shaped by their contrast: an objective truth that has nothing to say to "subjectivity," a subjective expressivism unmoored from any "objective" condition of being.

Do we not need a more ample sense of mindfulness, one in some way already at work and that does not have to be "created," since it offers something like the nurturing ethos where the imagination is at home, an ethos that is not just a space we can construct for the imagination to find its free release? Would not the idea of the intimate universal I connect with being religious have importance here? But it is only too true that we live in an ethos of univocity where the finesse needed for the equivocities of being is more and more contracted. Part of our problem in late modernity, even in postmodernity, is that freedom is dominantly interpreted as autonomy or self-determination, hence as self-legislating, hence as wary of otherness that may intrude on that self-legislation. Imagination is not self-determination, though it is an opening that may make self-determination possible and qualify it. In this context, imagination's indispensability in all forms of mindfulness tells against the excessive specialization of modernity, and the fixities of autonomy claimed by, say, philosophy, art, science, history. Perhaps one of the reasons for imagination's "popularity" is just that it overlaps all of them, and hence transgresses the boundaries fixed by a univocalizing autonomy.

What if something like religious imagination, as bringing us closer to the primal origin, were at work in all of them: religious imagination now meaning the place of original porosity between the divine and the human; the place that is also noplace in offering that porosity; the place/noplace where the origin communicates original power to the human? Suppose "autonomy" clogs up such elemental porosities? Being religious would entail the safeguarding of these porosities—keeping them open to communication. (I make an analogous point with regard to religious reverence in Chapter 8 below.) Maybe some postmodern thought tries to do something like this. Still its efforts to open the clogged porosities, if they are such, are often done with modern tools, and so we get the self-antagonism, the self-laceration of "autonomy." This gives us a postmodern "autonomy" that is no "autonomy." It does not come clean about being religious. We need to go further.

Consider the possibilizing power of imagination relative to the plurivocity of being religious, and what I call the counterfeit doubles of God. Imagination gives first form to the transcending energy that constitutes our being and that initially emerges in mindfulness as a kind of powerful formlessness. It must be given form, sometimes through an other or others, sometimes through itself. *Mimēsis* is extremely important for the first forms of articulation which the energy takes on. It cannot be anything definite without first taking them on, or finding itself impressed with them. Hence the importance of the early education of the soul, and the later always-needed presence of exemplars to spur the individual to emulation. But imitation is not enough, and the energy comes to give itself form. The very lability and plasticity of that energy inevitability means that the forms of being religious will be diversified, and this even in the context of monotheistic practices. There need be nothing wrong with that. The point is not the reduction of the plurivocity to univocity—though without some determinacy, and in that respect qualified univocity, we can fall into an extreme equivocity in which the soul, claiming to find itself, is actually lost to itself.

The possibilizing power of imagination is connected with what one might call archaic manifestness: manifestness having to do with the *archē*. Such manifestness implicates us, as much as the other being manifested; nor are we the *archē*. But how we envisage the other and *archē* is conditioned by what we can receive and that to which we can give imaginative form. The equivocity in our most intimate souls will surface in the images of the divine other we ask to stay for contemplation and praise. This equivocity will surface in our own double posture toward what is manifested: never perhaps pure adoration or idolatry but a mingling of them. One could say even that pure idolatry, were it to know itself as such and knowingly execrate the divine, would indirectly pay its compliment to God. Its knowing hatred would be its perverted love. A more dozy idolatry, asleep to the sleep of finitude, might not even realize that its devotion to God was its treason.

We come to the nub of the problem of the counterfeit double: the image mimics the original, but it presents itself as the original; indeed it seems so like the original that we have difficulty telling it is an image; if such an image, so to say, usurps the original, how can we tell this, since it looks the same as the original? The daimon and the angel are intermediaries, but the daimonic can become the diabolical, and the first angels fell. "Angels are bright still, though the brightest fell" (*Macbeth*, 4.3.22). Lucifer is the bearer of light, first son of the morn, but is it not just light that we seek in our condition of night? What then could an evil light be, how tell a light as evil? By what light tell this counterfeit light, since it too is in the light? How could light counterfeit light?

In other words, the plurivocity of being religious is always open to the temptation of the equivocal, and hence is itself an ethos of possible idols or counterfeit doubles. This is inescapable, which does not mean we are trapped in it: given what we are, it will arise, but we can face it, and see it through. Religious finesse is needed to understand the images, to discern the doubles. There is a call made on the imagination, but since imagination cannot of itself but be in the equivocal doubles, it always risks the canonization of a false double in giving the form. This is the old problem of the truth or falsity of the image. It has not to do with a univocal proposition where we could say, *this* true, *that* false and so on. It has to do with the communication of equivocal possibility. But there is a call on *being true* in this communication of equivocal possibility. To what are we being true, or called: ourselves, or more than ourselves; or both; hence true to the *fitting relation or community* between us and what is more or other than ourselves? This last is what I think is most true. It has to do with a being true to the ultimate relation *between* ourselves and what is ultimate.

Nevertheless, we can construct a second middle in the given middle. Call this made-up middle a crystal palace—with a bow to Dostoevski. The images in the second, made-up middle can be false doubles, doublings of ourselves and the circuit of human self-transcendence clogged with itself. We still must discern the original. A religious person may say this is God. Postmodern thought will say there is no original. But then we are in the midst of images of nothing—except of ourselves—and we too are nothing. We seem to come to the ultimate double: either God or nothing. If we opt for God we are not opting out of the plurivocity: we still have the task of a life—to discern the images, and to live according to the communication of the original. How? In accord with the promise of the good of life. Is this not the significance of being religious—the keeping open of the ultimate porosities in the middle between the human and the divine?

On Counterfeit Doubles

Consider further the question of the truth of imagination in this modern, postmodern context. We tend to find a kind of equivocality all along the line. Is the doubleness between us and the divine being counterfeited? I must say more on what a counterfeit double is. It is an image that is almost exactly like the original, but something has been altered that vitiates its claim to be true. Suppose I have a counterfeit banknote. It looks good, but there is something missing, or something added that is not right. How to see this? Close discernment is needed, and more and more so the *better* the counterfeit. The better a counterfeit, the more it is *true* to the original. Its *achieved falsity* is dependent on its *being true to the original*. This is a very paradoxical situation where *perfected falsity is a function of being true to what is not false*. The perfect counterfeit looks exactly like the true currency. But somehow (and much of the difficulty lies in this "somehow") the claim it makes, or the authority it claims, is not to be sustained.

The following story raises interesting questions about how the perfect counterfeit can reveal its imperfection just by being too perfect. During World War II the Germans produced extremely good counterfeits of the English currency, and for a time were successful in sowing confusion. The counterfeits were so good that it was very hard to tell any difference between the genuine currency and the forgery. How then was the difference finally told? It is said that people began to tell the difference because *the counterfeits were too perfect*, while the genuine currency always revealed *some flaw or other*. The "too perfect" was not "perfect," while the "imperfect" was the more true, or "perfect." The story makes one wonder about forms of philosophy and religion: the truer forms of philosophizing and being religious are not those that are, so to say, "too perfect," but those that confess more honestly our imperfection, and theirs. This would mean properly guarding the difference of the human and the divine, the finite image and the absolute original, without choking the communication between them.

Of course, much hangs on whether there is any original to which reference can be made to sustain the claim to be true, or false. If there is no original, there is no counterfeit; there is not even an image, since any image, without original, images nothing, hence is no image. If this were so, there would be no question of truth, and no question of discernment. There would be no question of *being true*, in the many senses this can have.[3] That this cannot be so follows from our very being, which is to be called to be true. Every denial of truth happens *within* the exigence to be true, and this exigence is not something we first determine or construct, but it determines us to be the kinds of beings we are. Every truth we claim to "construct" happens within this exigence we do not construct.

This call of "being true" is not a matter of this truth or that truth, yet it is evidenced in that we are unavoidably drawn to ask about what makes this either better or worse than that. We ask this most especially with respect to being religious, where some of the images may be idols, that is, counterfeit doubles of God. If every image is self-authenticating, then there is no authentication in which differences of better and worse have a grounding. It will amount to "say-so": it is because we say it is. Everything is "made-up," but when everything is made-up, we cannot even speak of something being made-up. Equivocity so absolutized is self-subverting. It is analogous to this paradox we find in the modern ethos of "creative" imagination: If every human is now a genius, this means there are no more geniuses.

The question: Do we need an *original as other* to sustain the claim made by an image to be a genuine image—a genuine image not sim-

---

[3] On the different ways of being true, see *Being and the Between*, chapter 13, "Being True."

ply of itself—for then it would be only a self-referring image, a self-reflexive image, a self-creating original, a work of art giving birth to itself, Nietzsche's claim for the world. And is it not strange how the exclusion of God as the other original leads to the self-divinization of immanent finitude as its own self-original? From where do we get that sense of the original as other? And how do we discern claims that this or that is the original, since every such claim seems itself open to the suspicion of being a counterfeit double? In such an equivocal situation, is there any finesse that will help? From where would that finesse come?[4] The religious image itself, even if it is genuine, is here also tested by this perplexity of the counterfeit double. I know antireligious thought will point the finger at religion as itself counterfeiting the human being. It is true that religion cannot just point the finger back at its antagonist, but must put the question to itself. And most especially it must, if indeed its vocation is to keep open, cooperate in the keeping open of the ultimate porosity between the human and the divine.

If this porous between is to be kept open, from a religious point of view one might define a counterfeit double in terms of an image that somehow seeks to extrude reference to transcendence as other: divine transcendence as other to our self-transcendence, even though in our self-transcendence we may find that space of porosity where the communication between the human and the divine is offered to us. Recall above the double view of imagination: not just our power to mediate with ourselves, but the happening of an intermediation, between us and what is other, certainly the opening of the space of free possibility for that communicative intermediation to be given. If I am right about our tendency to reduce the double mediation to a singular self-mediation, it will not be surprising if we often confront the temptation to the counterfeit double, especially in a culture that makes an idol of autonomy: where the *nomos* of *to auto* closes itself off, sometimes more crudely, sometimes much more subtly, to the

---

[4] In the background here is also the question of authority. We seem to need genuine authority if there is to be stability in the economy of counterfeits, a regulation of discernment, and ways of telling the difference. But if in a society, or epoch, everything seems to be under the rule of equivocity (as seems to be implied by the postmodernists), then the absolutization of equivocity will not get us the finesse we so need; for finesse is not the absolutization of equivocity but its mindful discernment. An analogous problem of authority under the sign of equivocity affects political communities, as well as religious, intellectual, and cultural communities.

other, *to heteros*. Religious imagination is creative porosity to the original *heteros*; but just that porosity as equivocal allows us to remold it as the ambiguous space of our own self-communication. In that sense, it is we who make ourselves to be the counterfeit double. We want to "make ourselves up" absolutely, by denying we are first and primally creatures: given to be, and endowed with the original power to make something up, before we make anything up, either in a truly creative sense or in a lying.

But maybe this is too simple. Perhaps all this is not just due to us alone. Perhaps the plurivocity of religion is inseparable from the excess of the divine, the "too muchness," the overdeterminacy of its light that both broadcasts itself, and yet dwells in its inaccessibility beyond us. Do counterfeit doubles, again paradoxically, suggest something about God as One? Consider the following line of reflection.

Suppose this One is communicative. The communication would be within Godself, but also, relative to us, the communication of being to creation; and the communication between God and creation would define the space of difference and relation within which our being religious takes shape. This difference between God and creation need not be construed as a dualistic opposition, but more as an ambiguous matrix in which God cannot be absolutely evident. For what could this absolute univocal evidence be in finitude? God's communication to finitude and in finitude will be relative to the form of finitude, and hence the difference always means that it will never univocally be God's self. If it is not God absolutely, this does not mean it is nothing. Maybe this communication is absolute relative to what is not absolute, absolute relative to finitude; hence it is between, equivocal between the absoluteness reserved for God and nothing. And yet it is robustly there as communicating more than can be fully made present in the form of finitude itself. One might say: the communication of God in the between is also a reserving of God: showing is also hiddenness; just as there are recesses to manifestness that do not themselves become manifest, though they are ingredient in making manifestness possible.

The between of God and creation is thus an ethos of ambiguity, in which we are given our freedom with respect to communication. This is our free being: communicated to be; but as being in the between, possibilized as being in communication with the source of the primal communication. We are an immanent middle: an equivocal opening of freedom and new possibility; and in that sense, a middle between

God and creation. Suppose we think of creation as the gift of the agape of the origin. Then what is given is let open. In other words, the One is not determinative in a univocal way of the being of the creation; and this is most evident with intermediate beings such as humans, where the creative power of the overdeterminacy in our being awakens to itself and beyond itself. This arising of creative power in finite immanence is confirmed in the endowment of original imagination.

The communication of the One is not the self-duplication of the One. The agapeic One is not a self-cloning God. A self-cloning God would always give rise to the same again: no genuine newness or originality would arise in creation. Thus human beings who are eager to be cloned only want to redouble themselves as the same. They have no interest in creating the new. A self-doubling, self-cloning God, in that sense, would be absolutely *autistic*. There would be no finite creation as genuinely other, and no finite powers of origination endowed with the free power to bring the new into being, after the form of finitude—in a word, no imagination, and no imaginative originals such as we human creatures are.

There is a genuine two-ness of God and creation. It is in that otherness that the overdeterminate plurivocity of divine communication can come to show itself. A counterfeit double would then be a happening of finitude in which the true doubleness between God and creation is distorted, indeed corrupted. It would be a finite one taking over the double space between itself and the One, and doing away with this double space in terms of its own singular claim to be the ultimate. This true doubleness would be reduced just to self-doubling, and we humans, the usurping original of immanence, would stake our claim to be the only self-doubling God: bound in a nutshell, kings of infinite space, but inmates of autistic immanence.

And this is the temptation of finitude itself: given to be for itself, it contracts its being for itself into its being for itself and nothing but itself—the being given for itself as gift, as first given, is blurred or denied. Obviously, this only arises properly with beings capable of assent and refusal to their own being given to be, the finite nature of their own being for self. The temptation here is the refusal of everything entailed by our first being given to be as *passio essendi*, a refusal riding on a certain self-determination of our *conatus essendi*, our endeavor to be. The temptation is prepared in the equivocal being of finitude itself: between its being given to be, and its being given for itself; between its relativity to the ultimate origin and its own self-relating being for itself in immanence.

God plurivocally communicates with creation; but we communicate with ourselves; and we take that to be communication; we take our self-transcending to be transcendence itself; and in its energies we envelop finitude and invest it with the infinitude that truly is other; but we have not lived up to the difference between our infinite seeking and the infinitude of the One sought. The plurivocity as over-determinately communicating the divine has been turned around into a "closing," self-enclosing equivocation rather than granted as an "opening," self-releasing equivocity. Our desire to fix it on our terms generates the closing. The fixing seems to make us master, but what we think we master has just escaped us, in our very claim to fix it.

Some Counterfeit Doubles?

What if there are diverse reconfigurations of the porosity between the origin and the human original, porosity endowed with plurivocal promise and open to be determined now this way, now that? I now want to ask whether the counterfeit doubling can take a scientistic form, a fideistic form, a rationalistic/idealist form, an aestheticist form, a moral one. Science, faith, philosophy, art, and morality are part of what we are, but none is immune from deep-seated equivocity.

The scientistic counterfeit double of the religion image? Here I mean the tendency in modernity to emphasize science, its methods and findings, to such an extent that a merely negative attitude is taken toward the image, be it religious or other. We find a dominant objectivist approach. Images are aftereffects of sensory impressions or expressions of subjective emotion and value: their epistemological value is low, and their ontological claim all but nonexistent. It is not that the image is done away with—this is impossible. That science itself is grounded in evidence as sensorially recorded, and indeed on images, analogies, models, and so on, is undeniable. But the significant power of the imagination here is to be the subjectivist matching track to the true objectivistic line. There is truth and it is objective; there is imagination and it reflects our subjective needs, emotions, wants. The first now can come to minister to the second: the achievements of cybernetic culture can be turned to serving our comfort levels, our

need for novelty, distraction, and entertainment. It is as if Enlightenment and Romanticism enter into a pact in which the science and
technology of the former prove their necessity by ministering to the
satisfactions enjoyed in the self-expressions of the latter. The human
uses of objectivity are not themselves objective: they are the hand-
maids of the subject, even though officially they claim to have nothing to do with subjectivity. Think of what the Internet serves: the
highest achievement of our cybernetic science, and it has led to the
proliferation of pornographic sites galore. Hard heads and a mess of
eros.

What of the religious image? It has no cognitive or ontological
claim. Religion used to be the opium of the people, but now we have
better opiates and they are not religious, even if they mimic, or claim
to mimic, its consolations. The image has been instrumentalized—not
necessarily to serve the deeper exploration of the inward otherness
of the human being, but to cream off the most surface of apparitions
that curdle at the top. The intrinsic power of the image to return us
to the deepest ambiguity immanent in our being, in the inner otherness, is debilitated. This ambiguity is the double space of communication between the human and the divine. The exploitation of images,
their instrumentalization, mimics the opening. The true opening
would be more like prayer—but there is no technology of prayer,
or univocal method, and it appeals to an intimacy of being beyond
"subjectivism" in the subject itself.

Great images come out of that more intimate space. That is
why they have always the fresh power to surprise us. Images as instrumentalized by scientistic reason quickly lose that freshness, because they lack that intimacy. Today's originality, too loudly
"announced" as unprecedented, tomorrow stales as old hat. Images
become clichéd, or hackneyed for propaganda purposes, or advertis-
ing, or imaginative muzak for relaxation, and so on. Even the great
images of extraordinary art are press-ganged into being thus serviceable and disposable, their fresh loveliness abused in being overused.
They are robbed of the diviner innocence, or purgatorial suffering,
of their truer glory.

There will be those who even go so far as to sell religion, in all
good faith, as leading to lower blood pressure, less drug abuse, increased longevity, and so on. These may be effects, yes, true images
coming from change in a way of life and understanding. But to think
that the truth of religion is *to be used* that way is to misunderstand its
truth. There is a literalist univocity at work here that treats the scien-

tific and the religious as simply homogeneous on the same continuum. We collapse the qualitative difference of geometry and finesse. The religious image is more intimate with the origin in its otherness than all scientific theory, which comes later, emerging itself out of that intimacy, though it proceeds to forget, to be blithe about, to disparage, or even to hate what gives it to be. The univocalists of religion do not help us when they think religion is merely homogeneous with scientific theory. The defect of finesse holds true not only of the scientistic types, but also of those who want to defend religion thus. The seriousness of their literal-mindedness lacks the plurivocal mindfulness of the religious image.

The fideistic counterfeit double? What I intend here concerns a certain reaction to the scientistic counterfeit. Truth is given over to the sciences while religion takes up residence in the interior soul, not to be touched by the calculations of the former. It is in the heart. I think there is much to this, in so far as the mind of finesse must remain in communication with the heart, as indeed must the religious imagination. But what of the intimate universal? Is the universal, as neutral homogenous truth, given over to the univocal possession of the scientific, while the intimate becomes a private affair making no claim to truth? But if the claim of truth, not for the image, but of the image is given up, we find ourselves less with faith, as midway between faith and an *aestheticization* of the religious image. Faith may not need to justify itself to calculative *ratio*, yet mindfulness is where the heart is, and here too is the porous space of *being true*. The intimate universal is not the neutral, homegenous universal. Nor can being truthful be confined to its objectivist modes. To confine it so has a pernicious effect on religious imagination in the long run. It becomes a matter of "say-so." And if this is so, we are running closer to the wilder will of unashamed will-to-power. It is so because I will it so. Obviously, willing is crucial, but will cannot be just such an "I will it so." Willing must also put its roots deep into the original porosity of being that frees will in us to be free and for itself. There is a willingness prior to and beyond determinate will, and will-to-power; and it must abide in fidelity to our *passio essendi*, all the (self-)driven energies of *conatus essendi* notwithstanding.

Here again imagination is crucial: if it is a primordial freeing, the religious willing must always find that place of imagination where freedom comes to emergence, as if for the first time; and in this first emergence, there may be much more communicated than "I will it so." What? A sense of "innocence" before definite will—turn and be as a child. A sense for nakedness and vulnerability; an attunement to the porosity. A feel for the *passio essendi*. These reveal more of the truer ground of willing rather than the self-affirming will of the *conatus essendi*. Important is a fidelity to the inward otherness as given to be by the more original origin. Important also is a patience to an overdeterminate solicitation that is made upon one's free responsibility, for which one can never answer absolutely, since one is not absolute, and not the absolute good (Dostoevski and Levinas saw something of this).

Fides must return to this root and not take up permanent, unmoved residence in later derivative determinations of the basic *con-fides*. What we come across is not solely a *fides* but a *con-fides*: a confidence in the sense in which there is a "faith with": a confiding. Something is confided to us, and we are given to be as confident. This again shows something of the happening of the primal porosity. The counterfeit double of the confiding can be the faith that confidently determines itself as thus and thus. This latter confidence can come from a more primal confiding; but it can also counterfeit this more primal confiding, such that it will not even know what is meant if reference is made to it. It is not Thy will, but its own will, its own "say-so," that it will do, even when it says "Thy will." Were it to return to the porosity, or be returned, it would be more diffident about asserting *itself* with the confidence that seems so impressive. The primal happening of the ultimate porosity, as a confiding, grounds con-fidence, and this grounds faith in a more determinate sense of *fides* in this or that. There is something overdeterminate about the original confiding confidence.

And is this not a mark of religious faith? It is not simply confidence in this or that, but a confiding confidence that is brought to this or that which, as such, is more than this or that: overdeterminate as exceeding every determinacy, though it takes flesh in this or that determinacy. The truth of religious imagination is here extremely important in that genuine imagination seeks to find expression for this sense of the "more." We are reminded of a great work of art that has both singular determinacy and an inexhaustibility that we cannot pin down to this or to that. This is even more true of a living exemplar of ethical goodness and religious holiness. There is a living spring of freshness in this thing itself, alive in this good person, this holy person. Perhaps the con-fides makes us intimate with the living spring, out of which the living imagination also flows. Scientistic literal-mindedness will not understand this. Nor, I am afraid, will a merely asserted fideism. The con-fiding has to do with a primal patience to God, in place of which self-assertion, whether scientistic or fideistic, puts an idol—each itself as its own counterfeit double of God. In finding itself and thus asserting itself, it has lost itself and its endower.

The rationalistic/idealistic counterfeit? A number of possibilities are here evident. Some are relative to more simple forms of modern rational enlightenment, others are more sophisticated, and concern less a scientistic opposition to fideism, as a claim to give a better version of *fides quaerens intellectum*. Think about the above story of the "too perfect" counterfeit currency. This might be here applied to the way philosophical reason will sometimes claim to "perfect" religious imagination. But, as with the German counterfeit currency, philosophy's being "too perfect" may well betray its not being perfect, while the "imperfection" of religious imagination may, in truth, be closer to the more perfect. I mean something like an attitude that is most clearly exemplified by German idealism, especially Hegel's.

There are religious images, and qua images they are ineradicably equivocal: they mean something but do not deliver their meaning with full lucidity through themselves alone. Philosophy, it will be said here, will perform this last act of midwifery in which religious meaning, struggling to be born as true, will at last be assisted to its last birth. In an act of charity to its inability, philosophy will deliver religious imagination from its own equivocity. Understanding completes this incompleteness of faith.

Notice the double posture of philosophy. The religious image has some truth, but it is incomplete since intrinsically wrapped in equivocity; it must be freed from this potentially falsifying form, and given the true rational form of freedom. There is a "yes" to the religious imagination; there is a "no"; but the "no" claims to continue the "yes"; and hence the "no" and the "yes" of idealistic philosophy claim to be faithful to the religious imagination itself. Its truth is more truly expressed in philosophical form and hence it can be affirmed when recontextualized within the frame of philosophical concepts.

I must put aside many issues. Here is the core. This recontextualizing especially bears on something about the original image that resists incorporation into concepts. I mean the transcendence of God. The religious image even in its immanent otherness points beyond itself to an otherness of the divine that is not reducible even to the immanent otherness. This is its poverty, if you like; but its poverty is precisely its power, for its power is not its own. The "powerful" poverty of the religious image is to not draw attention to itself alone but to be the passageway of the human and its mindfulness to the divine as other. It is true to its call in confessing its poverty, even in its greatest success; for this always keeps open the space of difference of the divine and the human, even as communication comes across the gap between them. The religious image is a double between in that respect: not reducible to one side or the other, since it is a space of intermediated communication of the human and the divine. Its poverty is the guardian of the difference of divine transcendence, even as it finds opening a way of communication in that difference.

The idealistic recontextualization risks being a counterfeit double because it is this dimension of transcendence as other, and this poverty, that it finds intolerable. For the opening or porosity cannot be generated by reason itself; reason itself presupposes it. If reason then claims to be completely self-determining, its "yes" to the religious image must dissimulate a more aggressive attitude toward transcendence as other. For its "yes" is to what it can reincorporate in itself as self-determining reason. What it cannot, it must either reformulate in its own image, or else excise, or silence, or in benign condescension consign to "mere"contingency, not truly relevant to "philosophy proper." In other words, its claim to be a "yes" to the religious image is peculiarly equivocal toward the positive power that is equivocally shown in the poverty of the image, namely, as keeping open the difference of the human and the divine.

Hegel: the philosophical *Begriff* possesses the form and the content of absolute truth; religious *Vorstellung* may have the content, but the form is external, creating a gap between us and God. But his conceptual *Aufhebung* counterfeits the religious original, in order to make it fit in with the concept's own efforts to be self-determining thinking. Hegel's god is a counterfeit double of God: all the more seductive in that it claims to be true to the original, claims to be the truth of the original.[5] In some regards it is so like it that one can easily be taken in by it; but there is something altered or left out or distorted in the transposition from the image to the concept: the otherness of God as other. Hegel is a powerful instance of what I said above about a counterfeit double: the achieved falsity of a counterfeit double is dependent on its being true to the original. Since a "perfect" counter-

---

[5] On this more fully, see my *Hegel's God*.

feit looks almost exactly like the true currency, perfected falsity is a function, paradoxically, of being true to what is not false; but this counterfeit "being true" falsifies what is not false.

I would rather say: The religious image is truer to this, the otherness of God as other, both in form and content; truer to the double opening which religious imagination reveals; and truer to the excess of the divine to conceptualization and the richer plurivocity that is communicated by the divine. Put otherwise, this idealistic way of claiming self-determining thinking seems to close a circle in which God and the human being are one, but this circle is a way of closing down the original porosity between the human and the divine and falsely lodging it in philosophy itself.

This way of philosophy seems to show great courage in knowing itself, but does it really know itself and understand the sources of its own courage of knowing? I doubt it does. For these are in the original porosity with which being religious is more intimate, not in thought thinking itself as allegedly beyond that porosity. The claims of reason are not self-grounding, not self-determining; they are based on a confidence that is not in the first instance generated by reason itself. Reason has courage in its search for the truth, because first it is marked by *confidence*, but this is related to the primal *con-fides* I mentioned above. This is not the product of self-determining reason, but more original, as endowing reason with the confidence in its own power. There is a "being en-couraged" before a "being courageous." Reason has confidence in its own powers, because it is *already empowered by this con-fiding source*. This is a primal endowment, and again brings us back to the porosity of the human and what is transhuman. (I return to the question of courage in a later chapter.)

It seems to me that religious imagination keeps us in communication with this original source of con-fiding. Without it, the courage of reason would soon dry up, or mutate into a self-asserting that claims to rely on itself alone, or that turns to a defiance of an (ab)surd universe that we now seek to know, and even overpower, *despite* our impotence to ground reason on itself. The self-grounding of reason in this way leads to its ungrounding; its self-empowerment leads to its disablement. When we remember the source of the courage of knowing in the confidence of the original confiding, we henceforth have to be on guard against the propensity of the rationalistic/idealistic philosophers to substitute their version of reason for God. It is not God but a false double.

What we need at this point to discern the philosophical counter-feits is not only a different *fides quaerens intellectum*, but an entirely other *intellectus quaerens fidem*. The poverty of a truer philosophy (as we saw) is its new ecstasis into the night of divine mystery, which no thought thinking itself can even capture.

Moralization of the image—is there a counterfeit double here? Inevitably one thinks of Kant. Kant is in the business of producing secular dou-bles of religion. For instance, his *Religion Within the Bounds of Reason Alone* (*Die Religion innerhalb der Grenzen der bloßen Vernunft*) can be seen as giving articulation to a secular double of "ecclesiology," a double meant to be the successor and replacement of the more historically "positive" Church. It is all very earnest in a rationalistic way, even touching, but it does test one's credulity—somewhat in the way those rewritings of the life of Jesus as an exponent of the categorical im-perative make one pull a polite face, for fear of breaking out into impious laughter. (The younger Hegel tried his hand at this comic genre of demythologizing moralizing fiction.)

I will also mention Kant's efforts in "Conjectural Beginning of Human History" (*Mutmaßlicher Anfang der Menschengeschichte*, 1786) to create a secular double to the religious story of the book of Gene-sis. Interestingly, he claims absolute fidelity to that book, as if it were his map—but this is one place in Kant's writing where I think the tone borders on the facetious.[6] He nods and winks, and makes it

___

[6] I want to cite a few lines from the second paragraph of Kant's essay, since they chime in so well with our theme(s): Kant's conjectures "must not lay claim to being serious business, but perhaps rather only to being the exercise of the imagination in the company of reason, carried out for the sake of the mind's relaxation and health. . . . [B]ecause I here undertake a mere flight of fancy [*Luftreise*], I may hope to be granted permission to use a holy document as a map and, at the same time, to imagine that my flight—taken on the wings of imagination, though not without a guiding thread by which, through reason, it is tied to experience—follows precisely the same line as is sketched out in that historical document. If the reader will check the pages of that document (Genesis, 2–6), he can see whether the path that philoso-phy follows by means of concepts coincides every step along the way with the one set out by history." I. Kant, *Perpetual Peace and Other Essays*, trans. Ted Humphrey (Indianapolis: Hackett, 1983), 49. Note that the Bible is not a sacred scripture, it is a historical document; and even if Kant does follow it line by line, he says nothing about what results, be it sympathetic or antipathetic. Humphrey translates the essay as "Speculative Beginning of Human History." I prefer "conjectural," as found in other translations. Given the paragraph here cited, does one see a seed of Hegel

quite clear to those in the know that such asseverations are not to be taken too seriously. That Kant acknowledges this story of beginnings to be conjectural places us squarely in the space of postulatory fictions—in the sense of something "made-up"—and hence in a secular space rivaling religion in *imaginationd*. Kant will dampen our anxieties about "imaginative fictions" with reassurances of the supervision of reason. The word Kant uses in his title—*Mutmaßlicher Anfang*—is exactly the same word Zarathustra uses when proclaiming that God was a conjecture, or supposition (as we saw in discussing "postulatory finitism" in Chapter 1—see note 3 there). Zarathustra could not care a fig for the supervisions of Kantian reason. But not entirely unlike Zarathustra, Kant's conjecture offers a secular *muthod* to counterpart the religious *muthod*. And since the secular *muthod* appeals to us in the mode of *ald ob*, inevitably its appeal is (quasi-)religious.

Without religious and metaphysical finesse such a project of counterparting quickly converts into a project of producing counterfeit doubles of religion, or of God. Because Kant is inept when it comes to metaphysical astonishment before the "that it is at all" of being, and because religion is univocalized by being moralized, he is not well positioned to see that creation, as a religious story, points to something hyperbolic to scientific theory. There is not a univocal continuum between the two.

Now to the question of the moralization of the religious image. Is the moralistic form one of the most pervasive counterfeits of religion in modernity? That this might be so is understandable. Being religious issues an ethical injunction to be for the other, and indeed up to the extremity of being there for the other in the mode of agapeic service. Is there a moralistic counterfeit of the power of the religious image when there is, so to say, an inversion of the two great commands: Love God first; second, love neighbor as self, for the love of God. The second command is more proximate, more immanent, it seems, so we can immanently be engaged with it. What can we say of the love of God as other compared to the love of ourselves and the neighbor? While all the loves may be inseparable for us, they are not the same. We can take a route here that divorces morality from the religious entirely. We can take a route that substitutes the moral for

---

(and the speculative) in this older Kant? There certainly is the hint of a philosophical *Aufhebung* that claims absolute fidelity to the religious *Vorstellung* by the rational *Begriff*. Sublationary infinitism seems also to be a member of the same family as postulatory moral deism and postulatory finitism.

the religious. An unconditional call is sounded in being ethical, and it is difficult to take issue with the unconditional. But perhaps the unconditional too can be counterfeited, if we do not properly relate to it? Does this happen if autonomous morality itself becomes the ultimate; and not a service that the ultimate asks of us, but which is not the ultimate itself?

This will be hard to accept for those who see nothing beyond this claim to autonomous morality. Indeed, for suggesting something more one might even be accused of a lack of morality. In *Religion Within the Bounds of Reason Alone*, Kant himself takes as a "principle requiring no proof" that any service beyond the moral conduct of a good life is nothing but "religious delusion and counterfeit service to God." It is merely "pseudo" service. To appeal to God will become scandalous for the moral person. For has this person not already his or her absolute, why does he or she need anything more? Anyway appeals to God are likely to produce wars, we are told over and over again; but we are true universalists, the intimacies of religions are mere divisive, private particularities, and so on and on. The greatness of religion, of course, does make it also most dangerous. Its intimacy roots it in the depths of the *passio essendi*, and no doubt this can be overridden by a vehement *conatus essendi* whose fanaticism reveals, in truth, the betrayal of our porosity to the divine, hence also a defection from the agapeic patience of being that is more truly love of the divine and the neighbor.

Otherwise put, if the ultimate is God, and not the moral law regardless of God, something else is asked of us here on the moral heights. It is as if we would do without God, if we could. Kant fits my description here in the sense that religion is not the ground of the ethical, even though he claims morality can lead to God. Remember for Kant we must do our duty regardless of God, without reference to God. And if moral duty leads us to postulate God, this God is not the God of the first great command. Kantian man must dare to know, and dare to do his duty, but this is not the daring of love. The transmoral audacity of the agapeic God receives no reverence. Kant's God fills out the moral system such that the scandalous disjunction of virtue and happiness in immanence is not to remain scandalous. The moralistic use of God risks making morality itself the counterfeit double of God.

(I would not accuse Levinas of offering a counterfeit double of God, but I do have worries about how the ethical relation in his thinking seems to take over the whole of the religious relation.)

The aestheticization of the image — is there a counterfeit doubling here?
There is something inherently equivocal about the image: its double-ness, indeed its possible plurivocity, cannot be reduced without re-mainder to univocity. What if we take this to be the truth of the image: that it has no truth, that is, that the truth of its truth is un-truth. Then we will be inclined both to elevate the image, as what we have by way of essential expression, while at the same time depreci-ating any claims to truth made on its behalf. This is particularly a temptation when people recoil from very strong claims made on be-half of religious images: such claims are now seen as reflecting a domineering dogmatism that would impose its (allegedly arbitrary) will on human freedom. We find this aesthetic freedom attractive, since it seems to point to depths of significance beyond the flatlands of the univocalized world. Something more in the image seems to call us to our creative promise, and with an openness to otherness we find congenial. Hence the aesthetic influence on religious ways of thinking that want to pursue more robustly this opening to otherness, whether immanent in the self, or between the self and what is other.

There is an aestheticism of the image that exploits its free play with possibility, though always in the background is the play of power that fends off authorities claimed as dogmatic, while for itself it both protects and expands its own space of maneuver. I associate this with someone like Nietzsche: against the moralization of the image that closes down the free play of possibility, we must open up that free play, and, in that, release untapped sources of creativity in humanity. An analogous posture is to be taken against the scientistic literalists, the fideist dogmatists, the speculative systematizers. As is to be expected, the artist becomes privileged in this view. Indeed, the artist seems to take on many quasi-religious characteristics: genius as a divine power, the artist as elected or destined for an elevated task, a singular being excessive to mere everyday morality, and all this in the name of holy art and its higher mission.

This involves an aesthetic glorification of the equivocity of the image and imagination, and there are many sides to it.[7] I will only mention that it risks turning the artist into a counterfeit double of the

---

[7] I have already indicated how there are more family likenesses between Kant (postulatory moral deism), Hegel (sublationary infinitism), and Nietzsche (postula-tory finitism) than is often granted, but see also *Ethics and the Between*, chapter 4, where I discuss their continuity in terms of autonomous self-determination and the will willing itself.

priest—the religion of art. There is also the intoxication with human creativity considered as absolutely autonomous unto itself. Art and the religious cannot be finally separated, but if the first substitutes for the second, and seeks to absorb all the power of the religious, we risk falsifying the plurivocity of the religious image. We make art a "saving" power, but the salvation it gives us has a hollow ring when it dissembles its relation to being religious. We make art absolute and end up with nothing absolute. The unanchored power of the human eviscerates rather than creates. See how in our time creation seems to have become destruction: "creativity" seen not in what we originate, but in what we negate. Art's mission becomes the outrage. Today's outrage is tomorrow's boredom, and so the stakes of provocation have to be continually raised—or lowered. We end up numb. The aesthetic becomes anaesthetic.

First we ask too much of art, and then end up asking almost nothing of it. This aestheticization of the image does not come fully clean in regard to its religious power, and especially the mysterious intermediation between human originality and its source.[8] For this originality is an *endowment*.

Imagination as Threshold Middle and Prayer

Needless to say, science, religious faith, philosophy, art, and ethics are all genuine human endowments. The issue concerns how we understand the endowments, and what they serve, what good they serve. By way of conclusion let me offer a last remark about religious imagination and its porosity to transcendence as other that can be clogged by the above counterfeit doubles.

Imagination is a *threshold* endowment. It points to an inward otherness, an immanent originality that emerges into freedom from a source it does not initially determine itself. The giving of it to itself by this other source makes possible its own giving of itself, either to itself in the form of its self-determination, or to what is beyond itself in the form of various possibilities of self-transcendence. In any case, it is not closed into itself on either end: the origin where its source retreats into enigmatic reserves; and what it reaches toward as beyond itself, be this outreaching in the form of aesthetic, ethical, scientific, philosophical, or religious self-transcendence.

---

[8] On this more fully, see *Art, Origins, Otherness*, passim but especially chapter 8.

Kant suggested that imagination partakes of both the stems of sense and of understanding, being their enigmatic root lost in the depth of the soul. The visible as sensible has a root that retreats into invisibility; while our reaching to the sensible as visible also points beyond visibility to the invisible. We might say: Imagination is a middle power, putting its roots down into our own bodies and aesthetic being, and yet reaching up and out to the shared space of more public communication. Between a singular intimacy and a universal communicability, in this regard, threshold imagination might be seen to originally incarnate the promise of the intimate universal.

One can see how important such a middle power must be for being religious, if its roots retreat into the intimate ontological depths of the soul, and if the freedom it begins to release opens up communicability, pointing beyond even the "visible," the "sensible," understood here in the sense of the determinately given, pointing beyond with some clairvoyance of transcendence itself. Its roots are in the intimacy of being, where God is secret; its fruits grow up into the space of the word, where human communicability is, where the works of communication of art, ethics, and religion are broadcast, and where the communication of God also may be. As a middle power, it is a threshold power; but because the middle, like it, is equivocal, its free standing on this threshold is always also fraught with equivocity. Hence the dangerous possibility that true images of the divine will be generated, or idols: a show of the original or a counterfeit double. We make up the main hindrance: we get in the way of ourselves, so to say, and block what passes; and in this, we clog the porosity that allows a way to be made for the communication of the divine.

Imagination is metaxological, as I would put it; but the complex doubleness of this metaxological empowering power can be reduced to forms of self-mediation in which the intermediation with the other is shortchanged or distorted. It is intimate with the origin, but as other in us it attracts us with the seductions of *our own otherness*. We can fail then to let our inward otherness be the passageway for the religious porosity and the other other. I am most intimate to myself and that is that: we have clotted on ourselves in claiming to find ourselves and nothing but ourselves. As an immanent middle power, rooted in the intimacy of being, imagination is a threshold that connects us with the *passio essendi*; but if we wrongly make it only an activist power, we only see *ourselves* on this side of the threshold, and wrongly assimilate imagination to the *conatus essendi*. There is something before that and more than that, and to which *conatus essendi* alone cannot answer.

The threshold rather reminds us of the happening of prayer. Suppose true prayer is the most porous to divine communication: inspiration is graced. One wonders if imagination, being true, and finessed with respect to the counterfeit doubles, can be likened to prayer—if prayer is our being awakened to the happening of the primal porosity.[9] Imagination, like prayer, must woo; but the wooing is less for the divine to hear us, as for that intimate threshold to be crossed; and it is rather we who are granted into hearing.

---

[9] On wooing, see *Art, Origins, Otherness*, 47–48, 288. Eros and mania, and notions like inspiration, enthusiasm, the daimon, and the muse are relevant to the religious roots of the imagination.

5

God Beyond the Whole: Between Solov'ëv
and Shestov

For and Against "All-unity"

The idea of the whole has immensely influenced the thinking of God
in the wake of German idealism. This is not unconnected with the
claim that we live in a "post-theistic" time, and that if we are to have
a God, it should take some pan(en)theistic form. Yet there are fundamental ambiguities attached to the idea of the whole, especially in
relation to God. I want to explore some of these philosophical and
religious ambiguities, with the aid of Vladimir Solov'ëv and Lev Shestov. Solov'ëv (1853–1900) is considered by many to be the greatest
of Russian philosophers to seek a harmony between religion and philosophy. By contrast, Lev Shestov (1866–1938) was a Russian religious thinker who bitterly excoriated dubious collusions between
religion and philosophy that masked nonnegotiable differences between the two. The contrast of these two figures epitomizes something of the essential difficulty, as well as allowing us to state more
explicitly the fundamental issues at stake. The issue between them
seems clear. Solov'ëv wants philosophically to affirm an "All-unity
[*vseedinstvo*],"[1] claimed to be compatible with the traditions of revealed religion, including Christianity. Shestov acknowledges the

---

[1] In his introduction to *A Solovyov Anthology*, trans. Natalie Duddington, ed. S. L.
Frank (London: SCM Press, 1950), 10, S. L. Frank claims that "the intuition of this
unity determines the whole of Solovyov's world-conception."

first about Solov'ëv's philosophical ambition, while denying the second claim to compatibility with revealed religion. He holds that any surface resemblance between these two belies a deep distortion of the biblical God. Against the "All-unity" (and against what he calls "omnitude"[2]) Shestov protests on behalf of the free singularity of the human, and the personalism of the creator God. If the speculative notion of "All-unity" were the ultimate truth, that God would have to be rejected as a merely relative anthropomorphism.

First, I want to outline some general considerations in relation to what I will call the holistic God. I want to counterpose the sense of the transcendence of God as creator and the more pan(en)theistic sense of the divine whole. I want to underline some considerations of the former difficult to accommodate on the terms of the latter. Second, I will focus on Shestov's criticism of Solov'ëv, and its justice. There is a truth to Shestov's critique; nevertheless, at times it does run the risk of caricature. Caricature has its justified uses, especially if one feels it is urgent to highlight the slippery seductions of certain ambiguous notions. But there are also dangers—and Shestov did not always heed them—of simplifying certain unavoidable demands made on philosophical reflection in relation to the divine. One worries that his protest does not guard sufficiently against relapsing into too simple a dualistic opposition to the God of the philosophers. Is this the best way to the God beyond the whole? Does Shestov help us open up a way between, and beyond, on the one hand a reductive totality, and on the other, an affirmation of divine transcendence insufficiently purged of dualistic opposition? Do we need more than an existentialist protest against the idealistic proclivity to absolutize the whole? What would that "more" entail? Does Solov'ëv's view point us toward a God beyond the whole?

Shestov's struggle to highlight a sense of singularity beyond the whole helps us with these questions, and this will be my third consideration. A fourth consideration will concern whether Solov'ëv is quite as philosophically hostile to the idea of divine transcendence as someone like Hegel. Openness to divine mystery is not attenuated in Solov'ëv. Yet for all that, the question still must be posed as to whether his "All-unity" does lend itself to being interpreted as a counterfeit double of God. Overall, there are considerations in the God of biblical personalism that are difficult to account for on Solo-

---

[2] This follows Dostoevski's use of the word "*vsemstvo*" in *Notes from the Underground*.

v'ëv's notion of "All-unity" and any metaphysical metaphorics of "organism." What would it mean to say that the otherness of transcendence is irreducible? Must we do more than protest in Shestovian terms? Is the more systematic treatment of a Solov'ëvian sort by no means to be repudiated as per se inimical to thinking the God of the religions of revelation? If we are to do this, however, must we not reflect more thoroughly on the *dialectical equivocities* about the divine that are the legacy of the idealistic thought of the whole?

Fifth, in my final remarks I will offer some thoughts on why we are pointed to a God beyond the whole. Can we think of creation as what I call agapeic origination? Rather than a speculative unity do we need a *logos* of the *metaxu*: a metaxology of the between rather than a dialectic of the whole? What sense of human singularity goes with this? Is there a between that holds open the space of qualitative difference of God and creation, which enables creation to be as other while yet allowing communication between the two? Do we need *more* than "All-unity" and rather a community of open wholes that is not itself a totalizing whole? Is not some sense of the *intimate universal* of religion implicated here?

Idealism and the Holistic God

Idealism occupies a crucial importance for Solov'ëv and Shestov, though the importances are opposed. Modern idealism tends toward what I will call a holistic God. It sets itself against any dualism of immanence and transcendence, nature and supernature, and returns to an old view, older than Christianity and its heritage. *Hen to pan*: One the All. This view, profound with meaning both for philosophy and religion, is not only ancient: it names a perennial possibility, resurfacing in modernity in relation to Spinoza, connected to the *Pantheismusstreit*, inspiring great thinkers to revivify the ties binding the divine and the whole. Not surprisingly, *Hen kai pan* (One and All) was the spiritual rallying cry of the youthful Schelling, Hölderlin, and Hegel, the sign of their new "Church Invisible." None of them were ever really apostate to this church. We also find resonances of this holistic God in Solov'ëv.[3] One might say also that a good deal

---

[3] Here is Solov'ëv, from the *Lectures on God-Manhood*, in *A Solovyov Anthology*, 36: "The eternal God forever realizes Himself in realizing His content, i.e., in realizing all. That 'all,' in contradistinction to the living God as absolutely One, is plurality — but plurality as the content of the absolute unity, as dominated by unity, as reduced to unity. Plurality reduced to unity is a whole. A real whole is a living organism. God as a Being that has realized its content, as a unity containing all plurality, is a

of contemporary panentheism has more of a family likeness to this approach than it seems willing to acknowledge.

A particular formation of the *dialectical way* of thinking is important here. For dialectic allows us to think about the many without tarrying with merely dispersing diversity. It claims to let us address oppositions without trapping us in dualism. It claims to open a mediated pathway beyond dualism in the direction of the togetherness of the opposites, and hence toward a more encompassing unity of being that embraces manyness within itself. Overall, it encourages comprehension in terms of wholes which are not reducible to the sum of their parts. At the same time, it claims to allow us to view the partiality of limited wholes as themselves contributions to more encompassing wholes, all the way to the whole of wholes, the absolute unity of the many. What is stressed here is less a denial of manyness as a placing of manyness within what is said to be its fuller context. The true context of all contexts is, on this view, the whole of wholes. The negative, it will be said, is not contradictory to this. Quite the contrary, exposure to contradiction serves the development of a more concretely rich truth wherein the one-sidedness of opposed positions are held together in the comprehensive unification of the embracing whole. God is identified with the whole of wholes.

This view of God as the ultimate whole suggests the ring of rings that completes all finite integrities of being. Nevertheless, we must also speak of *origin* in appropriate terms. The mode of origination in this holistic view tends to favor some form of emanation over creation. Why? Emanation stresses the *continuity* of the world and God, creation seems to underscore their *discontinuity*. The first suggests the *immanence* in the world of the divine, and the whole, or of the world in the divine; the second suggests the *transcendence* of the divine, hence the nondivinity of the world. The danger of the former is the conflation of the world and God; the danger of the latter is the deflation of the worth of the finite world, thought to follow if we infinitely inflate God in value. The holistic God stresses the sameness of world and God, the God of creation the difference. Most famously, Spinoza will speak of *Deus sive natura*; the *sive* will be seen by some as the deflation of God to the world, and by others as the inflation of world to God. Sameness may become an identity robbed of any dialectical difference, and hence also of the "otherness" between the two, even

---

living organism. . . . The elements of the divine organism, taken together, embrace the fullness of being; in that sense it is a universal organism."

as this "otherness" is eternally mediated into the togetherness of the two.

Hegel is famous for his claim that "the whole is the true" (*Das Wahre ist das Ganze*) but he also took pains to disentangle himself (as did Solov'ëv) from an unnuanced version of such pantheism. He claims that no thoughtful person ever was guilty of "pantheism" in the sense of identifying God with finite things. Some of Hegel's disentanglements I find dialectically disingenuous.[4] Hard questions do remain, even if we do place on ice an unsophisticated "pantheism." In particular, the question of transcendence does not go away. It never goes away, even when we want to think the community of the origin and creation. Just as there may be an unsophisticated pantheism that lives off an undiscriminating identity, so there may be an unacceptable sense of transcendence that lives off an unsustainable dualism. But—and this is important—to *identify* transcendence with that dualism does as little service to the truth as to fasten, from the opposite direction, on the identity of pantheism.

Yet, if we ask about what is "inside" and "outside" the whole, it seems we must answer that there is nothing finally "outside" the holistic God. To be "outside" is to be absolutely nothing. To be "outside" is only a relative condition that signals *more internal relations* within the divine whole, rather than any external relation between the divine and the finite creation. Being "outside" is being "inside," but "inside" in a manner that does not fulfill the truth of "being within"—it is "being within" that does not recognize that it is within, and that, as within, is nothing apart from being a part of the absolute divine whole. One sees here the Eleatic view: "outside" of absolute being there is nothing, and it makes no sense to speak of that nothing, for just as nothing, it is nothing. Hence speech about it is speech about nothing: empty sound. And yet astonishingly the sound said to be nothing is yet something—somehow. And seems to have some meaning.

By contrast, the view emphasizing creation—if it is creation from nothing—stresses the difference of nothing, as not within the divine

---

[4] See my *Hegel's God*. An interesting study in contrast might be done between Solov'ëv and Deleuze, particularly given Deleuze's notion of the "One-All," his stress on immanence, his univocal notion of being, and his reverence for Spinoza. Solov'ëv makes some way for transcendence, though not radically enough for Shestov. Deleuze seems to be at one with Hegel at least in this one regard: there is no God beyond the whole.

life, rather as between world and God. God is, and is not the world; the world is, and is not God. And while this "not" separates, it also brings together; for this is an "outside" that conditions communication of a different sort from holistic self-communication. It is communication between others—an intercommunication, not a self-communication, though it is not exclusive of self-communication. The world is not relatively "outside" God, it is essentially "outside" God. Admittedly, it is hard to find adequate words for this "outside," for once one names this "outside," one immediately has to add that the world is nothing "outside" of God, hence nothing without God, and so even in its being something as "outside" God, it is still in community with God, for were it not, it simply would not be at all.[5] Yet, by contrast with the holistic "reassimilation" of world to the source, world does not "disappear" into the creator. Assimilation invokes similitude, likeness, but we can push likeness to the verge of merging into identity. Similitude is a form of participation also but in the holistic view participation verges on the disappearance of difference, like drops falling back into their source, the *fons et origo*.[6] With creation, likeness and participation keep open an essential difference. World and God are not of the same essence; creation is not the self-creation of God. God cannot be cloned.

The question we come to then: Within the limits of this dialectic of the whole, can it make any sense to speak of God *beyond* the whole? To be beyond the whole seems paradoxical, if not outrightly contradictory. For this beyond seems again to be within the whole, since nothing is beyond the whole: there is no beyond at all. This is the point of idealism generally, and especially in Hegel, where finally any *Jenseits* (residual in religion) is completely sublated in the philosophical concept, entirely at home and at one with itself. The defect of the religious consciousness is said to be just that residual *Jenseits*,

---

[5] I discuss this complex "not" that separates and allows communication, this metaxological "not," in "Hyperbolic Thought: On Creation and Nothing," in *Framing a Vision of the World: Essays in Philosophy, Science and Religion*, eds. Santiago Sia and Andre Cloots (Leuven: University Press Leuven, 1999), 23–43. See also chapter 7 of *Being and the Between*.

[6] Something like this is one of the things that Levinas finds problematic about "participation," identified with Lévy-Bruhl and "primitive" holism, animism. We can see Levinas as trying to think of a God beyond the whole. The very title of his work *Totality and Infinity* indicates this. See my "Philosophies of Religion: Jaspers, Marcel, Levinas," in *Routledge History of Philosophy: Contemporary Continental Thought*, ed. Richard Kearney (London: Routledge, 1994), 131–74.

even though the claim is made that the truth of Christianity, as the consummate religion, is just the overcoming of the dualism of immanence and transcendence, time and eternity, the human being and God. To try to make sense of a God beyond the whole seems either to perpetuate nonsense, or else to bring this God back within the whole, and hence not to think the God beyond the whole. It seems a doomed enterprise.

Suppose you object to contradiction here? But what of dialectical thinking, which claims to unify opposites? Why fear contradiction then? Why fear contradiction especially if the being of God cannot be determined in a logic of exclusive opposites, more suitable to finite determinate things? One might equally say: Just the difference of God to finite entities, indeed to the entire totality of finite entities, might point to what cannot be captured in univocal logic. This would signal the necessity to risk the contradictory—contradictory from the standpoint of univocal logic. God cannot be made intelligible in terms of finite, univocal things. My question: does dialectical thinking itself recur to a univocity at a higher speculative level, when it claims there is nothing beyond the whole? Must we not also risk the contradictory relative to this "higher" dialectical-speculative univocity of the whole? Would this not be needed if there was, so to say, a metalogical otherness of God beyond the whole, a metalogical otherness that calls for a thinking not only beyond univocal finitude, but beyond a speculative dialectic of whole and part? This would have to be a logic of a *different between*: between finite creation and its origin as other: a *logos* of the *metaxu*, not only relative to the immanences of the given *metaxu*, but also with respect to the beyond of the given *metaxu*: for God beyond the whole is not the *metaxu*, but its original creative source.

Singularity Beyond the Whole: Shestov

In light of the above, what of Shestov's interpretation of Solov'ëv?[7] Shestov is a provoking and inspiring thorn in the flesh of rationalistic

---

[7] This is contained in "Speculation and Apocalypse: The Religious Philosophy of Vladimir Solovyov," in *Speculation and Revelation*, trans. Bernard Martin (Athens: Ohio University Press, 1982). Hereafter *SR* in the text. This essay also reflects Shestov's style, which touches on a wide range of thinkers, including Spinoza, Schelling, Hegel, and Nietzsche. See also my "Philosophical Audacity—Shestov's Piety," in the *Lev Shestov Journal*, no. 2 (Winter 1998): 45–80.

philosophy and its saner securities. He attacks what he takes to be the idolatry of philosophical reason. When philosophical reason claims absolute autonomy, in one sense it is autocratic, but in another sense it is not sovereign at all but servile to a fate indifferent to the singular person. It is indifferent to the person in agony about ultimate good in the midst of often tragic circumstances. Its rational universality ends up hostile to the intimate singularities of life. If there is no standard beyond or higher than autonomous reason, religion and the God of biblical revelation will have to present their case before its tribunal for justification and approval, and perhaps condemnation. Condemnation is the more likely.

Hence Shestov's repeated engagement with Spinoza: father of the subordination of the biblical God in modern philosophy, source of a modern Eleaticism, followed in the essentials by all the major thinkers. Where religion seems to be exonerated, as in Schleiermacher, and indeed in Solov'ëv, Shestov might be seen to suggest that it is a *changeling* that has been patted on the head. It is a philosophical twin of religion that superficially looks the same. It is a *false double*. I take this to be central to his accusation against Solov'ëv. The false double of philosophically reconstructed religion is one that sheers off the beyond of the God beyond the whole, brings that God into the whole, hence makes Him part of the whole, or perhaps the whole itself, but thereby makes God not God. The God that is not God is, of course, an idol. This too, it seems, is the secret sin of the pious Solov'ëv.

I will return to the problem of the false double, or the counterfeits of God, but first I note the connection of reason and the whole. The whole is said to be marked by the immanences of worldly intelligibilities: rational necessities to which reason must submit, such as $2 + 2 = 4$, the dead cannot be brought back to life, and so forth. These worldly intelligibilities, when absolutized, are the self-evidences against which Shestov inveighs. These are the necessities of the whole; and while reason, our reason, seems to master them, in fact they master us: we submit to them, eager to extirpate our singularity. We seem to be kings but in fact we are the serfs of the whole.

Shestov liked to cite the adage of Cicero, repeated by Seneca (*SR*, 67; see also 39, 245): *Fata volentem ducunt, nolentem trahunt*—Fate leads the willing, the unwilling it compels. Shestov humorously likens the philosopher of fate to the drunken man being dragged off to the police station. Is it too mischievous to add a thought like the following? One imagines some philosophers (say, Kant) still trying to keep their dignity as they are dragged; and they say, "Now, now,

I am coming. . . . " They consent, *as if* (*als ob*) they really wanted to go. But at a deeper level, they are *pretending* they want to go. They have no choice, but they want to rescue their dignity by dressing up coercion as free consent.

When Shestov bridled against such submissions to fate or necessity, I think it was in the name of an ultimate God beyond the whole. Shestov names his own endeavor to be beyond the immanences of the whole as a struggle for the impossible. One can see the point if the only logic available is one of univocal unity, or even perhaps a more sophisticated logos that speaks of the dialectical self-becoming of the one or the whole, such as we find in Hegel. The possible, then, seems exhausted by what happens, or what might happen within the whole. There is no possibility beyond the whole. Beyond the whole impossibility reigns—that is to say, nothing reigns, there is nothing possible beyond the whole.

This certainly would be the death-knell of any revelation. For this comes to us within the whole but not from the whole: within the whole but from beyond the whole. That it comes within the whole might easily be converted into a claim that is it just another part of the whole. But then it is not revelation in a genuinely irreducible sense. This is the perennial difficulty: revelation must come within the whole, if it is to come from beyond the whole. Even if it erupts in the whole, and comes from beyond the whole, the medium of its communication is the within of the whole. Hence, even if we defend a God beyond the whole, we cannot be satisfied with a mere dualism of the whole and this beyond. More is required, and Shestov is not always attentive to the problems here, since his style of thinking tends to be "either/or." This will not entirely do, relative to the communication of the God beyond the whole to the whole.

Of course, dialectical thinking, as in Hegel, claims to address this problem, and from within the whole. It claims that since the God beyond shows itself in the within of the whole, it is the latter that is the ontological reality fuller than the God beyond. This last is an empty *Jenseits* prior to communication, and hence once again is *as nothing* without its immanences in the whole. I could show in detail how this move represents Hegel's position, but that is not the point here.[8] The point is that there is a predilection to think the communication from the God beyond just in terms of the immanent whole, and this risks contracting, distorting the truth of the beyond that is

---

[8] On this, see my *Hegel's God*, as well as *Beyond Hegel and Dialectic*.

being communicated. It is just the miscommunication that forgets the beyondness of this beyond, and assimilates it to the worldly self-evidences and intelligibilities, and indeed to human-all-too-human desires, will to power, and so forth. But clearly this is to step on the path toward the idol; that is, if the truth of this beyond is *not to be assimilated* to the evidences of the immanent whole. What then is the truth of the communication or revelation beyond the immanent whole, or the whole of immanences?

This question—not quite in this form—is rightly pressed by Shestov. His questions are intended to unsettle the complacency of thinkers of the whole and the autonomy of reason, and quite rightly. But it is one thing to unsettle, another thing to address the unsettling question. Shestov: a voice in the wilderness of idealistic, rationalistic self-satisfaction; but a voice calling us into another wilderness; and a voice that seems to grow progressively silent as we approach the borders of this other desert, albeit that this wanderer carries the Bible in his hand. This may be all Shestov thinks we can do at this verge, at this entry into a darker beyond. But there may be more to say about that extreme edge, more beyond the oscillation between idealistic hubris and religious protest, and more beyond the powerful complacency of one and the tortured dissidence of the other. Undoubtedly in Shestov's eyes Solov'ëv represents the first option, while Job, Paul, Luther, Pascal, Kierkegaard, and Nietzsche represent the second. But is it so simple?

Shestov's protest is drummed out again and again. Like the drumming of an elemental beat, it has a hypnotic effect. We fall into its rhythm, the rhythm of Shestov's passion. This is the danger: a different kind of enchantment, a different kind of bewitchment under which one can fall. The flood of his passion is moderated by a superb intelligence and an ironical tartness, not to say bitterness. But there seems no stopping this flood once the stream is set in motion. There is something right about this, and one does not want to "tut-tut" Shestov for the fire in his soul when it comes to the religious urgency of ultimacy. I agree: When philosophers smugly assume the role of Job's comforters it is hard to hold one's patience. Yet religious fire does also need philosophical finesse—finesse beyond the sometimes sophisticated rationalizations of Job's comforters.

Consider the suspicion of an element of personal bitterness in some of Shestov's remarks about Solov'ëv. There is something about Solov'ëv he *finds hard to forgive*: his seeming moralism in relation to Pushkin's fate, when Solov'ëv pontificates about the light of providence evident in his justified death, justified because Pushkin was morally flawed. Shestov shows a raw irritation with any suggested moralization of geniuses like Mozart. One might say: The philosophers (shall we say the Kantians?) always seem to have more sympathy with the Salieris than with the Mozarts. The Salieris have *worked* for their reward—they earn it through their own labors, their own autonomous work. They have *a right* to say—"It is mine." The Mozarts, in a way, are helpless through themselves alone. The Mozarts are *gifted*: finally they show—"It is not mine." They play or are the playthings of a power beyond. They are singular exceptions but *blessed* by gifts beyond the measure of human earning; perhaps also cursed by such gifts. Kant revealingly said: Plato is play, Aristotle is work . . . and Kant clearly valued work the more. The satisfying works of immanence are superior to the sudden gifts of a blessing beyond. If such philosophers were asked to choose between the wages of work and a godsend, I fear they would disdain the godsend.

There are other ironies here. Shestov sometimes counterposes *thunder* and *philosophy*. When he despises Solov'ëv's judgment against Pushkin, he hates Solov'ëv's moralistic thundering. But does Shestov not himself thunder against Solov'ëv, and in a manner not unreminiscent of the judge who condemns? Moralistic thunder, religious thunder, philosophical thunder: but the divine flash of lightning brings a humbling silence. Nor is the thunder free from equivocity—a point to be remembered.

Between "All-unity" and the Counterfeits of God: Solov'ëv

Shestov is right, of course: Solov'ëv's thinking was deeply touched by idealistic currents. Furthermore, Spinoza was a lifelong influence, even unto Solov'ëv's later lecture "The Concept of God," in which he comes to the defense of Spinoza and his concept of God. Though imperfect, this concept is nevertheless indispensable for Solov'ëv. Shestov seizes on these commitments (see *SR*, 74ff.), and relentlessly excoriates them not only for their questionableness generally but, in Solov'ëv's particular case, for lack of self-consciousness of what for Shestov is the great issue dividing the God of the philosophers and the God of the Bible. Solov'ëv was of the party of the serpent in the Garden of Eden, as were all the philosophers since. At times one almost thinks that for Shestov philosophy was the original sin, certainly the most deceptive temptation insinuated by the serpent. Knowledge is chosen over life—and God.

We can get in better perspective the idealistic influence in Solov'ëv's holistic approach to the idea of God. Thus his notion of the God-man (*Bogochelovek*) takes up the claimed reconciliation of the human and the divine in Christianity, and he sees this in terms of a movement toward "All-unity" and divine humanity (*Bogochelovechestvo*). As with idealism, opposition and fragmentation are not denied, but they are situated within the compass of a more inclusive unity, toward which differences and manynesses themselves point as their telos. The becoming of immanence shows this movement toward the "All-unity" and the eschatological realization of divine humanity. In the God-man (*Bogochelovek*) the divine and the human are one, and the divine transfiguration of the human into divine humanity (*Bogochelovechestvo*) is already prefigured. And one can find numerous instances in which the model Solov'ëv uses to describe the final community, or the ultimate telos of divine-human interaction, is one of *organism* (see the citation in note 3), in which the different parts or members are to be assimilated to the integral governing power of the whole.

Admittedly, this "All-unity" is not the block unity or absorbing God that we might ascribe to more univocal and unsophisticated Eleaticisms. Solov'ëv, like Hegel and others, tries to grant some qualified independence to the members of the "All-unity": differences are said not to be done away with, though they are nothing outside their being what they are within the whole. Indeed, the original sin seems to be primarily the self-assertion of difference and singularity over against the whole. In a line of inheritance stretching from Anaximander, the original ontological *guilt of being* is expressed in the daring that affirms individuality for itself over against the whole. By contrast, the true whole preserves the differences of the many within itself. Evil is the usurpation of the absoluteness of the whole by the singular part. Salvation from evil consists in the sacrifice of this false absoluteness and submission to the truth of the immanent movement of the whole toward the consummating "All-unity" which will be all in all.[9]

---

[9] From *The Meaning of Love* in *A Solovyov Anthology*, 173: "God as one, in distinguishing from Himself his 'other,' i.e., all that is not He, unites that other to Himself, positing it before Him together and all at once, in an absolutely perfect form and consequently as a unity. This *other* unity distinct, though inseparable from God's

One notes here Solov'ëv's continuity with the more progressive historical teleologies such as we find in idealistic thought. One is also struck by the song of praise he raises to August Comte in which he comes close to identifying his own divine-human "All-unity" with Comte's Great Being — Humanity as the *Grand Être*. This absolutization of humanity might strike some of us as a supreme idolatry of the human, but such a worry seems not to have strayed enough across Solov'ëv's mind (though, as we shall see, this is not true of his sense of ominous foreboding toward the end of his life). He is intent on relating Comte's *Grand Être* to his own claim about the suprapersonal character of the divine being. I think Solov'ëv's blindness to the idolatry of Comte's *Grand Être* is analogous to Shestov's blindness to the idolatry of Nietzsche, whose will-to-power he astonishingly identifies with Luther's *sola fide*. I return to this below.

Nevertheless, there are some indications counter to the undoubted influence of the holistic God on Solov'ëv. One detects significant differences of tonality from Spinoza, as well as Hegel and Schelling. I mean especially Solov'ëv's explicit religious commitment to a community of worshippers — proximately the Orthodox Church and more inclusively the universal church. While his language describing that community might rely too heavily on the idealistic whole, and the God of the whole, something of these other commitments produces (in my mind) quite a different effect than the reading of Spinoza and other philosophers of the whole. I would say that participation in the intimate universal of a worshipping community puts brakes on the temptation to render the "All-unity" in terms closer to a homogeneous, neutral, impersonal universal. Solov'ëv might seem to be innocent of some of the more intractable difficulties here, but Shestov in no way adverts to this dimension. Solov'ëv's commitment is to the Christian community, expressed in his challenging effort to think the ecumenical community. It is closer to this that his heart lies rather than to the idol of rational necessity or indeed the holistic God of idealistic philosophy.

---

primary unity, is in relation to God a passive, feminine unity, for in it eternal emptiness (pure potency) receives the fullness of the divine life. But though *at the basis* of this eternal femininity lies pure nothing, for God this nothing is eternally concealed by the image of absolute perfection that He bestows upon it. This perfection, which for us is still in the process of being realized, for God, i.e., in truth, actually *is* already. The ideal unity toward which our world is striving and which is the goal of the cosmic and historical process cannot be merely a subjective idea (for whose idea could it be?), but truly is the eternal object of divine love, as God's eternal 'other.'"

There is a genuine tension of these two: not only in relation to the irreducible character of robust otherness and the inherent worth of plurality itself in the ecumenical community, but also relative to the belief that there is a God beyond the whole. I mean if the ecumenical community is thought as "All-unity," then we risk shortchanging the otherness of the divine; and maybe for that reason also, we might not be able to do justice to the full affirmative worth of difference and plurality *within* the ecumenical community itself. Likewise, the ultimate transcendence of God might be so radically immanentized in the worldly "All-unity" that the putative ecumenical community becomes but the *seeming* of the most exalted: a community that *poses* as the highest, but its posing is imposture, and hence this highest risks really being the lowest, that is, an idol. I think this is the problem that Solov'ëv began to suspect. It is not as simple as Shestov's reason versus revelation, or the God of philosophy versus the biblical God. It is the perplexity, perhaps even more intractable, concerning the *counterfeits of God*, and the counterfeits of the absolute community.[10]

This is related to the problem of the anti-Christ, a problem more intractable than the terms of Shestov's critique allow. Here it has to do with the holistic god usurping the God beyond the whole. This is not simply the usurpation of rational philosophy, but a more intimate and radical usurpation of spiritual *superbia*. This is a *superbia* that takes worldly form in the claims to initiate the absolute, the ultimate community within the whole of immanence itself. Solov'ëv's sense of Apocalypse, and immanent catastrophe—and the foreboding of some such catastrophe seems to have overtaken him toward the end of his life—is with respect to the suspicion that the god of the whole is really this monstrous idol. The idol is incarnate in the projected ideals of certain forms of worldly community itself, forms that in mimicking religious community threaten its corruption.

I will come back to this, but I want to continue to ask if there is more to Solov'ëv's doctrine than the "All-unity," and hence some

---

[10] In *A Solovyov Anthology*, section 2, "The Essence of Christianity," is an extract from the article entitled "On Counterfeits" (1891; see 253). Solov'ëv speaks of pseudo-Christians, and the counterfeits of Christianity (see 48–51). See also 68–71, where he speaks of the medieval worldview, pseudo-Christians and the casting out of devils; also 80ff. on the union of the churches where one might connect the issue of heresy with the finesse needed to discern the counterfeits of Christianity; and these again with spiritual power and worldly dominion. These all connect with the issue of the anti-Christ.

sense of the God beyond the whole. What of the doctrine of *Sophia* here? Putting to one side a number of complex issues of its meaning and justification, does not the formulation of such a doctrine testify to a power *between* God as the ultimate other and the finite between as the milieu wherein the community of the human and the divine is coming to be? Is not the doctrine of Sophia a pointer to a *middle between* utter transcendence and an otherwise godless immanence?[11] One might wonder if the doctrine of the Mother of God, *Theotokos*, perhaps takes up some traces of mother religion, even the pagan love of Gaia, over against an utterly aloof father who simply stays aloof, as a God beyond the whole. This latter beyond is easily set then in opposition to immanence, resulting perhaps in either an utterly un-mediated transcendence of mystical negation or the finally redundant transcendence of the deistic divinity. The mother Sophia—one sus-pects this would be for Shestov just another idol. But why not a name for a community of wisdom and love *between* the God beyond the whole and the divine-human community coming to be within the fi-nite whole?

That aside, the focus in Solov'ëv is not on the beyond of the be-yond suggested as the necessary other side of this Sophia. The focus is on this side. But then is not the doctrine of Sophia, especially in its feminine and maternal metaphorics, as *intimately personal* as the dominant paternal metaphorics of the Old Testament transcendence that seems to be Shestov's preferred emphasis? Some might call this pagan idolatry, but is not God the divine mother also an image ap-pealing to the deepest intimacy of our being as singular persons, loved personally and intimately and singularly? One can call upon one's mother as much as on one's father. Indeed the love, in a sense, is more in a fleshed bond, hence has an incarnational dimension that is mediated through less intimate embodiment, as via the father. So-lov'ëv: love of the mother, and the feminine? Shestov: love of the ab-sent father?

And Solov'ëv in his spirituality had an intensely aesthetic, embod-ied sense of the feminine Sophia. One recalls his visions of Sophia and their life-changing power for him. I think of his final vision in

---

[11] Sometimes creation was viewed in a related way: the divine Word (Son) as exemplar; wisdom as similitude, eternal reason turned toward finite creation. This difference of the Word turned back to the origin (Father) and wisdom turned toward creation might be seen as intending to *keep open the ontological difference* of Creator and creation.

the *desert*. Solov'ëv answered a call in a manner that makes no rational sense: he decamped from the British Museum and its sober civili-
ties for the dry deserts of Egypt, where he was captured and robbed
by Bedouins, and then granted, upon being released, his third vision
of Sophia.[12] Such an adventurer does not quite answer to Shestov's
depiction of the philosophers as risking the idolatry of the rational
concept. Shestov praises the prophets and others who had a "God-
craziness," but surely if we take note of the extraordinary influence
of Solov'ëv's visions, we must at least ask if his name too must be
entered in the lists of those set on fire by a *theia mania*. And this, even
though Solov'ëv might then try to make sense of this fire and madness in the idealistic language of the "All-unity."

These existential and spiritual, indeed mystical sources of Solo-
v'ëv's quest are not really taken into account by Shestov. Solov'ëv
knew poverty—he owned nothing, and lived often as a wanderer, the
beneficiary of the generosity of friends. Perhaps he knew something
of the poverty of philosophy. Moreover, he was sometimes seen to
be in the Russian tradition of the "Holy Fool"—touched by idiot wisdom. There are times when one wonders if Solov'ëv has more claim
to be listed among the madmen of God than Shestov: I mean as the
recipient of a godsend, one touched by a blessing of spiritual and
philosophical gifts, a blessing that always brings its torments too. The
blessing of gifts in Shestov's case seems to arise more in torment than
in vision, since it is his deepening dismay with the perceived blindness of philosophers that is his blessing and curse. Solov'ëv seemed
to see beyond dismay. I agree that the language of the whole is not
adequate to this beyond. But to find the better language may be as
much a task for philosophy as it is a matter of willingness to listen to
the sacred languages of holy scripture.

---

[12] See Frederick C. Copleston, *Russian Religious Philosophy* (Notre Dame, Ind.:
University of Notre Dame Press, 1988), 82–83. These visions were felt as a call to
explore the idea of "All-unity," since Sophia as beauty holds all in one. If this is a
speculative construction, one would also have to ask about its *liturgical* sources.
See Copleston, 87–88, on the icons of Wisdom, and on Florensky relative to the
seventeenth-century liturgical Office in honor of Sophia as divine wisdom at Nov-
gorod—Feast of the Dominion of the Blessed Virgin on August 15. I cannot recall
any reference in Shestov's writings to the possible liturgical sources of some philosophical thoughts. One might look at speculative thought differently in this light.
See Catherine Pickstock's excellent book *After Writing: On the Liturgical Consummation of Philosophy* (Oxford: Blackwell, 1998).

Perplexity About the Anti-Christ

Dismay brings us back to the problem of the anti-Christ, as it does to the God beyond the whole.[13] Shestov briefly grants at the end of his essay that there is a generally acknowledged "change of mood" in Solov'ëv's last writings. He spends little time on it beyond suggesting Solov'ëv's complete repudiation of his earlier work, and his discovery that the God of speculative philosophy was dead and not the source of life. Shestov is willing to grant that a new going out into the darkness and the desert is suggested, like Abraham not knowing where he is going, and not asking either. I think this is to the point, but the matter is more complex still and indeed full of peril.

First one has to grant here a certain continuity in Solov'ëv's thought, in the following regard. One has to take account of Solov'ëv's concern for the church and its claim to be the *ultimate community*. The church may claim to be this community in spirit but it is also a worldly reality, and always has been. Here there may be opportunity, but also always tremendous danger. If this community is beyond the whole of immanences, it is also resident within the midst of these immanences: it is within and without; it is a *meta* in the double sense of the Greek: in the midst but also beyond.

These are not the terms of either Shestov or Solov'ëv, but they help us to see the present difficulty. The intertwining of spiritual community and forms of worldly power is also inseparable from Solov'ëv's lifelong concern with ecumenical community. One might say that the problem of power takes its most ultimate form with regard to the anti-Christ. The problem of the anti-Christ is the problem of *superbia* as the usurpation of spiritual power. This is not the question of the "All-unity" as putatively reconciling the human and divine. It is the *production of the counterfeits of God and the usurpation of reconciliation* in the form of communities that have all the appearance of being ultimate and unsurpassable. Think here of how there is nothing beyond that is envisaged by the last Emperor of the world in Solov'ëv's story of the anti-Christ. There seems nothing beyond this *nec plus ultra* of spiritual-worldly power. Those who will not bow to this last Emperor do so in the name of a Christ beyond this *nec plus ultra*. Their faith is in a God beyond this power claiming "nothing beyond."

---

[13] Copleston notes in *Russian Religious Philosophy*, 47, n. 13: "According to his nephew, in the last year or so of his life Solov'ëv experienced several 'visions' of the devil or the principle of evil." These visions of evil are perhaps the dark double or twin of his younger visions of Lady Sophia.

If we consider the three temptations of Christ in the desert we are here primarily concerned with the third temptation—this I think of as the temptation to spiritual power, or the usurpation of spiritual power. First temptation: Turn stones into bread. This might be called the first temptation of will-to-power to minister to human desires for contentment and domestic comfort. Call this the will-to-power of Nietzsche's last men. Maybe today we might call it the temptation of perfected technology. Second temptation: The tempter shows Christ the cities of the world: You will be master of these. Call this the second temptation of will-to-power: dominion over the earth, expressed in political rule. You will become Caesar. Third temptation: Throw yourself down and the angels with bear you up. This is will-to-power as commanding the powers: this is the temptation of spiritual pride. It is higher and more perilous than the will-to-power of the last man and the will-to-power of the political lords. It is beyond the rule of Caesar, and the cities of man, and in struggle with the ultimate powers: this is the highest struggle, spiritual struggle. This last temptation of Christ is also, I think, Nietzsche's great temptation. It is a temptation that he felt in relation to Jesus: namely, to decide the issue of superiority of spirit. As we know, Jesus refuses the temptation, saying one should not tempt the one Lord and God. There is a freedom from spiritual pride, as well as consent to the ultimate. There is a more ultimate other: God as an agapeic giver of all, but not the all. There is none of this in Nietzsche: No God and no man above me! And no Christ above me either! *Non serviam!*

Relative to this third temptation, there can be a spiritual violence involved that even the storm of Shestov's polemic cannot quite match. One wonders if he fully appreciated this, not least because he seemed incapable of seeing Nietzsche as anti-Christ: this means as incarnation of this temptation to spiritual *superbia* that claims a superiority to Christ, as well as claiming to be Christ's higher successor and replacement (on this, see Chapter 6). But this is the concern of Solov'ëv: he clearly indicated that the issue with the last Emperor, this superman, is spiritual pride, growing out of the absolutely extraordinary character of his gifts. It is at the highest level of blessing that the greatest danger of curse and corruption emerges—and the greatest struggle also. Solov'ëv's last Emperor also sees himself as Christ's successor and replacement. Indeed when he receives no confirming sign from heaven, his admiration of Jesus turns into envy and hatred. When the last Emperor freezes into despair, he throws himself from a cliff; but he is then unexpectedly saved and borne aloft by a power who anoints him as his only son. That power is not the power of God. We are dealing with a double of the third temptation and the giving of powers that save but do not save.[14]

It is impossible not to think of Nietzsche when reading Solov'ëv here. In the last years of his life Solov'ëv was disturbed by implications stemming from Nietzsche's thought.[15] Solov'ëv is concerned with the equivocal promiscuity of spiritual power and worldly dominion, concretely embodied in a counterfeit of ultimate power and absolute community. This is not discontinuous with his previous work, though perhaps some of the dismay comes from a blindness to, or underestimation of, or even earlier complicity with what was at play here. One cannot but wonder if Solov'ëv is doing some penitential work for himself in writing his story of the anti-Christ.

What is at play is not outside the churches, but intimately in them, to the extent that they are less servants of God as they are incarnations of a "god" tempted with the usurpation of God. If we have some presentiment of God beyond the whole, and of the qualitative difference between finite creation and the absolute origin as other, then this dismay will never entirely leave us. Just in that difference there is given the promise of the highest freedom but also the most infernal temptation; and both are granted to freedom by the allowance of the agapeic origin or God.

Put differently, against the dialectical-speculative overcoming of their difference as claimed by the idealistic philosophies of the whole, there is here (for Solov'ëv perhaps) a realization of the *difference* of the City of God and the City of Man (Augustine). In time, these two cities will be always promiscuously mixed. Time is just that mixture, or the medium of that mixture, of weeds and wheat, sheep and goats. The last judgment is not the judgment of time (contra Hegel who, borrowing from Schiller, said that *die Weltgeschichte ist das Weltgericht*). Apocalypse is the realization of the truth of that difference. The problem is not only the counterfeits of God but of the City of God. These counterfeits are now made by man for man: autonomously, with repudiation of transcendence as beyond and other to our auton-

---

[14] See the story in *A Solovyov Anthology*, 231, on this incident. See also Chapter 6 below.

[15] See Nell Grillaert's very helpful "A Short Story About the *Übermensch*: Vladimir Solov'ëv's Interpretation of and Response to Nietzsche's *Übermensch*," in *Studies in East European Thought* 55, no. 2 (June 2003): 157–84. I want to thank Philip Gottschalk for his help on this matter.

omy. The counterfeits seem to look just like the divine original, or seem to realize in truth the promise of the divine original. For they are made historically concrete in the name of the highest moral ideals.

Thus in Solov'ëv's story, the last Emperor is unimpeachable in terms of his highest moral intent to realize on earth all that is best. But these ideals are inwardly corrupted by the will-to-power of *superbia*. This is also what one fears corrupted Nietzsche. Contra Nietzsche, the problem of the anti-Christ does not bear on the transvaluation of values out of the inversion of the highest values. It has to do with *simulations* of the highest values, which have been inwardly hollowed out. The simulations look exactly like the true thing, but in seeming the same they are radically other. They are false originals, so to say. They look like absolute originals, and pass for true currency, but they are without any ultimate resources to back their claim. There is no credit or faith to be invested in them, though they present themselves as the most credit-worthy. They appeal for confidence, but work a confidence trick rather than deliver true reliability. Lucifer is the bearer of light (*lux*) who, as *light simulating the light*, becomes the ape of God, and does so at the highest level of *spiritual mimicry*.

Parodia Sacra

What is here enacted is a *parodia sacra*: a parody of the sacred that may not even know or acknowledge that it is such a parody. This parody of the sacred rebounds on itself, if it is the aping of God. The perplexity of the anti-Christ revolves around just such a *parodia sacra*. Nothing is more full of holy irony than the fact that Nietzsche enacted just that *parodia sacra*, all the while thinking that his message was spiritually superior to the teaching of the holy he parodied. The anti-Christ is the sacred parody of Christ, but there are sacred parodies that are also desecrations.

Solov'ëv had developed an idea of the superhuman (*sverkhchelovecheskoe*) well before Nietzsche's *Übermensch*, and before Nietzsche's idea had gained currency in Russia from the 1890s onward. The superhuman Good (*sverkhchelovecheskoe Dobro*) is to be associated with God, and the appearance of the superhuman in the God-man (*Bogochelovek*).[16] The question of counterfeit doubles emerges here, and it

---

[16] On this see Nell Grillaert's art. cit., 159ff., and see also 178, note 11, where she points out that the Russian *sverkh* implies a qualitative elevation of the human, hence the word *sverkhchelovek* "signifies an improvement, a perfected state of the human

troubled the later Solov'ëv. The fact is that Solov'ëv's idea of the superhuman (*sverkhchelovecheskoe*) and Nietzsche's *Übermensch* seem to be very like doubles of each other. Yet while seeming very close, they are entirely opposed: in the refusal of God in the second, and in the impossibility of the first without God.

One thinks of Dostoevski and the mirroring between those who seek the God-Man and those who seek to realize the Man-God: the mirroring can mask a qualitative difference in seeming likeness. A *parodia sacra* can be a mirroring likeness that reflects an original, but the directionality of the spiritual energy is *reversed* between the two. Shestov seemed to have been entirely asleep to the possibility that Nietzsche's will-to-power, in terms of just such a reversal, might have harbored a form of spiritual monstrousness. And this from the standpoint of faith in the God of biblical personalism to whom Shestov wants to recall us. Nietzsche himself, in fact, was much more aware of what is at stake and indeed one fears that he went more than halfway to embrace the monster.

The problem of counterfeits is a major one with forms of *postmodern thought* that deny any originals and affirm only images. The images are images of nothing but other images and there is no original. What results? If there is no original, is there any image then? Or is it that the image seems to image only itself, and hence mimics an absolute being for itself? Or if there is no original as other, and the image is the image of nothing but itself, is it not then just the image of nothing? Is not then the image that mimics absolute being for self nothing but an image of nothing? But is this not an idol: an image that seems everything and is nothing? If so, does not this postmodern issue bring us round again to religion, even while we seem to be going away from religion? The idea of an idol makes no sense finally outside of religion. And the question comes to us: What do we love as ultimate and original? If the answer is nothing, we are still in the condition of nihilism. How then do we read the equivocal images? Nietzsche is said to have brought us to the twilight of the idols, but did he? Or did he manufacture a new idol?

I think one can connect this deep equivocity with the import of Solov'ëv's last vision: the corruption of moral good (universal community turned into its counterfeit double) through spiritual corrup-

---

type." By contrast, the German prefix *über* points to what is "above," "over," "beyond"; hence the *Übermensch* can refer to something higher above humanity, or beyond humanness, in which the merely human is somehow overcome.

tion (spiritual *superbia* as the counterfeit double of spiritual power). In its own way, postmodern thinking might be seen to beckon back to an elemental condition: being in a glass darkly. This is our religious condition—as seeking God. The problem of the counterfeits, one might say, is not at all the "death of God" but blotting out the light in the dark glass, and it is not that we no longer see, but that *we no longer seek*. For one might be in the dark and seek even while not seeing. But not to seek at all: this would be the attempted closure of our porosity to the divine. Something like this thought appalled Shestov, though he blamed it too much on "philosophy." There are forms of postmodern thinking, deriving from Nietzsche mainly, that seem so to exult in equivocity that they no longer seek. We must seek the finesse needed to discern the divine in the equivocity. Otherwise we lack any intimation of the divine. We lack the urgency that what we most require is what we most lack: true divination.

Comte provides an illuminating illustration of this matter of the sacred simulacra or parodies. Solov'ëv, as I mentioned, was once taken in by Comte's vision of Humanity as the *Grand Être*. Comte is famous, or infamous, for his efforts to propagate the final religion, the religion of Humanity. There will be a consummation of religion in the new positivist "Church," the last and ultimate community of Humanity, and this will be the scientific successor of Catholicism, with its priesthood of scientists, its liturgical calendar of the great heroes of Humanity, and the supreme positivist Pontiff above it all, Comte himself. Perhaps Solov'ëv, at the end, was doing penance for being taken in by something of this *parodia sacra*.

Dostoevski's Grand Inquisitor, of course, also brings up the issue of the counterfeit doubles of Christ. Solov'ëv was himself intimately related to Dostoevski who, it seemed, attended his lectures on God-manhood, and who took Solov'ëv as the original for his character Alyosha Karamazov. Solov'ëv's story of the anti-Christ is impossible to read without thinking of the Grand Inquisitor. And this despite the fact that Shestov derides his silence about Dostoevski after his death. Yet clearly the Grand Inquisitor is also bound up with the perceived Caesarism of the Roman Pontiff. I think of Nietzsche's image of the highest will-to-power, the *Übermensch*: A Roman Caesar with the soul of Christ. The Grand Inquisitor: A Roman Pontiff without the soul of Christ. (I come more fully to Nietzsche's image in the next chapter.)

Once again one cannot gainsay Solov'ëv's longtime concern with the relations of the Eastern and Western churches, and his views of the primacy of the See of Rome. These concerns are not merely "ec-clesiastical" in a narrow sectarian sense. Quite the opposite, they have to do with catholic community beyond sectarianism, in image of the God who is beyond all sects, and cannot be reduced to the terms of any particular human community. Solov'ëv is on the side of those who refuse the gifts and temptations of the last Emperor. Yet their resistance seems senseless, since this ruler has got the whole world in his hands, and there seems nothing else beyond. He is the worldly god of the whole. (Hegel says one must honor the state as an earthly-divinity—*ein Irdisch-Göttliches.*) This worldly god seems to have all moral justification on its side: its ideals seem morally noble in the highest sense, for it is *the good of the whole* that it is working toward and is in the process of realizing here and now. This seems senselessly rejected in terms of a faith in Christ and the God beyond this whole, whose kingdom is not of this world. Is this the apocalyp-tic realization that seems to have struck Solov'ëv, and with an intima-tion that catastrophe might have been in the making?

You might say Nietzsche also had this intimation, but his own prognosis and cure contribute to and embody the coming catastro-phe. I mean the mushrooming of the will-to-power to monstrous pro-portions. Shestov is incredibly blind to the potential for corruption contained in this Nietzschean view, and indeed the corruption that is already there, if one accepts that there is finally an absolute qualita-tive difference between Christ and Nietzsche's anti-Christ. Nietzsche succumbs to the third temptation that Christ rejected with the words that affirm there is only one God. This returns us to a radical mono-theism, but this One is not the "All-unity" of the becoming of imma-nence toward its own self-completion. It is God beyond the whole, as always qualitatively other to finite entities, even while being with them in the most intimate of communities, even in the undergoing of death itself. I take this to be part of what the word "Father" means. There is One beyond the whole, yet more radically intimate to the whole than any being within the whole, who cannot be captured in the languages of the holistic God.

Nietzsche speaks the language of a superior will-to-power rather than the pan(en)theistic language of idealism. But he is not averse to the latter in so far as he seems (in *Will to Power*) very sympathetic to a new pantheism. This is not the rational whole of idealism, but the rhapsodic Dionysian whole of will-to-power and *Amor fati*. The world is this ring of rings with nothing beyond, this self-differentiating and self-gathering "monster of energy" (*ein Ungeheuer von Kraft*), as he puts it in a very revealing image. We glimpse the other side of this monster at the end of *Thus Spoke Zarathustra* ("The Intoxicated Song") when Zarathustra speaks of all things being enchained with each other, in love with each other. How this monster and this love join together, or are perhaps the same, remains a mystery ringed around by two riddles.[17]

In sum, the anti-Christ has to do with the *equivocity of the divine*, raised to the highest pitch of spiritual tension. This equivocity cannot be separated from the *beyond* of the divine. In other words, *transcendence is not transparent* in the whole: it shines in and through it, as in a glass darkly. In a glass darkly: but all this darkness seems to evaporate in the holistic God (see, for instance, Hegel's *Aufhebung* of religious *Vorstellung*). To attend the dark glass in the spirit of truth: this is the struggle for watchfulness, for mindfulness of the God beyond the whole, in and through the equivocal signs within the immanent whole.

Pascal is right in relation to *disproportion*: there is no *one whole* of the human being and God; for that whole would then claim to be more than God, and there is no such "more." God is the unsurpassable "more," beyond which nothing can be thought, but which is beyond all our human thought of the whole. We are between the finite whole and this unequal "more": between the finite world as an *open whole*, and a more radical transcendence that is always itself in its own otherness, even when its being gives to be the finite between as the place of given promise where human community with God is offered.

What do we need to read these equivocities? We need *singular finesse* (Shestov is so far right). But we also need some *systematic* understanding. This will not save us, but it will help save us from false identifications within the matrix of the equivocal mixture of finite being, save us from the indiscriminate identification of opposites (such as Shestov's foolish identification of Nietzsche's will-to-power with faith alone in the God of the Bible). Solov'ëv may not save us here, but he may help.

Shestov's too indiscriminate attack on philosophical reason is not finally helpful in relation to seeing through the counterfeits of God.

---

[17] On this see my "Eros Frenzied and the Redemption of Art: Nietzsche and the Dionysian Origin," in *Art, Origins, Otherness*, 165–208; on Nietzsche's claim that the world is will-to-power, and nothing besides, as a "monster of energy," see 205–6; see also Chapter 6 below, note 23.

We need finesse to do that; but philosophical thought is an indispens- able aid also. For there can be a *philosophical finesse* that is also trou- bled by the idolatries of reason, such as troubled Shestov, tormented him. Shestov has his own philosophical finesse, but his polemic against the idols of reason can have the effect of simply abandoning us in a wilderness of equivocity. There it is as likely, more likely, that another idol will take shape to quell the chaos or fill the vacancy. This may not be the philosopher's idol but some more infernal mon- ster. One can be led into the desert, but there are different deserts. It is just in the desert that the torment of the counterfeits of God makes itself most felt; for it is in our deepest emptiness that idols seem to appear as if from nothing, and tempt us with their different salvations.[18] Who will show us the difference between salvation and salvation, salvation and perdition? This is another side of the radical perplexity the issue of the anti-Christ raises.

To put it another way: we can connect our reading of the equivocal signs in relation to God to the question of the *false prophet*. The ques- tion is not, as with Shestov, just a matter of *thunder against philosophy*; it is also a matter of *thunder against thunder*.[19] This latter problem is also raised to the highest pitch of tension in light of the radical equi- vocity of the anti-Christ. Radical equivocity: the fact that the "same- ness" of Christ and anti-Christ is absolute difference. How then tell the difference, if the "sameness" seems to comprehend all, seems a kind of "All-unity"? If that is the last word, there is no way to tell the difference. Shestov stops us in our philosophical tracks when he sets the *prophets over against the philosophers*. But what when we have *prophet against prophet* (think of Zarathustra against Jesus)? Our quandary then is not merely that of philosophers who substitute themselves for the prophets. It is of *war among pretenders to prophecy*.

What guidance does Shestov give us then? I am not sure he can give us much. He can recall us to prophets in the Jewish-Christian

---

[18] In Solov'ëv's story (*A Solovyov Anthology*, 246–47) it was after fasting and prayer on the desert heights of Jericho that "the union of the churches took place on a dark night, in a high and solitary place," as night's darkness was suddenly lit up with a bright light, and a great sign of the woman clothed with the sun.

[19] The magician Apollonius, apostate Catholic bishop, later to be made last Pope under the Emperor, possesses the power to bring down fire from heaven; he over- awes the waverers with this power, indeed with his ability to command the infernal powers. Thunder and lightning can also be on the side of the powers of darkness. The point again: the thunder is equivocal; it proves nothing univocally; it too re- quires finesse—philosophical, ethical-political, as well as religious.

tradition now recognized as such. But when it comes to the equivocal ethos of our own time, what then? Once again I find it thought provoking when I contemplate what I see as the disastrous misidentification of Nietzsche. In my view, Nietzsche is right to call himself the anti-Christ. If we take seriously all that this entails, Shestov seems unable to distinguish between Christ and anti-Christ: that is to say, he is himself enchanted by the spell of the equivocity of "prophecy." *Within* the war of the "prophets," he seems to be as analogously vulnerable as he claims philosophers are in relation to prophets.

This indeed is why we cannot give up philosophy. No doubt, we need better philosophy: truer to the prophets, more open to the disturbing message of Jerusalem. Can we see Solov'ëv as doing this? Shestov seems so to define the essence of philosophy that it must pervert the communication from Jerusalem. Even if that were necessarily true, which is open to question, one still cannot sidestep the above quandary. More things besides thought may be needed to address this (sojourn in the desert, a radical reorientation of life, say, a conversion . . .), but we also certainly need thought, and hence philosophy.

God Beyond the Whole?

In a final reflection, let me try to gather together the threads of what we have learned of the limitations of the holistic God, as suggested by Shestov's protest on behalf of the God-impassioned singular, as well as by the counterfeits of God called to mind by the last work of Solov'ëv. I will put the matter in terms of six questions, which also connect with my remarks at the beginning about the general character of the holistic God. My remarks will echo some reflections elsewhere on God as the agapeic origin. The language of the whole is insufficient to this God, though maybe we might speak of God as "over-whole," namely, as in excess of every determinate whole, even the absolutely self-determining totality of Hegel and idealism. There is a *hyperbolic dimension* to this over-wholeness of the agapeic origin.[20]

---

[20] See *Being and the Between*, 207–22, on transcendence and the way of hyperbole; see also "Hyperbolic Thought: On Creation and Nothing." An "over-whole," "open whole"—this is paradoxical language: a whole that is more than a whole: a whole beyond the whole: transcendence itself. It is present throughout my work since *Desire, Dialectic, and Otherness*; it is even in *Art and the Absolute: A Study of Hegel's Aesthetics* (Albany: State University of New York Press, 1986), where I am perhaps too indulgent of Hegel, and ventriloquize certain thoughts too much through him.

First, what about the origin of *difference*? If difference is described as a fall from the One, we see it too negatively, or at most as a provisional reality, vanishing as it is arising; and then we see too negatively the prodigious plurality of the world. The very plurality that roused us to thought of the One is put into the pale by the One. Being put in the pale is not entirely wrong, but we want a One that will lead us out into the sun, and give us to affirm, reaffirm the plural.

Second, why the so-called fall into time at all? This has been a question put to Solov'ëv, as indeed to the longer metaphysical and theological tradition which resorts to this notion. Does not this too degrade the temporal, instead of elevating it as the gift of finite becoming in the between? Why does the One have to alienate itself at all, if it is the absolute it is? Why not be one with itself from eternity? Why then temporal differentiation at all? Suppose there is no fall, only the giving of being to the other, being-other as good. Clearly, the language of fall is not adequate to this good. To the contrary, we talk about the *arising* of being in the between. It does not fall; it arises into being; it is an elevation, a floating on nothingness, a lifting to the heights, a glorification of creation. Arising is as if every moment were a resurrection from the dead; or a preserving from the threat of death, a guarding the goodness of beings; as if God were torn by grief for every death, and yet on the instant resurrected the beloved this into the goodness of life. We do not see this steadily in present life; we get glimpses of it. And they do not come on command; they arrive as godsends.

Suppose one were to venture that time is supported on the love of eternity, what kind of love might this be? Is it the love of the agapeic origin that frees time into the goodness of its own otherness? Is it the love of an erotic origin that needs time to be itself the consummated absolute? The holistic view tends to eschew the first for it introduces a pluralism not reducible to a monism of the whole. In *The Meaning of Love* (in *A Solovyov Anthology*, 175), Solov'ëv talks of *amor ascendens* and *amor descendens*, as Plato's two Aphrodites: the ouranian and the pandemic. It is hard, however, to see his view here as fully an agapeic understanding. Yet it is not simply an erotic view as instancing a movement from lack to completion. There are traces of this view: thus *within* the Godhead there is the eternal overcoming of nothing; *within* the cosmic and historical process, there is the temporal overcoming of lack and fragmentation, and the dynamic toward completed unity. But the agapeic release of finite creation as other? And the "nothing" between God and world? And the community within creation and *between* creation and God—as not to be mapped onto holistic terms? These emphases I do not find here.

Third, what of the *necessity* of the arising of the many? Are we restricted to a more standard juxtaposition of sheerly univocal determinism and equivocal indetermination? Is God simply identified with an impersonal necessity that must be as it is, and such that things must be as they are? This is Shestov's protest. In many traditions God has been defined as the necessary being: the being who cannot not be, the being whose essence involves existence. If the arising of creation were necessary in the same sense in which God's being is said to be necessary, it becomes hard to understand the contingency of finite beings in the between. If we recognize some contingency, we are tempted to redefine it relative to the more encompassing necessity. Hence arises the suspicion that contingency, such as we experience it in the between, is being shortchanged. This suspicion has been expressed relative to Hegel. For if contingency is thus redefined, is it really contingency, relative to the mark of nothing, and the openness of possibility to being other, and indeed to the singularity that cannot be fully rendered in the concept of a more embracing universal necessity? Creation as a *happening* ceases to be a happening; it becomes a necessity that could not be otherwise. And all that happens in it is not a happening, but is univocally as it is and could also not be otherwise. *Amor fati*—life becomes a fatalism in which the darker possibilities of contingent happening are canonized as themselves the fated expression of the eternal laws of necessity.

Shestov is engaged with this issue in terms of its repercussions in human existence. If this necessity rules, why do anything that will upset the ways things are? Indeed how *do* anything? Things are as they must be; and what we do counts only as expressing the necessity of which we are manifestations. Quietism, fatalism? These words can be too easily endorsed, as they can be too easily dismissed. For the acquiescence named here *can* draw on a recognition that there is a power in the deeper course of happening whereby things, as we sometimes put it, "come to right." To speak of the fateful need not be entirely wrong, but it is wrong if it ethically neutralizes the ultimate power, and excludes our being cooperators in our destiny, which must be as much chosen, as well as in being chosen.

The importance of the intimate universal is evident here. Destining and destined universality would be no more than a monstrous universality, a quiet indifference the resting face of an enemy, if it merely crushed the singular in its intimate being for itself. An agapeic destiny would communicate, in the intimate universal, the promise of a gift. We must accept the gift, though we can refuse; since the gift is itself a promise, we must serve the good to redeem its promise. Otherwise, the promise of being is crushed by univocal necessity in a resignation not reconciled but merely cowed or apathetic—just as certain sufferings take the light from one's eyes, and make one want to die. Such necessity does not "come to right" but offers the poisoned chalice of death. No wonder then that, as a further response to this, there is often revolt.

Fourth, what is the space for freedom in view of the holistic God? Where is the allowance for the unfinished and the open? Is the indeterminate not engulfed by the self-determining whole? Is not the indeterminate more than mere indefiniteness, offering rather the overdeterminate promise of a self-transcending that is to be realized most fully in the community of agapeic service: transcending to the others as the fullest freeing of human possibility, beyond any circular self-realization? Suppose there are spaces of openness embraced within the holistic God. But is there another freedom not so "within," but released into its difference with all its hazards, as a parent frees the child to walk on its own feet, even as it watches with love as the child stumbles? Without the allowance of its own tottering, would the child ever weave itself into a dancing?

Our notion of freedom is closely aligned with our understanding of God (see Sartre's existentialist dualism and atheism, on just that issue). Is there a freedom beyond consent to holistic necessity? This might look like perverse anarchy to the rationalist, but perhaps it has the greatness of the idiotic in it. The God of holistic necessity frowns on the idiotic, as rationalists would rein us into line in terms of their idol of univocal or speculative necessity. The agapeic God loves the idiotic, and delights in the sweet singularity that dances or dares before it. The idiotic singular is the child of play, and the agapeic God laughs with its pleasure.

Fifth, what of the status of the singular individual? In holistic views there is a tendency to define singulars through a network of differential relations with others, and hence the singular as irreducible center of distinct being is hard to uphold. Its singularity is idiotic in a bad sense, that is, merely idiosyncratic relative to the more encompassing and general context of intelligibility. The affirmative richness of idiotic singularity is hard to understand on this model, becoming something that is vanishing and that should vanish into the more encompassing whole. This also means we miss the promise of the intimate universal. Hence, relative to the holistic God, the singular tends to be associated with *estrangement from the whole*, indeed in some cases as the center of *evil*. In Hegel, for instance, the singular qua particular is the source of evil. The singular's claim of absolute independence as turned against the more inclusive whole, this is the source of evil. The point is echoed in Solov'ëv. One can see the point: the singular as a being for itself can set itself in opposition to all other being, and hence deform the community of relations that still actually binds it to all the others. It can refuse its community with the origin, and with the others in the between. But to see this as evil is barely half the story.

Put with maximum conciseness: *The very power of evil shows a freedom from the whole that is hard to interpret in holistic terms.* This is a metaphysical way of posing an essential perplexity connected with the anti-Christ and the counterfeits of Gods, as discussed above relative to the later Solov'ëv. How can light counterfeit light? How is it that a part within the whole sets itself up against the whole and asserts itself as the true whole? It cannot be a mere part to do this, and hence the language of part and whole is not itself true enough to the evil of the finite whole that stands against the more inclusive whole. Evil testifies to a recalcitrant power that, looked at from the other side of the singular's promise, is the power of a freedom to be for itself, and to be for itself rightfully. Singular selfhood is a kind of world unto itself, not a mere moment of a larger whole. The holistic way paradoxically undermines the fullness of that wholeness, turned in a different direction to the profound abyss of its ontological intimacy, that is, to its divine idiocy. We need a God who can turn the other way.

The idiocy of the singular person is an overdetermined intimacy of being that is not to be rendered in terms of a neutral, homogeneous generality (Shestov's "omnitude" again).[21] The dialectical language of parts and wholes is not fully fitting for this idiotic intimacy. One needs something closer to metaxological terms to articulate a community of open wholes in the between. Nor need we view this matter with a typically Western emphasis on the individual as standing over against the other, and often with a kind of willful insistence on self. The holistic perspective, in common with other views, rightly sees a certain willful self-assertiveness as a block on the true mindfulness of the divine. The assertiveness hardens singularity into a mere knot of resistance to otherness beyond itself, or worse, it exploits the powers

---

[21] On the idiocy of being, see *Perplexity and Ultimacy*, chapter 3.

of being given to it to lord over the gift of creation as other, or other humans whose very existence offends its usurpation of absoluteness. In the East maybe the destructive truth of such self-assertion has been known better than in the too willful West. It has been known in the West, though within a horizon of interpretation where singularity is not an illusory center of being that must vanish for the truth of the whole to shine through. Such willful self-assertive humanity is not the truth of singularity. To come anew to the porosity of being it must pass through a penitential un-selving.

The true idiocy of the singular involves its being as a communicative integrity of existence, and hence its communicative togetherness with others, even in the deepest intimacy of its inwardness. In that intimate idiocy the communication of the absolute other is most deeply felt, if and when it is felt at all. For it is in its awakening that we know the porosity of our being, and come to ourselves as *passio essendi*, prior to *conatus essendi* become will-full. Communicative being is not outside one, but both inside and beyond one, at one and the same time: most intimate to one, most solicitous that one step out of the confined selfhood curved back on itself. If there is a primal porosity to our being, it could not be simply either inside or outside itself, but gives passage between these, and in passing is both. If we must give up a certain willfulness, this willfulness is, in fact, one of the masks of idiotic singularity, whose promise as a porosity of being is here turned away from its community with the other into hollow self-glorification. Such an idiocy, as at the opening of our porosity to being in communication, finds its home as prayer in the intimate universal.

Sixth, what of the character of *community* of God and creation? Obviously the holistic way does think in terms of community, but this is the embrace of a more inclusive whole. The model of the community is the whole that mediates with itself through its members. Ultimately community is ("organic") self-communication, even if the "self" in communication is the divine, or the divine-human. Is this adequate to the communication *between* beings in the finite middle? Or between the origin and the beings in the between? Or indeed between the divine and itself? Surely, the other as standing in the *integrity of its otherness* is necessary for community as more than self-communication. But if so, there is a community of metaxological togetherness that is beyond dialectical self-mediation, and hence beyond the embrace of divine holism. Divine holism does not deny the oppositions in relations, indeed it turns them into the opportunity of a more reconciled community. But all otherness is not opposition, and there are othernesses even in the community of reconciliation that are not merely provisional; they are essential to defining the communication of reconciliation itself. The agapeic origin suggests a mode of communication that is self-communication yet *more than self-communication*, for it is communication of being to the other as other. This other communication is the opening up of creation in its finite integrity as given for itself, and not for the origin that gives it.

Does not this relate to a traditionally noted difficulty, namely, that the holistic way suggests the absorption of the world into God? The world is "within" the life of the divine, and hence both the independence of world and the transcendence of God are put in question. What "within" means is hard to say, as hard or as easy as "independence" and "transcendence." The latter terms, as we saw, do not have to be thought in dualistic fashion. Hence our choice is not between a dualism of the two, or a holism that asserts an identity more fundamental than their duality. There can be a community of the two that does not reduce their duality, without making that duality a dualism. There are doubles beyond dualism and counterfeit doubles, as there are communities beyond holism. There is a pluralism entirely resistant to absorption into a one, but not for all that a source of alienation, or void of the promise of community. This community of togetherness beyond dualism and not reducible to one is metaxological.

In fact, this question of the *absorption* of world into God is only one side of a general problematic of the whole, the other side of which is the *reduction* of God to the world. For we can tilt the identity in the direction of a worldly evaporation of God, as equally as we can tilt it toward a mystical worldlessness which evaporates into God. Spinoza's *Deus sive Natura* is again instructive. This *sive* is equivocal between the two sides. Thus Spinoza was the notorious atheist in his own time, *Spinoza maledictus*. The reduction of God to the world was suspected, especially since the idea of creation was despised by him, as well as the notion of a personal providence and deliberate free will. The one substance seems in the end to be indistinguishable from the mechanism of the materialists. The impersonal universal of geometry does not save the intimate person in his or her singularity.

Now recall the turnabout toward the end of the eighteenth century, the time of the rising sun of modern pantheism: no longer *maledictus*, now Bendictus Spinoza, the *Gott-vertrunkene Mann*. Instead of reduction of God to world, the absorption of world in God, or God in world, it does not matter, for nature seems again divinized: instead of the godforsaken mechanism, the sacred organism that in its naturalness is the living body of the divine. This absorption of world into God, or God into world, shapes a new naturalistic piety of the whole, putatively free of the strain and discords of traditional transcendence and its dualisms. There might seem a kind of intimacy to this "warmer" pantheistic universal, but it finally too is a universal in which the intimate personal as an irreducible singular is also dissolved.

The fact that Spinoza could engender these opposed interpretations, and continues to do so, indicates both a versatility and instability in the identity of God and world, which tells against the equilibrium of the whole. We seem to find what looks more like a dialectical equilibrium in Hegel, but given Hegel's legacy we wonder if his speculative equilibrium conceals the difficulty in a new *dialectical equivocity*. The instability between reduction and elevation still persists. The metaxological way seeks to avoid both reduction and absorption, trying to find the right words for a sense of the One and the plural, beyond both dualism and the self-mediating whole. In this regard, it stands somewhere between Shestov and Solov'ëv. In appreciating these respective emphases, it is other than both in the way it seeks, beyond their respective exclusions or overemphases, in the between of the intimate universal, for the God beyond the whole.

6

Caesar with the Soul of Christ: Nietzsche's Highest Impossibility

Equivocal Philosopher, Philosopher of the Equivocal

Nietzsche has been a companion to my thinking as long as I have tried to reflect philosophically. I read him as a teenager when I first became aware of philosophy and he has come and gone as a companion for over thirty years. It is hard to speak of someone so close—and yet, for me Nietzsche is and was finally distant and alien. If one takes him seriously, it is hard not either to love him or hate him—or perhaps both. Indifference is hardly an option. I record rather a double response: fascination, and yet resistance. How few there are who do not feel something of his fascination? And this not only for the brilliance of his writing; more for being drawn in to the enigma of his character and the joy and pain of his life. And yet resistance is what I can remember as long as I have read him—resistance specifically on the issue of religion and the violence of his "no" to Christianity. One attitude I could never quite appreciate is that of the Christian who seeks to *co-opt* Nietzsche, for purposes oriented finally to an *apologia* for Christianity. Nietzsche should be honored as an antagonist, not as a secret fellow traveler for forms of religious reverence he himself so vehemently repudiated. This does not mean any simple "yes" or "no," or simple "either/or." Nothing is ever univocal in relation to Nietzsche. And least of all his atheism and his piety.

Nietzsche is an equivocal philosopher and that makes him all the more difficult to interpret. Everything deep loves a mask, he confesses. But *that* he takes us into his confidence about the mask should make us wary of everything he says—and not only the surface of what he communicates. For where does the mask end, and the true Nietzsche appear? He tells us he has a second face behind the first, and perhaps another face again behind that.[1] But as with some masked actors, the suspicion comes over one that there is no face, finally. It is all surface, and there is no surface. Of course, Nietzsche did know there was a superficiality itself profound. "Those Greeks were superficial—*out of profundity*" (*Gay Science*, preface to second edition, §4). This is a profound thought about surfaces that, on the surface, eschews profundity. But how respond to such equivocity? Superficially? Or profoundly? What now could these terms possibly mean?

Nietzsche is also a philosopher of the equivocal in being peculiarly adept at the process of reversal,[2] which exposes the recessed, darker side of what presents itself, superficially, as bright and noble. This reversing power he revels in nowhere more than in relation to the Christian: They have a way of rolling their eyes up to heaven that drives me mad—so he submits. They would have to sing better songs, Zarathustra says, to make me believe in their Redeemer; his disciples would have to look more redeemed. Love your neighbor: command that secretly enforces one's own sweet will? Nietzsche is a philosopher of the *nose*:[3] he claims to smell out, in high ideals, through subtle traces and trails, the secret stains of rottenness. Example: the categorical imperative *reeks* of cruelty.

---

[1] F. Nietzsche, *Ecce Homo*, in *Nachgelassene Schriften* in *Werke*, ed. G. Colli and M. Montinari (Berlin: De Gruyter, 1969), VI, 3, 253–372, § 3 of "Warum ich so weise bin": "Diese doppelte Reihe von Erfahrungen, diese Zugänglichkeit zu anscheinend getrennten Welten wiederholt sich in meiner Natur in jeder Hinsicht,—ich bin ein Doppelgänger, ich habe auch das 'zweite' Gesicht noch ausser dem ersten." (*Werke* hereinafter referred to as *W.*) This appears in an initial version of this section, written in October 1888. A revised version was sent two months later to the publisher. My thanks to John Hymers for bringing this to my attention, and for his help in checking references. For detailed analysis of *Ecce Homo* see *Sämtliche Werke: Kritische Studienausgabe*, ed. G. Colli and M. Montinari (Berlin: De Gruyter, 1980) 14, 454–512. I will refer to Walter Kaufmann's translation of *Ecce Homo* in *On the Genealogy of Morals and Ecce Homo* (New York: Random House, 1967), 225 (hereinafter referred to as *EH*).

[2] *W*, VI, 3, 263ff.; *EH*, 223. One thinks of Pascal when he speaks of a reversal pro and con: when we have spoken one truth to the end, then we have to state the opposite truth, and indeed state the opposite truth because of the first truth.

[3] On smell, see *W*, VI, 3, 262, 265; *EH*, 222, 224: A well-turned-out person smells good.

I do not think of Nietzsche as the naughty Peter Pan of postmodernism. He called himself a Pied Piper, but describes Zarathustra as a "Dionysian monster"; he speaks of himself as "calamity become man"—his name will be associated with terrible things, perhaps the most terrible thing. "I am not a man. I am dynamite" (see *W*, VI, 3, 363; *EH*, 326–27). This was a phrase initially used by a critic reviewing his work, but Nietzsche loved what it implied about the explosive power of his thought. There is the irony to which he seems a bit dozy—when dynamite does explode, we are left with shards and bits, not the man. Nietzsche strained to be the assassin of the spiritual ideals of the millennia, yet there is a spiritual seriousness to him, and for which one must search in his postmodern devotees. If this seriousness breeds finally a spiritual *superbia*, this is a pride that springs from a genuine longing for nobility. Nor should we slight the *laughing, mocking* Nietzsche. How could one be spiritually noble without knowing intimately something of the spirit of laugher and mockery—mockery of one's own laughable pretensions, if nothing else.

If Nietzsche was an equivocal philosopher, he was also a philosopher of the equivocal: as much a victim of equivocation, as a master of ambiguity; who wrote a book for everyone and for no one; who spoke to the few but who has exercised influence in a mass sense. I will pass over in silence the academic industry in which the many and busy last men, now wearing the mask of the professor, turn the gold of his aphorisms into the dross of pedantic prose. (If I do that myself: *mea culpa, mea culpa, mea maxima culpa.*)

Deep equivocity also runs through his relation to Christ, and surfaces in the phrase I take as my text: "A Roman Caesar with the soul of Christ." But how deal with this equivocity? Often the dazzling ambiguities of Nietzsche have a bewitching effect. In an exact sense, Nietzsche is a bewitcher: he casts a spell, he works an enchantment. How does the magic work? Often by means of the lure of the extreme, as he himself well understood. We live in an epoch when, paradoxically, transgression has been made à la mode. How is this to avoid ending up as only simulated transgression, perhaps symbolic, ritual gesture? Or even in counterfeiting revolutionary provocations that turn everything upside down but leave everything exactly as it was? To what end then is all of this?

Nietzsche gloried in his transgressive role, and nowhere more than in relation to the received pieties of a bourgeois Christianity. This self-styled untimely thinker proved to be very much of his own time on that particular score. That time extends as much backward as forward. At work in Nietzsche are sometimes disguised because more rhapsodic residues of the left-Hegelianism of thinkers like Ludwig Feuerbach and Max Stirner (*Ego mihi Deus*). His view of religion is not unrelated to Hegel's unhappy consciousness that projects itself into a "beyond." There are remarks in *The Will to Power*, for instance, where religion is connected with our own self-division, with our inability to accept as our own certain unusual and surprising powers, and with their attribution instead to another, a superior other, a divinity. The dynamics of what Nietzsche sees as the nihilistic outcome of Christianity are already to a degree encapsulated in Hegel's version of the unhappy consciousness, for it is *the beyond* that condemns us to unhappiness: God as *our own beyond* is the source of the devaluation of the earth and ourselves. Compared to Hegel, the left-Hegelians offer a humanistic coarsening of the dialectic in a manner that produces a reductionist theory of religion as projection. The dialectical identity of God and man becomes the recovering of the human at the expense of a killing of God as other, leading to a new self-projection into *one's own higher otherness*: the superhuman as self-apotheosis, the transhuman, if you will. The glory of the lord is the project of self-glorification—transhuman, if you will, but there is nothing transcendent about this transhumanity, for it will be entirely immanent. But if entirely immanent, how then "trans"?

On this view, instead of an otherworldly "trans," we require an entirely immanent "trans," that is, the superman must be projected into the future as a *this-worldly* "beyond." Why should we prefer that new immanent "beyond" to the old "beyond"? Why should we not continue to offer trust to the old God rather than to the superman-producing power of the new "god"—humanity? Notice how the somber, even desolate proclamation of the "death of God" in the *Gay Science* (*W*, V, 2, "The Madman," §125) is connected subsequently with an overflowing paean to human creativity, and the now newly opened horizon of the future (*W*, V, 2, "What Our Cheerfulness Signifies," §343). How you make this *transition* from metaphysical somberness to unbridled creativity is not at all clear, beyond suddenly now singing a more upbeat song from a new hymn sheet. One wonders if a postulatory finitism that insists we "remain true to the earth" has done its work, and necessitates this immanent transition to preempt any different transition to transcendence as other to the human, in a divine sense other to Nietzsche's *Übermensch*. And what can *that cheerfulness* signify for us *now*, if the songs from that hymn sheet no longer ring true?

Nietzsche's transgressive magic goes some way towards explaining his power of bewitchment in a culture that still thinks of freedom as unloosing itself from the manacles of the millennia. And yet there is also an urgency of ultimacy in Nietzsche that at times is overpowering. How does one deal with a wizard or bewitcher, or indeed a *seducer* (*Verführer*), as Zarathustra is called (*W*, VI, 3, 258; *EH*, 220)? But suppose one divines that one must ward off the enchantment? Suppose one has the intimation that the spell being cast on one is really a magic stupor from which one must struggle to wake up? Think of falling under the spell of a hypnotist: one loses oneself; one's will is paralyzed; one floats, one has no will. And further suppose the spell tells one that now finally one is waking up, waking up to one's own true will. In truth, such a waking up would be all a matter of sleepwalking. If I am not mistaken, Nietzsche has this hypnotizing effect on not a few, including, marvellous to behold, some of the better minds of the last century.

How then does one wake up? How does one snap out of an enchantment? Can one do it on one's own? One is in a dream and struggling to wake up; one moves one's legs but one does not move; it is *als ob* movement, quasi-transcending. What one needs more than anything is someone or something other *breaking in from the outside*. But what if the wizard or dream has enchanted one with the belief that there is *no outside*? One is tempted to give up on the quasimovement and sink back into the enchantment. And then one is surely lost.

Do I exaggerate when I say Nietzsche does have this strange effect: sending us to sleep, after first seeming to wake us up to ourselves? Charming us with the belief that at last we are waking up and no longer asleep in the nightmares of the millennia, even though waking up is only another sleep or dream? We look into Nietzsche and we seem to gaze into a magic mirror and we seem to see ourselves. We are persuaded to see ourselves as now budding creators, and so we feel irritated with anyone who will deprive us of the mirror and our unprecedented promise of originality. Readers of Nietzsche do not frequently identify themselves with the "many-too-many" he derides. Is this why so many have *their own* Nietzsche: a thinker for everyone and for no one? Before the magic mirror, we all crowd eagerly to admire our own untapped creativity. But as with most gazing into mirrors, this too is vanity—mostly.

One final image of equivocity: Nietzsche has been variously credited with *prophetic* powers, for instance, in forecasting a century of great wars. He did detect delayed effects of an atheism in remission. Still, there are times when I suspect it is more true to say he wrote *horoscopes*. Horoscopes are riddles that seem to tell our fates by the stars. So they mime what it means to be possessed of a prophetic quality. And at times they can seem to answer a deep riddle in ourselves. Indeed they can be quite right, on occasion. But they can be everything, and they can be nothing, depending on what we bring to them. Mostly nothing. And then the prophetic quality turns out to be a platitudinous reassurance of post-Enlightenment impiety—or piety: You too have creative potential that has been stifled by belief in God or by some other at last bygone crudity! But suppose it is not in the stars, but in ourselves? And in ourselves, there too the truth of God—and disaster?

In sum, Nietzsche strikes one as an impossible combination of opposites. I do not mean logical impossibility. I mean the human sense when we say, in a mixture of exasperation and affection: "You are impossible! Incorrigible and lovable at once!" Nietzsche is thus impossible: a mixture of hyperdiscernment and crude caricature; a singer and a shouter. One can value singing and not denigrate exaggeration, hyperbole, excess, caricature. They are sometimes needed to provide effective revelations. But they too have their *protocols*. Nietzsche does not always observe these. Again there is the lure of the extremes: intoxication with exaggeration.[4] I agree: sometimes one has to communicate by exaggeration. Especially in times of urgency, to get people to listen, you may have to raise your voice. People are sleeping. Some sleep lightly—all that is needed is a whisper and they start up. Others are in a deep torpor: whispering will not do; you have to shout to wake them up. I will say: whispering is the language of love; shouting is the language of war. Is there too much war in Nietzsche, too much shouting? Especially in relation to Christianity, we find him barking out his claim. For instance, one notes this kind of style in *The Anti-Christ*: at the outset, Nietzsche is calm, cold, almost icy, but by the end, he is close to being beside himself, firing off in all directions. This might seem to be like a mania maybe, but is it

---

[4] As Nietzsche himself admits in *Der Wille zur Macht. Versuch einer Umwertung aller Werte* (Leipzig: Kröner, 1930), 255 (§374), and *The Will to Power*, trans. W. Kaufmann and R. J. Hollingdale (New York: Random House, 1967), 202: "Plato, for example, becomes a caricature in my hands." How many worse caricatures we might have been spared, if some of Nietzsche's interpreters had had some of his honesty and self-consciousness.

divine? Nietzsche hectors[5] in the name of the anti-Christ; he *curses*. Do not misunderstand me. Nietzsche is also a whisperer; a lover, a seducer; he speaks softly; he murmurs; then he bewitches. And shouting? Shouting means we must return to the question of curse and blessing.

Caesar with the Soul of Christ (1): Vulgar and Superior Will-to-Power

"The Roman Caesar with the soul of Christ." This striking phrase occurs in the following passage in the notes published posthumously as *The Will to Power*.[6] Here is how it goes:

> Education in those rulers' virtues that master even one's benevolence and pity: the great cultivator's virtues ("forgiving one's enemy" is child's play by comparison), the affect of creator's must be elevated—no longer to work on marble!—the exceptional situation and powerful position of those beings (compared with any prince hitherto): the Roman Caesar with Christ's soul.

What is Nietzsche talking about? About what it means to be a creator, and the requisite education in the virtues proper to rulers. These virtues are to include but also to exceed those virtues associated with Christianity. Compared to these virtues of rulers, it is suggested, the Christian virtue of forgiving one's enemy is mere child's play. Yet, it is also suggested, these ruler's virtues exceed certain qualities we often associate with the princes of power—these worldly overlords do not know the height of the creator, so it is intimated by

---

[5] I find this hectoring, barking tone in Heidegger's political writings.

[6] "Die Erziehung zu jenen Herrscher-Tugenden, welche auch über sein Wohlwollen und Mitleiden Herr werden, die grossen Zuchter-Tugenden ('seinen Feinden vergeben' ist dagegen Spielerei) den Affeckt das Schaffenden auf die Hohe bringen—nicht mehr Marmor behauen!—Die Ausnahme und Macht-Stellung jener Wesen, verglichen mit der bisherigen Fursten: der romische Caeser mit Christi Seele." *Sämtliche Werke: Kritische Studienausgabe*, ed. G. Colli and M. Montinari (Berlin: De Gruyter, 1980) 11, 289; *The Will to Power*, 513. Kaufmann mentions his disagreement with Jaspers. For Jaspers, the phrase embodies Nietzsche's tendency to yoke opposites together; for Kaufmann, it is to be interpreted in terms of an ideal like Aristotle's man of *megalopsuchia*. Jaspers has probably the better sense of what is at stake, but neither digs deep enough into the more profound significance suggested by the phrase.

Nietzsche. The imputation is of something *hyperbolic*: something in excess of, though inclusive of, what is entailed by the will-to-power of the princes; something superior to the putative spiritual superiority of those who are superior to the hatred of their enemy.

As usual, Nietzsche is raising the stakes. To say there is something hyperbolic here is not intended as a criticism—not now anyway. Finally everything in Nietzsche has to do with the hyperbolic—and not least with respect to the hyperbolic demand made on human creativity in the projection of the *Übermensch*. We are being directed to the projection of a highest possibility, a hyperbolic possibility in the literal sense of being concerned with the *"huper."*[7] This *"above,"* this *"über,"* seems to embrace the extremest promise of human creativity: highest superiority of spiritual power. In my view, this highest possibility, understood in its Nietzschean modulation, is Nietzsche's highest impossibility. How so? Ultimately, the issue turns on how we judge the spiritual superiority of Jesus or Nietzsche. It also turns on how we understand the Nietzschean modulation of the above possibility. This is no easy matter, not least because there are subtle consonances and dissonances, affinities and divergences between spiritual superiority when this is referred to Nietzsche and when it is referred to Jesus. Finally I have to confess Jesus to be the superior, but how pursue the decision between them in a form that is not merely assertoric, not just a matter of "say-so"? At the least we must look at the deeply equivocal possibilities of will-to-power.

As a first approach, we might glance at the three metamorphoses of spirit unfolded by Zarathustra: first spirit is a camel, then a lion, and finally it becomes a child. The camel stands for the servile yet strong spirit: it obeys, it does not command. The lion breaks free from servility: beyond duty and command, it asserts its own will, though in the more negative form of creating the space for creation, while not itself being fully creative. The child is the third: the self-affirming spirit that is a sacred "yes" and self-propelling wheel; it is a new beginning of the will willing itself.

I think we need to distinguish two forms of will-to-power (this will be further qualified below), call them the vulgar and superior, the

---

[7] On "being above," see Nietzsche's description of the festivals and arts in the ancient world: "They also aimed at nothing other than to feel *on top*, to *show* themselves on top. These are means of glorifying oneself, and in certain cases of inspiring fear of oneself" (*Götzen-Dämmerung, Twilight of the Idols*, W, VI, 3, 151, "What I Owe to the Ancients," §3). See also his "psychology of the artist" and his account of Raphael's inspiration (W, VI, 3, "Skirmishes of an Untimely Man," 110–13, §§8–11).

lower and higher forms. The lower, vulgar form might be described as the will to *impose oneself* on the other, to bend the flux to one's will, to assert one's freedom from impediment—and this by *being above* any constraint on the will expressing itself, even to the point of using violence on the other, as it is appropriated, expropriated. By contrast, the higher form has to do with the freedom of self-affirming will: its energy is less directed to dominating the other, as in the overflow of itself in its own self-rejoicing. Very broadly, the lion and the child give us the metaphors to make the point about these two versions of will-to-power. The lion is, so to say, the more "ordinary" Nietzschean will-to-power: dominating, imposing, inflicting cruelty and violence if necessary, and on the other, as subordinated to one's power. I assert myself but in the mode of subordinating the other, even to the extreme of subjugation and exploitation. Since this sense is to be found widely scattered throughout Nietzsche, it is perhaps the basis for the more vulgar Nietzsche, as the advocate of the blond beast. It might also seem that many of the princes of the world, the Caesars, answer to this form of will-to-power: like all kings they are regal lions.

By contrast, the *more than ordinary*, the extraordinary form, has to do with will-to-power as self-affirming. As with the child, there is a self-affirming that constitutes, in Zarathustra's discourse, a sacred "yes." Note this higher will-to-power is not any release toward the other as other: it is not for the other; it is for the fullness of self-affirming. Clearly, throughout Nietzsche this is what he wants to affirm as the highest: any seeming release to the other must resist any reversion to the camel, which does the will of another, and thus becomes the sly reintroduction of the servile will, albeit disguised as service of the other.[8] Thus Nietzsche/Zarathustra will confess to not knowing about receiving. He knows about giving; and giving out of an abundance. This giving out is in the form of self-affirming; it is not for the other as other; it is the fulfilled power of the child simply overflowing, through being full with itself.

In the case of the Nietzschean creator, it is quite clear that the overflowing of the self full with itself is for purposes of self-glorify-

---

[8] *Der Antichrist. Flucht auf das Christenthum*, in *Werke*, VI, 3, 161–251; I will refer to *The Anti-Christ* as translated by R. J. Hollingdale in *Twilight of the Idols and the Anti-Christ* (Baltimore: Penguin, 1968); see *W*, VI, 3, 178–80; *Anti-Christ*, 125ff., §15, on Christianity as trafficking in imaginary causes, and the implication that the Christian alienates himself to an unreal other that falsifies and disvalues actuality.

ing. This is literally the *apotheosis* of will-to-power. Superficially, the image of the child recalls Jesus's claim about the turning needed for entry to the kingdom of heaven. But the children of Jesus and Nietzsche are very different, just on this issue of highest self-affirming, and release beyond self in which the affirmation of self is not just of and by self and for self. I will return to this below, when I speak of the difference of Nietzsche's version of the gift-giving virtue and agapeic giving. The sacred "yes" to self of the Nietzschean child is finally a self-creation: this is in the line of a self-determining autonomy, albeit rhapsodic rather than rational, which in its stress on self-affirming must always consign the affirmation of the other as other to an equivocal position.[9]

When Nietzsche talks about Caesar with the soul of Christ, he is suggesting something like the union of the lion and the child. But if this child, as Nietzschean, in fact lacks the soul of Christ, we are talking about something that may well be closer to the spirit of the anti-Christ. This is a special name with which Nietzsche was happy to baptize himself. What anti-Christ means as a name for Nietzsche, of course, has its own enigmas. One of the great enigmas here is that it is extremely difficult to discern the difference of the Christ and anti-Christ, since *one mimics the other almost perfectly.* The problem of the anti-Christ is, to put it ambiguously, one of a *parodia sacra.*[10] It is not

---

[9] I see a line of descent from self-legislating will in Kant, through will willing itself in and through the other in Hegel, through the darker erotic will in Schopenhauer, to the will that affirms itself in Nietzsche's will-to-power: the true will that mediates with itself *wills itself,* even if it seems to engage with another. Not any longer the self that submits to the law, but that legislates the law, that creates the law, because as the will affirming itself this will is simply the law of itself (*autonomos*). Thus self-activating will passes from its rational forms in Kant and Hegel, through an industrial productive form in Marxist historicism, through the darker sense of its own origin of itself as origin in Schopenhauer, to its seeming resurrection of itself out of its own Dionysian darkness in Nietzschean self-affirmation. It is the rhapsodic circle of itself. Hence finally Zarathustra's exclamation: How could there be an *"outside-me"*! See *Ethics and the Between,* chapter 4; also "Autonomia Turannos: On Some Dialectical Equivocities in Self-determination," in *Ethical Perspectives* 5, no. 4 (1998): 233–52.

[10] "Cesare Borgia as Pope" (*W,* VI, 3, 249, *Anti-Christ,* 185)—this is a buffoonish version of the *parodia sacra,* though for Nietzsche it is the true meaning of the Renaissance, its only symbol, he says. Cesare Borgia as Pope, for Nietzsche, would be the triumph of life in Rome on the papal throne itself; but this triumph was aborted by Luther and the reformation—Luther restored the Church (*W,* VI, 3, 249ff.; *Anti-Christ,* 185ff.). "Am I understood? . . . Very well, *that* would have been a victory of

that the highest values devalue themselves (Nietzsche's claim about the process of nihilism). *It is that extraordinary mimicries of the highest values are hard to separate from what they mimic.* The image becomes its own original and leads us away precisely from any original other to it as image. But is this not to bring us close to a condition of radical equivocation in which the dazzling image usurps the power of the genuine original—and looks *genuine* by doing so?

Put differently: Suppose the infernal is not coeval with, but *second born* of the divine promise of freedom. Since we humans are in the between, there is always a struggle to discriminate the equivocal image, a struggle to prevent the tilt away from the good. One might endorse Pascal's point here: atheism is an indication of spiritual vigor but only up to a certain point. Or Dostoevski's point: there is an atheism that is just a little lower than faith, an atheism in a way superior to the faith of the many who are too mindless. I connect both points with the perils of our intermediate condition, at the height of transcending, or in the depths of the idiotic intimacy where the soul is alone with God. The vigor of these atheists carries them beyond those who are indifferent to the great strife of the human heart. But they have decided the strife in their own favor rather than in terms of a more radical exodus from themselves into the admirable night of the divine, and the terror of the holy. What is their vigor? Is it their intoxicated fall into bewitchment with the magic of their own demonic powers?

Caesar with the Soul of Christ (2): Erotic Sovereign and Agapeic Servant

"The Roman Caesar with the soul of Christ." Let me try again from a somewhat different angle. I immediately think of Jesus's own words: Give to Caesar the things that are Caesar's and to God the things that are God's. The words are not without their own ambiguities, yet on the surface Caesar and God are set apart. Nietzsche's phrase seems to move in an opposite direction: bringing to unity the figure of worldly imperial power and spiritual (perhaps unworldly) power. This too would be too simple, without some further qualification. If Nietzsche's words deal with his figure of the higher human,

---

the only sort I desire today." Nietzsche repeats the phrase "Cesare Borgia as Pope" in a letter (Brief 1151) to Georg Brandes, November 20, 1888, *Nietzsche Briefwechsel*, 3 vols., ed. G. Colli and M. Montinari (Berlin: De Gruyter, 1984), III, 5, 482f.

perhaps the *Übermensch*, we might be startled, especially in its invocation of Christ. Why? We are familiar with Nietzsche's praise for conquerors, we are familiar with his contempt for Christianity, but we are maybe less familiar with his hesitation before Christ. Certainly in *The Anti-Christ*, there is an ambivalent note of admiration and distance. There was only one Christian and he died on the Cross, we are told; and he had nothing to do with the gruesome mythos of the punishment for sins and justification in another world beyond this life. Jesus was a symbolist of the inner presence of the kingdom of God, a practitioner of a way of life who knew nothing of dogmas and doctrines. He did not know the "no"—he was innocent of the will that stands against, that negates, and in that sense empty of *ressentiment* and revenge. All that unholy holiness begins with Paul, so claims Nietzsche.

"Rome versus Judea." What of Nietzsche and anti-Semitism? We know Nietzsche despised contemporary German anti-Semites, his own brother-in-law not least. Still, I find impossible any *univocal* "yes" or "no" to the question of his anti-Semitism and his anti–anti-Semitism. I am not at all as sanguine as those who would entirely exonerate Nietzsche of any anti-Semitism. There is a more intractable difficulty here. One might speak of a more "vulgar" form and a "higher," more "philosophical" form. Nietzsche admired the early Jews when he claimed their God was a national god, at a time when they had not yet fallen under the powers of the "priest." He also admired many contemporary Jews, not least for their extraordinary powers of survival in hostile circumstances. He hated his contemporary anti-Semites as "vulgar" continuations of Christian *ressentiment*. Nevertheless, his own *philosophical* interpretation of morality risks being a *philosophical anti-Semitism*, in the very specific sense that he wants philosophically to expose or undercut or root out slave morality, which is Jewish first and Christian second. Philosophical anti-Semitism means: depreciation of the Jew and the Christian and elevation of the Greek (not Plato who was a "Jew"), or the Roman ("Rome versus Judea"). Pontius Pilate had a "noble Roman scorn" for affairs Jewish, Nietzsche avers. I will say another word about Pilate's nobility at the end.

This *second* "higher" philosophical anti-Semitism is quite compatible with his hatred of the first "vulgar" contemporary anti-Semitism—in hating that first "vulgar" anti-Semitism, he was also hating the slave revolt in morality; and so in an oddly contorted way, this hatred of "vulgar" anti-Semitism is anti-Semitic in the second, "higher" sense! This is also why his "higher," philosophical anti-Semitism could be turned to coarser uses by the "vulgar" anti-Semites. The "anti" motif runs throughout his work, and specifically relative to Semitic concerns, whether in "Platonic," Jewish, or Christian forms. This "anti" of Nietzsche follows from his naturalism: his hostility to the Jewish arises from its inversion of natural values (*W*, V, 2, 164f.; *Gay Science*, §135: origin of sin—a Jewish feeling and a Jewish invention). This is evident in *The Anti-Christ* in his description of the "gods," as well as of the Christian as "only a Jew of freer confession." Nietzsche even seems to make Jesus a "higher" anti-Semite: Jesus uttered his "no," his "anti," not only against the "Church" and the "priests" but against the "Jewish Church" (*W*, V, 2, 166f.). Once again we find the equivocal stance toward Jesus. For this just cited evaluation seems to be the opposite to what he says in the *Gay Science* (*W*, V, 2, 167; §140, "Too Jewish"), where it is said that "The founder of Christianity showed too little of the finer feelings in this respect—being a "Jew"—finer feelings here with respect to God as *judge*.[11]

Nietzsche's Jesus, of course, is also characterized as closer to the *idiot*, and commentators have noted the striking effect that the reading of Dostoevski had on Nietzsche—the only person who might have something to teach him in psychology, he says. Yet Dostoevski is the artist of such figures as Prince Myshkin, Alyosha Karamazov, Tsarets Zossima, and so forth.[12] Like Jesus, they seem to lack the will that negates, and so in a sense they lack will-to-power in a prop-

[11] For some recent representative discussion, see *Nietzsche and Jewish Culture*, ed. Jacob Golomb (London and New York: Routledge, 1997).

[12] Nietzsche compares the idiot to the genius and hero, the latter being entirely inappropriate categories for Jesus (*W*, VI, 3, 197; *Anti-Christ*, "Against Renan," 141). Jesus was a "political criminal," a "holy anarchist" (*W*, VI, 3, 193; *Anti-Christ*, 140). References to epilepsy and epileptic states, as characteristic of Christians, especially early Christians, are frequent in *The Anti-Christ*. As we know, Dostoevski suffered from epilepsy; indeed it provided him with an opening to ecstasy that both shattered him and left him longing for transfiguration. In *The Anti-Christ* Nietzsche's own finesse often deserts him in these crude "naturalistic" references to epilepsy. Idiocy is counterposed to the *superbia* of a healthy spirit (*W*, VI, 3, 230; *Anti-Christ*, 169, §52). Dostoevski, of course, also created the figure of Raskolnikov who, believing himself beyond good and evil, talked a little like Lady Macbeth, and Nietzsche himself on occasion ("No deed can be undone by being regretted; no more than by being 'forgiven' or 'atoned for.' . . . [W]e immoralists prefer not to believe in 'guilt.'" Kaufmann translation of *Will to Power*, §235, "Against remorse").

erly robust sense. They are almost harmless innocents, on *this* side of the difference of good and evil, not higher men of creative will-to-power, on the *other* side of good and evil, in the innocence of becoming. It is to this last that Nietzsche is gesturing, using this striking combination of seeming opposites to communicate the point.

I think it is questionable to identify the soul of Christ with this idiotic innocence on this side of the difference of good and evil. If there is an idiocy to Jesus, it is a *different idiocy*, on the other side of good and evil, beyond the servile will that defines the slaves in their struggle with the masters: this is the divine idiocy of agapeic service. This service is beyond both sovereignty and servility. In the language I use, Nietzsche's formulation suggests the union of the erotic sovereign and the agapeic servant. What I mean by these terms I cannot fully explain here, but the following can be ventured, particularly in relation to their proposed union in Nietzschean terms.[13]

What I mean by erotic sovereignty is connected with the expression of power in its highest representatives, with the overcoming of the lack in our desire, with the activating of our energies as self-transcending and toward their fullest affirmation. Sovereignty is connected with the desire to be "above," but not necessarily by denial of what is below. Erotic sovereignty does not have its origins univocally in power, but in a mixture of power ("to be") and precariousness (of our "to be"), of the exigence to be and the lack in finite beings. Our self-affirming and elemental insistence of being is inseparable from its lack of its full self. So it is tempted to insist on itself in the face of its own lack, and to overcome its threat. This is to will the overcoming of fear of one's own death. This cannot be accomplished at one fell swoop; for lack returns, ontological lack, and dread of death, no matter how remarkably hidden. *Fear and I were born twins*—said Hobbes. But the birth of the human is also a temporal rebirth, as newly becoming itself in the unfolding of its free power, and with each rebirth the rebirth of new fear, and the new need to overcome fear.

You might say that the struggle for erotic sovereignty emerges out of our being as *passio essendi* which in the present case is not accepted as such. Rather the endeavor to be of our *conatus essendi* seeks to overcome the fragility of our elemental givenness and assert itself as more than the given conditions of life. Erotic sovereignty gives head to the *conatus essendi* as seeking to be the measure of, even to master the

---

[13] See *Being and the Between*, chapters 10 and 11. These notions are more fully amplified in *Ethics and the Between*.

patience of being. In truth, to do this it must dip into the *passio essendi* for sources of energy that carry it beyond its current given condition. Otherwise, there is no self-surpassing. But the self-surpassing itself has the tendency to hide its indebtedness to sources of energy in its own passion of being. For this self-surpassing tends to be overtaken by *impatience* at limits on its self-transcending, and hence the deeper significance of the patience of being is easily lost, or denied, or indeed mutilated.

By the erotic I mean more than sexual eros, though this is very important. At issue is our ontological exigence to be, in despite of our own possible nothingness, and the concretion of this doubleness in our desire, and hence also in all our becomings as forms of self-transcending. Eros refers us to the inordinate restlessness of the human being as desire without determinate limit, restlessness in finite being that shows the sign of its own infinity. There is a quality of absoluteness about it, even as in its disquietude it searches for what is absolute. Its will to be is singularized in this finite self, and yet it exceeds all finite determinates. We are the paradox of this double nature: the mixing of power and precariousness, grandeur and wretchedness, elevation and debasement, superiority and abasement, serene beauty and the ferment of an ugly chaos.

Eros seeks sovereignty over this doubleness. Selving struggles with its own amorphousness, its twilight nature, the equivocal chaos out of which it would create. To know the turn of twilight into dawn, it must go into its own night. What does it mean to "come to oneself"? It is not any simple selfishness. Sovereignty is often pursued in view of a *purpose greater than the singular self*. There is even the danger of a *fanaticism of purpose*: it takes over the whole self, seems to be greater than the self. It is often so with sovereignty that the search is to overcome the shabby condition of one's present limits. There is something "more" in self, expressed in the passion of its eros and its restless search for something more than itself, something above itself, something above by which it comes to what is more in itself, what indeed may be above itself. Thus the higher selving, either as in the *Übermensch*, or as preparation for the *Übermensch*.

Erotic sovereignty here can be connected with the figure of *the hero*. Let "hero" be metaphorical of the restless sweep of human self-transcendence in its search for the "more," in its will to live the "more" in its own self-becoming. Self-becoming is a self-overcoming; it releases the original power to be sleeping in the potency of our "freedom to." This release, in the overcoming of limits, cannot be a

Nietzsche
crit, "heroic

mere indefiniteness, for then one would have the sheer futility of self-becoming without any purpose. This means that purpose here cannot be any merely finite aim. The hero is the singularized selving of more than finite purpose. He or she may not be able to say this, it may remain a longing, or a calling, or the solicitation of something more that only progressively can become more determinate. Self-becoming that is called to something more beyond the limit comes to itself in the discipline of the limit. The coming to itself is immediately converted into a self-becoming that knows it can never come to itself in an entirely determinate way.

There can be a grandeur and nobility about such an erotic sovereignty. It is proper justice to grant this. But I would also claim that there is an agapeic freedom that is released beyond this higher autonomy of erotic sovereignty. Beyond sovereignty, this release is also beyond servility. It is released in a being for the other that is for the other and not for any return to self. It is released by renewed accession to the sources of human self-transcending in the *passio essendi*: in this accession selving finds again its own porosity to what is other to itself, whether this be the intimate otherness of the divine, or other human beings toward whom one is called into a communal space of a more compassionate service. Even the self-affirming of erotic sovereignty would itself be impossible were not the sovereign *already given to itself* through the other, were not its promise of being itself already solicited by the love of others that loved that sovereign for itself and as other. There is a freedom in agapeic service in which we are genuinely self-transcending, since it is less the self that counts as the very energy of transcendence of self. In erotic sovereignty, there is a transcending that leads to a higher selving; in agapeic service there is a release of transcending that is higher than selving, no matter how glorious. The glory of selving is not what is at issue.

What is at stake, then, in the living of agapeic service is not at all what Nietzsche excoriates in regard to the servility of the slave. The community of agapeic service is beyond the impulse to revenge, for it is defined neither by servility nor sovereignty. Nietzsche did not see far enough beyond erotic sovereignty which overcomes this slavish servility. He squints when he tries to see a service beyond all servility, and beyond erotic sovereignty, not below it.

Nietzsche associated Jesus with those who might be described, in his mocking phrase, as cases of delayed or "retarded puberty" ("*unausgebildeten Pubertät*," *W*, VI, 3, 201ff.; *Anti-Christ*, §32). As Zarathustra puts it: "He [Jesus] died too early"—as if, with more time and maturity, Jesus might have become a more acceptable Nietz-schean sovereign.[14] What of retarded puberty? Think of people who have not passed through the shaking vehemence that awakens with our erotic energies: they have an odd softness; one shakes their hand, and it is as if there is nothing there; the hand offered is flaccid flesh, like a dead fish: like a child in a certain sense, not perhaps as lacking a kind of self-insistence, but as *lacking a will*. Will here means the decisive energy of singular being, incarnate in the I, and directed to goals chosen or loved, or turned away from them. The upsurge of erotic energies makes demands on the mature becoming of will in us. The child before puberty has no will in that sense, hence our rejec-tion of child labor, or our repugnance to paedophilia.[15]

Implication: Jesus for Nietzsche embodies something *prior* to eros, not a further possibility beyond eros. There is the innocence and the absence of a will, in the sense of an overtly directed energy: an ab-sence of erotic selving and hence one in whom the surging vitalities of life are still sleeping. This is a will-lessness *prior* to will; hence prior to any quest for sovereignty and one's own self as sovereign. But sup-pose Jesus was more mature than erotic sovereignty? Suppose aga-peic selving is a being beyond self as willful and as willing itself? As such, it would imply a kind of unselving, if you like, but not in terms of an innocent will-lessness before erotic will, but with a willing be-yond willfulness and beyond will-to-power, and indeed beyond good and evil, in so far as these are defined by a determinate, humanized moral measure. This is to be, not in the innocence of becoming, but in the agapeic good beyond moral good and evil.

If Jesus is put *below* the erotic sovereign, one in whom the eros of will-to-power seems not to have developed, Nietzsche shows himself to have failed to comprehend fully the promise of agapeic service *be-yond* erotic sovereignty. Not that he lacked an intimation of the mo-mentous issue at stake, as I believe his striking phrase evidences:

---

[14] *Also sprach Zarathustra*, in *Werke*, VI, 1, 91. I will refer to R. J. Hollingdale's translation of *Thus Spoke Zarathustra* (Harmondsworth: Penguin, 1961), 98. Where necessary, I will make reference to the German. I have made slight adjustments to the translation.

[15] *Child labor*: properly to labor or work, you have to have a will in the more deci-sive sense. *Paedophilia*: this is a violation of the innocence wherein the erotic energies still sleep—in that sense, paedophilia is not unlike raping someone in their sleep, or like desire for a will-less body, not unlike a necrophilia in which death appears to function as the counterfeit of innocence.

"Caesar with the soul of Christ!" These names together signify an effort to state the union of the erotic sovereign's power with the soul of agapeic service. This is my point: The service of the second, in transcending the power of the first, transfigures the meaning of power, in a manner that can never be mastered by erotic sovereignty, or captured under the name of Caesar. Caesar will have to cease to be Caesar, to have even an inkling of the soul of Christ. But this means we must understand Christ differently than Nietzsche does.

Agapeic service, one might venture, is beyond any version of the master-and-slave dialectic, whether Hegelian or Nietzschean, beyond its historical concretization in the Marxist class war. Its inspiration comes from an other dimension beyond the power and violence of world history. It works vertically to the horror of world history, into which it pierces and seeks to uplift. It tries to enact in the worldly between and the meantime of historical time the generosity of a vertical transcendence. It is a service beyond finite reckoning, beyond reduction to determinate calculation. It lives a noninsistence, but what sustains its hope? The trust that at bottom being is an agape. This is not to blink away the suffering, the evil, the heart-shattering tragedy. This is not to be asleep to losses beyond finite recovery. Such agapeic service is not unmindful of the way we scourge creation and each other. It knows our demonic power to revolt against the goodness of creation and the origin. And yet the horror of evil itself is parasitical on the agape of being that the horror tries to corrupt. To be the horror it is, it must be let be by the agape of being itself. This is to appeal to a faith beyond finitude, in a hyperbolic good whose allowance of freedom is not its endorsement of evil. Evil is, because of the forbearance, the patience of the good. It is not crushed because the good does not crush, for the good is not a master or an erotic sovereign; it is an agapeic servant.[16]

Caesar with the Soul of Christ (3): Rank and Spiritual Leadership

"The Roman Caesar with the soul of Christ." I try to make sense one more time. I call to mind the important fact that Nietzsche was concerned with the problem of *leadership*, indeed *spiritual leadership*.[17]

---

[16] See *Beyond Hegel and Dialectic*, chapter 4, on good and evil beyond world history; see also *Perplexity and Ultimacy*, chapter 2, on tragedy and the beloved this.

[17] This is why certain "aestheticizations" of Nietzsche do him an injustice. If there is an aestheticization, it is in an *archaic*, not post-Kantian, sense: archaic in the respect that poetry is inseparable from the religious, and indeed from pedagogic, legis-

This reflects his persistent desire for a new order of *rank*. It reflects a vision of the difference of the lower and higher, the many and the few; a vision to which the equality of each before God was uncongenial, indeed profoundly flattening of the differences that Nietzsche held should be strengthened rather than weakened. The point is urged against Christian religious equality, scientific homogeneity, democratic or socialist egalitarianism. Differences properly strengthened are more likely to separate the Nietzschean goats from the Christian sheep and provide the nurturing matrix for the higher self-affirming will-to-power of the *Übermenschen*.

The point applies equally to the socialist sheep, or the democratic sheep, but we don't hear much about that now. Our own egalitarian age, even while it loves Nietzsche, finds such talk about leadership and sheep uncongenial. That talk implies that some know what others do not; that some see where others are sightless; that some have a more ultimate goal, while others are engrossed in the proximate; that these few have not an obligation but a right to lead. We think only in terms of vulgar will-to-power. We warm egalitarians break out in cold sweat at the thought of *being told*.[18] Is it not strange that Nietzsche is popular with people who would squirm at the thought that what we need more than anything else is *obedience* to a new ideal? Is it that old black magic: bewitched by all the blather about "creativity," we think that Nietzsche is talking about *us*?[19] Who does Nietzsche obey, who is he willing to obey? I will return to the issue of obedience.

With regard to the two forms of will-to-power, above distinguished, we need to be more refined. We must distinguish further: first the vulgar will-to-power in a more normal sense; second the Caesars' will-to-power in a more normal sense; third the creators' will-to-power in a *more than normal* sense. It is the extraordinary will-

lative, and conservative functions concerning the fundamental values of the ethos of a people. Plato's poet is to be understood in this sense, as well as his concern with the plurivocal power of the equivocal image. Shelley: "Poets are the unacknowledged legislators of the world." On this archaic sense of the poet as legislator, *vates*, sage, and so on, see *Philosophy and its Others*, chapter 1.

[18] Zarathustra's animals notice that he *speaks differently* to them than he does to himself. See especially the section on the announcement of the eternal return: the animals say almost exactly the same as Zarathustra, but they repeat it as hurdy-gurdy and organ grinders. The same is different in the mouths of different speakers. Zarathustra addresses different people differently. Consider the moment when he looks into the face of his animals and says nothing but shakes his head.

[19] On obedience and autonomy, see my "Autonomia Turannos."

to-power of these *third* individuals that consumes Nietzsche, and that really is at stake in his "Caesar with the soul of Christ." The first are concerned with proximate domesticities. The second are those who do impose their will, but as leaders of peoples or political realms. These latter are the Caesars—in a more normal sense. These "ordinary" Caesars are midway between the vulgar and the higher will-to-power—the will to domination is mixed with the will to dominion. (Do not forget that each expresses a will that wills itself as the measure of what is to be imposed as valuable on the flux.) Such Caesars are not the highest for Nietzsche. The highest are creators who are more fully released into the self-affirmation of their own will-to-power.[20]

If, in the language of the three metamorphoses, they are children rather than lions, what kind of children? Both children and lions metaphorically express what I call erotic sovereignty, but they do so somewhat differently. We might say: The Nazis emphasized the second as reflecting their own will to mastering power, which was enacted with an evil below the vulgarity of the first, an evil below the brutality of banality; meanwhile at the same time they exploited the suggestion of the cultural and spiritual superiority of the third form of will-to-power. This third has to do with spiritual leadership—this is the temptation to which Heidegger succumbed, and from which Nietzsche was not immune. Other interpreters, who want to free Nietzsche from Nazi distortions, emphasize the third, but without proper treatment of the other forms, they sometimes make it more humanistic and egalitarian than it is in Nietzsche himself. They conveniently cover over the brutality in any struggle of will-to-power— indeed the brutal character of the highest spiritual struggle. In Anglo-American interpretation, this can sometimes mean an anodyne Nietzsche, sanitized for a civilized seminar in the humanities, conducted according to the comfort levels of the presiding last professors.[21]

The question of spiritual leadership and superiority must always go hand in hand with the possibility of spiritual corruption. Ultimately Nietzsche attributes such corruption to Christianity, as well

---

[20] Something like this threefold differentiation is also suggested by some paragraphs, concerning elites, toward the end of *The Anti-Christ*, §57; *W*, VI, 3, 239ff.

[21] In English commentary, Kaufmann has some responsibility: though now not to the fore as during his life, he has an afterlife in a Nietzsche relatively innocuous, on the whole. Danto, in his incarnation as an analytical interpreter, and Nehamas in his aesthetic, literary incarnation, do not heed the brutality of this spiritual struggle.

as other philosophical and religious inheritances. Nietzsche himself is not above suspicion. He had a will to spiritual superiority and leadership that is monstrous from the standpoint of vulgar domestic ambitions. He wanted to stamp himself on the millennia, in a manner rivaling and surpassing the stamp of Christ or Plato on the last two millennia. Even if we do not endorse that ambition, or judge it to be monstrous, let us at least be honest about what is at stake.

The extremity of Nietzsche's desire for spiritual seriousness is evident in his will to be a creator of the new values, and to stamp his will on the millennia. Among many other communications, there is a letter to his sister chiding her for not understanding that literally he himself holds the fate of the world in his hands. The hyperbolic ambition appears also at the end of the *The Anti-Christ* (and not only there): we must start to count time anew, he suggested; previously time was marked from that *dies nefastus* of the first day of Christianity. Why not now begin to mark time from today, and the revaluation of all value initiated by Nietzsche? The back of history is being broken, and whoever comes after Nietzsche belongs to a higher history.[22]

What sense can we make, on Nietzsche's terms, of *any* distinction between "higher" and "lower"? Leadership points to an ethics of rank, but can such an ethics be possible if we hold to a *monism of will-to-power*? Even though the one will-to-power is said to diversify itself, as the above differentiations seem to indicate, is it possible finally to sustain any qualitative difference of inferior and superior? I do not think so. Why? Nietzsche asks: Do you want a *name* for this world — this "monster of energy"? "A *solution* for all its riddles?" He answers: The *world is will-to-power — and nothing besides!* And you yourselves are also this will-to-power — and nothing besides![23] This is the soul of the

---

[22] *W*, VI, 3, 251; *The Anti-Christ*, 187. In *Ecce Homo* (*W*, VI, 3, 371; *EH*, 333), Zarathustra, by uncovering Christianity, is said to break the back of human history in two. In a letter Nietzsche wrote to his sister in his last lucid months (mid-November, 1888, Brief 1145, *Briefwechsel*, III, 5, 473f.) he said: "You haven't the remotest conception of the fact that you are closely related to a man and a fate in whom and in which the question of the millennia (*die Frage von Jahrtausenden*) has been decided. I hold the future of humanity, quite literally, in my hands." The philosophers of the future in *Beyond Good and Evil* are referred to as tying the knot of millennia.

[23] See *Der Wille zur Macht*, 696–97; *The Will to Power*, 549–50. On Nietzsche's vision of this world as "a monster of energy" (*ein Ungeheuer von Kraft*) and the monism of will-to-power, see my *Art, Origins, Otherness*, 205–8; see also 184–85 on the question of will-to-power and wills-to-power in the plural (Müller-Lauter's emphasis). Consider also: "*My purpose*: to demonstrate the absolute homogeneity of all events and the application of moral distinctions as conditioned by perspective; to demon-

[handwritten: local powers. / P Sade.]

world, as well as its body. The incarnation of the truth is the aesthetic expression or show of will-to-power, goods or values are also the aesthetic bodies of will-to-power.

If *all* value is projection of will-to-power, how do we establish *rank*? For if all is will-to-power and there is no inherent value (as Nietzsche believed), the whole is valueless and the truth of rank in value is actually *homogeneity*, since high and low are each a projection of will-to-power. Suppose we say that the higher is a *more valuable* projection of will-to-power, then something *inherent* in will-to-power is expressed more truly, more affirmatively in such rank. And then we are back with some form of inherent value. The will-to-power must have some inherent exigence for good, if there are values that are inherently higher; that is, if like Nietzsche we want an ethics that can *discriminate and discern differences*. Surely this is what rank means. If we are to defend an ethics of rank, we must reformulate will-to-power to make it inherently hospitable to the discrimination of higher and lower values. Nietzsche wanted to offer a great "Amen" to all that is. But what resources does he have for enabling such a hyperbolic "yes"? Apart from the granting of some inherent hospitality of being to worth, apart from some granting of being's inherent worthiness to be affirmed, every assertion of will-to-power seems to be just another reassertion of nihilism.

If, as Nietzsche held, the whole of creation is devoid of inherent value, we cannot sustain the claim that humans alone can be the epitome of inherent value. The result has to be the opposite. Opposite not only in the hypocrisy, indeed the impotence of this will-to-power—impotence to acknowledge the good of other-being, the good as other to us—but opposite also in this straightforward sense: if the whole is valueless, then every project of will-to-power to legislate value to the whole or to whatever is within the whole, is doomed to failure. For every project of will-to-power is itself a manifestation of the truth of the valueless whole: will-to-power in creating values is itself ultimately valueless.[24]

Caesar with the Soul of Christ (4): Neighbors, Agapeic Giving, the Gift-giving Virtue

"The Roman Caesar with the soul of Christ." Another approach may help, this time by looking at Nietzsche's view of the *neighbor*, as ex-

---

strate how everything praised as moral is identical in essence with everything immoral. . . ." *The Will to Power*, 155.

[24] See "Autonomia Turannos," 245–48.

[handwritten: Sade in Lacan]

pressed through Zarathustra, since this is intimately related to the difference between erotic sovereignty and agapeic service. When Nietzsche/Zarathustra speaks of the neighbor, he is clearly intent to break with any subordination of the "I" to the "thou." Zarathustra says: the "thou" is older than the "I," but the "I" is to be the crowning achievement of the creative individual. The "thou" is rather submerged in the herd, and has not yet broken free to be itself. The implication is that love of neighbor is a form of servile relation in which the glory of self-affirmation is lacking. The daring to stand out, and to stand against, is lacking, as is the courage not only to be what one is, but to create what one would be. Lacking is the will to be oneself. Zarathustra advocates love of the most distant, not love of the near, the neighbor. I call attention here to what strikes one as a rather odd saying of Zarathustra: "higher still than man I account love of causes and of phantoms." (*Sachen und Gespenstern*, matters and ghosts). What are these *Sachen* and *Gespenstern*? The phantom/ghost, more beautiful than us, runs alongside us, we are told. We do not give it flesh and out of fear we run back to the neighbor. This is the ideal we lack the daring to make incarnate. Our love of our neighbor is our lack of creative courage before ourselves (*W*, VI, 1, 73–75; *Zarathustra*, 86–88).

None of this is any form of crass selfishness, of course. The friend is taught in place of the neighbor. "May the friend be to you a festival of the earth and a foretaste of the Superman." "May the future and the most distant be the principle of your today: in your friend you should love the Superman as your principle."[25] Note the redeeming power of the promise of the *future*, and the superman in the other. We are not honoring humanity in the figure of the other as in Kant, but the promise of the superman in the friend. Nevertheless, there is here a complex *circle of self-mediation* in which, in the end, we come back to ourselves, even if as our higher and redeemed promise. "Yet your friend's face is something else besides. It is your own face, in a rough and imperfect mirror" (*W*, VI, 1, 68; *Zarathustra*, 83). Indeed, a circular process of dispersal and return is enacted in the friend, a circle that brings the becoming (*Werden*) of good through evil, and of purpose (*Zweck*) out of chance (*Zufall*)(*W*, VI, 1, 74; *Zarathustra*, 87–88). Elsewhere Zarathustra will say: What finally comes back is my

---

[25] See my "Tyranny and the Recess of Friendship," in *Amor Amicitiae: On the Love that is Friendship*, ed. Thomas Kelly and Philip Rosemann (Leuven: Peeters, 2004), 99–125, especially 120ff. on Nietzsche and the friend.

own self! He also exclaims: "For me—how could there be any 'out-side-me' (*Ausser-mir*)? There is no outside! (*Es giebt kein Aussen!*)" (*W*, VI, 1, 268; *Zarathustra*, 234). Recall earlier remarks on being under a spell, being bewitched: how could you be released, or woken up, if there is "no outside"?

There is something here in Nietzsche that is intermediate between erotic sovereignty and agapeic service, midway between an eros that overcomes its own lack and in relation to the other comes to itself, and a self-transcending that gives to the other out of a fullness already real. Giving from a full heart seems central to the meaning of a friend. This is not unlike agapeic giving, which gives out of a pleni-tude already real. It does not relate to an other out of a lack that the other is to fill. Nietzsche's erotic sovereignty is not a lacking eros that has to fill itself in and through the other: it makes a claim to be al-ready a fullness in itself, and out of this it overflows. The decisive question concerns the nature of this overflow. Is it finally for the self that overflows? Or is there a communication beyond self from abun-dance that is given for the other as other and not just as an excess of self-affirming power? I think the latter can be called agapeic giving; I think Nietzsche's gift-giving virtue (*die schenkende Tugend*) is rather of the first kind.[26] And the difference of the two decides the differ-ence of the gift of Christ and the gift of Zarathustra.

What can we say of Zarathustra's gift-giving virtue? Significantly, the matter is broached in the last and culminating section of part I of *Zarathustra* (*W*, VI, 1, 93ff.; *Zarathustra*, 99–104). Also significantly, in the previous section "On Free Death" (*W*, VI, 1, 89ff.; *Zarathustra*, 97–99), Zarathustra refers to Jesus and his death. Genuine giving has an intimate relation to how we face into our death, and live be-yond it, even in going toward it: how we will it or choose it, or how we need a *metanoia* of willingness to consent or say "yes" to life in the face of it.[27] Zarathustra makes the suggestion: Jesus died too young—he was wise enough to repent and change his mind, had he lived. The fact that this section is followed by the discourse on the gift-giving virtue is clearly intended to suggest something more ulti-mate than the Christian teaching on love of the neighbor. It intends also to name the successor of Jesus: the teaching of the gift-giving virtue is to hand with Zarathustra, its bestower. This is the new dis-pensation of the higher self-affirmation.

---

[26] Translated by Hollingdale as the "bestowing virtue."

[27] This relation to death is also evident from previous discussion of erotic sover-eignty.

Superficially the gift-giving virtue looks like agapeic giving. The thread of equivocity is here evident again in the issue of the *counterfeit*. Is one the counterfeit of the other, a kind of *parodia sacra*, and perhaps a false double? Nietzsche clearly thought of his own as the genuine article, but what if its attractiveness borrows from agapeic giving, if this is the real thing?[28] In fact, the gift-giving virtue is not at all a generosity given for the other as other. It is an overflow of the self-affirming soul that rejoices in itself and that can do no other than give beyond itself, and this giving beyond itself is simply its self-affirmation. It glories in itself as it seems to give itself away to the others, but it is not giving itself away, it is simply its own overflow that once again rejoices in itself.

This is what I called above the higher form of will-to-power. The question to be asked is whether the deeper truth of giving is being redefined and distorted, despite the surface of affirmation. If the overflow of the giving is fated so to overflow, where is the space of generosity that allows the other to receive or refuse? If there is no such space, does the gift-giving turn into a fated force that might even be tempted to force its gift on the other? Is that then a gift? It seems to me that no understanding of giving is possible without an understanding of receiving, and an understanding of receiving as itself a kind of giving or gift. The giver has to allow for the space of receiving in the other. For instance, a giver who won't take "no" for an answer can turn out to be rather tyrannical. The generous giver has to make way for the freedom of the receiver. But such a "making way" is not just a fated overflow.

Further, it is not only the generosity of the giver that is important but the generosity of the receiver. We are the receivers, and, strangely, it is the generosity of the other that possibilizes our comportment of generosity toward the other. Generosity entails no servile reception or abjection before the other. In fact, the other's generosity does more than occasion our gratitude; it charges us with the living of generosity. Only a generous person can properly receive

---

[28] I suspect something similar with respect to Hegel's discussion of "forgiveness" in the *Phenomenology*: it is an extraordinary *subtle mimicry* of real forgiveness. On this more fully see *Beyond Hegel and Dialectic*, 192–95, 217, 232–33, 238ff., 300; see also *Hegel's God*, chapter 6, especially 156ff. on Hegel's *Geist* as *self*-forgiving. On counterfeit doubles, see my "Dream Monologues of Autonomy," in *Ethical Perspectives* 5, no. 4 (1998): 305–21. These monologues revoice the story of the prodigal son, as if re-told by wayward sons, with some resemblance to Kant, Hegel, Nietzsche, and Marx.

a gift. The *receiver* must have generosity to receive the generosity of the giver. Otherwise, the gift is either not truly received or perverted in thankless grabbing.

Think of a person who cannot receive a compliment. They refuse what they take as being in the debt of the person offering the compliment: generosity would shackle them to the other, they think, for they lack the generosity to receive the other's generosity. Think of those who are unable to be gracious—their inability turns the gift into something else, turning it aside. I have even known people who clamp themselves tight against laughing at a good joke—laughing might put them in the position of receiving something they have not first determined themselves. The gift needs the graciousness of the receiver to be fulfilled as gift. Thus the gift is the promise of a fulfilled community. Receiving itself is gifted. The promise can be lost in more than one place. The gift is an occasion that occasions giving, as much by the receiver as the giver. There is a reception that is a giving, for it is an opening of the self to the other, and this opening is the greatest gift—not the thing given, but the mode of being of the giver and receiver; as with the widow who gave her last mite—she held nothing back for herself, and so was close to God.

Those who cannot receive a gift lack the spirit of generosity; generosity is not only relative to the giver. We must be generous to allow the generous other to offer its gift. It is the spirit of generosity that is more than us and makes us more than ourselves, and that comes over us in the gift. If we are obsessed with doing all for ourselves, with proving that we are in charge or in control, even if we seem utterly noble in insisting on giving to others, we may, in fact, have perverted the occasion of generosity. Our "generosity" may be the pride that insists on itself, and hence not be generous at all.[29] The depth of generosity is sustained by a humility in relation to the ultimate.

We are not degraded in dignity by such humility. This is not "impotence," and is not without its glory, in that even beyond wretchedness we can be visited with glory, in the breakthrough of the gift of the origin, the vision that the between is truly beyond our power, and that this is a good thing, that it is just the good of the between that

---

[29] Is this not Descartes's *générosité*? This is really the pride that is more concerned with self-worth, self-esteem. Consider the ambiguity in "being full of oneself"—Zarathustra is full with himself as giver, but "being full with oneself" also suggests an insufferable self-regard. Once again one thinks of a giving that will not take "no" for an answer, but what kind of giving is this, what kind of generosity?

its good is not our production. Its gift is good, albeit ambiguous to us, sometimes threatening, sometimes destructive. Appreciation of this gift can nurture a gratitude to the ground of good, the enigmatic God who possibilizes all, even the breakthrough into ultimate trust. What is most our own we do not "own."

This we know in a religious porosity, and in the release of freedom in a wise patience. This is not a matter of any hyperbolic striving of our endeavor to be. Receiving the gift of the "to be" in the *passio essendi*, we can rage, or whine, or be thankful. We can find sly means to get our own way, to the end of finding that it is not our possession, as we go as naked into death as when we first came to birth. Naked, we spend life covering ourselves, but in the end, as at the beginning, there is nakedness: exposure beyond all human power, beyond the power of nature as a totality; vulnerability and exposure beyond the whole. The nakedness can be lived with hard-won consent, or perhaps with a gift of "yes" that comes out of nothing, or with anxiety and trembling, or with wrath. An ethics of gratitude can be called forth, lived as a life of generous offering. Thanks is incarnated as a form of life. Since such thanks, not just for this or for that, but for the gift of life as such, and the good of the "to be," finally makes no sense without God, it is other than the Nietzschean gratitude.

Such a generosity of agapeic offering means the willingness to put oneself in the relative position, not the unconditional. Strangely, the relative position is the absolute position, in so far as it is the position of relativity, in which being there for the other becomes an ethical reality. Being relative in the spirit of this generosity is the unconditional relation, and not the self-relation that would only relate to the other out of its prior securing of itself. This prior securing is a perversion of what the prior is, for what is prior is the gift of being as good. Securing ourselves as mastering powers cuts us off from the fullness of the gift, even though it is the gift that itself allows for this cutting off of the gift.

Zarathustra's gift-giving does not really know the meaning of receiving in the above sense; he gives from a fullness but not for the other; the putative fullness simply overflows and glories in itself, affirms itself.[30] The other seems an *occasion*, not properly a beloved in

---

[30] See also *Beyond Good and Evil*, §260 (W. Kaufmann trans., *Basic Writings*, 395): Nietzsche speaks of master morality, the strong, "we truthful ones" who determine being and create values: the noble one is "proud of the fact that he is *not* made for pity." "Everything that it knows as part of itself it honors: such a morality is self-

deepest otherness. One might here consult Zarathustra's "Night Song," where this gulf between giving and receiving is evident. *Das Nachtlied* (*W*, VI, 1, 132ff.; *Zarathustra*, 129–30) is perhaps one of the most beautiful things Nietzsche has written, and yet for all its energy of self-affirmation, it is full of a nameless sadness, of something missing or missed. *That* Nietzsche was aware of its immense significance is sure: he quotes it in full in *Ecce Homo* (*W*, VI, 3, 343ff.; *EH*, 306–7). That he was aware of *what* its full significance was, I am not so sure. The "Night Song" is a hymn to solitude. But the involuntary confession of a kind of despair hums around this hymn, betrayed to us in an outcry for love from the other. This is coupled with Zarathustra's own lucid claim that this love for him is an impossibility. The song has a double effect of both communicating the flame of creative inspiration and yet it chills one to the bone: solitude loved as muse, solitude confessed as almost unbearable emptiness. We warm to the tender singer and fear for his desolation. Listen to this:

> But I live in my own light, I drink back into myself the flames that break from me. I do not know the joy of the receiver; and I have often dreamed that stealing must be more blessed than receiving. It is my poverty that my hand never rests from giving. . . . Oh wretchedness of all givers! . . . A gulf stands between giving and receiving; and the smallest gulf must be ridged at last. . . . Oh solitude of all givers! Oh silence of all light givers. . . . Many suns circle in empty space: to all that is dark they speak with their light—to me they are silent. Oh, this is the enmity of light toward what gives light: unpitying it travels its way. Unjust toward the light giver in its inmost heart, cold toward suns—thus travels every sun.
>
> Ah, ice is around me, my hand is burned with ice! Ah thirst is in me, which yearns after your thirst. It is night: ah that I must be light. And thirst for the things of night! And solitude!

glorification (*Selbstverherrlichung*). In the foreground is the feeling of fullness, of power that seeks to overflow, the happiness of high tension, the consciousness of wealth that would give and bestow: the noble human being, too, helps the unfortunate, but not, or almost not, from pity, but prompted more by an urge begotten by excess of power. The noble human being honors himself as one who is powerful, as one who has power over himself. . . ." This self-glorification is more like an urgency of ultimacy without the porosity of being and the *passio essendi*—reverence turned toward self not toward a superior *other*. I return to reverence in Chapter 8.

... and longing for speech breaks forth, and the song of lovers; Zarathustra's soul is the song of a lover.

Among other things, one notes the enmity of light toward what gives light—something enigmatic we noted (in Chapter 5) concerning the production of counterfeit doubles. There is another deep ambiguity about this: the unwilled joy of a willing of self that overflows, with yet the intimation that this fullness is still not enough:

Oh wretchedness of all givers. . . . Oh eclipse of my sun! Oh craving for desire!
Oh ravenous hunger in satiety! . . . my joy in giving died in giving, my virtue grew weary of itself through its abundance.

We can detect also the desire for "more": longing for the love of the other as a giver; and yet it seems there is the rejection of this, in so far as *this sun refuses every other sun*, even the light giver in its inmost heart. The impossibility of receiving the light from the other not only extends to those sources in the starry sky *above*, but also those sources *within*—the light of the other within the recesses of the most intimate soul.

If Nietzsche is genuinely beyond, there must be something other beyond this, some other affirmation beyond what is suggested here. Otherwise the gift-giving virtue is a retraction from the fullness of agapeic offering, retraction to the verge of an erotic sovereignty full of itself and yet also weary of its fullness, but one that cannot make the further movement, because to do so would cause the collapse of the whole enterprise of self-affirming will-to-power. Otherwise every movement beyond is a quasi movement, and like the sleeper fleeing in a dream, one remains fixed to the spot. And yet this collapse of the project of self-affirming will-to-power is necessary, if Christ is superior to Zarathustra. Out of this collapse may come a return to zero, a different interface with creation beyond nihilism, and a different voluntary death may be accepted, from which a different selving and transcendence can come to be.

Curse, Blessing, Temptation on the Heights

I return to Nietzsche's spiritual seriousness in relation to Christianity. In the ultimate provocation, Nietzsche utters a condemnation, not utters but howls a kind of *curse* on Christianity: Christianity is the one great curse.[31] The violence of his indictment of this curse makes the indictment a kind of cursing of this curse. Nietzsche curses Christianity, and he reiterates the curse. Wherever there are walls, he tells us, he will inscribe his indictment. This is the extremity and urgency and ultimacy of the stakes at issue. "Dionysus versus the Crucified."

What does it mean to curse? It is not only to utter one's most violent negation, it is to will to blight the cursed. It is to withhold and deny all welfare and good from the cursed. It is to damn. Of course, to deal with curse is also to deal with blessing. On this side too we approach close to what is the ultimate. If to curse is to pronounce an ultimate refusal or negation, to bless is to give voice to an ultimate consent and affirmation of good. To curse or be cursed, to bless or be blessed: each is beyond utilitarian self-satisfaction, beyond happiness, beyond eudaimonia, except in this regard. The daimon brings us into the middle space between mortals and divinities: it is in this ultimate between that the struggle between curse and blessing is fought; it is wrestling with the ultimate powers, or in supplication or prayer. Curse and blessing come in the most ultimate struggle of spirit when the human being wrestles with, or enters into converse with, divine or daimonic powers beyond itself. This struggle is always on the heights, where curse and blessing either elevate or cast down, redeem or doom.[32]

Curse and blessing are ultimately uttered by human beings in face of mortality: we will die, but can we still say "yes, yes" in the most comprehensive sense? The power to say "yes" is not only a fruit at the end, it can be the fructifying power that ferments in the entirety of a life that is released to consent in life itself. For Nietzsche, consent means to redeem time from the spirit of revenge (see the section on redemption in *W*, VI, 1, 173ff.; *Zarathustra*, 159–63). The religious language of woe/doom and redemption is entirely appropriate to the

---

[31] Initially, the subtitle for the *The Anti-Christ* was "A Revaluation of all Values," but this was crossed out and "A Curse on Christianity," "*Flucht auf das Christenthum*," inserted instead, albeit in the spiky handwriting portending the disaster of Nietzsche's impending madness. I know also that Nietzsche's condemnation falls on Christianity, not directly on Jesus; but such a condemnation is hard to finesse. Especially given the criticism of Jesus as inferior to Zarathustra, and Nietzsche's own assumption of the name anti-Christ, the curse scatters wider than the target of a supposedly perverting Pauline Christianity.

[32] I explore this struggle of erotic sovereignty more fully in *Ethics and the Between.*

task Nietzsche understood as his fate, and the ultimate "yes," or consent he sought to sing.

How compare this with Jesus? Consider again these claims about Jesus in *On Free Death* (the discourse prior to the one on the gift-giving virtue, *W*, VI, 1, 91; *Zarathustra*, 98–99).

> Jesus knew only the tears and melancholy of the Hebrews, together with the hatred of the good and just—the Hebrew Jesus: then he was seized by a longing for death. Had he only remained in the desert and far from the good and just! Perhaps he would have learned to live and learned to love the earth—and laughter as well! Believe it, my brothers! He died too early; he himself would have recanted his teaching had he lived to my age! He was noble enough to recant! He was still immature. The youth loves immaturely and immaturely too he hates man and the earth. His heart and the wings of his spirit are still bound and heavy. But there is more child in the man than in the youth, and less melancholy: he has a better understanding of life and death.

Jesus would have repented if he had lived; if he had stayed in the desert. But what happened in the desert? This is where, we are told, the evil one tempted Jesus. Look at those temptations. Are there more ultimate temptations? How might we see them in light of Nietzsche? Or Nietzsche in their light? Might Nietzsche's own temptations be themselves contained within the possibilities of Christ's three temptations? I offer the following suggestions. Note especially what I say with respect to the ultimate temptation, for it has to do with the highest possibility, or impossibility of Nietzsche's higher will-to-power.

Christ, we are told, went into the desert for forty days and was tempted there three times.[33]

Turn stones into bread! Call this the temptation of will-to-power that will minister to the desire of humans for contentment and do-

---

[33] The temptations can be found in Matt. 4:1–11, and Luke 4:1–13. The order of the three temptations differs in these two. I refer to Luke, since there the last temptation is what I called the temptation of spiritual pride to which Jesus answers: Thou shalt not tempt the Lord thy God. This can be understood as the refusal of provocation of the ultimate power; for one answers to it; one cannot command it. Of course, the wasteland or desert is central in Nietzsche's thought, not least relative to the three metamorphoses.

mestic comfort. One might call this the will-to-power of the last men, one that today perhaps takes form as the temptation of a perfected technology. Instrumental reason and technical ingenuity will satisfy all our needs and we will be happy. Nietzsche rejects this: it is not ultimate. He despises it. This is the wretched contentment of the mediocre.

The tempter shows Christ the cities of the world: You will be master of these! Call this the second temptation of will-to-power: dominion over the earth, expressed in political rule. You will become Caesar. This is one of the temptations involved in Nietzsche's sense of will-to-power and the lure of grand politics. Nietzsche was indeed drawn by the seduction of great politics, especially in his later years, yet he retains a certain freedom from it: it is not ultimate or highest.

The third temptation: Throw yourself down and the angels with bear you up! This is will-to-power as commanding the powers: call this the temptation of spiritual pride. It is higher and more perilous than the will-to-power of the last man and the will-to-power of the political lords. It is beyond the rule of Caesar and the cities of man, and in struggle with the ultimate powers: this is the highest struggle, the spiritual struggle, in the desert and on the heights. This last temptation of Christ is also, I think, Nietzsche's great temptation. It is a temptation that he felt in relation to Jesus himself: namely, to decide the issue of superiority of spirit.

Jesus refuses the temptation, saying one should not tempt the one Lord and God. If this displays a freedom from spiritual pride, it is not a servile submission, but an expression of consent to the ultimate. There is a more ultimate other that gives one to be and to which one is given over, and to whom one is freely to give oneself over. That God is an agapeic giver. What do we say of Nietzsche? There is none of this in Nietzsche: No God and no man above me! Zarathustra: "Six thousand feet beyond man and time!" And not Jesus above me either! But who is really free, or freed? And what then is spiritual superiority? Can one claim it, affirm it for oneself? Is this not already to pervert its meaning, and hence to fall from it? Is this self-affirmation only masked refusal?

There is a question here concerning *power and the good*: without the balanced togetherness of these in life, the extremes we face seem to be either a power that is evil, or a good that is impotent. Mostly in life we are the beneficiaries of *mixture*—sometimes the victims. The Caesar with the soul of Christ focuses on the nature of their mixture and the peril of corruption in their mixing. Mostly here also we think of power as power to command. This is the importance of the third temptation. It tempts with *highest commanding power*: spiritual command. But what of *obedience*: its power or impotence? The third temptation is the temptation of commanding power; and if we surrender to this temptation, the price of command of the powers is enslavement to the power of the evil one. Jesus refuses thus to command. There is a *higher obedience*. What is the higher obedience in Nietzsche? What or whom does Nietzsche obey? No God, and no man above him! *Non serviam!* Unconstrained *self-service* then? Does he then obey *himself*? If so, how distinguish this from a double condition of command and obey: where being master of self means being slave of self; where the more commanding the self, the more enslaved it is to itself, for there is no release beyond self, no "outside-me." Obeying self as commanding self means—I too am "God."

I cannot but think that the consent of Jesus is superior to the will to superiority I find pervasive in Nietzsche. Nietzsche lets the mask drop more and more toward the end of his productive life. The highest form of will-to-power in Nietzsche, as we saw, concerns a self-glorifying will to self-affirmation. While Nietzsche is engaged with the other forms, and is not immune from the temptation of the second, it is the third that is most of moment for him. By comparison, the other temptations are either vulgar or a matter of inferior superiority. The deepest engagement with Nietzsche must be with reference to this third level.[34] Only in relation to that temptation do we approach the religious heart of Nietzsche.

What does Nietzsche tell us is Zarathustra's last temptation? Pity. Zarathustra resists the temptation to be drawn away by pity. Drawn away from what? From himself (*W*, VI, 3, 268; *EH*, 228).

What is "God" for Nietzsche? He puts it without adornment in *The Anti-Christ* (*W*, VI, 3, 180; *Anti-Christ*, 126): "One is grateful for oneself: for that one needs a God." What is this "God"? If I have read the equivocal signs rightly, I fear this is an idol.

For being grateful for oneself can have all of the ambiguity of "being full of oneself" (see note 29). One might be grateful to another, or other source, for oneself; or one might want to be, so to say, both self-giver and self-receiver, thankful for oneself but *thanking*

---

[34] We can domesticate this into a kind of cultural war, or into an "aestheticism"; the latter might be dovetailed into a sympathy for fascist politics, Nazi or otherwise—I do not discount this; but the deeper source of these is the struggle with the temptation of spiritual pride.

oneself. One is grateful not only for oneself, but to oneself. Nietzsche is entirely equivocal if there is an other to self whom one thanks, even for oneself. The invocation of *amor fati* settles nothing. Reviewing what he announces as the immortal achievements of his forty-fourth year, he says in *Ecce Homo* (*W*, VI, 3, 261; *EH*, 221): "How could I fail to be grateful to my whole life? —and so I tell my life to myself." To whom is Nietzsche giving thanks, if he is telling his life *to himself*?

Counterfeiting Christs: The Grand Inquisitor and the Anti-Christ

Are we off the mark then to deem Nietzsche's highest possibility— the Roman Caesar with Christ's soul—Nietzsche's highest impossibility? Consider again if the *Übermensch*—as the transhuman apotheosis of will-to-power—functions as a *parodia sacra* of Christ—as the human transhuman: the God-man. Such a parody need not always be intended, though there is much of intentional parody in Nietzsche, perhaps even parody of himself.[35] Certainly there is intentional parody of the Gospels in his *Zarathustra*, but there can also be an involuntary mimicry of what claims the more ultimate truth. What seems the sameness of the two, anti-Christ and Christ, is in truth an absolute difference, for the spiritual energies of each are turned in directions opposed to each other. If we try to unite the two, the result may not be a progression through contraries, as Blake would have it, but the posing of an impossibility: the impossibility of having both, on the terms proposed. Trying to unite them on the wrong terms leads to a kind of canceling out, and we are left with nothing—a nothing that claims to be everything. By contrast with this nothing, one might suggest rather that we are put to the question of choosing either for one or the other. Being put to the question, there can be nothing univocally straightforward about the choice. For whichever one we determine to be the superior original, mimicries of the one will seem to appear in the other. Which then is the more original, which the image? We grow perplexed and need finesse.

I put the question this way: Does the Roman Caesar with the soul of Christ mutate into Dostoevski's *Grand Inquisitor*? Not the Grand

---

[35] I am thinking of the preface to the second edition of *The Gay Science: incipit parodia* supervenes on *incipit tragoedia*. Does Nietzsche, doing the fool, mimic himself? Reading this preface, it is hard not to think that Nietzsche is beside himself—in a playful way. He is more than a little manic, but is it *theia mania*?

Inquisitor of the cities of men, but the recessive legislator of the usurped city of God? I find that when Nietzsche describes the Christians as the *vampires* of the *Imperium Romanum* (*W*, VI, 3, 243; *Anti-Christ*, 180), I am minded to think of the Emperor, Julian the Apostate (331–63), warrior and philosopher (Neoplatonic, to be sure), who hated the effeminacy and enfeebling effect of Christianity, and sought to restore the virile virtues of paganism. I am also reminded of the very charges that motivated Augustine to write the *City of God*. Augustine rejects the charges against the Christians, and again and again finds grounds for the decay of Empire in the corruption of will-to-power whose most original source is in the envy of the good as "not-mine," the envy that is pride. For Nietzsche, by contrast, the building of the Imperium is the highest pride, the highest art, art in the grand style. And now with the Christians? The entire labor of the ancient world is *in vain*, he says (*W*, VI, 3, 245; *Anti-Christ*, 182).

I imagine an Augustinian response: The point of first importance is not such vanity but rather the revelation of agapeic service from beyond the will-to-power of erotic sovereignty, and a new glory in that "beyond." The things of Caesar might remain the things of Caesar, but nothing, not even the things of Caesar, can claim absolute possession for itself, through itself alone. The endowing gift of being is more primal than the power realizing its promise, or usurping, or betraying, or counterfeiting it. For us to grant that gift as gift is to be reoriented toward the things of Caesar that, if now treated as absolute, show themselves rather as counterfeit doubles of God.

Nietzsche's pride is the envy of Christ. An envy that admires, that does not quite comprehend, that refuses what is beyond it, and that puts itself in the position superior to the superiority of what escapes it.

The question of counterfeiting Christ obviously emerges in relation to the Grand Inquisitor. Like Nietzsche, the Grand Inquisitor believed in the necessary lie, though not for exactly the same reason: we need illusions, lies, lest we perish from the truth. Nietzsche despised the feebleness of Christian pity, but one could ask if this is not Nietzsche's pity? I mean his claim that we have a need of lies, of art, to save us from the truth. Is this a pity Nietzsche could not finally but despise, just because it lied, even if he deemed it necessary to save us from horror? A pity he finally also could not stifle—as we see in the extraordinary episode when he embraced the thrashed horse on the streets of Turin? In his breakdown, what breaks through? Is it not the reverse of his proclaimed doctrine of hardness:

a new accession in madness to the porosity of being; a resurgence of the *passio essendi*; and then a release of compassion for the suffering of this worthless other, the broken animal? Is this folly sacred? Or does it show the sacred, even in folly?

The Grand Inquisitor lies for the sake of the people; meanwhile the few know the disillusioning truth; they are beyond, in being strong enough to bear it. The Grand Inquisitor is one who has succumbed, but in no crass sense and for the highest of motives, to the temptations Jesus rejected: bread for the people, rather than spiritual freedom; the Caesarism of political power; the spiritual pride of knowing better than Christ.

The need to lie is evident in *The Anti-Christ*. Nietzsche does not at all reject this, only lies for what he considers to be base ends—the lies of Christianity are such ignoble lies. We need different lies, but it all depends on the end or purpose they serve. "Ultimately the point is to what *end* a lie is told" (*W*, VI, 3, 237, see also 243; *Anti-Christ*, 175, see also 179). Are there times when Nietzsche seems to be warning against succumbing to the temptation of the Grand Inquisitor? I doubt it, but if so, I can find nothing, finally, in his entire outlook sufficient to make one hesitate in succumbing—and *without shame*.

Nietzsche's remarks on Pilate in *The Anti-Christ* are very revealing. Of course, that Nietzsche entitled his own "autobiography" *Ecce Homo* binds him to both Pilate and Christ. "Ecce homo"—so Pilate exposes the man to the crowd, and then gives up the innocent Christ to death. What is Nietzsche giving us, what exposing, what giving up, what innocence giving to death? Is Nietzsche offering us another *parodia sacra* in which he is *both* Pilate and Christ? Is it by being both the executioner and sacrificial victim, the union of Pilate and Christ, that he is anti-Christ?

Nietzsche's remarks on Pilate in *The Anti-Christ* are relevant not only to the "needful lie" and the Grand Inquisitor but to the issue of "vulgar" and "higher" anti-Semitism, as I put it earlier. Nietzsche says that Pilate was the *only decent figure* in the New Testament: his decency seems to consist in his hard, cold indifference to affairs Jewish. Pilate is not unlike the Grand Inquisitor, except that Pilate allowed Jesus to be crucified, the Grand Inquisitor did not want to have to crucify him a second time. Pilate is more like a Caesar without the soul of Christ: servant of the expedients of a more vulgar will-to-power.

But if Pilate is no Roman Caesar with the soul of Christ, I must stress how Nietzsche praises Pilate's *superiority*. He embodied the at-

The last man' that kills himself

titude that showed the "noble scorn of a Roman" who was "unable to take a Jewish affair seriously: One Jew more or less, what difference does it make?" (*W*, VI, 3, 223; *Anti-Christ*, 162). This recalls, as previously I put it, the "higher" anti-Semitism. Here one remembers too how earlier in *The Anti-Christ* (*W*, VI, 3, 221f.; *Anti-Christ*, §46) Nietzsche turns up his nose in disgust at the early Christians, mimicking perhaps this "noble scorn of a Roman." Nietzsche sniffs: "One would no more choose to associate with 'first Christians' than one would with Polish Jews: not that one would need to prove so much as a single point against them. . . . Neither of them smell very pleasant." A philosopher of the nose indeed! Who can read this and not shudder? Certain smells reek of world-historical effects, more monstrous than anything Pascal could have dreamt of in connection with Cleopatra's nose.

What is to prevent Nietzsche's Roman Caesar *with* the soul of Christ from becoming—as I suggested about Solov'ëv's last Emperor—the Grand Inquisitor as the Roman Caesar *without* the soul of Christ? For how could you tell any difference between the two, if the figure dominating the conjunction of the two is always the Roman Caesar? In fact, is not Dostoevski's Grand Inquisitor—as the Roman Caesar *without* the soul of Christ—the more *honest* form of the spiritual mimicry or counterfeiting of Christ? Does not Dostoevski's penetration of the darkness prove to be the more unflinching?

Oddly, Nietzsche himself cannot keep quiet about the need to lie. If you are going to lie effectively in these matters, surely the utmost reticence and silence is needed. Here his almost involuntary honesty pays indirect compliment to the truth: dishonesty is intolerable. At a certain extreme, we cannot evade the unconditional claim truth makes on us, and the unconditional call made on us to be true. But how make any sense of such unconditionality in Nietzsche's perspective? There is no basis for *anything* unconditional in his understanding of being.

Dishonesty is intolerable to a noble soul, and yet a certain dishonesty is finally the condition without which, for Nietzsche, life is impossible. Nietzsche is hence finally torn between the Grand Inquisitor and Christ: not the Roman Caesar with the soul of Christ; not perhaps the Roman Caesar without the soul of Christ; but an inward laceration of spirit, a torment between Caesar and Christ; and all the while the insinuation is communicated that he is beyond both. And this laceration is *not* at the level of the Caesars as the princes of the world, but at the level of the soul of Christ, and the struggle there with the ultimate power. Despair of God mutates into forced praise of a counterfeit double of God one has constructed oneself.

In Dostoevski's story, Christ kisses the Grand Inquisitor silently, and goes. Could Nietzsche thus kiss the Grand Inquisitor? How would the anti-Christ kiss the Grand Inquisitor? Exactly as Christ did, but with the opposite spiritual energy. But then there would be no need at all for the anti-Christ to go, or be sent away. Is it possible for the anti-Christ to kiss Christ, and not as Judas did? Or is this perhaps what *we* should now do with Nietzsche—kiss as Christ kissed? Can one kiss Nietzsche silently? Can one, so to say, show Nietzsche the way out? And allow him now to go—but not with curses on his head, but blessings?

7

The Secret Sources of Strengthening:
On Courage

Courage and Knowing

Courage is something we take for granted as understood, something recognized and recognizable in everyday life. Clearly courage is also ethically important, and one might wonder what significance it has for both philosophy and religion. Yet once one tries to say quite what it is, one finds oneself quickly in the middle of perplexity. The perplexity less bewilders one as makes one wonder what is *there* at all to be understood. A person shows courage, but what is *being shown*, and what are its sources? It seems to elude one the moment one tries to make determinate what just a moment ago showed itself so strikingly. There is here something strikingly elemental, yet the full dimensions of what strikes us evade fixation. Why is this?

This might seem rather discouraging, but as often happens with philosophy discouragement encourages us to come to grips with what eludes us. Of course, language like "coming to grips with" is redolent of implication for courage. "The human being . . . should and must deem himself worthy of the highest. . . . The initially hidden and concealed essence of the world has no power to withstand the courage of knowledge"—so proclaims the mighty Hegel about the courage of truth (*der Muth der Wahrheit*) in his inaugural lecture in

Heidelberg, repeated at Berlin.[1] There you have it: perplexity to begin with, but hold fast, call upon courage, and the initially hidden essence of the world will show its impotence to hold out. I hear Hegel preaching: do not be discouraged, knowing will triumph! But what of the courage itself?

Consider how we speak here. "Holding fast": as if it were also natural to "give way," not to confront what seems to oppose us; as if we *need* to hold fast, because something risks undermining us. So we call upon courage. But how do you *call* upon courage? What is this call? Can we call upon courage as if it were a resource that was within the command of our will? But is there not something about courage that exceeds that kind of determinate act of will? Courage does not simply come on us, and yet there is something of *happening* about it: it surges forth from sources very hard to pin down. We do not so much call upon courage, as that something is called forth from us in courage. What does our call on courage call forth in us? Is it a resource, a source, at once deeply intimate to our being, and yet other to our total self-command, even when we are commanding persons, and in self-command? Do we "hold out" because something other "holds out" *against* us, perhaps some enigmatic inner resistance that we must *overcome*? Or is it almost the reverse of this—we call on courage and something is *held out to us*, and then the initial recalcitrance no longer holds out against us? Is the language of something "against us" adequate? Is some other source aiding us in holding fast? If so, courage would never be just *my* courage. My courage would come out of sources that also involve one's *"being encouraged."* Is there a "being encouraged" before "being courageous"?

---

[1] "Der Muth der Wahrheit; der Glaube an die Macht des Geistes ist die erste Bedingung der Philosophie; der Mensch, da er Geist ist, darf und soll sich selbst des Höchsten würdig achten, von dem Grosse und Macht seines Geistes kann er nicht gross genug denken; und mit diesem Glauben wird nichts so spröde und hart seyn, das sich ihm nicht eröffnete; das zuerst verborgene und verschlosse Wesen des Universums hat keine Krafft, die dem Muthe des Erkennens Widerstand leisten konnte; es muss sich vor ihm aufthun, und seinen Reichthum und seine Tieffen ihm vor Augem legen und zum Genusse geben." This is the Heidelberg version, *Gesammelte Werke* (Hamburg: Felix Meiner, 1968), 18: 6; the Berlin version, 18: 18, is slightly more clipped and direct. Hegelian courage tries to enact more audaciously the Enlightenment motto of Kant: *sapere aude!* I return to Kantian courage below. I want to thank Professor Ray Hart for his insightful comments on an earlier version of my reflections.

Suppose Hegel is right: because we have had courage, knowledge comes. But from where then does the courage come? It does not come from the knowledge; for we must have the courage to have the knowledge. If knowledge comes from courage, from where does courage come? Is there a courage of knowing *before* knowledge? If so, how then is it a courage of *knowledge*? Is the courage of knowing encouraged by sources it cannot know in advance, maybe can never know in a fully determinate manner, since these sources are what make determinate knowledge itself possible? Does knowledge presuppose a courage that knowledge itself cannot make fully determinate, whose secret source it cannot completely comprehend? There is a tricky problem here because immediately we are tempted to think that once we have the knowledge the perplexity is overcome. In fact, we have only forgotten, in the knowing, the enigma of the source from which the courage itself has come. Knowing, it seems, is successful on the basis of a courage it invokes but that it neither fully understands nor can explain.

Grant this line of argument, and it suggests that our coming to know is a *being given to understand*, with emphasis on (unknown) sources of knowing that release us, free us into the understanding. Is knowing only possibilized by an unknowing empowering of understanding, an *encouraging of knowing* quite different from the courage of Hegelian knowing that claims to be self-determining, self-encouraging? Think of the *suddenness* of some happenings of knowing. *Eureka! Exaipnes!* It is as if one were being gifted with hearing things, or seeing things, in a sudden access of understanding. An access of understanding would be our access to understanding, but also an accession of understanding in which we are graced with vision or hearing. There is ambiguity, of course, in all this. For "hearing things" is also hearing nothing, as "seeing things" is not seeing things.

Courage and Willing

In the classical ethical tradition courage is spoken of as one of the *cardinal virtues*. A virtue here indicates the proper flourishing of a human power or powers. A courageous human being shows a settled character in holding fast in a certain way in deeds or undertakings that otherwise call his or her being into account. Is courage an action or a reaction, or both? It seems not possible to understand courage through itself alone, since it is called forth in situations where the person seems under threat. Were there no threats, courage would not be necessary. But then if it is a reaction, it is also an action, since it expressed itself in comportment that issues in deeds: I do my courage; I act courageously; and indeed because I habitually act in such a wise, I come to show, and indeed to be marked by, a courageous character. Are there still deeper sources to all of this?

Courage is *called forth*. The happening of a threat seems to indicate that we need to understand the nature of *the enemy*, if we are to understand courage. Courage stands fast, and issues in deeds, against a threat that is hostile or potentially hostile to my being. The hostility may be minor or major, but it is against something of my being that the threat is directed. In its major instance, it is the threat to my very being, to my life, that asks for courage as a countering movement. And this is why, if I am not mistaken, most understandings of courage seem to stress a form of *self-affirmation*, or *affirmation of self* in the courage itself. This we find in the Stoic view of courage, or in thinkers like Spinoza and Nietzsche, but there is something of it in Heidegger's "resolve," *Entschlossenheit*, as well. Courage reveals an energy of being called forth in the face of a potential enemy or enemies that threaten one: it is self-affirmation *despite* an other that is *countering* one. I will say more (in Chapter 9) about the enemy and the threat, but it does indicate a certain *intimate frailty* of our being in relation to others: a frailty that can easily turn from peace and accord toward hostility and war. To be courageous is to live in this precariousness in such a manner that one's self-affirmation is not stifled. But there is more.

What kind of response is this courageous self-affirming? Is it not a kind of willing? What I am as *will* holds fast; it maintains itself in the face of the threat. This is not a matter simply of knowing the threat; it is knowing the threat, comporting oneself toward it and oneself, and *willing* not to be destroyed by it. One may well be destroyed, but courage wills not to be destroyed. And there may be forms of courage that accept that one will be destroyed, but something other than just life can be willed. There may be an *unconditional* exigence intimate to the will itself that asks to be courageously reaffirmed, even at the cost of one's life. I will return to this relative to the witness or martyr.

Of course, there is here the classical problem of will and knowing. Being brave is a willing; but being rash is also a kind of willing—it looks like the first, but it is a willing that is foolhardy. Qua willing, being brave and being rash seem to mimic each other, but the quality of mindfulness is different. Being brave demands a discernment of the fitting expression of one's being, defensive or offensive. Courage seems to require a *knowing willing—a discerning willing*. Must there not be *some* form of knowing in courage? I mean that a threat must be *known as threat* in some way, for courage to be called forth. If one is not aware of any danger, there is no need for courage, and none is called forth. Rashness lacks this discerning and so is not properly courage.

And yet there are sometimes *intimations* which would be hard to call cognitions in a more determinate sense, intimations that yet are *indeterminate knowings* of danger by way of a presentiment of threat. In fact, is this not how threat often first presents itself to us: in the clairvoyance of danger that has the presentiment of something possibly hostile? Presentiment is not univocal presence or presenting; it is an equivocal intimation or suggestion that yet is not nothing, and that may take on firmer form, though it may also vanish as an anxiety of nothing that casts before itself the spell of unreal danger. There is a presentiment which is a kind of foreknowing that finds itself suspended in a space of equivocity where what is other is inherently ambiguous, in that it can present a double face of welcome and of possible hostility.

This indicates that for courage there must be some *openness* and *indeterminacy* at play. Indeed the calling forth of courage, as a *firming up* of one's will, stands in this equivocal openness itself. Courage takes a stand in this equivocal openness. That is to say, courage is inseparable from the opening of freedom in us, matched by the intimation of an equivocity in other-being that cannot be subject to our mastery. Though it can make a call on our powers of self-mastery, that openness exposes us to terror before the new beyond us, as well as inciting us to excitement before its very novelty. The blood quickens with the relish of danger.

If there is an opening of freedom, this freedom is *not* the more determinate and developed form of *autonomous self-determination*. Something half-hid in darkness is intimated. There is an opening of will in the equivocity that later may take the shape of that more self-determining freedom, but this opening and courage are not describable alone in terms of that form of freedom. Such autonomous self-determination is the diurnal side of a happening whose primal opening is half-hid in nocturnal recesses. Courage suggests a rooted willing that is *in* this will or that will, but is not just this act of will or that. A more univocalizing voluntarism seems not to work.

Likewise, in this light, this half-light, the rationalistic approach does not seem enough either. If there is a knowing willing in courage, it is something exceeding complete rationalization: a knowing in act that does not determine itself, that perhaps cannot fully determine itself in univocal propositions. This does not mean it is merely irrational, but more that it is planted in deeper ontological soil of the human being. The energies of being that come to rational form are not just forms but formings that are sourced in energies that are freely opening, energies releasing and being released, but that cannot be confined to form. The happening of courage sends its roots deep into the overdeterminate original sources of being. These make determinate happenings and knowings possible, but are more than all such determinations. Is not this why there is something *excessive* about courage? Neither the calculative intellect or will can fully determine its "why." And yet it happens, happens with its own powerful elemental determinacy, but in the happening something more is shown than can be univocally determined.

Aquinas is one of those who thinks of will as following intellect. But does intellect not rather follow will in another sense: not this or that determinate, deliberate will, but will in the form of an *ontological love of being*, a willingness before will, so to say? One need only remember that knowing emerges from a *desire* to know. This refers us back to a love at work *before* determinate knowing, and that cannot name itself as known in this its prior happening. If this were so, then courage would also entail a *willing before will*, inseparable from this basic and elemental love of the "to be." And the courage of this more indeterminate willing (I would prefer to say overdeterminate willing) makes determinate acts of courage and knowing possible. Given what has been said, should we not call this more original happening of courage an *encouraging*? For we do not produce it, but our very being gives witness to its already being at work in us. If this is so, there is a more original reference to a source of strengthening other to us, at work in the most intimate recesses of our own most intimate willing, be it of being or of knowing, or of this good or that good.

One might well ask here: Is this not just the basic *vitality of life itself*? Yes and no. One thinks especially of the vitalities of young persons: they will try anything, we say, risk anything. Are they courageous? In a certain sense, yes. They show a kind of natural, spontaneous courage: the very *bravado of being* that spontaneously marks the being as vital and self-affirming. That same bravado of being can as easily be merely rash, hence stupid rather than brave in another sense. It is surely when the knowing of threat has entered into this spontaneous bravado of being that a different courage to be is needed and perhaps called forth.[2] Intellect can indeed corrode or destroy this bravado of being. "Thus conscience does make cowards of us all, / And thus the native hue of resolution / Is sicklied o'er with the pale cast of thought" (*Hamlet*, 3.1.84–86).

Courage is not merely deliberate will, though that; and not merely rational understanding, though that. Deliberate will can *force one forward, but one may lack courage.* "Forcing oneself" may be one part cowardice and one part bravery. There can be a deep care in courage, and also a kind of carefree abandon, both of which can be usurped by a counterfeit double: grim earnestness on the one hand, crazy "devil may care" on the other. Courage becomes more complex with complex mindfulness of being, for the latter knows the fragility of finite being, and hence is more attuned to the occasions of risk, and hence more is asked of it to call forth the sources of continuing to be, regardless of risk. And maybe there is a knowing that comes to a point where it sees there is no point in thus caring any more—though now it does not care the less, but its courage passes a critical point, and its energy is released into meeting opportunity and danger, good and evil, as they come. Knowing the difference between what is in our power, and what is not, it lives differently beyond that difference.

Often it is not the knowing that brings courage, but the courage that brings knowing. Courage points to a willing of being prior to a knowing of being; not a willing opposed to knowing discernment, but willing that cannot be entirely determined by knowing; an enigmatic willingness out of which knowledge of enigmas comes. Courage arrives, comes—sometimes; other times, courage fails. Then it is not quite that I fail in courage, but that courage fails—as if the source had dried up. I am complicit perhaps, but also I am either the beneficiary of, or the one abandoned by, courage. Courage cannot be an explicit determinate knowledge; it cannot be a simple deliberate act of will; it seems more in between an indeterminate willing and a deliberate act of will. Courage is transitional. And the darker source of strengthening from which it transits to more articulate expression in deeds remains resistant to complete determinate expression. Even

---

[2] Paul Tillich, of course, speaks of the "courage to be," in his book of that title, *The Courage to Be* (New Haven: Yale University Press, 1952), but I do not use the phrase with quite his meaning; his emphasis seems again and again to fall on self-affirmation.

when courage becomes a knowing willing, it still shows something in excess of determinacy. Strength here is not a mere given; it is a given from a strengthening—an enigmatic giving not first known or willed determinately. In sum, whether the self-affirmation of courage is a willing or a knowing, there seems to be something more or other than self in it.

Courage and the Passion of Being

We speak of a *self-affirmation* in courage, and against the threat to one's being, but we now see there is a certain equivocity in all of this, not only with respect to the other-being, but also with respect to self-being, and its own immanent otherness. Perhaps the major tendency in understanding courage has been to emphasize the *conatus essendi*, the endeavor to be, and in the face of what threatens that being. Yet we can so emphasize *conatus* that we cover over the *passio essendi*: the passion of being or "to be." Thus Spinoza: *conatus is* the essence of a being. I think this is a univocalization of an essential equivocity or doubleness. To be is to be plurally, not univocally, mediated. To be is not only to be self-mediating but to be intermediating with what is other to us, and indeed intermediating with what is other in the intimacy of our own self-mediation.

Let us return to something elemental. There is a certain delight in the "to be" as good that beings qua being live. Thus each being affirms its own being; to be is to be good, and this "to be" as good is singularized in each entity; and so it wills to affirm itself and persist in being. This looks like Spinoza's *conatus essendi*, but I think it is more complex. Suppose there is a basic ontological love of being singularized in each being as being. What is this basic love of being? Is the self-affirming absolutely elemental, if the affirmation and singularization come to be in a milieu of being, an ontological ethos wherein the self-mediation and intermediations of beings come to be? We talk about self-love, for instance; and some will claim that this is all; love of the other, altruism, is only covert or masked self-love. But is it at all clear what the so-called primary self-love is? When we reflect on the happening of courage, something of its perplexing enigma strikes one in a similar manner, as does the perplexing nature of such a basic self-love.

If a being loves itself, is it not already in some *relation* to itself, in the irreducible fact of being given to be at all? But if to be given to be is to be in a relation of love, is this love *mine*, and alone mine? The human being does not *produce* this love in the first instance; it already *finds itself* as being, as this self-affirming being; it *finds itself already* in this love of being. Does this mean that something other than self is at play, before the self even wakes up to itself as loving itself? It is given to be, and thus given, it wakes up to itself in self-affirming, and as self-affirming. Is this "being given" also describable in terms of the affirming love of being? If so, and if this affirming love shows a giving that is *other* to self-affirming, is there a sense of the love of being that, already from the outset, is *more primal* than the primal self-affirming form that, on the surface anyway, seems the most irreducible? Does self-love emerge from sources of affirming that cannot be quite called self-love?

If there is a *being given to be*, before the being given affirms its own "to be," or before being *determined* or *determining itself* to be, must there not be a *passio essendi* more primal than any *conatus essendi*? This would be a suffering, or passion of being more elemental than any endeavor to be, or striving to be. Suffering here does not necessarily mean *pain*: we can *suffer joy*, be "surprised by joy," as Wordsworth put it. The delight in the "to be" as good is such a suffering of ontological joy. Suffering calls attention to *happening* that exceeds our self-determination, though some happenings possibilize our powers of self-determining. Passion also refers to the (ontological) *porosity* of the human being in the deepest roots of its being. Porosity also means being opened in a space of elemental communication, a space of opening that indeed possibilizes our own being as self-communicative. We *are* in communication with self, and with what is other to self, because we are already opened in a space of communication. In this space the powers of receiving and giving, of consenting and transcending are communicated in the very happening of our being given to be at all.

This *passio* puts its roots most deeply into the idiotic sources of selfhood, and it is not clear that you can directly reach them. "Idiotic" here carries something of the Greek sense of the intimate: not the neutral general, but something suggestive of singularity as lived from within out; something resisting complete objectification, indeed complete subjectification also; the more determinate "subject" comes to be out of this more intimate, idiotic energy of selving.[3] And yet this idiotic source has also everything to do with the *singular communica-*

---

[3] On the idiotic, see *Perplexity and Ultimacy*, chapter 3; on the idiot self, see *Being and the Between*, chapter 10. The theme is diversely explored in *Ethics and the Between*.

bility of the living being itself. Often this *passio essendi* comes to more overt attention only indirectly. Necessarily we live out of it, and just as inevitably it seems we do not mind it. We mind it more when the more surface determinations of selving dissolve, and we are returned, often painfully, to the idiotic, intimate, also more vulnerable source.

Suppose then that the *conatus essendi* presupposes the *passio essendi*: being given to be is before striving to give oneself to be—a suffering of being as gift is more primal than the courage to be that more overtly affirms the good of the "to be." If this is true, then even this courage to be cannot be confined to the terms of self-affirmation. It may be affirmative of what *passes beyond* self, since relative to the *passio essendi* we now see that what it means to be a self, to be a selving, passes beyond self also, indeed passes into selving from intimate sources of ontological giving that we do not produce ourselves.

There is a great temptation when we turn to courage to focus so much on the foreground of the *conatus* that the import of the *passio essendi* is made secondary. We should be looking the other way round, relative to the primacy of the *passio essendi*. This temptation reflects a desire to stake a mastery over selving and the precarious conditions of life. Yet if we do this only in terms of the *conatus*, we cover over the elemental givenness that indeed makes the *conatus* possible—possible even as capable of dismissing the givenness as impossible. I mean we might be tempted by a defiant "courage" that will entirely *revolt* against the ontological gift of the "to be" at all. For the foregrounding has foreshortened that givenness into an absurd thereness, meaningless until I stamp my meaning on it.

Think here of a kind of courage that prides itself on *being determined*. Thus Lady Macbeth's unwavering determination, when Macbeth's courage was failing him: "We fail! But screw your courage to the sticking-place and we'll not fail" (*Macbeth*, 1.7.59–61). This determined courage determines the person to be thus and thus. These are faces of "courage" that often impress us with their resoluteness. But they are foreground faces—masks in which something more than the foreground face enacts itself. A very important issue here would be the courage of *daring evil*, or of *evil daring*. This is something one fears Nietzsche fakes in his call for courage beyond good and evil. The evil daring is the courage of Macbeth. *Macbeth* is a play about warrior courage and its overreaching, and the hatred of the *passio essendi* (for instance, in the form of "pity," or the "milk of human kindness"). It is also about the karma of the equivocal, about sticky evil. There is an evil daring whose pride in determining itself leads to perdition in the darkest sense: damnation.[4]

If there is another courage that remains faithful to the *passio essendi*, then this courage that forces the self-guarding closure of the *conatus essendi* on itself must be seen to be a counterfeit version of courage. Its affirmation of itself has, in fact, failed to open itself fully to what is communicated in the presentiment of threat, both with reference to its own inward otherness, the outer other, and the sources of being, whether immanent in itself or transcendent to it. It has not faced up to and endured the full disclosure of its own ontological *porosity* of being, and what is communicated there. And it is in this porosity of being that the secret sources of strengthening are attendant on us.

Many views of courage overstress the *conatus essendi* and either subordinate the *passio essendi* or else misunderstand it in too negative terms, and not more affirmatively as constitutive of the good of the gift of the "to be." It becomes univocally our vulnerability to threat, our exposure to the encroachment of other-being. Its essential equivocity as *between self-being and other-being*, as *between what one is and what is not one's own*, is reduced. Other-being, what is not one's own, as what is *not* one, becomes a presencing of hostility, against which one must be on one's guard, either suspiciously or defensively aggressive, or destructively hostile. Courage, on this view, must always be a standing fast against, and "in spite of."

If we grant the affirmative role of the *passio essendi*, then we have to think of courage in terms of an *en-couragement*. Before being courageous there is a being en-couraged. The "en" refers us to the immanence of the source of the courage within oneself; but the source, as communicated or offered from attendant powers, is not to be called "mine," or one's own. (Consider the "en" as like the "en" of enthusiasm.) The "en" refers to the communication of ontological power in the elemental porosity of being in which one comes to be, and comes to stand, comes to ex-ist, as the being one is. One is courageous because one has been encouraged. To be is to be encouraged to be. There is no courage to be without this primal encouragement to be.

---

[4] See my "Sticky Evil: *Macbeth* and the Karma of the Equivocal," in *God, Literature and Process Thought*, ed. Darren Middleton (Aldershot: Ashgate, 2002), 133–55; see also Chapter 1 above.

Four Forms of Courage: From the Vital to the Transcendent

What light does this equivocal condition, mixing *passio essendi* and *conatus essendi*, shed on some different forms of courage? I will say something about the following four forms: courage relative to *vital self-insistence*; courage in the form of *affirming life*, in face of a threat; courage in the form of affirming a *way of life*; and courage in the form of affirming *worth beyond* my life and ways of finite life.

First form: Courage is intimately related to the *vital self-insistence* of a human being. Some individuals exhibit more natively an energy of being that faces more forthrightly into the world, and into the hazard of what is other to them. They exhibit a certain vitality of being that seems irrepressible. Every being shows this, but some stand out more than others, who by comparison seem merely timid. The timid hold back, as if overanxious or afraid. The affirming energy of the "to be" is more than self-affirming, and while this energy is singularized as this self, some selves singularly concretize that affirming energy of the "to be" more than some others do. This is why we call them "full of life." It is as if the native *conatus* is spontaneously an overflowing of any sense of threat, or indeed of hesitation brought about by sensitivity to the *passio essendi*. This is a kind of givenness of character, not much acknowledged by those who claim all is nurture, but evident enough if we are not bewitched by such theories. Some individuals seem to have natures more vitally self-affirming in this more overt sense. Surely it must be acknowledged, since if not, then further forms of courage would be deficient in the dynamic that gives them something of their élan.

An interesting question here is to what extent this form is more tilted toward a kind of *masculine* extroversion, where the *conatus* all but smothers the *passio*. Feminine feel for the nuance of the *passio essendi* must surely yield a different formation of these vital energies; the self-insistence will not be quite the same. Is this why philosophers—male philosophers—have so admired courage, as seeming to epitomize the power of the *conatus*? Think of Nietzsche's injunction to be hard, and his contempt for the effeminacies of his time. Or Aristotle: the coward runs away when danger appears—he is *soft*. The Greek word for "courage"—*he andreia*—has the tinge of what used to be called "manliness"; the cowardly were often referred to as "womanish." "Manliness"—a word not now much in use. Why? Until recently, armies—communities of trained killers, be they defensive or offensive—were the exclusive preserve of men. Would this mean women have less to do with courage? Surely not. When discussing women and courage, more would have to be said about the *passio essendi* and the giving of life.

Is this dynamic vitality properly courageous, if it is simply one's nature so to give expression to itself? Does not the notion of courage necessarily entail the emergence for us of some sense of threat, threat that must in some manner be known as such? If the original vitality is simply a spontaneous overflow, it does not quite fulfill this condition of knowing a threat, and hence is not quite courage either. And yet it is intimately related to courage, since there is something ontologically constitutive about such vital energies, since they are the given overflow of the affirming energies of the "to be," lived intimately as good by us. Could one have genuine courage if it were not undergirded, under-grounded by this elemental ontological affirmation of the "to be" as good? For surely genuine courage must have something worthy to be defended, to be fought for? And is this not again inseparable from the worthiness of the "to be" to be preserved, that is, affirmed again as good? Vital courage is not the end of the matter, but it does call to mind something of this ontological worthiness at work, in our self-affirming being.

Second form: This bears on a more *determinate affirmation of a life,* but in the context of a threat known as such. That threat can take different forms: it can be a more or less nameless anxiety that insinuates itself in the very intimacy of our being; or it can be a more determinate threat, such as an assault on our aesthetic being, our bodily integrity. It can also concern threats to the kind of second character we have become, beyond the first character of the given vitality of being. We have *become* such and such a person, not out of knowing threat, but by learning to face it, endure it, and transmute the vulnerability into an occasion of further self-transcendence. I am afraid, but courage in the face of what I fear not only overcomes fear but makes me a kind of person I was not before. Courage is intimately essential in how, as we put it, "we prove ourselves." If one had nothing to prove, would one need courage at all? Or if one thinks one has nothing to prove, might it be because one thinks one has met the greatest challenge and proved equal to it?

Notice the language here: it is the language of the *conatus essendi*. And, in fact, this surface of *conatus* causes us to forget once again what always lies in the background, namely the *passio essendi*. The need of courage, the claims of courage realized, all presuppose the vulnerability of being that is constitutive of what we are in terms of this *passio essendi*. Once again, if the *conatus* is dipped into the *passio*, must not this courage of second character also have to dip into this *passio*, and not now in the form of the above vitalities, but in the form of a kind of existential, lived honesty about what one is: deeply fragile, even in the very courageous surmounting of fragility.

One might wonder here about forms of *boyish* courage: it is not that they show courage, but rather every such form of courage risks deluding itself about this fragility. This fragility returns and hence the boy has to prove himself again and again. A man of sixty might still be a boy. There is no point at which he finally has nothing more to prove. For every time he proves himself, he has hidden what drives him to prove himself, namely, the ontological vulnerability of the *passio essendi*, and this must come back, whether in victory or defeat, for this is simply his being. Those who have nothing to prove are either, as it were, as unmovable as a stone, and hence dead; or those who have more radically come to terms with the ultimate fragility rooted in the *passio essendi*: they are not dead, but have taken a step beyond their own death by coming to terms with this *passio*, where the origin of life is, but also the twinseed of death.

Notice how we are always drawn back to something more indeterminate in the very determination of courage. I would prefer here to speak of the overdeterminate, as exceeding determination, rather than the indeterminate, as lacking determination. The overdeterminate origin has everything to do with the secret sources of strengthening. For it is not death that strengthens us, but the source of life that in affirming the good of the "to be" is more than death, more courageous than death. Courage of a life, of this life, in the face of a threat, is more determinate than the often formless overflow of vital energies, but it too is secreted from sources that root into more overdeterminate reserves.

Third form: This is courage in the face of a threat to a *way of life*. The determinations of middle life come more and more into play here. A way of life is not an overflow of vital energies, though this is needed; nor is it my or your life, though it is that too. It is the social incarnation of shared ways of being, often immensely plurivocal in themselves. It is a communal configuration of the ethos of being, and the human potencies of the ethical, in which individual and social value, or the sense of the worthy and worthwhile, are communicated in an immensely complicated intermediation, or plurality of such intermediations. There are many forms of communal courage here: within the community, and between different communities in a larger intermediation, but also between this community and another, for instance, this nation and another. This form of courage has often occupied philosophers: the courage that is either defensive of a society and its communal way of life, or offensive against a possible threat that left unattended may balloon into a monstrous enemy and destroy the society. What is courage here? I mention two aspects, one internal to the community, the other more "external," between a community and an outside other.

First, there is the courage of a community that will fight forces of disintegration within itself. A police force can embody this kind of immanent social courage. The enemy within is often the most insidious, it is said. It is true because what is entailed here is not only rival formations of *conatus essendi* (this faction against that), but also imposing forms of social *conatus* that force themselves on others—these others reduced to subject *passio essendi* whose receptive vitality is made to serve the dominant social *conatus*. What is courage for one is repression for the other. Think of the different modulations of courage as understood from the point of view of the Confederacy and the Union: what is for one an honorable courage is for the other a bloody intransigence. Both can be right, and therein lies the tragedy.

Though this is a social intermediation of courage, it is an intermediation that serves the self-mediation of the people. Hence it may be immanently defined by the encouragement of outstanding insiders: think of the way Churchill—a leader right for war, but an unsuitable braggart for peacetime—kept the spirits of his people up. His charisma intermediated the immanent social encouragement of the nation's courage. Or the communal courage may take shape through the definition of the outsider as the enemy, the worse the better to mobilize the secret sources of strengthening in a society. In other words, the self-insistence of a people, now called its historical right to self-determination, requires the courage to insist on itself and its own way of life (call it a culture or tradition) over against the alien way, either encroaching from outside, or occupying it as an invasive force. How is courage called up here?

The *conatus essendi* has to call upon secret resources in the *passio essendi* of a people[5]—for this is closer to what it loves more elementally, and often can only be appreciated by living it from within, living it in the intimacy of its happening. The language of a people, while something overt and determinate, is often the carrier of these secret resources, especially in its religious and poetic reserves. Hence the importance of language in liberation movements, fledgling nationalist causes, and so on. The *passio* of a people is spoken by its poet, who most deeply must be religious, as someone porous to the ultimate sources of origination. Language, the right word, calls forth courage; encourages a people to be itself, to become what it is in promise.

Of course, there are languages that encourage what is base in a people too. And in our time we have known the outrageous daring of great demagogues such as Hitler. That all of this is more than determinate cognition is evident in the practices of propagandists and advertisers—something well known to the Nazis, though not only them. If one controls the images, one may tap into secret sources of strengthening, or weakening. A charismatic leader has an intuitive power to speak to those secret sources; the *conatus essendi* can be impotent without recourse to the *passio essendi*. Think also of the way enemies to "national security" are sometimes conjured, as if out of nothing. That they are conjured as if out of nothing is crucially important, for the "nothing" ultimately refers us back to the forgotten fragility in the *passio essendi* that under-grounds even the most powerful *conatus essendi* of an empire.

In times of peace and stability, this self-determination in communal intermediations may not be exposed to unsettling disturbance. But then something at odds with an absolutized social self-determination can emerge, either from beyond a community's own boundaries or from within its own social intimacies. "The other outside" is not always an enemy demanding courageous resistance. The other may be the communicating face of a more universal intermediation beyond this self-determining community. Here political courage meets the demand for a transformation into religious courage. We will come to this.

Within the intimacies of a society, there may be those who have been violated, or consigned to conditions incompatible with the

---

[5] I speak of "general eros" rather than "general will" with regard to a people's sovereignty in *Ethics and the Between*, chapter 15, "The Community of Erotic Sovereignty."

human dignity we so jealously guard for ourselves. Ethical courage is needed to acknowledge the deficiencies of our given society. Ethical courage—this need not be the orchestrated rhetoric of universal victimhood. It says: we can and will do better. This is more than a social knowing, though it asks an honesty of a society it is not always willing to endure. It solicits a communal willingness in excess of the stabilized norm. Nothing of this willingness grows to effective life unless it exceeds the more cautious ploys that preach satisfaction with the present form of social self-determination. We see its power when it takes on the momentum of what we call a "movement." In an ethical "movement"—to the surprise of the jaded wisdoms of the already discouraged—secret energies of the *passio essendi* emerge into social showing. These can transcend the vital and the self-affirming toward a more universal ethical concern.

Fourth form: This form of courage relates to steadfastness in the face of threats to "values" beyond ways of finite life. As much is suggested above in the opening of a more universal intermediation beyond the second mediation of a particular society, and also in the acknowledgment of the unconditional worth of the human being to which we are asked to hold in ethical courage. If the first form of courage is a certain extreme that recedes into the half-hidden roots of vital life, here is an extreme at the other end, beyond whose verge death veils its mystery. The "beyond" of finite life is at stake, and the glorious vitalities of the middle space have to be given over, given up, to an equally, though differently, half-hid source. This means moving on the boundary between life and death, between being at all and not-being.

One might object that this is to overstate the matter. Yet, in truth, all forms of courage are imbricated in the mix of life and death, and the threat of the latter to the former. The boundary between these is not at the end simply, but is in the middle, and indeed in the beginning, in that being given to be is contingent happening, not necessary occurrence. The line of this boundary runs through all life in the between, and in the middle range of human concerns. It becomes most evident in moments of supreme threat, where the always immanent possibility of not-being shows itself with devastating effect.

I think that here there is a reawakening of the *passio essendi*, beyond the *conatus*—for instance, in compassion for the other's suffering, or in granting that the barbarian other, the hostile other, even the enemy, is also my brother. What courage would be needed to live these realizations? What would strengthen one to place oneself before others in such a potentially radical vulnerability? One throws away one's weapons. What encourages one to throw away one's weapons? Is it not foolhardy? Or is it that a good higher than the finite goods of the moderate humanized middle makes a call on us? We are visited by an intimation of transcendent worth that is no aesthetic frill; that disturbs the self-satisfaction of human existence; that cannot be determined through ourselves alone; that cannot be univocally known with the self-certainty we often crave; that places us in a constitutively equivocal space of having to risk what we cannot prove in advance; and that, if confirmed at all, can only be confirmed in the wager of courage itself. This is *religious courage* beyond ethical courage, certainly on the ambiguous boundary of the ethical, in that it is, most of all, not subject to our complete self-determination.

Think of this religious courage as a reawakening of what is promised in the *passio essendi*. The matter might be expressed relative to the *transcendental*, the *transcending*, and the *transcendent* potencies of the ethical.[6] Let me elaborate.

Relative to the *transcendental* potency, we find ourselves under the constraint of unconditional obligation that the moral imposes (Kant is right in this, though his language of autonomy is not adequate to the givenness of the moral law). This concerns the transcendental givenness of unconditional worth relative to the human person. It is not just respect for the moral law that is here needed, but an ethical courage that is more than vital self-affirmation. For ethical courage to do the good may in some situations put that vital self-affirming energy in jeopardy, and yet this risk is granted as a *must*. We undergo that "must" in that we "must" do what is asked of us. It seems to me that Kant does not have anything much to say about this as courage and the secret source of strengthening here, except simply to command us: "Just do it!" *But what if we cannot "just do it" through ourselves alone?*

If we were to take this question seriously, Kant's claims for *autonomy* would have to be qualified. There is an extraordinary footnote

---

[6] For a fuller account of the potencies of the ethical, see the introduction to *Ethics and the Between*, and *passim*. If the first and second forms of courage above relate more to the idiotic and aesthetic potencies of the ethical, the third form relates more to the dianoetic and eudaimonic, while the fourth form more explicitly relates to the transcending potency and the transcendent. The transcendental potency of the ethical might be situated somewhere between the third and fourth forms, though the eudaimonic could also be situated there.

in the *Critique of Practical Reason*, when he is discussing God as a postulate of pure practical reason.[7] What Kant says has bearing on the question of courage and the sources of strengthening. He speaks of Stoicism and strength of mind, and its elevation above the "base incentives of sense." He speaks of the Stoic "heroism of the sage who, raising himself above the animal nature of man, was sufficient to himself." He refers to Christianity to place it in the same line as Greek ethics, even though he does mention holiness. And then he says: While Christianity may destroy man's confidence of being wholly adequate to the ideal of moral perfection in this life, it nevertheless reestablishes this confidence by "enabling us to hope that, if we act as well as lies within our power, what is not in our power will come to our aid from another source, whether we know in what way or not." Aid from another source, and perhaps in a way that we may not even know? How can Kant, banner carrier of autonomous will and rational enlightenment, dare say such a thing? Or is that other source just the enigma of the secret source of strengthening? If it is acknowledged, the ideal of autonomy must be severely revised, and the tendency to elevate the courage of Stoic self-sufficiency criticized. Otherwise, the enigma of the *necessary ethical courage* is hardly even acknowledged.

Relative to the *transcending* potency of the ethical, our eros is inspired by an opening to what surpasses our own self-transcending. Nevertheless, we can so insist on autonomy that we make courage into a refusal to appeal to an other source of aid, or strengthening. I see this as very widespread after Kant. The *conatus essendi* claims it is the most courageous by standing fast against the vulnerability of the *passio essendi*, but this of course also means against itself—in the name of itself! This can be deeply ambiguous. There is a self-transcending that insists on itself alone, but more deeply as against itself, since the native eros to what is beyond itself is refused. What looks like self-transcending is no transcending, since it merely traverses a circle back to itself again. There is a heroism of self-sufficiency that secretly is this false form of courage.

There is a genuine self-transcending that has the courage to find against itself, and so seeks to be released beyond itself. In the inti-

---

[7] I. Kant, *Kritik der Praktischen Vernunft*, ed. Karl Vorländer (Leipzig: Felix Meiner, 1929), 146–47; *The Critique of Practical Reason*, trans. Lewis White Beck (New York: Macmillan, 1993), 133. This is in the "Dialectic of Pure Practical Reason," section V, "The Existence of God as a Postulate of Pure Practical Reason."

mate heart of *conatus essendi* as striving to be itself by being beyond itself, the *passio essendi* surges up with the mysterious solicitation that it is the "beyond" of self that self-transcending seeks, and not just itself again. The *conatus essendi* would, so to say, *burn up its own selving as a kind of offering to this "beyond" of self.*

This surge of transcending requires its singular courage (yes, singular), since it may have to go down into its own darkness to find that fire, to await communication of the secret sources of strengthening; and even when the strengthening comes, the exceeding of self beyond itself is not guaranteed of a success—certainly not on its own terms alone. It must be steadfast in a darkness of self-exceeding that may shake everything stabilized about its own consolidated form of being. Its intimacy with the *passio essendi* strengthens its courage for an exceeding in which its very being is placed on the line. I risk everything. I risk blessing or curse. I risk redemption or disaster. There is no "proof" in advance. The courage of the risk comes from what is most intimate to me, but also from what is other and strange to me. Within me it comes to me from beyond me. In the immanent otherness of my most intimate *passio*, an other otherness communicates a call and the secret strength to answer it. One is not alone.

Relative to *the transcendent*, the *passio* here is a passion of being that cannot hide behind the masks of its own forms of self-determination. It is as if God were also behind those masks created by the *conatus essendi*; as if God were behind them, in the intimacy of the *passio* and its secret mutations, so secret we as humans have only an inkling of what may be happening in our own most intimate being. When we know ourselves, we also know we do not know ourselves. Something is happening and one is not sure. What finesse and courage it takes to attend to this extremity of nuance in the soul. The enigma of encouraging sources is inseparable from our elemental vulnerabilities. What would protect us from nakedness before God in the ultimate porosity of being? Our only "weapons" here seem to be lies. But these are not "weapons," they are false defense measures against being true.

Our passion before God is most violently stressed when we come to face death, our own death—though not only this, since the death of a loved other can also be one's own death. We die the death of others too. What is the courage before death, if we here have the *conatus essendi* at the extreme where *conatus*, endeavor, reaches its own limit? One may endeavor to be, but the endeavor faces its own "not": I will *not* be, I am now "not to be." *Passio essendi* becomes a suffering of the "not," singularized in its own being as this I that is to die, whose to be is not to be. One can be awakened through suffering, through this suffering.

Once again this is a space of equivocity, for it can awaken one to despair, as it can awaken one to a hyperbolic trust that might be called courage before death. This is not the courage of the defiant Stoic, which is not courage before death but courage against death. I am talking about an encouraging that is in death itself, not against death, but through this most dark of all undergoings. Courage as an extreme trust; trust risking its "yes" in the undergoing itself. Its "yes" to what? To itself? But if only to itself, then it is finally to nothing, since it is to be nothing. If to what is beyond self, then perhaps it is to be itself in this being beyond itself. Either to nothing or to God. But a "yes" to nothing is not quite a "yes." The "yes" to God may have to come to itself beyond nothing, by saying its "yes" to its own nothingness, and then trust that a hyperbolic "yes" may strengthen it from beyond its own mortal destiny.

The Courage of the Philosopher, The Witness of the Religious

I realize that philosophers often now squirm if anyone mentions religion or God. In charity to their comfort levels, I come down into the lowlands of the finite middle. How apply these reflections to philosophers themselves? Generally, philosophers are more at home in the ethos of the warrior. Many of their reflections on courage refer to the paradigm of the warrior.[8] The risk then is a hypertrophy of the *conatus essendi*, and an atrophy of the *passio essendi*. Think of Plato's coupling of the spiritedness (*thumos*) of the warrior with the spirit of the philosopher. Of course, the Platonic philosopher is not a warrior, since his care for justice makes peace his concern, the peace of the soul harmonious with itself and the cosmos, the peace of the society wherein the different groups are at amity over the enterprise of the just social whole. And also of course the eros of the Platonic philosopher is, in some sense, intimate with the *passio essendi*, though also guarded about it. Clearly in the *Republic* the destructive rashness of

---

[8] Socrates was a hoplite, Descartes a soldier, a camp follower. Heidegger's three services include military service: *Arbeitsdienst, Wehrdienst, Wissensdienst* — all three equal in rank, and equally primordial for Heidegger. Plato would rank the philosopher superior to the warrior.

unknowing courage is to be tempered by the wisdom of the philosophers. But what is the courage of the philosopher? Is it just a courage
of knowing, if courage itself is not just a knowing? If not, what then
are the sources of strengthening of philosophical courage itself? If
they do not merely come from philosophical thinking itself, from
where or what do they come?

Nietzsche is unlike Plato in that his call for courage is much less
moderated by the necessity of *phronesis* in tempering the rashness of
eros that overreaches its own limit too impetuously, and is more
likely to precipitate disaster thereby than higher blessings. Nietzsche's call to war urges forward the *conatus essendi*, in the form of will-
to-power, alternatively contemptuous of and alarmed by the *passio
essendi* that might reveal its debt to the other, or bring on compassion.
These latter are weaknesses for the cowardly. Could one say that the
Nietzschean philosopher is willing to throw his weapons away? Is it
the Cynics who in antiquity seem most to have done that? And yet
their *words*, and perhaps their *performances of an elemental wisdom*
served to weapon them in a culture open to the truth of extreme
human vulnerability. And Socrates? Here we find the unweaponed
courage of knowing that it is better to suffer evil than to inflict it.
These are hard wisdoms properly to live.

And yet what are the weapons of philosophy? Words, words,
words. But are they weapons? What is the courage of words? Does
anyone know the secret source(s) of the true word? If philosophy is
an erotic activity, one has to ask again what are the sources of its
own strengthening for knowing? Not knowing itself; for to know we
have to be strengthened in the confidences that we *can know*, and this
we cannot know *before* we know. We can only trust that we can, en-
couraged, impelled by an unknowing confidence that it is possible.
If "being en-couraged" is before "being courageous" is there not a
"confiding" (*con-fides* — a "trust with") before "being confident"?
What is the confiding? The confiding is an endowment, an entrust-
ment. Is the speaking of the true word impossible without such a confiding endowment? But then the true word makes no sense if it is not
referred to its endowing source. But we are the endowed, not the
endower. We do not give ourselves the ultimate confidence, but are
given to be what we are as knowing *within the endowment of this confidence.*

Sapere aude! So proclaimed the careful Kant in urging Enlightenment and autonomy. What possibilizes that daring, that courage? Is
this daring not dark to itself, and is its possibilizing source *not* at all

determined by our autonomy? And yet Kant was one of the most cautious of thinkers when he arrived at the extreme and hardest questions. This timidity Nietzsche despised. Kant wanted to secure himself at every step, not to risk himself. If he had to risk himself with his postulates, even then he wanted the security blanket of moral necessity. Nietzsche's courage is a daring or audacity that exceeds rational enlightenment, and in this he is more rational than the rationalists are, for their securities are self-deluding. Nietzsche went more nakedly to war. But if the courage forgets the *passio essendi*, and seeks to absolutize the striving of the *conatus essendi* in the form of will-to-power, then it is deficient in the finesse needed for the harder question of the endowing source. Then the essential reverence of the philosopher is corrupted into the hubris of a domineering thinking, a dictating thought. Why do you say so? Because *I* say so! When I say *I*, I mean Nietzsche, of course. Nietzschean courage has too much of that "say-so."

Does Hegel's absolute knowing help us? But where is the courage then? Courage demands the *risk of the unknown*, and, as we saw, it cannot be accounted for in terms of our knowing alone. What then is the "yes" of the philosopher? Suppose God has absolute knowing, one might still ask: Does *God* show courage? Being all-knowing would seem to require no courage. Or would God's knowing be absolute courage in a sense other to ours: courage to give, courage to encourage what is radically other to itself? Human courage needs non-knowing—needs the openness of freedom. But is it not also dependent on this original giving of difference? Does not this bring us closer to the "being en-couraged" before "being courageous," and the endowing source that confides confidence?

These are difficult thoughts I cannot pursue further here. I conclude with a final remark on two instances of human courage that do have reference to the ultimate: the courage of the *warrior* (see the third form above) and the courage of the *witness* (see the fourth form above). There can be a philosophical warrior; there can also be a philosophical witness. Socrates' testament was not just a warrior's courage; it was that of one who apologized for a philosophical life. This is the venture of a *martyr: one who witnesses*.

There is a courage of truth asked of the witness. One is to stand by the truth, so far as it has been vouchsafed to one. Vouchsafed: this means an endowment, something given into one's trust. Courage here is the enactment of a fidelity to the endowment, to what has been given to one. The vouchsafing of truth entails an encouragement to courage. The source of the giving as other to oneself is communicated there in one's very being a witness, a testament. One might have to risk one's life in terms of this courage of the truth. This is not only applicable to canonized philosophical martyrs like Socrates. One thinks of more daily trials, where witnesses can be "interfered with," say, by bribe or intimidation. That some witnesses do speak the truth in circumstances entailing risk to life is itself testament to an unconditional call on us. It is because we can freely say "no" that courage is needed and enjoined. One can betray the call, and tell the untruth; the courage of being true fails one, or one fails relative to trusting the sources of strengthening that offer themselves.

Is the religious witness or martyr beyond the warrior? And beyond the philosopher? Blood is not an argument, Nietzsche rightly said. But is it a matter of *argument* here? In practice, Nietzsche's "warrior" rhetoric often does stir up the blood. But the question is not only the *how* of dying for something, but *for what* would one die? Are the witness of the philosopher and that of the religious person in the same family, if both come down to the courage of an ultimate trust—in truth, in the good of the ultimate? Testament entails the courage of *being truthful*; courage to be truthful, even though one might have to die. Courage here is connected with the *unconditional*. The ultimate needs no courage, being encouraging rather than being courageous in our sense; we need courage for the ultimate. But since we are *not* ultimate, can we *give ourselves the ultimate in courage*? What would that ultimate in courage be? Maybe that trust is more daily granted than we philosophers grant. Being religious has everything to do with our ultimate porosity in the *metaxu*, between God and nothing. Is it only here that the "yes" is granted?

8

On the Betrayals of Reverence

A Prior Reverence?

There are many models for the interrelations of religion, philosophy, and science: separation, complementarity, reconciliation, nonchalant indifference, and so on. I turn away from these models to turn back. I turn away from the enchantments of determinacy—its fixation on fixity, its will to secure. Here fixed philosophy, there religion fixed, there again science fixed; and then we see them stand as determinate, and now we set to and ask how we are to relate or mediate or reconcile or divorce or settle them in comfortable collusion or apartheid, and on and on. We become marriage counselors or police officers of territorial integrity, or border patrollers who inspect passports and travel documents for legitimacy. And it is only too true that regimes exist that will call forth their inquisitors and torturers.

We must not be too overtaken by the belief that science, philosophy, and religion are fixed determinations, and that our task is to join, or dissociate, or mediate, or reconcile, or police the boundaries between unbending determinations. Such determinations are the results of processes of coming to be determinate; and such processes are not simply a matter of determination but express more original and dynamic determinings, which exceed complete determination, indeed point to sources of determining that are in excess of all fixity, and univocalization. The later developments hide from us their equivocal roots in a more promiscuous mingling: a mixture in motion, out of which differences come to be, as well as a holding together extremely difficult to pin down. I think reverence may have more to tell us about this more primal source than the later-born reasons of science and philosophy. Religion is closer to the mother that gives us to be what we are. We become old and do not love our mother. We look and see a ruin that had its time of glory and now it is past. We do not look with reverence. We have forgotten or betrayed this early gift of the mother.

My line of thought begins from this consideration: A human being without reverence turns into a monster. To be a monster is not simply to be without reverence, but also to live its corruption; this corruption too lies at the heart of human reality. The quest of science is not our *unequivocal release* from that corruption; it may be complicit with it. A monster need not be a foaming brute, but can be silky and sleek and sophisticated.

A second line of consideration: I do not find myself at home with those who sing an easy and comfortable alliance of religion and science, nor between either of these and philosophy. I do not deny their kin character. But families, all resemblances notwithstanding, provide the ethos of grossest violence and spiritual deformation, as well as their opposites. We now inhabit an ethos within which the more objectifying mentalities enjoy an unprecedented dominance. The developments of science, coupled to the practical successes engendered by technology, consolidate this dominance. Let that trend be accentuated to an extreme, and I fear we have signed the death warrant of reverence, and hence the birth of man as monster. As I say this, I remember Vico and the turn of the gyre that brings the second barbarism of reflection, that gyre whose ominous turn the troubled Yeats envisioned.

A third line of consideration: The issue here is philosophical, not one for those within the religious simply, nor those simply within the scientific framework. When we reflect about the economy of the "whole," or, as I would prefer to put it, become perplexed about our being in the between, a perplexity such as marks philosophy, or ought to mark one's thinking can come to be *at an angle* to science or religion: inside and yet outside, in the midst of and yet other. This does not preclude porosity between them, or thinking that passes to and fro between them. But the question of the significance of science is not a scientific question—it is philosophical. Hence the appropriateness for it of modes of mindfulness not scientific, not objectifying.

Admittedly, modern philosophers have often aligned themselves more with science than religion, but this alignment is not at all self-evident.

But why focus on reverence *at all*? My impression is that most discussions of the interplay of religion, science, and philosophy place primary emphasis on what seems most important to the latter two. Hence we become absorbed in questions about the *reasonableness* of religion, or about the extent to which it matches the search for *law and intelligibility* as epitomized in science, or about the *autonomy of thought thinking for itself* in philosophy, and so forth. Not always do we have the dialogue that asks in all seriousness: How do science and philosophy stand, if we take with the utmost seriousness matters like reverence, matters seemingly more of moment to the religious? How do science and philosophy stand up?

Science and philosophy celebrate their initially hard-won autonomy. Do they grow complacent in their putative independence? Do they perhaps participate in the slow withering of the root of transcending? Is something being hollowed out by the progressive sterilization of the soil of reverence? Today there are extensive discussions of the relations of, say, metaphor and science: there are many signs that these discussions are going the way of aesthetics—science itself as a kind of "art," unintelligible without the leap of constructive imagination. Could one vary the question and ask about reverence and science: Should discussion of their relation be going the way of the religious? I mean: Why not begin to see philosophy and science as determinate crystallizations of a reverence that more basically is religious, or to which the religious may be more immediately close? I want to take the angle of vision that considers how things appear from the outlook of reverence: reverence seemingly tangential and at an angle to philosophy and science, but all the more thought-provoking for that—and yet most intimate to these others to whom it has come to seem most strange.

The Betrayals of Reverence

Why speak of the *betrayals* of reverence? This can mean at the very least two things: that we betray reverence; that reverence betrays us. I start with the second, for it has something to do with a temptation in one of the widespread self-images of scientific knowing. I mean this: it will be said that reverence puts us in thrall to another; say, the authority of the church and its obscurantist traditions, or supposedly

264 ■ Is There a Sabbath for Thought?

outmoded thinking. *Reverence betrays us* because we cease to think for ourselves and we fall into a kind of spell or bewitchment. What will scientific knowing do? It will wake us up from our bewitchment, our sleep in the spell of reverence. Taken in a certain way, this is the death decree of religion.

I know the issue will be fudged. It will be said that only certain religious presuppositions make possible the confidence in rational knowing that science exhibits and develops. I know, I know. I will return to the point in this claim: the deeper roots of science are themselves in reverence. My point now: the univocalization of being that signals the development of that confidence in rational knowledge entails the progressive extirpation of the roots of reverence—its own roots. Implication: unless science itself is rooted more deeply in the sources of religion, namely, in an ontological reverence for what is superior in worth to us and our science, in time it will be a plant trying to grow itself from the top down, from its own constructed heaven down to an earth it seeks to overlay. But then it blots out heaven, and covers the fertile ground in which the darker sources of its own healthier growing really reside.[1]

Suppose religion were closer than science and philosophy to the ontological roots of things, though mostly it does not know this, and would be puzzled to hear the matter put down thus. Its proximity to God is its intimacy with the ontological origin. Its genuine prayer is its being in communication with that origin. Betray that proximity and the monster in us is incited to its autonomy. Admiration is related to reverence, as I will indicate: *miranda*: what is to be admired. But the monstrous is also admirable: it takes our breath away; for it is excessive and hence our fascination with the monstrous is a cousin of reverence proper to the religious. The dark twin of the divine sometimes looks almost exactly the same as the divine. How to separate the twins? A problem for *finesse*. There is no univocal reason, no *geometry* to separate them. Religious practice is the devotion that sustains this finesse. Reverence is a finesse. If science loses reverence, if it betrays reverence, because it holds that reverence betrays it, then has it also cut itself off from finesse?

---

[1] Think of Jonathan Swift's tart image of Laputa in *Gulliver's Travels*—that land of the absentminded minds where projectors dreamed up, along the lines of the new science, schemes like constructing houses by putting up the roof first, building the rest of the house from there on down. See also Swift's remark about Socrates in his basket in *Tale of a Tub*.

Many scientific enlighteners have implied: reverence is self-incurred tutelage; it betrays us, for it stops us thinking, and *thinking must be critical*; reverence is submission and consent; it is the sanctification of what is other, and hence a complicity to let the unreason of the other off the hook. To become scientific, suspend reverence. Reverence leads us astray, fosters the wishful thinking that would think the other in the images of its own wish (God as wish-fulfillment). We need a cold shower of scientific rationality to awaken us to the gray dawn of the disenchanted world. What does science do? It presents itself as the *breaker of spells*. What were some of the spells? Among them, the witchcraft that saw Europe enveloped by the monstrousness of religious sects at war with each other in the name of the God of holy love. What is a spell? It is a pervasive enthrallment. And those within the spell cannot snap out of it of their own will. Something must come from the outside, like a clap of thunder, to bring them to their senses.

What if the spell is *culture-wide*? When an enchantment marks an era, or epoch, as a whole, from where is the thunderclap to come that will break in from the outside? A question to be remembered. For we are awakened from one spell, but soon we begin to fall under the power of another spell. While before we preached against witchcraft, now since we think of ourselves as enlightened about witchcraft, we cannot even entertain the possibility that we might now be prisoners of another spell. We preach our autonomous knowing and worry not at all that we are being led by the nose by nameless powers that rarely show their faces, and whose presence is barely suspected, except by some rarer souls who are sensitive to the sinking feeling of being drowned in a sea of illusion, a sea that by others is taken for the supporting truth of enlightenment. (Change from spell to spell: how does this differ from a "paradigm" shift?)

Science: reverence betrays us; we must reject reverence; and we will not be betrayed; we will know; and the gates of hell shall not prevail against a rationality that has come into its enlightened maturity; its illuminating power will be with us all days, even to the end of time, and even if in these times it develops and changes paradigms; a mighty fortress; an undying god. But is it too much to ask if the temptation of scientific knowing is itself always to betray reverence? Is its rejection of the reverence that allegedly betrays us *itself a betrayal of reverence*, whose extreme consequences are not enlightenment but a new descent of darkness? The new spell: enlightenment is itself darkness. We insist on making all of being intelligible in a certain way, and we end up in a situation where nothing has any point, where everything is senseless, our own selves most of all. Excess of light produces blindness. The happier we become, the more miserable we seem to be.

Why? Is it because we have been perfidious to reverence, and the chiaroscuro of reverence, in whose play of light and darkness we lack the patience to live? We insist on turning its doubleness into the mirror of our own light, and we end up accentuating the darkness we willed so heroically to dispel. Suppose then that nihilism is the truth of scientistic enlightenment: the feeling at the high noon of enlightenment that it comes to nothing, that it all is an empty extravagance of wind. For if we love nothing, reverence nothing in an ultimate sense, there is only a mocking silence to our question on this shadowless noon: What is the point of it all, what is the good of it all? We extinguish reverence, come to ourselves as autonomous knowers, and fear finally it all comes to nothing.

Reverence and Respect

What is reverence? There are forms of reverence directed to a particular person: I revere my teacher or my father or my big sister. One looks up to someone. Or one might have a reverence for things, in the sense of a special care and tenderness for the very worth of their being: not their price, but their worthiness, a worthiness beyond instrumentalizing. An artist can show something of this reverence for things in his imaging of them in his work (why the relative absence of such reverence in modern art?).

We speak of reverence for life. This seems less specific, more indeterminate. This more pervasive sense of reverence is related to the religious. Religious reverence cannot be defined in terms of any specific finite object: were it so, we would be in idolatry rather than reverence. A doubter might say: nothing specific, nothing in particular, nothing. Religious reverence is devotion to nothing. Reverence for God might look like that: a blank love of what cannot be finitely specified. And yet this same nothing is more than nothing, and more than what can be finitely specified, because its non-objective object is more than can be finitized. This is an indeterminacy that is not ontologically defective in determinations, but rather an overdeterminacy enigmatically in excess of determinacy, with a fullness impossible to overpower and fix.

Something of this same excess is evident when we revere someone like a great teacher: the teacher is there determinately as this person, but what is shown in and through him or her exceeds what can be determinately fixed. Similarly, the reverence for things: as an artist shows this (see there the still life, quick with strange energy), there is something exceeding there about that bowl of apples, and yet what is there cannot be pinned down there univocally, for it exceeds all fixation and indeed determinate analysis. It is this more excessive reverence, this overdeterminate reverence, that is at issue for us here. For it offers itself as a porous attunement to what gives itself as worthy to be admired, indeed to be loved, an attunement that cannot be made completely determinate, though it provides something essential to the context or ethos within which our more determinate fixations of finite life take place. In that respect, it is a source of more determinate formations that come out of it.

The question: Does what we call the desire to know, in its different forms, have its roots in a more primal ontological reverence: a reverence not fixed on, confined to the determinate intelligibility of what is, but in attunement to the good of being, the glory of creation, the gift of the "to be"? If so, such roots are intimate kin of the religious attunement to the divine and its gift of finitude. Scientific and philosophical thinking, in their more determinate and rational formations, grow out of these roots.

Reverence is *more than respect*. There is love in it, as well as trepidation. Respect is a more circumscribed relation in which I also maintain my self-respect. I can stand at a distance and maintain my integrity. Thus the great importance of respect for Kant: I can preserve my autonomy, even while acknowledging something other as worthy, be it the moral law or another person as end in itself. To treat with respect also means "to beware," to stand on guard. *Achtung!* Watch out! "Revere," for instance, might be traced back to Latin *"vereri"*—to hold in awe or fear; this is a possible distant relative of the English "aware," "beware." Respect is a vigilance not quite reverential: more standing on its own dignity than giving itself over to a worthy other. Reverence is more than standing on one's dignity, for there is a worthiness beyond dignity, as there is beyond "price." Because reverence has *love* in it, it is also a yielding of the fixed boundary of one's affirmed integrity.

Reverence is beyond autonomy, but it is not a form of servitude: it is a freeing, a being free in relation to the superior other. It always has some relation to the superior other in it, even when ostensibly the reverence is addressed to another finite creature or happening or event: to these reverence relates in the light of a secret presentiment of the supreme other. In that reverence is related to *veneration* for a thing or place or person held in awe, of an exalted or sacred character, the responses it engenders, such as deferential bowing, or kneeling, enact the surrender that is the germ of worship—I am given over to the worthy superiority of the other. Finally, all forms of reverence yield pride of place to reverence for God, and indirectly free us toward this. That reverence is more than respect is related to the fact that the God of the agapeic origin is more than the God of the moral law, such as Kant maintained.[2] Reverence forgets self in a release that exceeds integrity; respect maintains self in integrity that keeps its distance.

Reverence and Scientistic Univocity

How does this fit with the quest for scientific knowledge? I see this quest as driven by the desire for the most complete univocalization of being possible. What is this univocalization? To reduce all equivocities to as clear and distinct uniformities as possible, to eradicate mystery as much as possible, for mystery is a problem that, reformulated as a difficulty, seeks its determinate solution, short of which the quest for scientific explanation is frustrated. The radical character, in principle, of this quest is quite compatible in practice with a humility on the scientist's part in his or her admission of, say, the tentative or provisional or revisable nature of now given results. The dynamic: an initial perplexity, perhaps full of ambiguity, is made less equivocal by being made a problem, which is the perplexity progressively univocalized and given as precise as possible a determinate form. But determinate problems seek their commensurate determinate solutions, generating in turn more determinate problems, and more solutions. That there might be *root indeterminacies in the ontological situation* that we wrongly approach in the spirit of univocalization, this thought is not to the fore along the way of science. What we can univocalize we

---

[2] On the notion of God as agapeic origin, see, for instance, *Being and the Between*; on autonomy, see "Autonomia Turranos: On Some Dialectical Equivocities of Self-Determination," in *Ethical Perspectives* 5, no. 4 (1998): 233–52. That "being free" takes plural form, and is not confined to autonomous self-determination, is diversely explored in *Ethics and the Between*, especially part III.

will univocalize; the rest awaits better methods, further research, and so forth; the maximum of univocity will still be the desideratum.[3]

Reverence moves in a different direction to the spirit of this univocalization. It lives in ambiguity. It also lives in a milieu in which there are excesses to determination: there is something too much that is not a determinate problem simply; the excess asks to be let be as excess; to seek to grasp with the determinacies of our conceptual tools is precisely *not* to understand what is at play here.

Again this example: I revere my teacher. What is my reverence? Is it fear? No. Is it lack of independence on my part? Why so? Surely reverence is not servility. Is there a problem to be solved? How so? Is my creativity being stifled by this reverence? Why should it be? My reverence again is not just respect, for I can respect another and not love that other. Reverence always entails some love of the other, and so it is more than respect, though not then less than respect. When I revere my teacher, I acknowledge a superiority that I silently admire, and not admire only, but love. Or perhaps there is an admiring that is an unstated love. *Admirare*: the word *mirare* is there: *miranda*: wonder: an astonishment that is agapeic. My reverence frees me from myself in a love that transcends toward the worthy superiority of another, in whose aura I find myself, whose charisma enthralls me, in its own way. I consent to a superior otherness with whose worthy value I do not claim to be on a par. This is even true of reverence for things: reverence does not make idols of them; it lives in appreciation of the fragile gift of their finite being; thanks for their being given makes us porous to something further. There is a joyful heteronomy.

Is not scientific knowing more closely allied with the cognitive ideal of the autonomy of thinking for oneself, knowing that, so far as possible, one will determine for oneself? The dominance of science in modernity is not unrelated to an unprecedented stress on autono-

---

[3] Recall here how not long ago we sweated with *cybernetic anxiety* with the approach of the millennium: change one number, from 1999 to 2000, and there was deep disquiet abroad that the supreme exactitude of the system would not work or would be thrown entirely out of kilter. The desideratum was the absolutely workable, the absolutely reliable, the supremacy of exactitude. But this *one little number* might have had more world-historical significance than *Cleopatra's nose*! Our cybernetic anxieties betray how much we have taken for granted. On being and univocity more generally, see *Being and the Between*, chapter 2. Could any approach tending to naturalistic uniformitarianism even begin to understand what is at issue relative to God's being as *other* to finite univocities?

mous self-determination in that respect. We now inhabit these ideas—they are like the water in whose element we swim, so that we find ourselves choking and gasping with disbelief if someone suggests that we are really drowning in our own self-determination, and that we need the hand of another to lift us out of the pit where the waters have risen to our necks.

Reverence for the truth: What is this, and how relate it to the scientific quest? Is it reverence for this or that fact, or law, or "truth"? Is this reverence not our being in *the spirit of truth*, itself expectant with respect to something unconditional with regard to truth? We all hate to be deceived, though we often deceive without compunction. Why hate? Is this hate not the sign of a love: our love of truth, at least with relation to ourselves? Is it not because we want our trust in truth not to be broken, at least with respect to ourselves? Of course, to contract this trust to ourselves is perhaps already a betrayal of our being entrusted with being in the spirit of truth, and the reverence for truth. Again, there are complex relations here; but finally we find it hard to fix reverence for truth to this or that, or for this or that self, or community; something more is in play.

Consider the question this other way: How do truth and falsity relate to reverence? Truth as correctness to fact clearly seems not adequate. What facts? Again can one revere facts or information? A *literalist mind* knows no reverence: wooden, rigid, lacking imagination. This is true of scientistic types, true of fundamentalist types. Or do we find in genuine reverence a "realism" in the truest sense? The real is not the reality of dead facts. The more literalistic mind will wave its wand of obviousness over facts, but there is no magic in that wand; and that is why this mind knows no reverence; or if there is magic, it is one that dispels the proper "charm" of reverence. Keats asked: "Do not all charms fly at the mere touch of cold philosophy? Philosophy will clip an angel's wing." But charm is not a word of falsity, however, since it is related to the *charisma of the reverent*: charm is the courtesy of charisma.

There is no testing procedure for reverence, and yet there is an elusive fittingness: reverence can be appropriate or not, depending on many factors. The response of appropriate reverence has much to do with the ontological status of the revered "object." In another sense, there are no "objects" for reverence; it is transobjective. It is a transsubjective response to what is transobjective, though sometimes embodied in this or that revered other. This transobjective status of the being that is revered concerns its *worthiness* to be revered. So there is no testing procedure, yet reverence can be tested. Thus one can be *betrayed* by a wrong reverence, a false reverence, as when the "object" is invested with too much, with more than its worthiness can in truth bear. Thus the revered hero comes to be seen as having feet of clay: something does not hold up. And this can be the fault of the one revering, as when I find myself *infatuated*. It is partly my fault that I hold this other in too high an esteem. I am falsely bewitched by the charm or the aura of charisma, which turns out to be gold more fool's than true.

Thus *reverence brings us into the ethos of bewitchments*. But bewitchment is also a religious category: a witch is an agent or practitioner of powers beyond the human, nefarious powers, benign powers. Reverence is inseparable from spells cast, or spells welcomed by infatuated desire, spells that can loose demons on the world or unleash the dogs of war. This is perhaps a contributory motivation in the will to neutralization, marking early modern science: to be exorcised of religious spells whose demons were the dogs of religious wars. The will to neutralization preaches: do not burn the witches; let us put witches and their inquisitors on ice; and we will be free from spells, as well as from the bewitching reverence that betrays us to darkness. The repudiation of reverence itself shows a test or ordeal of reverence which can be known by its fruits. There is an inevitable element of equivocity here, asking of us the utmost in finesse. One might say that the irreverence that produces destruction of the unworthy is the dark twin of the reverence whose inner essence is a love that venerates the worthy. What is truly to be revered is not the vessel of our investment; we are the celebrants of its worthiness; we are given something to be revered.

When early modern science struggled against bewitchment, those witches were often feminine; the new science will be "masculine"— hard-headed, tough, and tempted to abjure entirely our *passio essendi*. For this hard science, reverence shows too much of the equivocity of the tender feminine: its "softness" now is "nebulous," "fuzzy" like "clouds." Hard science gives us the "solid ground" of, say, primary qualities and their combinations: not "mushy" with soft secondary qualities, but "clean," and "value-less." A world washed clean. Seemingly univocalized without ambiguity. But the healthy organisms are those that thrive in earthy, dirty conditions. Recent studies indicate that children more robustly exposed to relatively dirtier conditions are healthier than children protected in more antiseptic conditions, who are more liable to asthma, allergies, and such like. What would a world without smells be like? Would we have to fragrance it with *false perfumes*?

I stress that my view is not that there is a simple *univocal* loss of reverence, nor indeed a necessary telos determined always in advance by a relentless objectivizing scientism. The project of univocalizing the world is itself deeply equivocal. The issue rather concerns certain equivocal potencies in the ambiguous milieu of being. The crystallizing of some of these potencies does not destroy other uncrystallized potencies. More often, the uncrystallized will precipitate as a *mutant form*. Reverence will take mutant shapes: a denied religiousness flowers in exotic and seemingly incomprehensible bewitchments. A betrayal is not a univocal loss; nor is its happening always self-consciously explicit. Betrayal means that we turn away from the reverence, and though the turn looks quite innocuous, yet its denied presence does not completely put it out of play. I betray a friend, and again it need not be overtly done in some dastardly treason. *But my turn away or betrayal stays with me*, even though I know it not now, or consign it to oblivion, and the one betrayed seems not with me. *The betrayal that does not know its own treason is often the most insidious and long-lasting in its toxic effects*. The toxic effects can be intoxicating, that is, can bring new bewitchments. So also with the betrayal of religious reverence. It is with us when we name it not, and it corrupts us most when we know it not. This is a betrayal we cannot wash out, finally. Nor do we know we are intoxicated with bewitchments. We cannot even name the bewitchments, for now these are what seem to give a point to all we do.

That a betrayal is not a simple univocal loss also relates to my rejection of simply accepting, as given, seemingly fixed determinations of philosophy, science, and religion. This fixing is the result of a modern "autonomizing" of each, without perplexity about deeper sources: sources prior to the more fixed determination, sources overdeterminate and out of which each comes to formation and definition. Return to the origin is a return to a more fluent overdeterminacy where there is an unexplicated togetherness. The religious is closer to that primal source.

Reverence and the Sources of Knowing

Regarding the *sources of knowing itself*, what can one say relevantly here? The desire to know is a source of the scientific quest, but what is the source of the desire to know? As we know, this latter desire can take many forms; for there are many knowings, of which the scientific is but one. When we wonder about the sources of the desire to know, our question is not any straightforward scientific question. In asking the question, we show ourselves already to participate in that which is the "object" of our inquiry, hence we can never stand objectively outside it. In that regard, science is not a question to itself, though it questions everything else, and even though at moments of limit and crisis the question of its own nature and methods does come alive for it. *But this perplexity about its own sources* is not the element in which it lives, or wants to live. It is carried by the desire to know, which it takes for granted as its enabling power, without astonishment or perplexity about what grants this power at all. Thus too it is not always attuned to the perplexity that this enabling of mind may be deeply equivocal and dangerous, for it releases monstrous possibilities, precedents for which we look in vain among the other creatures of nature. Our will to know scientifically, in potentially opening up to comprehend all that is, is *disproportionate* to all the objects it makes its concern. It is not perplexed about its own disproportion; not perplexed about the sources of this disproportion and the perils.

If you say the sources of the desire to know are in a continuation of *biological adaptation*, clearly this is true to a point, but it seems to me disproportionate to the intensiveness of penetration and the extensiveness of range that our scientific knowing projects. There is something useless here, relative to more proximate biological concerns. Uselessness is disproportion: it reveals the trace of infinity in the finite knower; and hence it mediately connects with reverence of the finite religious person for the infinite.

Or you say: the source is to be found in neurophysiological causes; science will lay out these causes. But science itself is also caused by neurophysiology, which here it invokes as explanation of itself. But what status has it *itself* then? Another formation of neurophysiology? But what gives it a status as the true, or the better, formation of neurophysiology? How to distinguish between the better and worse, the truer and less true, formations of neurophysiological causes? But these are all *qualitatively the same* relative to neurophysiological causation. There seems no explanation of mind that does not presuppose mind. And indeed, if claims to truth are made, this presupposes that fidelity to reality or being is better or superior to infidelity; but these are irreducibly qualitative distinctions or differences which seem impossible to uphold on the homogeneous terms claimed *within* the theory. If this theory were true, its truth could not be upheld. If it were true, it would lose its claim to be the truth about mind. Its overt claims are urged in terms of covert presuppositions that truth is better than falsehood. But these covert presuppositions cannot be explained in the particular terms of this theory, since they are presupposed by every theory claiming to be true.

You will say that philosophy is a reflective discipline that makes knowing its own thematic, and hence it is more explicitly capable of the self-knowing here required. This is true, and philosophical perplexity can move in a different direction to the more objectivizing curiosity of the finite sciences. But the perplexity above, regarding the enigma of the sources of the desire to know, can be put also to philosophy in this form: Is not philosophy often tempted to make a little god of reason; and when pressed to justify its faith, does it not infrequently reply that reason is self-justifying? For the only way to justify reason is to use reason; and so if we find ourselves in a circle, it is a benign circle—reason puts itself to the test, reason passes its own test, it confirms itself by its own self-confrontation and self-confirmation. Is this not so? Hence the god of philosophers is Aristotle's god: the thought that thinks itself.

Something is not quite right about this, something put in recess: the marvel of our thinking that is given from sources that are not themselves thought; an other to thought thinking itself; a source that releases our thinking into the freedom to seek the light, the light that gives it the power to be itself a participant in the light. Philosophical reason can easily fall asleep in its own self-bewitchment. It will dream its dream of reason within the spell woven by reason's own enchantment with itself. The enigma that we are given to be as beings with the promise of reason will be dispelled in rationalistic self-congratulation. We revere ourselves as rational beings (see Kant), but there is a self-reverence which is the counterfeit of reverence, as the walking undead might be the counterfeits of the living.[4]

---

[4] Consider this contrast not entirely unrelated to reverence and self-determining reason: on one hand, Schleiermacher's basing religion on the feeling of *dependence*; on the other, Hegel's apotheosis of self-determining thinking, and his corresponding contempt for Schleiermacher's view, expressed in the (in)famous comparison—if religion were grounded in the feeling of dependence, the dog would be your best Christian. Without entering into the differences between them, nor endorsing Schleiermacher, reverence testifies to what one might call a kind of releasing dependence. Certainly one cannot self-determine oneself into reverence. The polarity of dependence and independence, and their dialectic, whether in the Hegelian dialectic of master and slave, or in some other form, does not offer us the right way to be true to what is released in reverence. This is beyond such a polarity and such a dialectic.

Reverence, properly understood, can give signs about the source that further comes to determinate form, as the extraordinary desire to know that is our native endowment. These signs suggest that this source cannot be contained within the circle of thought that thinks itself. For again the release of reverence to a superior otherness is a granting that is not self-produced by us; it is a happening, in which we are as much gifted as we are carried by a transcending beyond ourselves. Reverence for the superior other is always a being given of release from the other toward which we are released. It cannot be imaged as any circle of the one that is simply at home with itself. Reverence is a being at home, but it can also seed a restlessness with every pretension of self, a restlessness without the violence that turns against that self, a restlessness of love that is carried beyond itself, a distension of selving in the sweet pleasure of being caught up in transcendence itself. Reverence, "that angel of the world," as Shakespeare called it,[5] shows a serenity before the superior other that is aching with a love.

Reverence points to a source deeper than determinate religion, philosophy, science. Each grows out of that source, and each shows something of the opening granted in the source. The greatness of scientific knowing is just its participation in that opening: its laying itself open to the happening of the world in its intelligibility; its realism. Its refusal of merely wishful thinking is itself sourced there; as is its own refusal of reverence—this refusal is itself fed by a reverence for truth that would not sleep in the bewitchments of mind that determinate religions and philosophies can also effect.

When we grow perplexed about the sources of the desire to know, we are driven to wonder whether this desire to know can know itself completely. One thing is true: it cannot determine through itself its own sources completely, since it must *already be* as desire before it can ask about itself and its sources. It always finds itself after a beginning which initially is not lucid to itself, and which never becomes fully lucid to itself so long as it is in the movement of desire, which for humans, as long as we live, is never finally terminated.

Hegel's insult raises questions about his idolizing of self-determining being, about his lack of finesse about dogs—and maybe about religion too. As we saw in connection with the poverty of philosophy and the Cynic philosophers, dogs might be appreciated otherwise (see Chapter 3, note 6).

[5] Shakespeare, *Cymbeline*, 4.2.246: "Though mean and mighty rotting / Together, have one dust, yet reverence— / That angel of the world—doth make distinction / Of place 'tween high and low."

Our desire for light itself emerges out of the chiaroscuro of being: we do not determinately know the sources of our desire to know and we cannot make them completely determinate; for even the desire thus to make everything determinately known is itself more than determinate. I am not talking about the unconscious, which is a hypothesis already framed in the horizon of determinate knowing. I mean the sources in being, the ontological roots of this desire. If these are dark to determinate cognition, all desires to know are more opaque to themselves than might be comfortably granted by these different forms of knowing. We think we know ourselves, and we are ignorant of the sources of thinking and our own self-knowledge. Each is rooted in an otherness in excess of thought thinking itself, or the terms of its own self-aware norms.

The desire to know always points us also to the paradox indicated in Plato's *Meno*: we must *already* be in some relation to what we seek to know, though as seeking to know we seem not yet to have a relation to it—we would not seek to know, did we not already know, if only as presentiment; but if we already know, why seek? There must be an unknowing knowing, or a knowing unknowing, in the complex intermediate character of our desire and ignorance. My suggestion is that there is a more *primal ontological reverence* out of which knowing as determinate cognition takes form; and it is with reference to this reverence that the double condition can be approached, the equivocal condition of being in relation and yet not being cognitive master of it. The development of certain forms of determinate knowing turn their back on this double condition, and its participation in an equivocal character, in a kind of chiaroscuro where a love and a trepidation coexist and promiscuously intermingle. Reverence points us to this sacred chiaroscuro.

If our condition here seems more to relate us to Plato's Cave than to the Sun, there are complications. Some searches for the Sun are resolved to turn the Cave entirely into a glare of garish light: scientistic enlightenment. What is produced? A different darkness. The more intelligible we make the world other to ourselves, the more meaningless we ourselves seem to become in it. Other searches for the Sun come more deeply to grant the truth of the Cave, the equivocal truth that will always be our lot as finite beings. The Sun is not denied, but neither is the Cave, even when we try to make our way to the surface of the earth, and even if we have been gifted by an elevation into a higher sphere, we will be asked to journey back down into the place of shadows again. Many interpretations of modern science lack the Sun or God. Rather they see here the secular will to enlighten the Cave purely through the self-produced light of the human intellect. The interesting thing is not only the continuing chiaroscuro of the Cave, but the blindness of the illuminators to the fact that we ourselves are grown in the Cave. So we ourselves necessarily in our being are *exemplifications of the chiaroscuro*. We are our own underground. We want to dispel the equivocity completely, but we the dispellers are equivocity incarnate, and even our will to dispel the equivocity is the host to a myriad of unnamed, ignored, despised, betrayed equivocities.[6]

Those who desire to univocalize the world hate the thought of the chiaroscuro of being. This chiaroscuro is the problem they will dissolve, it is not the milieu of being we inhabit always. Such a desire to know is a refusal of the truth of equivocal being. It claims itself to be in the truth or in its spirit; it is equivocal being that is in untruth. One worries that such a view of science harbors a certain ontological violence of the univocal mind. In fact, it too is indebted to the despised reverence from which it has come and against which it has turned, an ungrateful child of the mothering ontological reverence.

Suppose we say the desire to know is a *late-born child of reverence*. How late-born? Religion and philosophy are older children—and in that respect closer to the source. The late-born child is allowed to take determinations of life as already granted. It produces marvels of its own, with and within these already granted determinations. But it is not always as intimate with the original granting source prior to this form or that form. This is, in part, its temptation: idolatry of the already formed, false reverence for the determinate. Suppose religion is the oldest daughter of the more primal reverence. Then if we lose religion, our reason is more likely to end up *an orphan without home*. What will it do in its abandonment and without parents? It will remake the world as *its constructed home*, but without reverence. For who or what has it to thank, except itself? And do not preach that the relentless objectifying ways of science are *not* complicit in the

---

[6] Think of Socrates in the *Phaedrus* (229): He wonders if the winds of Boreas and so on should be "demythologized" through a neutral, univocal cosmological explanation. His response is rather: No, I must know myself first and call what I am into question: Am I a monster more swollen and furious than Typho or a gentler being endowed with a divine or gentler lot? Notice that self-knowing is named together with this double possibility of the monstrous and something more divine—a doubleness entirely fitting in considering reverence, for we are this doubleness.

flattening of the human being. We grow one-dimensional souls—and with complex theories to buttress our rationalizing preaching. We shield our eyes from forms of practical life spawned by the technological outcomes: homogeneity incarnate, hiding from itself the sameness in it all with a lush profusion of rhetorics of difference and uniqueness. This too is a form of bewitchment. Say this, and you may well be set upon by those woken grumpily from the sleep of knowing.

Reverence and Ontological Nihilism

Reverence has importance vis-à-vis the issue of *ontological nihilism*. To be reverent is to be beyond oneself: devoted to the other as worthy. In religious reverence, it is to be beyond oneself in devotion to the superior, the supreme other. Yet this being beyond is a strange intimacy with what as mysterious is strange, and what as strange is in deepest community with us. Reverence is related to wonder, where this shows a free contemplation of worthy otherness: the ontological value of its otherness as other, and the aura of the source that plays around its givenness. Reverence for the finite is in the light of the play of that aura. Does all reverence ultimately return to the primal reverence: reverence for God? We revere finite worthies just because of their goodness of being as having been given to be from out of the generosity of the surplus source. "It is good, very good." Reverence is *within* the happening of that primal affirmation. Philosophizing that begins in wonder rather than in doubt is more kin to that reverence. Doubt is entertained in the loss of love. Doubt reveals the dying of reverence. If we erect it into the primal source of true knowing, we corrupt our presentiment of the agape of the divine origin.

Kill reverence and intellectual curiosity *undergoes a mutation*. Curiosity then does not become a merely neutral instrument; for even if it is an instrument, it is subserved by purposes, by an agenda, by presuppositions about that on which it is to work. Neutrality mutates into indifference, indifference into contempt, contempt into hostility, hostility into aggression, and then we have the full assault that will subject being, as an other to be dominated. The loss of reverence is at the source of such an ontological tyranny wherein the human being is not at all one neutral being among others, but rather is the autocrat of the neuter. And so the throne is occupied by usurpers. Knowing, we will say, is a project, and the project of modern curiosity is closer than we always grant to the temptations of ontological usurpation. For if the world is worthless, we cannot stand a worthless world, we must make it worthy, worthy of us, and that means we must make it our instrument. The instrument of mind becomes itself lord in a dialectic in which lord and servant replace each other: everything other now serves us, even if we still sometimes speak of being servants of a truth that passes beyond us (the first is the corruption of reverence; the second a residue of the more original reverence).

What do we find at best? An equivocal mixture of openness to nature in its otherness (seed of agapeic mind) and our will-to-power over that other (knowledge is power). But corrupting the implicit reverence of the first unfetters an unbridled form of the second. Descartes may appeal to God, but we can get on well enough without God, we say. We can always say that, and do say it. This is to be oblivious to the gift as gift, the granting of being and our enabling powers, a taking it for granted. We are in the gift of the agapeic origin that lets us be to be free in our own difference, even to the oblivion of mindfulness of the generosity of the source.[7] Loss of reverence goes with this oblivion. Many postmoderns emphasize the will-to-power. Their hermeneutics of suspicion makes them less attuned to the reverence of agapeic mind. Many apologists for science cannot offer with sufficient finesse the account that would restore the reverence. For they are guilty, to a degree, of the claims made against them. The importance of an adequate philosophy here concerns our need for a mind of finesse to read the signs of equivocity: the equivocity of univocal science itself—as indeed of its postmodern deconstructors.

We cannot sidestep the issue of the *worthlessness of the whole*, a question brought on in the train of science. Scientifically, we cannot claim any teleology, nor establish inherent value: the happening of the world and its process is disjoined from worth. What then of the worth or worthlessness of the intelligibility that science discovers? What point has it? Has it also no point? Reverence brings us closer to the issue of what is worthy to be. If it concerns the worthy being of the superior, how speak of the superior at all, if the world as a whole is there as a valueless neutrality? How speak even of the superiority of science? Finally, it too is one more indifferent procedure among others in the valueless whole, talk on as much as we will about its vaunted "successes." "Success" can be a very vacuous notion. Hit-

---

[7] In addition to *Perplexity and Ultimacy*, chapter 4 on "Agapeic Mind," see also "Neither Deconstruction nor Reconstruction: Metaphysics and the Intimate Strangeness of Being," *International Philosophical Quarterly* 40, no. 1, 157 (March 2000): 37–49.

ler was successful in exterminating millions of Jews. Success is vacuous, indeed potentially vicious, if not subtended by a deeper sense of worth or worthlessness. Reverence grants the worthiness of being.

If nature as other is void of inherent value, what then? We as sources of value? Infinite value? But how make sense of unconditional worth in a valueless whole? The ecological attitude signals a return to a sense of the worthy there-being of nature as other. But there is no way to make sense of our respect for other-being, or for the human being as an end in itself, if there is not a deeper reverence for value that is not merely human: to be is to be good: it is good to be: ontological value, and reverence. Where does the notion of *ontological value* fit within scientific objectification? Nowhere. Science tells us nothing about these issues and does much to make human beings insensitive to them by taking them up into the dances of determinate explanations.

Does reverence hint at the promise of something like an innocence regained?[8] The fall would be our defection from an original unselfconscious reverence. The loss of this turns us against what is worthy as other, turns us back into our own desire as self-affirming which, in turn, quickly mutates, against the ambiguous presence of the other, into an erotic seeking, itself from the outset infected with the urge of unrestrained will-to-power. Reverence hints at the beyond of this fall into the dominion of unjust will-to-power. Science takes place within that fall also, and hence is double: tempted by will-to-power, rooted finally however in a gift which cannot be described in the economy of will-to-power, and to which its own fidelity to the real and to the spirit of truth pays witness—an always tempted witness. (You say that science is pure and its use is impure. Is this a somewhat self-serving exoneration? If so, the scientist must wear sackcloth for the impure possibilities he or she both knowingly and unknowingly brings to birth. . . . Science should confess its sins, it should repent and purge itself. . . . Weapons of mass destruction, pesticides developed to kill "pests," but perfected for use on humans in death camps. . . . Yeats again comes to mind: "Descartes, Locke, and Newton took away the world and gave us its excrement instead. Berkeley restored the world."[9])

---

[8] Tennsyon: *In Memoria*, prologue: "Let knowledge grow from more to more, / But more of reverence in us dwell; / That mind and soul, according well, / May make one music as before."

[9] W. B. Yeats, *Explorations*, selected by Mrs. W. B. Yeats (London: Macmillan, 1962), 325.

For reverence is related to *astonishment*, and this is importantly related to the *best fidelities of science* to being as it is.[10] Astonishment can easily fall away into curiosity, as perhaps reverence can fall away into unworthy obeisance. But in reverence there is clearly signaled the *worth* of the other. Reverence is a happening in which the worth and the being-there of the other are intimately conjoined. The disjoining of being and worth seem to me to be part of the project of modern science from the beginning; worth as subjective value is said to interfere with cognitive realism. Is there not a deeper sense of *ontological worth* communicated in reverence, and this too as the deeper root of the love of being that finds one of its worthy forms in the pursuit of

---

[10] In *The Passions of the Soul*, part two, section 73, Descartes says, and entirely in terms of the mechanics of movement of the "animal spirits": "Astonishment is an excess of wonder and it can never be other than bad." Also on wonder and method: he hopes "that those who have understood all that has been said in this treatise will, in future, see nothing whose cause they cannot easily understand, nor anything that gives them any reason to marvel." *Discourse on Method, Optics, Geometry and Meteorology*, trans. P. J. Olscamp (Indianapolis: Bobbs-Merrill, 1965), 361. See Auguste Comte, *Introduction to Positive Philosophy*, ed., with introduction and revised trans., Frederick Ferré (Indianapolis: Hackett, 1988), 38–39: "Immense as are the services rendered to industry by science, and although according to the striking aphorism of Bacon—knowledge is power—we must never forget that the sciences have a yet higher and more direct destination, that of satisfying the craving of our minds to know the laws of phenomena. To feel how deep and urgent this craving is, it is sufficient to reflect for a moment upon the physiological effect of astonishment, and to recollect that *the most terrible sensation we can experience is that which occurs whenever any phenomenon appears to take place in violation of the natural order that is familiar to us*. This need of arranging facts in an easily comprehended order—which is the proper object of all scientific theories—is so inherent in our organization that, if we could not succeed in satisfying it by positive conceptions, we should have to return inevitably to those theological and metaphysical explanations that, as I explained in the last chapter, had their origin in this need" (emphasis added). This passage betrays Comte's dread of astonishment as violating scientific reason at home with itself in its own order of comprehension, and his alarm that, left untreated, it will lead us back to theology/religion and metaphysics. One thinks of Lucretius long ago intoning (*De rerum natura*, II, 308): *Non est mirabile*. Jacques Monod is an example of a recent celebrated scientist who in his ventures into philosophical preaching is animated by the need for "a complete break with the animist tradition, the definitive abandonment of the 'old covenant,' the necessity of forging a new one." In effect, this is to want to have done with all reverence. See *Chance and Necessity: An Essay on the Natural Philosophy of Modern Biology*, trans. A. Wainhouse (Glasgow: Collins/Fontana, 1974), 159, also see 158ff.

scientific inquiry itself? Is not ontological value also an overdeterminacy of being that offers some intimation in reverence of God as the
overdetermined source of worthiness to be?

What of those scientists who, as it were, sing their hymns to the
universe, or the intricacy of its intelligibilities? (I have an image of
Carl Sagan in his studio spaceship, gazing starry-eyed onto the won-
drous emptiness.) The philosophical terms they have that might
make sense of such hymns seem nonexistent. Why does our hard-
wired neurophysiology feel the need to sing such hymns to the cosmos? No doubt, these hymns reflect the natural reverence that admires the glory of creation. But the issue here is philosophical, and
whether the absence of such terms is in deep tension with other pro-
clivities in the project of science itself. I do not seek to be reassured
by scientists, since they are in question.[11]

Did we have the needed philosophical resources, we might well
have to say that the deepest roots of knowing, philosophical or scientific, are religious. But the *Zeitgeist* does not give its *nihil obstat* to its
acolytes to say that, given the self-image of the philosopher and scientist as liberating their autonomous knowing from the self-incurred
tutelage of superstition and priestcraft. There is much equivocation
going on here, and some dishonesty too. We are still spellbound by
an image of the intellectual, surface differences notwithstanding, not

---

[11] Richard Dawkins in *Unweaving the Rainbow: Science, Delusion, and the Appetite for
Wonder* (London: Allen Lane, 1998), takes issue with John Keats's view of science
as robbing a rainbow of its wonder. The abject cringing of an uninformed wonder
is contrasted with the sophisticated, informed astonishment of the scientist. This is
not without its point, of course; but the issue, I think, is whether the *philosophical
resources* are to hand to help us understand the latter as much as the former. The
happening of scientific wonder is not in doubt; its meaning relative to our sense of
being as a whole, however, is in question, and whether the terms we find within
science are themselves adequate to what is at play in the happening of wonder and
astonishing. Astonishment, wonder, like reverence, are in excess of determinate
problems and their determinate solutions, and hence their happening cannot be fully
formulated in terms of the determinate univocities of science. We need finesse, not
"geometry." Dawkins seems to think that his superior geometry is on the same univocal continuum with the supposedly uninformed wonder of the scientific illiterates
or the perfumed aesthetes and the know-nothing religious Luddites. But is this not
just to lack finesse: to see the issue as a univocal sameness between, say, religious
reverence and the curiosity of the scientist that, were it possible, would resolve astonishment into a more clear and distinct geometry (I am speaking metaphorically),
and thus supersede religious reverence?

greatly changed since the eighteenth century, though our ethos (in its scientific and other determinations) in no way justifies the continuation of this self-image. I am not fooled by postmodern protestations. Let us come clean on religion first.

Reverence, God, Finesse

I conclude with some remarks on God, reverence, and finesse. I said that there was something about reverence in excess of finite determination, even when our reverence is directed to a finite being or happening. There is something about it disproportionate to determinate cognition. But the human being *is disproportion*. Disproportion that is proper: this is relevant to reverence; as disproportion that is improper is related to monstrousness. In both instances, there is the "more" than can be finitely determined. It is in the *hyperbolic dimensions* of disproportion that finesse is needed to read our place in being for signs of the ultimate excess, the unsurpassable beyond, beyond which nothing can be thought—God. Reverence already places us in this hyperbolic dimension of being: it is not the abject degrading that reduces us to the "below." It has everything to do with elevation and the dimension of height. When we revere truly we are carried by our love of the superior to a higher level. Monstrousness is also in the dimension of height. Monstrousness is our being debased in the dimension of the disproportionate. Reverence is a release, a being freed to the superior.

In passing: the hyperbolic dimension of reverence cannot be separated from *blessing and curse*. Curse involves the execration of irreverence. Those blessed also endure curse—but they hide the idiotic suffering of curse, and show the serenity of blessing—for the sake of the other. So Jesus: taking curse on himself, releasing blessing; and on the heights. Hence the *highest monstrosity* of the death of the saving God-man. Saving power: this is letting the curse fall—in fidelity to the blessing power. The divine accepts the execration of the monstrous—this is already redemption, offered—though the monster may refuse.

Reverence points to a genuine opening of self-transcending toward the other. This reveals a form of agapeic minding. Minding in its transcending opens beyond itself to the other and for the other as other. Agapeic minding also opens beyond the ontological nihilism that reduces being's otherness to a worthless thereness. For a world without smells would also be a world without perfumes, as an antiseptic world without dirt would not be quite healthy. Agapeic mind is a love of being: a love that knows that being is not sterile, but earthily hale, and worthy of affirmation as good in itself. This is obviously unacceptable to the dualism of fact and value, and the ontological nihilism endemic in modernity. The dualism reveals our deracination from our community with being in its otherness. The dualism is a result of this deracination, rather than being metaphysically primitive. As a theory it is, in fact, the expression of a loss of, perhaps hostility toward, our community with being in its otherness. It is a theory trapped in a fall from the elemental goodness of being and our given community with creation.

Even those who diagnosed this nihilism, like Nietzsche, often did not realize to what extent their own recommendations for *recovery* were the products of the same loss. Reverence for the goodness of creation will never be recovered through any apotheosis of the human being as the creator of values in a valueless universe. If the creation is valueless in itself, then we as participants in creation are also ontologically valueless, as are our human constructions ultimately. Our every effort to construct values out of ourselves will be subject to the same deeper, primitive, ultimate valuelessness. Human values collapse ultimately into nothing, if there is not a ground of value in the integrity of being itself. To affirm otherwise is only whistling in the dark. It might seem heroic to be defiant of a valueless universe, but this whistling is itself as dark as the darkness of the universe. Only subtle self-deception can avoid the collapse of our constructions.

If there is no primal regard in which being is good, then no being is good, including human being. The human being is a living nihilism masquerading as ethical, if there is no ontology of the good, if the good is not grounded in being itself, or if being itself is not primally good. This is strange to us irreverent denizens of modernity. The more we sup on the thin gruel of valueless being, the more the spirit of reverence is emaciated. Let this emaciation reach a certain point, and anything closer to health cannot be digested. We cannot take it in, it is excessive. The feast of being, the agape of being, will seem incredible. The husks and straws will seem more palatable to the anorexic spirit. But the husks and straws will only continue the slow dying, while the agape may restore robustness. And we now face the potentially catastrophic consequences of this ontological nihilism in what we call the ecological crisis. The excision of final causes from the explanatory schemes of modern science confines mindfulness to the fact of being, in itself without worth. Ontological astonishment is deadened, and we end up with a neutering, indeed deadening, of the earth. The ecological crisis more and more reveals the living sickness of this deadening.

The issue of ontological nihilism needs what I would call an archeology of the good as well as a teleology.[12] Reverence is inseparable from such an archeology of the good. Reverence stands against our totalizing of nature in the image of a kind of hubristic *ratio*. Reverence cannot be assimilated to the mathematization of nature with the view to becoming "its masters and possessors," in Descartes's famous words. This scientistic will-to-power is part of the problem, not the solution. Reverence needs a different sense of unity to account for the integrity of creation, which preserves the ontological good of being. To my knowledge, contemporary philosophers of science have not done much better than Descartes in addressing the issue of nihilism at the properly ontological level. Many philosophers seem blissfully unaware of the problem in this form. They may sing hymns to the brave new world of post-Einsteinian physics. But how does the cosmos as described within this physics provide the ontological basis for such hymns? A hymn is a song of praise that celebrates the sacred. Such a hymn could only make sense if being provides in itself its own worthiness to be praised, its own good, indeed its own sacredness. Within its own terms, science makes no room for this. The issue is urgent. Loss of urgency too often marks philosophical discourse, as well as a loss of resources even to understand the issue. Loss of reverence is among the losses.[13]

---

[12] As *archē* here does not mean a determinate finite cause, so there is a sense of transfinite teleology, which perhaps might better be seen as bearing on issues of eschatology. See *Being and the Between*, chapter 13 on "Being Good."

[13] Not a simple univocal loss, as I said before. Once again the claim is not at all that practicing scientists lack wonder or reverence. Astonishment might sometimes seem more indeterminate, though in truth it is overdeterminate—but reverence carries us more overtly into a space of "worth," into the ethos of the "worthiness" of being. There is also a stronger presentiment of the "personal," relative to this worthiness. One must ask: In what sense can one revere the impersonal? The nonpersonal absolute? The "whole" of pantheism? The evolutionary process? The marvel of the quantum world? One might admire, be astonished before these, be in awe, but could one worship them? Were one to worship them, one would have fallen out of reverence into idolatry. The idolatry might even hide this fall from itself, in presenting itself as the true rational reverence, but it would really be the counterfeit double of religious reverence.

Suppose we say: God is not geometry, God is *finesse*; and even if God is a geometer, as finesse God is *more* than geometry. Must we not also say: reverence comes with finesse? Of course, the scientist is overcome with marvel before the astonishing order and intricacy of the given world; of course, there is a sheer delight in coming to know more of the initially secret intelligibility of things; of course, there is an astonishment that the world is the extraordinary marvel it is. The marvel means the scientist remains human. Not to marvel would mean the scientist is not human, or had become the monster I claim we are without reverence. But there is more to be said. And here the affiliation of religion and philosophy is important.

First: "that it is at all"—this evokes a metaphysical astonishment, which is not exactly in the order of scientific wonder and curiosity about the "what" of what is there. That being is at all, something rather than nothing, is closer to the sheer marvel of being given to be at all; and this is always already presupposed by the scientific curiosity that investigates the intricate marvel of what is there. This metaphysical astonishment is closer to reverence than to scientific curiosity, though again none can be easily dissociated from the other.

Yet there is a scientific orientation that is a *mixture* of wonder and curiosity whose telos is the answering of curiosity, and in which answering the wonder itself is dispelled. There is a metaphysical astonishment in excess of such wonder and curiosity, and which no determinate answer or account fully dispels. Quite to the contrary, the more we know, the more this astonishment is deepened, because it gives birth to a nescience, a not knowing that again is not of the order of a set of determinate items which we now lack, or about which we are ignorant. It is not an ignorance to be dispelled, but comes to us in the acknowledgment of a sense of ontological mystery. This acknowledgment is closer to reverence. To the extent that we are genuinely in the presence of the superior, worthy other, God, there is no end to reverence. There is no higher cognitive state in which reverence is dispelled or overcome.

This astonished wonder that is closer to reverence is inseparable from the good of being, and not only its intelligible order. This reverence is closer to the *deeming* of the goodness of being, which puts us in mind of the God in Genesis, who consents to creation: "It is good, it is very good." This God is more than a God of geometry. This is a God of finesse. We live in a time of extraordinary geometry, geometries; but given our deficit of reverence, it is not evident that we have the finesse to match these geometries. Indeed, one suspects that our disproportionate geometry generates our deficit of finesse. There is no science or geometry of finesse, as there is no philosophical theory or method that will guarantee it. There is an art to finesse, and it is in the cultivation of religious reverence that its practice is most at home. And more than anything, we need finesse, as we need the God that is finesse.

As we need finesse to discern the monstrous, and to pose in perplexity Yeats's question in his great poem, "The Second Coming," echoing again the gyre of Vico: And what rough beast, its hour come round at last, slouches toward Bethlehem to be born? Our perplexity, alas, forebodes the forbidden. The gyre may well wheel round the second barbarism of reflection, but the coming of the second is not the second coming.

9

Enemies: On Hatred

Enmity and the Reverse Negative of Love

Love and friendship are of great significance for both religion and philosophy, and we might say the same for enmity and hatred. As I hope here to indicate, philosophical reflection can bring us to a boundary where something of the religious significance of enmity becomes more intelligible. While much has been written on love and friendship—and I have written myself on eros, agape, and, more recently, philia[1]—much less has been written on enemies or enmity. Some thinkers have written on war, some on the need of an enemy, such as Nietzsche and Carl Schmitt. But to my knowledge few have written on the nature of an enemy in a manner analogous to the way many have written on nature of love itself.

Yet we all have some instinctive or intuitive sense of what it means to be in a hostile situation, granting even that this too may not be at all unequivocal. But to understand something about what it means to *be* an enemy is not at all self-evident. And if we do not know what an enemy is, do we really know what a friend is? Do we really know what love is? We live some sense of each of these, and we can speak of enemies and friends and so on. But how much of such talk is de-

---

[1] See *Being and the Between*, chapters 10 and 11; *Ethics and the Between*, chapter 12; "Tyranny and the Recess of Friendship," in *Amor Amicitiae: On the Love that is Friendship*, ed. Thomas Kelly and Philip Rosemann (Leuven: Peeters, 2004), 99–125.

pendent on a network of concepts whose deeper sources remain clouded, just in our ability to use them, this way or that way? We talk about it, but do we understand that about which we talk? Perhaps to understand more about our talk we need mindfulness of what is at play in the happening of enmity itself, and this would demand an attentiveness to something that, for all its sometimes brutal power, is very elusive. The more one thinks of enemies the more enigmatic the happening of hatred becomes, and by the same stroke the more one becomes unsure about what one seems to have understood of friendship and love.

My proposal is to explore what it means to be an enemy in terms of what one might call the energies of being, and in terms of the fact that we live life as something that offers us a certain affirmative delight in the "to be" as good. I will say more about this shortly, but I am also motivated by the possibility that exploration of the enemy might offer us something like the *reverse negative* of love or friendship. From holding the reverse negative to the light perhaps we can also gain some sight of the "unreversed" original. I add that such a metaphor may be deceptive, especially if it turns out that there are no simple one-to-one correspondences between love and enmity. Maybe correspondences break down when we move from one to the other? Or perhaps the correspondences show certain structural likenesses, but the manners in which the affirming energy of the "to be" circulates in them are directed oppositely.

Perhaps we might even find that there is *no original* at all with respect to enemies; that while there might be a negative and a reversal, something is nihilating or being nihilated in this negative; and that we cannot see this *nihil* or "nihilating" directly or through itself, that it can only be "seen" if our being is in a more direct, intimate communication with the original itself, that is, with love. If so, this would mean that we can only see the enemy properly through the eyes of love, just as we can only see love through love; that hatred not only cannot see love, but in another sense hatred cannot even see the hated enemy. To see would be to love, or to love would be to see. Of course, there are times when we are so shocked by hatred that it dawns on us not that hatred is the opposite of love, but that it is more a nihilating absence. And this dawning can now wake us to a realization of what was there before the nihilation, there as granted but taken for granted, namely, an affirming love that lived itself, and took no notice of itself, no care for itself. Nothing is simple, at the outset.

What then might one say about the perplexing sources out of which enmity springs? Consider this as a first approach. I confront an other who faces me as an enemy. How does an other face me, front me, as an enemy? As someone who puts me under threat? But I can be under threat from someone who is not my enemy. A person who is benignly disposed toward me can threaten me, for I fear that in relation to them I will be exposed, and this I dread, for I have perhaps a guilty secret to hide. Or I may be threatened by the perceived superiority of the other, not in power and hatred, but in love. The superior excellence of the other threatens me, but is that superior other my enemy by virtue of that excellence?

Threat is manifold. In some instances, the threat may be intentional, and willed as such. Are there enemies that are neutral or indifferent on this score? Must an enemy somehow *will* my evil? Thus above: superior excellence arouses my envy, but my envy sees this excellence as my enemy, for it seems to negate me as satisfied with my own now suspected smallbeing. And my response to this enemy? I react with hostility to the perceived enemy, even here in envy of the superior good. I greet enmity, or good perceived as an enemy to me, with enmity. What threatens me brings forth in me the defensive hostility that keeps the threat at bay.

What are the sources of this seemingly entirely justified reaction? Does it make sense to speak of transcending such a reaction and to love the enemy? How love the enemy, since everything about the enemy is what I cannot love? If the enemy were lovable, he or she would no longer be an enemy; how then love the enemy as such? These are all very important questions, the answers to which would be very revealing about friends and enemies. I think that even more deeply the exploration has to be conducted in relation to more original sources out of which relations of friendship or love or animosity emerge. One wonders if these are, at least in part, the surface formations of energies of being that are now shaped in an affirming benignity, now in an assaulting malignity. What are those sources? This for me is a very important *metaphysical* question because it bears on the ultimate ontological energies that assume a variety of determinate forms with us, and which must be approached through these determinate forms. This is all the more important with enmity and love, since the energies of being here at play take us to a very elemental, perhaps irreducible level of being. In understanding something about them, we may have understood something of what it means to be, or not to be.

Enmity and Love of Being

Let me address the matter from another angle. Suppose we start again with what seems elemental: each being affirms its own being; to be is good, it is good to be, and this as singularized in each entity; each being wills to affirm itself and persist in being. Is this what Spinoza calls the *conatus essendi*? I answer "yes" and "no," and this double answer will become clearer. Yes, there is a basic ontological love of being singularized in each being as being. If this is so, then underlying all formations of being, and all singular beings, is a basic love of being. But what is this basic love of being? The question might suggest, in fact, that the self-affirming is not absolutely elemental, since the affirmation and singularization come to be in a field or milieu of being. This I call the between: the ontological ethos of plurivocal community of being in which the self-mediations and intermediations of beings come to be more determinately.

We talk about self-love, for instance; and some will claim that this is all; love of the other, altruism, is only covert or masked self-love. Such a claim could take, say, a more utilitarian form or a psychoanalytic form, but in whatever form it certainly seems so pervasive in modernity as to be taken for granted as the basic truth about what drives the human being. But putting aside for now the second claim about other-love, masked or overt, we must rather ask: Is it at all evident what the first or primary self-love is? I have to say that this is not at all so clear, and even less so what it might mean.

Each being loves itself; to be is to be this love, to be in this love of being; but what is this love? What does it mean to say that a being loves itself? Is it already in some *relation* to itself, in the irreducible fact of being given to be at all? If to be given to be is from the origin to be in a relation of love, what does this say about the claim that self-love is mine, and alone mine? The human being does not itself *produce* this love in the first instance; it already *finds itself* as being, as this self-affirming being. But if it *finds itself already* in this love of being, should we not be careful of taking it simply as *self*-love? For is there not something other than self at play, before the self even wakes up to itself as loving itself? It is given to be, given into the play of being, in the ontological ethos of the between, and thus given, it wakes up to itself in self-affirming and as self-affirming.

My wonder here: Is this "being given" also describable in terms of the affirming love of being? But if so, and if this affirming love shows a giving that is *other* to self-affirming, is there a sense of the love of being that already from the outset is more primal than the primal self-affirming form that, on the surface anyway, seems the most irreducible? If this were so, then would we not have to say: Self-love emerges from sources of affirming that cannot be quite called self-love? There is a being given to be, before the being given affirms its own "to be."

Put differently (and here is my "no" as well as "yes" to Spinoza), there is a *passio essendi* more primal than any *conatus essendi*: a suffering, or *passion* of being more elemental than any endeavor to be, or striving to be. This *passio essendi* is presupposed by the more overt forms of self-love; indeed self-love is itself a singularization of this *passio essendi*. Think of this example: the scream of the child first entering the world. This is not quite the scream of a Heideggerian *Angst* before being, or one's own being; it is the very *health* of self-affirming being that introduces itself as *passion* in the scream, and indeed thus also as both inherently self-insistent and vulnerable. Parents, doctors, and nurses *relax* when they hear the scream: life is there; healthy life is there; the scream communicates the good of the "to be."

What of more overt forms of self-love, I mean forms more explicitly lived and known as such? These too are not devoid of perplexing recalcitrance, and this is even more so if they refer back to the *passio essendi*, itself something enigmatic as elementally given. This *passio* puts its roots most deeply into the idiotic sources of selving, and it is not clear that you can directly reach them. What I mean here by the idiotic has something to do with its Greek sense of the intimate: something not necessarily available in the neutral general, something also inseparable from the tonality of singularity as lived from within out; something that also resists complete objectification; something indeed that resists complete subjectification as well, in that the more determinate and definite subject comes to be out of this more intimate, idiotic energy of selving. And yet this idiotic source has also everything to do with the singular communicability of the living being itself—listen again to that scream of the infant!

Often this *passio essendi* comes to more overt attention only indirectly: we live out of it, but do not mind it. We mind it more when the more surface determinations of selving dissolve, and we are returned, sometimes painfully, to the idiotic, intimate, and more vulnerable source. Consider *pain* in that light: pain has the power to bring us back to this idiotic intimacy. A toothache: we in pain feel this dull ache from within out; so much so that our involuntary moan can not only arouse the sympathy of the other but also the *irritation*; they do not thus know its idiocy from within out; *this* can irritate us. Think of the way Dostoevski's Underground Man moans in an exaggerated way, in order to spite the others, to drive them to anger. This moan says: "To hell with you, for not attending to me as I must attend to myself. I moan to spite you!" Here we see the sometimes perverse self-insistence of this self-affirming root. There are times when the agony of pain is so overwhelming that its return of us to the *passio essendi* is more like a trauma, or a concussion, a violent passivity. Interestingly, *erotic arousal* can bring us back to, bring back in us, the *passio essendi*, and here with relation to what is most intimate with humans. Love brings us back to the *passio essendi*, or lets its enigmatic energy resurface in how we relate to a beloved. (Apropos of the similarity of love and enmity: the communications of pain and pleasure here can sound the same—there are moans of pleasure and pain that qua moans sound just the same, though from the intimacy inside out they are radically different.)

Do we need to acknowledge this *passio essendi* to make sense of self-love, ordinarily so-called, self-love as often linked in our time with concerns like gratification, calculated self-interest, (consumer) satisfaction, and such like? If we need that acknowledgment, the bond that holds the self into an integrity, that binds it to itself as its own singularity of being, is not due to itself alone. The bond of being that is itself the singular self loving itself is passed to it from sources that are not its own. Self-love then proves much more mysterious and complex than the standard ideas of self-interest, and so on. There is a reference to an other source in it already, in so far as the *conatus essendi* presupposes the *passio essendi*. But most forms of understanding the *conatus* proceed immediately to forget or deny the deeper import of the *passio essendi*. Perhaps they want to stake their mastery over self and love, and hence cover over the elemental givenness that indeed makes them possible—possible as denying even the givenness as impossible. In my view, as we shall see, a variety of infidelities to the *passio essendi* can alter different forms of the *conatus essendi* from self-affirming love into enmity, and in these alterations enemies, the enemy, come to appear.

How does this analysis transform the usual contrast of self-love and love of the other? If self-love already is inseparable from an other source that gives the self-love, the meaning of the latter from the outset is more than self-relation; and this "more" is accentuated, made all the more intricate, the more the other as other has to be taken into account. If we remain true to the *passio essendi*, we will think that any closure of *conatus essendi* on itself is a defection from love; for with reference to the inward otherness, and the outer other other, there is always this source that exceeds such closure. This closure is what we call selfishness in the usual pejorative sense. The closure is always the *counterfeit of integrity of being*. It is a false wholeness.

Enemies, *Passio Essendi*, *Conatus Essendi*

What does this analysis have to do with *enemies*, and what does it tell us about the sources of enmity? I think the doubleness of the *passio essendi* and *conatus essendi* constitutes an essential equivocity of being out of which the relation of enmity comes, and in diverse forms. And most singularly, this doubleness shows something deeply equivocal about the being of the human. Let me first state the general point, and then turn to how it helps us understand different enemies and loves.

Think of it this way. *Passio* and *conatus* seem to be counterposed as a kind of lack and a kind of power: *passio* seems to name a reception, while *conatus* concretizes an action. And yet the human being is both: receiving and acting, lacking in absolute being and powerfully willing to be. A double subjectivity, a redoubling subjectivity that is also, one wonders, wounded. "Wounded" would not be the right word if by it we meant a harm that had later befallen it. Rather it draws our attention to the power "to be" as intimately vulnerable. The character of the power to be with us shows an intimate vulnerability that itself is doubled and redoubled, opening it to the other, but also opening it to *threat*. This ontological equivocity is the seed of a kind of ontological dialectic between trust and possible distrust, at the heart of the being of the human.

Consider here how ardent love sometimes can almost instantaneously mutate into a rage of jealousy on the *mere hint of suspicion* of the betrayal of the beloved. I think here of Othello: the mere suggestion of betrayal that the love of the beloved was not what it seemed to be, or only seemed to be what it was, namely love, is enough to plunge Othello into the pit of treason. The *thought* of betrayal unleashes an infinitely wounded rage. In the rage, what infinite vulnerability! How touchy the heart; how infinitely responsive to being touched, to being radically hurt; how insecure the heart, though, outside, one is all power. The murderous outburst of raging power is really the heart's manifestation of maximum powerlessness, helplessness.

Or think of the equivocity of the human face (and not in the terms of Levinas). The face shows the seeming of the other, and hence it is always suspended in a space of potential equivocity between hospitality and hostility. It may be true, as I think, that the anticipation of hospitality is more primordial than hostility; as seems to be shown by, for instance, the ontological "preprogramming" of the child for the *smile*, and the accord between the living being and the form of welcome (at an early stage, even a painting of a smile is enough to bring forth the smile in the child). But we come to know, as Hamlet knew, that "one may smile and smile and be a villain." And this we come to realize more as our own power of being comes out more fully into the middle space between ourselves and the others.

My suggestion is that enmity has its source in this radical intimate vulnerability of the *passio essendi*, when the *conatus essendi* comes to know, not only the equivocity of the self, but of the between, the middle space between itself and the other, into which it must necessarily communicate itself, and in that communication also risk itself, and the rebuff of the other. The *passio* can never be completely its own self-master, no matter how powerful its matching *conatus*; while, in tandem, the *conatus* is tempted just to intensify its own power to be, while negating or hiding the passivity of the intimate vulnerability. ("Growing a thick skin"—one mild version of this.) Moreover, since this double play between vulnerability and power is *redoubled between* humans, the vulnerability itself risks being limitlessly redoubled, just as vulnerability. Hence the potentially limitless vulnerability of the human being, in response to which the *conatus* may will limitlessly to redouble *itself*. If we are not careful or fortunate in this limitless redoubling, the beginning of a usurpation may already be set in motion. For since one can will oneself thus limitlessly, the other cannot but appear as a possible enemy, for it presents itself as a limit to one's own redoubling. Indeed the other seems actively to counterpose itself to my self-redoubling, and in this active counterposition seems to show itself not only a limit but an enemy. For the enemy is a limit that actively redoubles itself in negation of my own redoubling of myself.

Simply put: Enmity is the love of life that wills the negation of other-being as a threat to *its own* life, held on to now as *the* good to be preserved against the active limitation of the other. Of course, nothing is absolutely one's own, so there is always a radical instability in enmity on this level also, to say nothing of the instability in the pluralized redoublings that occur in a larger community. Enmity arises in the between: in one's own immanent equivocity between *passio* and *conatus*; and between one's redoubled self and the other presenting a face of ambiguity, wherein the *conatus* of the other threatens one, both as *passio* and *conatus*. Enmity comes from a mutation of the love of life into the hatred of the other, seen as the threat to my life. Enmity is a mutated form of the love of life, for it arises from sources in the deepest reserves of self-affirming life as good.

More might be said about the immanent mutations of willing that can here happen, and I have said something more elsewhere (see *Ethics and the Between*, chapter 8). I want now to say something about *different kinds of enemy*. I will take as my cue the suggestion I made of enmity as the reverse negative of love. I will look at the following negative reversals of these different loves: self-affirming love (self-love); eros as a self-transcending love that seeks the overcoming of its own lack in and through the completing, fulfilling other; philia as the mutual reciprocity of receiving and giving in all things good and excellent; agape as a love out of surplus that gives to the other but not with the intent to secure a return to itself, but simply gives goodly for the good of the other as other.

Enemies and Self-love

What of the enemy(ies) of self-affirming love? If the enemy is what negates me, how is it possible for the self-affirming love to mutate into self-hatred? Indeed some thinkers have claimed that the self cannot hate itself. I will note three forms.

First, self-affirming love loves itself as good but it is tempted to secure itself against the perceived threat of the other as enemy; and in this securing of self-affirming love there is implicit a seed of self-hatred, even in my own self-affirming love. How so? For this self-love has here been secured at the cost of trying to negate or diminish in myself the *passio essendi*. Hence my self-love at this most intimate level is also a *hatred of what I am most intimately*. I secure the mutated self-love only because I turn against what I am in the roots of self-being: idiot self and radically vulnerable. To close oneself to this is to begin to close the radical nature of one's porosity and openness, both to what is other and to one's own selving in its fullest promise. To overcome self-hatred asks for a return to this porosity, and a shattering of the self that has closed around itself in false self-security. Think of some practices of psychoanalysis; or think how the *passio essendi* surfaces in dreams, or drunkenness, or perhaps especially in moments of *unguardedness*: one lets one's guard down and a secret misery at the core comes up. Up comes the wretchedness of self-hatred at the heart of secured self-love. It must be let come if the selving is to come to itself again.

Second, there is the self-hatred that has allowed itself to be defined, though now by relation to others seen or known intimately as threats or hostile to my being. Rather than loving myself because I am not loved, now *I hate myself because I am hated*. The native self-affirming has had its very openness violated, not now through its own self-securing but through the violating hate of the other. I hate myself as the other hates me; for this other does not show me to myself as good but as evil, or deficient. The other is as much internal to me as external, and if the other is in enmity to me, my own self-relation may also mutate into self-hatred.

Here it is somewhat the opposite of the first possibility: there we flee the *passio essendi*, and protect ourselves by an enlarged *conatus essendi*; here the *conatus* has not been able to defend its true self-love, and its *passio essendi* falls under the dominion of a hating other. An alien germ of hatred has been deposited in this porous intimate ground, and it grows there like a cuckoo, battening on the life of its host, until the fledglings of genuine self-love are ousted. How be saved from this? Obviously the *conatus* can rebel, but the rebellion risks being also a form of self-hatred, especially since the alien germ is now rooted and grown in its own most intimate soil—it is hating something of its own, in the mutated *passio essendi*, when it rebels. Its will to be self-affirming love is twisted in its own turmoil.

More often than not, the *love of an other* is needed to counteract the hatred of another that has rooted itself in the intimate soul. That love may even be offered, but the self that hates itself may have great difficulty recognizing or acknowledging this, since its own self-hatred now makes it anticipate that the other will also hate it, and what looks like love will itself be seen as another equivocal face of hatred. *Patient* love of the other may be needed, patience that risks its own *passio essendi* in being there for the good of the self hating itself. For again it is needful that the breakthrough take place at the level of the *passio essendi*, if the *conatus* itself is to be reformed. Heroic patience, exemplary *passion* of love, may be needed to offer the promise of opening, slowly, slowly returning self to its self-affirming love. A hand knotted into a tight fist cannot receive a gift; but how do you unknot that tight fist, if it will not open itself also?

A *third* form of self-hatred is more complex. It might be addressed under notions like "guilt," but the precise modulation of "guilt" here implied is not always easy to fix. I do not mean guilt in face of the other that would negate or diminish my "self-esteem," such as we might find in the second possibility above. Example of this: The judgment of my disapproving mother or father makes me guilty, makes me hate myself, for instance: I hate myself for failing them. Of course, there may be *no judgment there at all*; but still I hate myself. Neither is the issue here the kind of guilt found in the first form of self-hatred, where one feels one has not lived up to what one is in promise: one has failed to be true to this promise, either by not risking what a properly unfolding *conatus* asked, or by stifling solicitations coming from a deeper appropriation of the exigencies of the *passio essendi.* A homely example of this: I am disgusted with myself, for I could have won that race if only I had tried harder, and been willing to endure the pain a little longer. I hate myself for losing, for I know *I could have won.*

By contrast with the first two forms, and to put the point with maximum conciseness, this third form has finally to do with God. In the original idiot selving the seed of being in relation to God is there: the diverse formations of *passio* and *conatus* that have come to be have departed from that relation, and vaguely this is felt as something lost, or missed, or perhaps betrayed, even hated, but in all of this I am hating myself, since this promised relation is given in the radical ontological intimacy of the idiot self. This is akin to, but not the same as, the feeling of having failed an unconditional command of the moral law; it is more than failing the law; for the ultimate power is not a law but something more original and living. (Suppose such a form of self-hatred defined not only individuals but also significant currents of an *entire era.* What would this imply about the era after the so-called death of God?)

Is there a hint of this third form when Pascal says, *"le moi est haïssable,"* (the self is hateful)? The self so hateful is the self that in affirming itself has made God into a hostile other, and made itself into an enemy of this ultimate love. Pascal's formulation is maybe too violent. Relative to the order of charity, it can be taken to mean that the hateful self in hating itself comes to love itself, as it is to be loved, that is, in the original and ultimate relation to God. In this form of self-hatred lies all the mystery of blessing and curse, of saving and perdition. But the possibility of this hell of ultimate self-hatred is itself in a mutation of love, and is itself allowed to be by love. There is a love that, as self-hatred, is damned, that damns itself to self-affirming hatred.

Enemies and Eros

What of the enemy(ies) of erotic love? What would the reverse negative here be? *Conatus essendi* here surges forth with *passion*, and as such the vim of the energy also reveals its nakedness and vulnerability more in the whole. That nakedness is the happening of an intimacy between one self and an other, in which *passio* and *conatus* are pluri-vocally coupled. What labyrinthine intricacies—advances and eva-sions—are secreted in these couplings, secreted and also kept secret. Erotic *passion* is very intriguing in that the *conatus* cannot build a self-security around itself: the *passio essendi* is in the *conatus* itself, intimate to it. I do not deny that humans may try to diminish the elemental vulnerability, try to manipulate the passion of the other, while re-maining themselves in control. The risks here are not only the instru-mentalizing of what is not instrumentalizable in the other, but of instrumentalizing oneself. We treat ourselves and our own eros as a mere instrumental means over which we claim control. We exploit ourselves. There is an intimate falsity to such a self who wields such an instrumentalizing control. For every such effort at such self-secur-ing is necessarily unstable, since the *passio essendi* is *intimately neces-sary* to the happening of erotic love. This is no less the case with exploitive eros. Desire is not being true to its full promise both as passion and as endeavor.

Eros is protean, as are the shades of hostility its enchantment casts. I will but note this possibility. My erotic *passion* for the other is expressed in my being in relation to that beloved in whom I en-deavor (here the *conatus*) more fully to be myself: to be more wholly myself in and through the beloved other. I love the other and *the other gives me back to myself as loved, hence lovable.* What if the beloved other does not give me back to myself as loved? Here arises the erotic enemy. This enemy is not only the one who negates me, but because I would be myself more wholly in and through that other, this enemy is the one who refuses or thwarts this self-mediation. I mean: this is not an enemy over against me, but an enemy *intimate* to the process of my own erotic selving. The *conatus essendi* as erotic passion can here arise with immense ferocity and insinuosity. The fury of my ha-tred is in the inverse measure of my thwarted or disappointed love;

and since this goes so intimately deep, in some way everything of my self-being seems at stake.

Recall my remark about Othello's jealousy. Think of how some divorces take on the character of an "all or nothing" war. Love at first sight turns into hatred at second. Hatred seems to awake as if from a spell, and one detests the enchanter who erstwhile held one fast. The hatred of those who once loved and now are in process of divorcing can sometimes show a kind of measureless animosity. The measureless animosity will even destroy its own self-interest, if only thereby it can injure, if not kill, the interest of the other. It can be a kind of perverse parody of sacrificial love: it would immolate the good just because the previously loved, now hated, other has it, or even *might have it*. Even the thought of the *possible* good of this now reviled other can arouse this destructive hatred. This destructive hatred wants to make even the possible good of the other impossible.

The point has applicability also at the level of a larger community. For this is a form of enmity that previously warring communities have to overcome: overcoming revolt at the idea that the former enemy *might* have a *possible* good that we do not now have. The overcoming of hatred in Northern Ireland, for instance, has had to face this. I think also of examples of those who love a cause (religious, political) and then some radical disappointment makes them hate it with a ferocity matching their previous ardor. Consider certain priests who leave the church, their previous love mutating into measureless hatred; or think of, say, former communists and their erstwhile comrades. Of course the hatred can arise in those who remain loyal to the cause and execrate the renegade.

One might find forms of this even with respect to *philosophical* eros. Rorty deserts Philosophy with a big P, as he puts it, in favor of philosophy with a little p; but the melancholy side of his affirmation of philosophy with a little p, makes one wonder if there is much of disappointment with a former eros for Philosophy with a big P. The acrimony of his former comrades would seem to confirm the point: after all, it is their love, their eros, that they feel has been belittled, been besmirched by the little p.

This form of the enemy has far-ranging application to political communities also, though I cannot develop the point here. A people's sense of sovereignty has its sources in a "general eros" rather than general will (see *Ethics and the Between*, chapter 15). If that "general eros" is thwarted, or rebuffed, or frustrated, a people can be consumed with hatred for the enemy, the other people that thwarted it.

In some situations it may have nothing to do with calculated self-interest; merely "being slighted" by the other might be enough to crystallize the animosity out of the ambiguous "general eros."

This hatred is beyond the measure of utilitarian calculation. Consider the manner in which great wars are astonishingly precipitated by seemingly trivial occasions or occurrences: secretly the "general eros" had already secreted the animosity, hollowed out the space that will be filled with offensive fury rather than utilitarian tasks. The excessive, immeasurable character of this hatred is evident in the fact that, given the outbreak of such war, it soon becomes evident that *no one* is in charge. There is no overmastering *conatus essendi* in charge, and even efforts at self-securing only increase the general insecurity. Outbreak (interesting word) of war: what has broken out? It is the power of the *nihil* that seems to take on its own life. The spirit of hatred has been let loose and everyone is dragged into the pit. This circulation of "general hatred" is itself the mutation of "general eros" and, like the latter, may have to discharge itself before people wake up from the infernal bewitchment. This often means at the point where the power of this hatred shows itself less as "darkness visible," as "nothingness visible." There is nothing to see. Great war seems to want to bring about a situation that will, as we say, "let nothing standing." With nothing standing there, nothing is to be let standing. The reverse negative seems to be driven to doing a work of absolute undoing.

Enemies and Philia

What of the enemy(ies) of philia? I offer only brief remarks on the turning of the friend into an enemy. I think one of the things here to consider about becoming an enemy is the temptation of a kind of *treachery to excellence.* Obviously, there are different kinds of friendship, as Aristotle classically makes clear. The treachery of enmity here is deepest with the third kind, the friendship based on excellence rather than on utility or pleasure.

There is a more symmetrical reciprocity to friendship that is thus not quite the same as the relation of one and the other in eros. In eros a certain asymmetry is more possible, in that the giving to the other can be with the view to receiving oneself back again. But the giving and receiving of friendship is less concerned with the possession of the beloved and more with the less self-insistently demanding character of friends *being together.* Friends enjoy being together, enjoy each other's company, but the *passio* of eros is not vehement and the *conatus essendi* is moderated relatively to overwhelming self-insistences. Again the point applies more to Aristotle's third kind: friends of excellence enjoy being together in excellence. The other two types of friendships, based on utility and pleasure, have unstable asymmetries in which the lurking self-insistences of the *conatus essendi* easily topple the reciprocity into onesidedness, with the loss of the high enjoyable ease of those friends who take joy simply in being there with the friend, together enjoying each other's good company.

Relative to the ease of this joy, when the friend becomes an enemy, there can be perhaps a more evil form of enmity coming from it than previous forms. Why? We know and have delighted in the *intrinsic excellences* of the friend. We have loved him or her as intrinsically excellent. If we now hate him or her, delight has become detestation, and we also risk detesting the intrinsic excellences. And if this hatred of the intrinsically excellent is not overcome or moderated, there can be a deep defection from love of the good: it is deep treason. "Treason"—the treachery of a friend—carries something of the horror of such a radical defection. Now as an enemy, we may feel we have to *malign* the former friend and his or her excellences. Think of the horror in that word "malign"—active malignity against the intrinsic excellence and the friend who embodies it.

We may hesitate to express this horrifying malignity, and instead be content to "find fault" with the appearing excellence. "Fault finding" is an interesting thing: it may present itself as honest openness, but it masks its aggression in its bluff concern. The deeper sources of the maligning, be they appearing or rooted, are in the soul or self or character. The enmity against the friend reaches into the intimate, the idiotic. The *being* of the other, before a friend, now an enemy, we now hate. We might consider, by contrast, the common enjoyment of excellences in a healthy agon: there competitors respect, even deeply admire, the excellences of the opponent, even those who defeat them. We find this with certain runners, for instance. This was to be seen recently at the death of the great runner Emil Zátopek (1922–2000): what was shown was not only the respect, not only the admiration, but the love of those, themselves outstanding competitors, whom he had beaten. Zátopek himself said: "Great is the victory, but the friendship is all the greater."

To malign excellence in response to the treason of the friend is an extreme, of course. To hate excellence is to be an enemy of good life, and so to be an enemy of being good, the good being excellent. How difficult this is! And if one's friend embodied a living excellence, how difficult for excellence to hate excellence! (Think about, for instance, the friendship, and falling out, of Thomas à Becket and Henry II. One might also ponder, in a different direction, Peter's triple denial of Jesus.) How perverse and deeply corrupting if the treason happens between good friends. Can one indeed have an entire reversal from friendship to enmity? Were it to happen, it would be an extraordinary corruption. A sense of tragic loss can pervade the mutation of friendship into hostility. Mostly ambiguity remains: sorrow for the loss of the friend, memory of the good of the other, involuntarily reawakened in a moment when the hardness of the enmity thaws.[2] So long as these ambiguities remain, the friend is not an outright enemy, and hence the relation is not completely irredeemable.

Notice we talk here of "redemption," or of a broken friendship as "beyond redemption." The hyperbolic nature of the language is no hyperbole in the invidious sense of an untrue exaggeration. It is truly hyperbolic—in the dimension of the excess of the intrinsically excellent. Friendship has itself redemptive qualities or potentialities, and the turn to enmity is itself a loss of those potentialities. A broken friendship beyond redemption is also a loss of this redemptive promise. There can be treacheries to friendship so deep that we are beyond brokenness even, and on the verge of a death. Such treacheries can *kill one*. One loved the friend to such a degree that his or her treachery is enough to deprive one of one's being. Should one live after the death of this treachery, one lives as one wounded forthwith, in the dimension of the hyperbolic, and on this side of death, perhaps irremediably.

Enemies and Agape

What of agapeic love and the enemy? What of the mutation of this last, perhaps first, form of love? Here we find not a love that seeks from lack, or that asks for proportional reciprocity, but that exceeds from surplus good, even in relations that lack or disable or seek to destroy

---

[2] I mentioned Richard Rorty above relative to philosophical eros, but he also confesses to having lost *friends* because of his turn to philosophy with a little p; sadly so, for instance in the case of Carl Hempel who saw what Rorty was doing as a "betrayal" of everything for which he stood. See the interview with James Ryerson in "The Quest for Uncertainty: Richard Rorty's Pragmatic Pilgrimage," *Linguafranca* 10, no. 9 (December 2000/January 2001).

reciprocity. Such a love from the surplus of being good has no motive beyond the good of it and the good of the other. In another respect, this love can also incarnate a willingness beyond this will or that will: an overdeterminate willingness of good, beyond the will of this good or that good. In that respect, it may be open to all, and yet be crystallized just in the love of the singular as singular, and hence find its determinate form in the love of this and the love of that, even to care for the sparrows of the air.

How could such a surplus good mutate into enmity? By its very being it seems to be love of the good and nothing but it. What enemy could it have? What *passio essendi* here that might experience the other as threat? Or *conatus essendi* that would assert itself and seek dominion over the other? For if agapeic love means the freeing of the other, it is hard to see how the language of self-affirming *conatus* suffices. And *passio essendi*? But would not this movement of love be more a *giving (as) giving*, rather than just a gift given; love more in the going toward the other than in a receiving? Where then is the *passio*? These are very difficult questions to answer if the agapeic love is absolute, that is, God. Here there seems to be no receiving in the sense of accepting a gift given. Why? All the receiving at issue here would *already* be a gift of this agapeic origin, this *giving (as) giving*. Is there then any divine reception, passion, suffering? I will remark on this at the close.

I know some will be uneasy with this hyperbolic talk of divine love. They will shift at the thought of something too theologically florid in this. In response, I would say that I have been exploring different sides of the issues at stake in many works, and in the present instance what I must venture to say is I think entailed by my exploration hitherto. As I said at the outset, philosophical reflection can bring us to a boundary where something of the religious significance of enmity can become more intelligible. There are no univocal certainties here; nevertheless some directions for thought are suggested. But let me first pursue the point by returning to the human being.

Some will deny the possibility of agapeic love on the part of humans, and the deniers will span the spectrum. There can be an interesting coincidence of opposites here. Some theologically minded will say only God is agapeic, humans cannot be, for this is divine love. Some psychoanalytically minded will say that agapeic love cannot be, for beneath all love is a more or less voracious self-love, which worms its way secretly into all the hidden passages of the heart, and not least those pluming themselves with higher motives. Some more naturalistically reductive will take a similar tack: surplus good is a fantasy, since nature operates according to an economy of scarcity, struggle for resources, and the programmed tyranny of self-insistent energies. The question then: Is agapeic love a promise for humans, a promise sometimes more or less redeemed?

We can throw light on the question by considering the opposite case, the case of "motiveless malignity," Coleridge's resonant words for Iago, the tempter of Othello. "Motiveless malignity": Is there such a thing? If there is this hatred, if there is, one might say, this *surplus hatred*—the strangeness of the phrase is apposite, we will see below—is not its negative reversal also a possibility? If motiveless malignity is not only a possibility but happens, is not the surplus agape of motiveless generosity, motiveless benignity, not in a similar situation? If not, why not?

If we say "no," does this owe something to our defect of seeing, of mindfulness, of love that grants? I suggested above that there is a regard in which only love sees. If this is so, the denial of agapeic love has something to do with defect of love in those who deny it, perhaps even as a possibility. Out of the heart, the idiot, comes its fruits, some sweet, some bitter, some pretending to the final truth about the heart grown hard in its self-insistence. Can we understand what, in some sense, we do not participate in? Is it such that we cannot think what we do not thank? If the thought of one is inseparable from the other, then evil itself offers a path through the reverse negative that suggests to us what evil refuses, namely, the agape of love: surplus being good.

One might apply Aquinas's deep sentence: *si malum est, Deus est*. If enmity as motiveless malignity is, then motiveless benignity is, that is, the surplus good of agapeic love. For human beings to affirm this cannot be a merely "objective" determination, for it involves our own ultimate loves and hatreds. Moreover, to deny "objectivism" is not to embrace "subjectivism," since what is at stake is the ultimate *relation* to the other as ultimate, to the ultimate other. This relation, as radically intimate, is "subjective," yet, just as radically intimate, it is also radically communicative, hence "transsubjective."

Return now to God, since this helps us ask the question about such surplus good. Can God then have an enemy? It seems not, certainly if we mean an enemy that makes God to be a power defined in hostility toward the other, if the other embodies some good. Such an enmity of God seems impossible. Can God have an enemy in hostility, if the other is evil? But if the other is a created other and in the gift of the good, then this would not be the case. If its being is a gift incarnating a certain ontological goodness, how could the created other *be* evil? Yet it might *become* evil. How so? Must we not again say that this comes from mutations of love into enmity, similar to those we have tried to outline hitherto in other forms of love and enmity? Recall that these enmities are in some fundamental sense "reverse negatives," mutations of love of the good of the "to be." And must *all* these mutations be finally defined in some form of contrast with this possibility of absolute love? Must they be defined, in some significant way, as closing off the fullness of the agape of the good? But how close off? The direction of my reflection points this way: by turning from, refusing, reconfiguring, deforming the promise of the gift of the good of the "to be." And do not these turnings take place in that complex middle space between *passio essendi* and *conatus essendi*? God is not the enemy, but the other to God can secrete an enmity to the agapeic good, by closing into itself, that is, refusing the full *broadcast* of the love, defecting from the promise of this communication of the unconditional gift of the good given for the other as other. But is this not our being: to be energized to be in the broadcast, in the communication, and yet given to close our share of the broadcast into ourselves? Finite freedom, as an open power of being, and as the potency of infinite self-redoubling, secretes enmity in that it is *not* the agapeic good, not the fullness of the broadcast of the good. We are not God, and we refuse what we are for not being God, and seek to make ourselves God in refusing God, in refusing ourselves.

Ask again: What could constitute an enemy here? Nothing, it seems, could be proportionate in a one-to-one correspondence. Yet in the agapeic communication between the love and its other, the other might will not to be that loved other, but the opposite, though now only by denying the absoluteness of the original good. The enemy would thus seek to make itself God by the nihilation of God. It would thus mimic or ape the original love, but the directionality of the energies of being would be opposed to the ontologically faithful broadcast of love. It would seek the undoing of the love and the good, and its communication; but the undoing would be by mimicking the love and the good and the communication. It would be the counterfeit double of the original surplus good.

In truth, this would mean that the enemy would be the broadcast of an *indeterminate hatred of the good of being*, as other to the one who hates. Thus as the surplus love is not confined to this or that, though incarnated with respect to this or that good, this hatred would not be confined to this or that, but every this or that might become the focus of its excess hate. One form of this (infernal) mimicry might be this: One might seem to hate nothing, yet might hate everything; but seeming to hate nothing, one might appear to love everything. Would one have the seeming of love that was really hate? But how could you discern the happening of such an extraordinary counterfeit double of love?

Example: Think of those who, proclaiming the highest moral motives, would make a better creation, though at the bottom of their hearts lies the passion that they can *better God*, outdo God's creation. For their hearts seem to say: better it were that such a creation were not; better not to be, than to be thus. This love that would *outdo* God hates God in hating what God has done: its love is a hate that would *undo* creation as given. Such is the radical equivocity of the mimicry involved: the reverse negative would thus seek to deface entirely the communication of the original, by displacing the original, with itself as the counterfeit double of the original love. This is what one would have to call an infernal hatred, since it looks almost exactly like the divine love. And infernal all the more, since to discern the difference between love and enmity here seems almost impossible, since the enemy dis-guises itself as the good. Is this why in folklore *the devil casts no shadow*? There is no "substance" there: it is a nothing masquerading as absolute life; it is the absolute whole of refusal, through which indeed the light passes, but only because the whole has made itself into a nothing. If one sees this, this is what one "sees": *there is nothing there*. This "nothing" is the counterfeit double of that original porosity of being that is the primal openness of the creature to God.

One might still press the question: *Do* we find, in fact, something like such an unconditional hatred? We come back to "motiveless malignity." Can one say an unconditional hatred is *motivated*? If it "moves," it is "motivated," hence not "motiveless." Is there such a thing as a "motiveless motive?" The question is also of relevance to understanding agapeic love. One might say that this love is motiveless, since it is not moved for itself, and yet it is moved, but for the good of the other as other: the love is motive but motiveless.[3] What

---

[3] Can we give a new meaning to God as the "unmoved mover" here, in terms of the "motiveless motive" of agapeic love? If so, God would appear as entirely other to the seemingly static, undynamic being, that many attribute, wrongly in my view, to the traditional view.

would move or be the motive of "motiveless malignity"? Hatred for the sake of hatred—the counterfeit double of love for the sake of love. So it seems.

More explicitly, this enmity seems to show that it is simply the "to be" that is hated, the "to be" as good, and now willed not to be. Remember again the claim that all love traces back to some affirming of the "to be" as good. In agapeic love we find this affirming in most unrestricted form. The enmity here would be unrestricted nihilation, by the reverse negative, of the good of the "to be": pure hatred. Such a movement of inversion, such a reversion of nihilation, would not be just a defection from the good of being, but, so to say, a *de-effecting* of that good. If the broadcast communicating the agape of the good is the granting of the "to be" of the other as good, this de-effecting would be *the counterfeit double of creation*: a de-creation masquerading as creation. It would be the counterfeit double of *being* in the most intimate and radical ontological sense. This enmity would be an icy malignity that wills to undo all being and good and all being as good. This would be satanic malignity.

But again, can we make any sense of this? It would be pure hatred of the *passio essendi*; pure because it radically wills it *not to be*, seeks to de-effect it, un-create it. The impossibility of this de-effection, this un-creation being fully effected by a creature, follows from the fact that to be created is to be *passio essendi*, and to be the promise of ef-fecting through the creative powers of *conatus essendi* as wedded to this passion. The aim here would be the aimless aim to un-create cre-ation, and this through a creature that is itself the communication of agapeic creation. Its hatred of everything is hence its mortal hatred of itself, itself as a creature. This is what its hatred finds absolutely intolerable—that it is a creature and not God. And its hatred is a certain flowering of the power of its *conatus essendi* that would be ab-solutely for itself alone. But being god over all being means being sovereign over the kingdom of nothing. And yet this de-creating is allowed by creation, as opening in love. This radical hatred is allowed by radical love. This is perhaps why Satan is called *the* enemy. But Satan too is a creature of God.

This last point suggests that intimate even to radical hatred there is something derivative from love. Though love itself is hatred, or has mutated into hatred, there is a love more intimate to hatred than ha-tred is to itself, and it is a love that first endows us. The point is rele-vant to what an immanent consideration of evil might reveal of good, or war reveal of peace (as we will see in the next chapter). "Angels are bright still, though the brightest fell (*Macbeth*, 4.3.22). There is a striking passage in Milton's *Paradise Lost* when Satan is on the verge of seducing Eve to transgress. Seeing the beauty of Eve, Satan is overtaken by marvel and involuntary admiration—arrested, brought to a pause: "Her graceful innocence . . . overawed / His malice, and with rapine sweet bereaved / His fierceness of the fierce intent it brought. / That space the Evil One abstracted stood / From his own evil, and for the time remained / Stupidly good, of evil disarmed / Of guile, of hate, of envy, of revenge" (Bk. 9, 459–66).

I would say: At a certain threshold, there is something more primordial in the enemy even than enmity, more intimate than the will to evil. "Stupidly good": I take stupid here to invoke "stupor"—itself recalling (think of the Latin word) something of overwhelming astonishment, not just stupid stupidity. Being "overawed" is to find awe come over one. There is something *idiotic* about this, yes, idiotic as more intimate than even one's own will. This idiotic good momentarily gets behind, as it were, the self-defenses of the will willing itself, the *conatus* seeking self-absolutizing, and reveals a more intimate and primordial patience to good, porosity to beauty. This happening of "being overcome" returns the evil one to something more primal than his own election of evil—for as created Satan too is good, good as given to be. In the interim of peace thus given, all malice is suspended. The interim is cut short. "[T]hen fierce hate he recollects" (470–71), and Satan resumes his purpose of mischief. He shakes off this idiotic peace, closes the porosity, and dedicates anew his will to malice.

And God and the *passio essendi*? Given what I have said, the following seems to suggest itself: God is patient to nothing, and in another sense patient to everything. Impassible and yet absolute patience toward everything. Impassible as absolute surplus good: unsurpassable plenitude of being good—nothing could exceed this absolute excess. Absolute patience: this is the surplus forbearance of exceeding agapeic love. Are we moved to this thought: God is the ultimate *com-passio essendi*? And this thought: this divine *com-passio essendi* bears all in forbearance? And perhaps to redeem from infernal enmity, God must be given over to the *passio essendi* of the mortal creature, and by entry into its most extreme vulnerability communicate agapeic love that re-effects the communication of the good of being in place of the de-effecting, the defection from the good, love that re-creates in place of the de-creation. The most radical agapeic love, communicated most intimately in and to this mortal *passio es-*

sendi, and in that place, opens itself to the extreme execration of the enemy, makes itself porous to the extremest vulnerability to evil, and in this undergoing of evil execration offers again, offers even there, the gift of the agape. But the offer, as radically free from hatred, is also an offer in freedom and of freedom, and as such it can be refused. The offer cannot but *let free* the evil one to remain as it wills itself to be, and, if it wills, to be enemy. There can be no *necessary* redemption of the evil, this enemy. The *letting be* of evil, as free, is entailed by the agapeic love, and evil's redemption can only come through freedom, when freedom consents to freedom. But this consent, too, is freely graced. The last "yes" to the enemy, the absolute "yes," would be an absolving offer.

10

Is There a Sabbath for Thought?
On Peace—Between Philosophy and Religion

A Sabbath for Thinking—A Round Square?

In the Bible the Sabbath is the day of rest reserved for God, a day calling human beings to unreserved rest, recalling humans to what is, and is to be, their first love, their being bound up with, bound by, God. The day also recalls human beings to the first commandment, which tells us that God is God, God alone is God, and nothing but God is God. The Sabbath is the day when we are to be most free of idols, that is to say, counterfeit doubles of God. The other days, one might say, are days when the seductions of the idols, and their daily insinuating loves, are less called to mind, less invigilated, though no less called into account.

There is the paradox, of course, that for many this seventh day is the most boring of days, for it so seems that nothing is to be done. A day in which rest is really lethargy, and peace the vegetating of human powers. One wonders then: Is it not the idols that actually energize us, rather than God? And maybe: so much the worse for God! Divine peace? Why nothing more than the apotheosis of boredom! Is the day of peace then the day of divine emptiness, the dead day?

Some remarks from this chapter were given as the Aquinas Lecture, March 2002, sponsored by St. Charles Seminary and John Carroll University, Cleveland. My warm thanks to Brother Don Lippert for his hospitality.

What then are days of peace? And is there any day at all that has its fill of the divine? Is there a festive peace in which rest is not lethargy, and the energy of love is not bewitched by counterfeits of insinuation or hyperactivity? Is the drag of Sunday boredom a token of the hollowness of a busyness that cannot recuperate an energy of being beyond instrumentalization, once the daily round of relentless activities be brought to pause? Pause, but what then do we meet? Tiredness, not peace; not release of an energy beyond instrumentalization; tiredness revealing something empty needing to be filled. How filled? Through relieved return to busyness? Or through breakthrough into another way of being alive to the given day, to the day of gift?

There is the view that the Sabbath is not the seventh day but the true first day: now things can truly begin. I mentioned boredom giving way to greeting in another place (Chapter 1). I recall a godsend, itself recalling for me a long ago. Listening to a Sunday-morning program on Irish radio, a long-running show, a Sunday institution almost, "Mo Cheol Thú" ("You Are My Music"), listening to it on playback, I heard coming over the Internet, the cybernetic between, and coming to strike me without expectation from the long past, suddenly, the song "Sunday in Savannah," sung with slow, measured Sunday passion by the "high priestess of soul," Nina Simone. It was thirty years since I had last heard it and it struck me as a godsend, transporting me into the thick boredom of a languid Sunday replete with a kind of humid divinity—the people singing, swaying, praying—and the lines of touching admonition—ominous, playful—not omitted: "Don't ya dare go fishin', son"—and then the last lines, and the long, the reiterated, the elongated amen at the end—amen—amen—amen—amen. One can sing this amen, but could one think it? Could thinking itself sing?

Questions about the boredom of the Sabbath, and the peace, could be multiplied, I do not doubt. One has to admit that such questions posed about the Sabbath speak, whether sympathetically or disparagingly, in the language of the religions of Biblical inspiration, and hence speak from the direction of the city of Jerusalem, not Athens. But Athens knew well its festive days. One group of Athenian sons, the philosophers, might well reply that this is the mythic language of a religious worldview, now overtaken by a more mature rationality. This maturity need not disparage that younger enthusiastic language, nevertheless the wiser heads of aged reason do suggest a more neutral, sober cast of mind, where the day is the day, and there is no difference of day and day, where thought is just thought, and there being no difference of day and day, there is no, there can be no, Sabbath for thought. Give over. Let be.

Can one let it so rest? Can anything here be said that these sons of Athens might recognize as a kindred language? Is there a Sabbath for thought, indeed of thought, in which understanding and peace are companionable partners? What kind of understanding, what kind of peace could allow that partnership? And if there were something of great moment here, what might it also say about the nature of *thought* itself? Or is to ask about a Sabbath for thought to court a gruesome promiscuity of religion and philosophy, where Jerusalem is not Jerusalem, Athens not Athens, and all differences screwed in a monstrous marrying?

Nevertheless, surprising marriages are possible, do take place. I illustrate from the case of art, and cite someone that might surprise, he being of the guild of card-carrying atheists: Schopenhauer. Schopenhauer tells us "all *willing* springs from lack, from deficiency, and thus from suffering," hence his judgment on human satisfactions is bleak. "[F]ulfillment is short and meted out sparingly[,] . . . always like the alms thrown to a beggar, which reprieves him today so that his misery may be prolonged till tomorrow. . . . Thus the subject of willing is constantly lying on the revolving wheel of Ixion, is always drawing water in the sieve of the Danaids, and is the eternally thirsting Tantalus." Endless want, futile passion, quenchless craving—this is our sorry lot. In Schopenhauer's desolate world, a good God would be too good to be true, and yet there are consolations. For suppose something—great art, say—"suddenly raises us out of the stream of willing, and snatches knowledge from the thraldom of the will. . . . Then all at once the *peace*, always sought but always escaping us on that first path of willing, comes to us of its own accord, and all is well with us. It is the painless state, prized by Epicurus as the highest good and as the state of the gods; for that moment we are delivered from the miserable pressure of the will. *We celebrate the Sabbath of the penal servitude of the will*; the wheel of Ixion stands still."[1]

Peace: we celebrate the Sabbath of the penal servitude of the will—and art offers us an access to this peace. The mingling of lan-

---

[1] Arthur Schopenhauer, *Sämtliche Werke*, vol. 1, *Die Welt als Wille und Vorstellung*, ed. Wolfgang Frhr. von Lohneysen (Stuttgart: Cotta/Insel, 1960–65; Darmstadt: Wissenschaftliche Buchgesellschaft, 1968), 280. Translated by E. F. J. Payne as *The World as Will and Representation*, vol. 1 (New York: Dover, 1966), §38, 196, emphasis mine.

guages is intriguing: A Jewish and Christian word is porous to aesthetic and metaphysical meaning, in relation to a philosophy of the will as ultimate, and offered in a kind of song of praise by an atheistic philosopher. What power this word "Sabbath" has if it allows even such an atheistic prayer! Schopenhauer is not at all wrong to draw on the power of art to give a rest beyond instrumentalization. Beyond the busybody will, this is a rest that is no lethargy. We clearly understand this if we consider the preeminent art for Schopenhauer, namely music. Music and lethargy are antipodes: where one is the other cannot be. And yet in the energy of music there can come to be a peace of being, beyond the relentless restlessness of the will. In the music, energy; and in the forming energy, peace can come.

I put aside whether, given the role will has in Schopenhauer's system as a whole, it can make any sense finally to speak of a *Sabbath* of the will. In Schopenhauer's system there is a reversal of striving into peace that is difficult to make intelligible on his terms, since at bottom being seems to be a will more primally at war than at peace, an insatiable striving rather than any resting.[2] Yet Schopenhauer is on the right path in praising art's power to still the relentless will, and offer it a kind of "Sabbath"—a festive joy, I would say, a release of serenity that consummates the energy of being and its delight in the "to be." There is, and should be, no nihilism here.

If atheist Schopenhauer can call on the reserves of the religious to make a point about the metaphysical power of art, why cannot we, who have taken our leave of the guild of the godless, call on something of that power to put the question to philosophy: Is there a Sabbath for thought? What forbids us from asking a question like that? I cannot accept the prohibition of Heidegger as the last word when, for instance, in tones of strong "say-so," he declares that a Christian philosophy is a round square. Philosophy is Greek and Greek only, and that's that. What a univocalizing of philosophy and its plural voices is thereby effected! *Athena (Deutschland) locuta, causa finita!*

I beg to differ. I wonder if Athenian ears have more surprising porosities, porosities that allow Athens itself to hear beyond its own self-sounding voice. Indirect testimony: Nietzsche, son of Schopenhauer, opined that "Plato, the great viaduct of corruption . . . was already marked by Jewish bigotry (—in Egypt?)" (*Will to Power*, 118). Indirect, in that while Nietzsche seemed to disdain the poros-

---

[2] On this complex question in Schopenhauer and his reversal from will to willlessness, see *Art, Origins, Otherness*, chapter 5.

ity, we thinkers between Athens and Jerusalem do not grant *polemos* the last word, or the first. All honor to the Athenian Plato: he honored the feast day and festive companionship of the human and divine (see, for instance, *Laws*, 653d). Mindful of the porosity of being, why cannot philosophy be a thinking porous to others, and not least as it tries to get a catch of what floats toward it on the breath of those winds blowing from Jerusalem? In the porosity of being there are divine promiscuities too, out of which are born noble issue. For that matter: What God or god ever decreed that the delights of eros are forbidden on the Sabbath?

(Surely someone has just now reached for his text to find that forbidding god. I hope a God of delight is rather found.)

Any fool can see that war is everywhere. Some who are not quite fools—call them philosophers—can see that war stirs things up, sometimes leading unexpectedly to creative outcomes. But what kind of fool could think peace more primal than war? The hard men of philosophy will snort: this is true idiocy indeed. But what if there is an idiot wisdom? Wiser, in its unknowing, about the intimate universal, and an enigmatic field of peace as first?

We need to look at what some philosophers have suggested about peace. What we will see will turn out to be ambiguous. Along the way, we will look at the idea of the Sabbath, in broad strokes; the warring practices of some philosophers, especially some modern philosophers; the relation of work, thought, and peace; the intimacy of peace and the porosity of being; and the issue of a sabbatical thought, in which the intimate affiliation, not the war, of religion and philosophy has to be (re-)considered.

Peace and Some Philosophers

The question of peace is of an importance that cannot be understated, given the many violent events of recent times, the ebb and surge of war around the globe, and an enduring constancy in killing and being killed. Nor should we forget the larger perspective. The twentieth century was a century of great wars, and that century is only yesterday on the time scales of history. We see great wars followed by exhaustion, and then followed by the outpourings of energies that rebuild devastated countries and continents, in Japan and Europe for instance. The theme of war and peace is coextensive with the human condition, and we do not need a Homer or a Tolstoy to tell us this. Interestingly, war often exerts more fascination than does peace, and not only in epic poems and novels. The philosophers also seem to have treated of war more often and more extensively. Here are some samplings.

Plato: the emergence of the city in the *Republic* is impelled by the threat of war. I mean that emergence that comes *after* we have left the rustic condition of primitive vegetarian peace, where we eat nuts and fruits and grains, and nothing living has to be killed for the living to continue green. This rustic peace might seem like the garden of life, pagan cousin of the biblical Eden (Greek, *paradeisos*; old Persian, *pairi-ꝺaeza*, an enclosed space open to the sky), and both a far cry from the garden of Gethsemane. But as Glaucon's intervention suggests (*Republic*, 372d 5–7): this garden city of vegetarians is more like a city of pigs than of men. The sharp point: we are always in, so to say, a carnivorous rather than vegetarian world.

This seems unavoidable, once desire in its unlimited acquisitiveness, or what Plato, like other Greeks, called *pleonexia*, has arisen. The desire for more and more, and for possession of more and more, is inseparable from the desire to secure ourselves against a threat, not only of the hostile others, but perhaps most deeply the threat to our being as finite. Something like fear of nothingness always lies at the back of possession and acquisitiveness. We secure ourselves by securing things and others and a way of life. The security is achieved by a posture of aggression toward what is other and hence the security is always an unstable peace. So it finds itself having always to shore itself up again by further suspicion and aggression toward the other. If this is our *primary* relation to the world, war inevitably defines human existence relative to what is other to us.

True, a simulacrum of peace can emerge from this posture of war, where there is a kind of balance or stasis between the powers in opposition. Nevertheless, I think one must still view Plato as a philosopher of peace, at least in this other guise: his notion of justice is articulated in terms of the harmony of the soul with itself, in the multiplicity of its powers, and the harmony of society with itself, in the concord of the different groupings and their common good. His view points to justice as a condition of being, a harmony, not first constructed by the exercise of our power but one making possible both the effective and ethical use of power. Power without justice reflects a condition of war and produces further war; power with justice can both express and contribute to a condition of peace. Peace here is a condition of being and a harmony of beings and their powers, be they individual, or communal, or indeed cosmic relative to the harmony of the whole. I am referring now to the *Republic*, but Plato's concern for peace as the best (*aristos*) good, and for the nature of a polis constituted for peace first and not for war, is explicit in the *Laws* from its first book (628c–e).

Even so, for Plato a warrior class seems always necessary, even if also it is subordinated to a group of wise guardians or rulers. Peace is the concern of the latter group, though the first is never dispensable, since the need of war, or the threat of war, to make harmony effective, is never entirely banished. The question then: How ultimate is this peace, since it is always in part made possible by war or the threat of war? It is not *absolute peace* but a precarious and shifting achievement, no sooner attained than new belligerencies emerge to throw existing arrangements into disarray. It is a natural question to ask if an absolute peace is a mere chimera for human beings. The question must come: Is our condition more primally one of war, with peace as secondary, the derivative of more ultimate polemical conditions? If so, Heraclitus would then be in the right: war is the father of all things. *Polemos* is *pater* (Frag. 53).

As a second example I take Aquinas. In the main, Aquinas is known for contributing to the formulation and consolidation of the theory of a just war. The entire discussion is with a view to peace, and in the context of peace unacceptably disrupted. War is waged for the sake of peace, Aquinas repeats Aristotle. There is no other justification for war. The idea of war for war's sake is nonsensical to Aquinas.[3] If war is for the sake of peace, and occasioned by peace disrupted, can Heraclitus be right, can war, in fact, be the father of all things?

Figures are not wanting who will side with Heraclitus. Nietzsche might be acknowledged as their modern drum-beater. True to his taste for the *über*-statement, Nietzsche declares war and announces victory, all in the same breath: "*we ourselves*, we free spirits, are already a 'revaluation of all values,' an *incarnate* declaration of war and victory over all ancient conceptions of 'true' and 'untrue'" (*The Anti-Christ*, §13). He is not a man, he is war and peace incarnate. Perhaps not quite: one might declare victory and yet there is no true peace. And again and again Nietzsche urges us to wage war. For what? For

---

[3] There is a discussion in *De Pace*, ques. 29, *Summa Theologiae*, IIa IIae, and there are some brief remarks when discussing the beatitudes in *De beatitudinibus*, ques. 69 in *Summa Theologiae*, IIa IIae. The primary thinker of reference in these texts is Augustine, and his exploration of peace in terms of *tranquillitas ordinis*.

the sake of peace? But peace is an insipid condition, a consolation of the feeble, the dreary salvation of the debilitated. If peace at all, peace should be loved as a means to new wars—and the shorter the peace the better, thus Zarathustra giveth out. Zarathustra's views of courage and the enemy suggest that the endeavor to be overtakes, takes over the passion of being. I have said something different.

The later Heidegger might seem quite opposite in stressing *Gelassenheit*, yet he always had a soft spot for Heraclitus, and he remained ambiguous toward his own earlier strong resolute stress on the *polemos* or *Streit of being*. I can only mention it here, but both Nietzsche and Heidegger are faced with the tension of will willing itself and will released from itself, a tension already at stake in Schopenhauer, father of Nietzsche, object of dismissal by Heidegger. The *polemos* of being seems finally more primordial than the peace. How then the release of art, or the serenity of a peace that is not just the issue of war?[4]

If we take Aquinas seriously, we are confronted with a great question: What is the vision of peace that makes sense of war, be it social war, or cultural war, or, in this instance, also ontological? What might "being peaceful" be: not only to be as peaceful, but to *be* peaceful? Is there any meaning we can give to the idea of a primal ontological peace? A primal peace as bringing us closer to community with the father/mother of all things, and an ultimate origin that is not war? In Aquinas, of course, there is the peace of the end: Beatific vision the true peace; the Sabbath of being, beyond life and death. Apropos of Sunday boredom, it is intriguing that Aquinas links *acedie* to the Sabbath: "Sloth is sorrow about spiritual good inasmuch as it is a divine good [*tristitia de bono spirituali inquantum est bonum divinum*]." "Sloth is opposed to the precept about hallowing the Sabbath day . . . [, which] implicitly commands the mind to peace [*quies*] in God to which sorrow of the mind about the divine good is contrary." (*Summa Theologiae*, IIa IIae, ques. 35, art. 3, response, and ad. 1). Sloth is opposed to joy (*gaudio*) (art 2, obj. 2). Why oppose joy? What is this strange sorrow of the mind about the divine good?

Interestingly, *acedie*, among the desert solitaries, tended to arise at midday, hence was named the noonday demon. This is the time of no shadow, the sun being at its height; and yet in the shadowless light, something daimonic appears, a lack of peace and dejection over the divine good. For Aquinas this sorrow sometimes "reaches into our

---

[4] See *Art, Origins, Otherness*, chapters 6 and 7, for fuller discussion.

rational nature which consents in the flight from, horror and detestation of the Divine good" (art. 3, response). Some of the vices that
accompany sloth are certain kinds of somnolence, but also surprisingly what seems the opposite to torpor, namely, a certain wandering
uneasiness (*evagationem mentis*), leading to importunity of mind, curiosity, verbosity, and bodily inquietude (art. 4, ad. 3). But perhaps
this is not surprising really, if the torpor and the inquietude are the
same—that is, both being without true peace.

A third example I choose is St. Augustine, whose vision is, in part,
an answer to the question of an original peace. Thus his vision of
peace in the *City of God* (see, for instance, Book XIX, chapters 11–
18). This is a multilayered account, as deeply ontological as it is
metaphysical and theological. Ontological: it is a vision of all things
being what they are by virtue of an ultimate ontological peace—to be
at all is to be in the gifted peace of creation as good. No finite being
could continue to be at all without a certain basic peace of that being
with itself and other beings. Metaphysical and theological: the ultimate ground of this ontological peace of finite being lies in God, the
giver of all conditions of the possibility of being at all, and the giver
of finite being in its integrity. This ontological integrity is first an *endowment* by the divine source: a being for self of the creation, or creature, that shows it to enjoy being on the basis of gift, and to continue
in being further on the basis of an ultimate harmony with itself and
what is other than itself, and most ultimately with God.

Augustine offers a vision of peace at the origin of all that is; a vision of peace at the end of all becoming; a vision of the necessity of
peace to be there in the middle, for nothing could continue to be were
the condition of war absolutized, since every integrity of being would
then dis-integrate. This is peace as an ontological condition of the
possibility of being at all. It is, I would say, like the intimate universal, the most taken for granted, and also the most difficult to speak
about. For it makes everything else possible but is not itself any
thing, and hence when we try to fix it, it always eludes fixation. How
fix this peace? In some ways it is like a word that in being spoken
communicates and passes; or a song sung that, in being sounded, res-
onates in transience itself, as it passes through. The primal harmony
of finite creation unfolds in time, dissonant in consonance, consonant
in dissonance, only because the musical tempo of finite being comes
from and goes toward a peace deeper, more resonant, quieter than
all finite dissonance and consonance.

Peace and the Equivocal "Yes/No"

In light of the above I would say we come to something equivocal, but in a pregnant sense. We are not up to the absolved and absolving "yes" of God. Our best "yes" always has in it something of "yes/no." To us the relation between original peace and *polemos* does not always come through. The mystery of evil arises in the space between the original peace and *polemos*. Reversing a more usual way of thinking, one must ask: Does *polemos* then arise from peace? But what mutation of original peace could give rise to *polemos*? Do we need a fuller account of the "space between" between original peace and *polemos*?

One might say, this between is equivocal for us: with us the "yes" and "no" interpenetrate. Sometimes a certain "yes" is really a "no," and a "no" can sometimes be a reserved "yes." We ourselves are a living "yes" to being, an ontological affirmation upon whose basis we can affirm ourselves or what is other in a further sense. But in this further affirmation, the second "yes" can be a "no" to what is more deeply promised in the first "yes"; as it can also be a "no" to the broadcast of the "yes" we are to others beyond ourselves. Then the peace of true self-love becomes a warring selfishness that has defected from the fuller promise of its own being as a love of being, and claimed its own being as *the* good. We have made our second "yes" to ourselves into *the primal "yes."* We claim to be the absolved "yes" of God but then we are least absolved, least free, for we refuse being released.

Is this where an original usurpation occurs: a "yes," but a "yes" only possible because it negates, because it is a "no," and hence a counterfeit double of the more primal "yes"? Is this where the idol comes to be? We have made ourselves the idol by saying "yes" to ourselves in a certain way that is not the true "yes," neither true to the original "yes" to being we ourselves are, nor to the promise of this "yes" that can never be just "mine," since the first "yes" to me is the endowment that possibilizes my being as "mine." The first endowing "yes" is beyond me before it is "mine," and is always beyond me just as mine, and most beyond me when I think it is just mine and mine alone. Gleaning the meaning of our own "yes/no," one comes to wonder about such a "yes" more primal than this doublet. This is the concern that charges us: If we can affirm, how we can affirm, a "yes" more primal than this middle equivocal "yes/no." (Dealing with the arising of *polemos* from original peace would require more extended reflection, though I have earlier touched on an aspect of it in the discussion of enemies.)

Peace can be found in many guises, of course. I name some guises in relation to what in *Ethics and the Between* I call the potencies of the ethical. Peace can be given in the *idiocy of being* where the intimacy of peace passes the understanding, because peace is before understanding. Peace can be offered in the *aesthetic marvel* of finite happening: the sublime glory of the world of sensible creation, given to the slave and the king, consoling in moments of relief the prisoner and the solitary and the ones burdened with power. Peace can come in the social concord when we live together in accord with the *dianoetic* potency of the ethical: the reign of law affords the stability of order, and peace must count on some constancy. Peace can come in a kind of *transcendental* form where one is at home with doing what one must, what it is one's obligation to do and to be. There is a *eudaimonic* peace: peace with enough: *satis*: enough is enough—satisfactory: fulfillment granted, and the granting of fulfillment is accord with measure, is consent. Peace can come in the energy of *transcending*: being-at-home in not-being-at-home; at ease with self in the unease of self-surpassing: uniting effortlessness and striving, passion and endeavor, the *passio essendi* and *conatus essendi* at one in selving. Finally, first and ultimately, the peace of the *transcendent* can come: the peace that descends, surpassing the understanding, surpassing our self-surpassing, a delectation of transfigured being. This is the peace of religion, and it is questionable if without it there can be any sabbatical for thought.

The poet Yeats wrote (in "The Lake Isle of Innisfree") of peace "in the bee-loud glade," peace that "comes dropping slow, dropping from the veils of the morning to where the cricket sings." Why dropping slow? Notice how we sometimes speak of the enjoyment of peace: it comes over us; peace descends, say, on the house, when night falls. It is hard to avoid the language of a *transcendence that descends*. We seem to be speaking of a gift from above. It is not that sometimes we do not have to work hard to bring about the conditions that help make peace possible. But granting these conditions, there is an energy of being-at-home, with others, with self, indeed with all that is, and that is released in experiences of true peace. Of course— and this is more important—there are times when no conditions are required: without advance conditions, peace comes—a godsend comes over us. (Who knows really what a godsend is?) When peace descends on us, we do not sleep but are overtaken and transformed, though if we were asked to give a definition of that peace it would be like the intimate universal—impossible to fix completely.

Are there forms of peace that wake beyond the sleep of finitude? Is true peace an awakening to a love of being, always given as a promise, or gift, though mostly we fall asleep to it? And in our sleep are our energies taken over by battles that bewitch us, as if that condition were more truly being, the darkling plain where ignorant armies clash by night? If it is true that it is *polemos* that is second-born, then *polemos* is the fugue state, and born of falling asleep to the first peace of being.

Notice that with the philosophers of peace I mentioned above we remain in either a classical or medieval ethos, where the porosity between religion and philosophy is more open and traversed than will be the case in modern philosophy. As I will indicate below, this ethos of modernity gives way to a more insistent prioritizing of work and war, one with mutations in the feel for the ethos of being that this betokens. One might take Hobbes as paradigmatic of this difference: the world is a stage of the contestation of powers, with struggle over scarce resources at the basis, and desire for power after power, ceasing only in death. Desire shielding itself from the enemy and death: this reveals our true nature as combatants. Life is no garden. To be is to be at war; beings are warring and at war, be it open or undeclared; peace is derivative of warlike conditions or preparative to war. Peace is a balance of powers derived from *polemos*, powers themselves the expression of *polemos*. Machiavelli: prophets with arms—only they succeed. But the armed success so attained can be such that prophecies of true peace are invariably counterfeited. The words that proclaim peace are only strategic—lulling smiles in a longer war whose length has no determinate limit.

I will come back to this, but I mention the point in advance, since if there is a Sabbath of being and it is lost, we not being observant, that is, we being asleep to what is given, then the possibility of sabbatical thought will also be lost, and thinking will take itself as a kind of warring negativity. It will take itself, say, as a warring negativity of determining, or self-determining, or perhaps of deconstructing determinations and self-determinations, rather than a gifted festivity of mindfulness. How possible is the Sabbath, or festive mindfulness in such an altered ethos? More impossible than possible. And if any kind of Sabbath seems possible, is not its counterfeit double more likely than true festive being? For if the truly divine is not there, does all festivity finally become fake?

The Sabbatical Amen

Let me say something further about the Sabbath. I am no biblical scholar, but even to a layman it is evident that the Sabbath is the day of God. It is celebrated ritually every seventh day. The seventh day itself is a symbol of the day of fulfillment and the day of rest. The connection with peace is intimate. The Sabbath as the seventh day of rest can also be seen as the first: now true life begins, fully can begin. I mention also the idea of the Sabbath as the *eighth day*—signaling, I would say, something hyperbolic to normal time, workaday time— hyperbolic even to the temptation to turn the seventh day into something simply homogeneous with workaday time. Sacred time is other, and yet intimate.

I would say that the Sabbath is not the first, but it follows from the first. God is the First. Hence the *first* and most hyperbolic commandment: I am God, and there is none other; God is God and nothing but God is God. This is the Extra-ordinary: absolute singularity. This also intimates the difficulty of humans staying with this singularity as singular. For we make seconds to substitute for the Extra-ordinary First. The Extra-ordinary First cannot be duplicated by us, as creatures, for we are seconds, and everything we make reflects our derivativeness. I would not deny that we may well be, as it were, *original seconds*: second as derived creations, but original as participants, indeed agents of a created creativity. We can also make *substitute* seconds, and when we do we make idols, seconds that substitute for the original First, that is, counterfeit doubles of God which we worship as God. It seems our nature to secrete these counterfeit doubles, since we are not God, and, living in this gap of difference between the First and us, we inevitably see God as other to what God is. The very otherness of God gives the space wherein idols can be created, for this space is also the porous between of being that is communicated by the first origin, and in which the first origin communicates to and with us—and therein our desire can become active in populating this space of difference with what our desire generates, and it is not always pure love of the First.

The *second* commandment shows this by stressing the danger of invoking the name of God falsely: this is a continuation of the first, yet also a recognition that after the absolute First, doubles emerge, genuine, glorious plurality yes, but also counterfeit doubles of God, or false names. For we are tempted to name, to attempt to name, but we cannot truly name the absolute First. With the doubling, we are in the domain of an equivocity, hence in the glorious pluralism of creation but also the milieu of a possible threat of war: war that falsely names the uniqueness of the One, and that loses its peace with itself. The harbingers of war are hidden in the false names of God.

Then the *third* commandment: Remember to keep holy the Sabbath day. It is a reminder: against the counterfeit doubles we produce, the substitute seconds we secrete, against the war hinted in the equivocal, there is a recall to the First, a recall to a peace more primordial than war. This is not a return to a reductive unity, but an encouragement to keep holy the day. It is a reminder of life, and how to live. This means: a festive being in which our communication with the primal and ultimate First is most energized. It is a call to holiness. This is not just a matter of moral earnestness. There is a hyperbolic aspect to it. It exceeds the human measure of morality; for holiness exceeds the human measure, being moral and more than moral. But what or who is to *keep* holy the day? We are to keep it, but is this not because we are in keeping?

And then again what of the Sabbath? Look back to the beginning, and to the seventh day at the beginning. God rests after each day of creation, and he beholds that "It is good." What can resting mean? It is not recuperation from weariness but enjoying peace before the good of what has been given to be. There is no sleep in it. It is a "being awake": a festive mindfulness. Resting on the seventh day, there is not just a single seeing or exclamation of "It is good." There is reiteration in it. What is beheld is celebrated in the dimension of the *hyperbolic*: "It is good, it is very good." This is the great Amen to creation. For God does not behold: I am good, and how happy I am with myself for making all this. No: "It is good." It, creation, is released from God, and from any self-congratulation on God's part. As I put it elsewhere, in creation God is not cloning himself. "It is good": this is not the erotic self-satisfaction of an autistic god, but an agapeic release of the otherness of creation into the goodness of its own being for itself. This is the great Amen: the creation itself is good. This great Amen is the sabbatical peace: peace because the creation itself is the gift of generosity; it is not shaped out of a more primordial *polemos* that always has the hint of war or threat hounding it.

I underscore this: there is something singular and unique about this "yes," this Amen. More even than the goodness of the first six days is the holiness of the seventh. Many have seen all of this as simply a naive and touching anthropomorphism. I would stress something quite the reverse. When we *behold* something, something of the otherness of the thing beheld is communicated to us: beholding is not a self-projection. Every anthropomorphism—call this our own self-projection on the other—is made possible by this "yes," as first giving creation to be for itself, endowing it with the promise of its own being for itself. Our self-projection, every anthropomorphism, is enabled to be, possibilized even unto its creative power, by this original giving. We get the hint of this to the extent that we take seriously the absoluteness of the first command: that the First is First, and nothing else; God is God and nothing but God is God. The primal "It is good" is, I suspect, inseparable from release from all idols, none of which would be possible without our anthropomorphic powers of self-projection.

True enough: every "It is good" we human beings utter tends to be entangled in some open or secret "It is good for me, for us." This "It is very good" points to something beyond the "for me," even beyond the "for me" of the divine. *It* is good, and good for itself, and this "it" is the creation as other to the divine source. This primal "It is good" is indeed *for the creation*, but in the mode of being released from every self-enclosed self-relation of the divine. It is given for the other as other, and the good as for us comes to us from a giver that is beyond any enclosure of "for self." Is this not connected with the sorrow of sloth over the divine good, above mentioned? *Acedie* falls into a kind of despair because the divine good is beyond our encirclement; we would have it for ourselves but cannot—cannot have it on our own terms. We must think the releasing "It is good" in terms of agapeic origination. This primal "It is good" points to something *hyperbolic* to any anthropomorphic making. It suggests that everything that is good for us is secondary to a primal sense of it being good: given good, yes, but the gift of the creation as other to the divine giver. It celebrates the creation coming to be, not out of *polemos*, but out of giving as giving, which releases the gift of creation into its own good; and this good is affirmed in the very Amen of Godself. To live in this Amen is to live sabbatically.

What, in line with this, would it be to *think* sabbatically? If nothing else, it would be to think, to be enabled to think, in and through one's participation in this ultimate endowment, or gift of (ontological) peace. But is this possible? Is it possible for philosophers? Or is it so that nothing, and no thought, would be at all possible without this primal and ultimate endowment? Is not thinking, as first given to be, a release of mindfulness that comes to us, before we later can give the thought to ourselves, determine thinking through thinking itself? Is not the deepest experience of thought often expressed in such ways of speaking as: "The thought *came* to me," or "Not I thought this, but I was *struck* by this thought." Beholding is being beholden.

Is there a primal *pathei mathos*, and not just a tragic knowing, where the freedom of thinking is not self-determined, but rather a release of mindfulness in which an access of light, an access to light, is given? And where this patience to the light, is not just at the end, say, at the height of tragic knowing, but in the intimate idiocy of the soul, from the origin? Gifting us with a primal porosity in which all forms of mindfulness take determinate shape or shape themselves? Gifting us with the possibility of being mindful at all, with its promise?

Philosophy's Own Agon and the Primacy of Peace

It is understandable why philosophers generally might give more credence to the necessity of antagonism, for is not philosophy itself inseparable from disputation? The love of the agon is well-cultivated, in words and argument. Peace is a dream; the harsher truth, the bracing reality is conflict. It stirs up the blood—stirs thinking up too. I do not forget that Athena is not only a goddess of wisdom; she is a goddess of war who sprung from the head of Zeus, fully formed, and brandishing a spear.

Heraclitus, though a pre-Socratic philosopher, again might speak for many moderns. A sampling of instances: Kant dreamed of perpetual peace, and yet for him there was something sublime about war: "a prolonged peace favors the predominance of a mere commercial spirit, with it a debasing self-interest, cowardice and effeminacy" (*Critique of Judgment*, §28). Boehme, heterodox religious thinker, divined a primal struggle in God's self-becoming, and Schelling, the heterodox philosopher, concurs. As a philosopher Hegel, no less theologically heterodox, puts dialectical method in the strife: contradiction is inseparable from the energy of thinking, and, even ethically, war wakes us from contented finitude. Hegel relishes "the ethical moment in war," in its power to disturb the satisfactions of finite life grown torpid in its self-complacency. I understand: war wakes us from this sleep of finitude—but to what does it wake us? Hegel is too blithe about what monsters might spring up, too facile about what a peace more absolute than war would be, for with him war still comes from peace, and there is no primal peace. To the contrary, *Geist* is at war with itself, in order to be itself at all.[5]

Marx might be a debunking son of Hegel, but the blood of the father flowed in him. Only recall his language of weaponry: "Just as philosophy finds its *material* weapons in the proletariat, so the proletariat finds its *intellectual* weapons (*geistigen Waffen*) in philosophy."[6] Philosophy is to come to the battle well-armed; revolutionary theory might have to employ its own purging terror. There is, of course, the class war as the ultimate engine of history, Marx's historicization of the *Kampf zum Tode* of Hegel's master-slave dialectic. One of Marx's revolutionary sons, Mao, is well known for his claim that "power grows out of the barrel of a gun," and these weapons are not just spiritual weapons (*geistigen Waffen*). China, the world itself, was no garden, but a site of battle. War is king, first and last. Paraphrasing a favorite saying of Lenin, Mao liked to say: "The unity of opposites is temporary; antagonistic struggle is absolute."[7]

I have mentioned Nietzsche more than once, but he detects agon in philosophy itself from its inception, and not without the aid of Jacob Burkhardt's vision of the agonistic character of Greek life and culture. Socrates was "Athens' greatest backstreet dialectician" (*Human, All Too Human*, §433). Socrates spurs Athens on through the "fencing art" of his dialectic, whose value is that of a new form of the agon (*Daybreak*, §195). One thinks too of *Streben* in Romantic

---

[5] See *Philosophy of Right*, §324 on the "ethical moment of war." Then also: "Thus Spirit is at war with itself; it has to overcome itself as its most formidable obstacle [*das wahre feindelige Hindernis*]. That development which in the sphere of Nature is a peaceful growth, is in that of Spirit, a severe, a mighty conflict with itself. What Spirit really strives for is the realization of its Ideal being; but in doing so, it hides that goal from its own vision, and is proud and well-satisfied in this alienation from it." *The Philosophy of History*, trans. J. Sibree (Amherst, N.Y.: Prometheus Books, 1991), 55. *Vorlesungen über die Philosophie der Geschichte, Werke*, ed. E. Moldenhauer and K. M. Michel, vol. 12, 76.

[6] Karl Marx, Frühe Schriften, *Werke*, vol. 1, ed. Hans-Joachim Lieber and Peter Furth (Darmstadt: Wissenschaftliche Buchgesellschaft, 1971), 504; *Early Writings*, trans. and ed. T. B. Bottomore (New York: McGraw Hill, 1963), 59. See my "Is There Metaphysics After Critique?" in *International Philosophical Quarterly* (June 2005).

[7] See Philip Short, *Mao: A Life* (London: Hodder and Stoughton, 1999), 459; on power out of the barrel of a gun, see 203, 368.

thought. Blake: "Without contraries is no progression." This attitude is archaic and has the allure of an aboriginal possibility. Thus Empedocles (Frag. 17): Friendship (*philia*) is in the course of things, as is also a kind of strife (*neikos*); there is alternation between the two, though there was a state of primal peace or innocence when "altars were not steeped in the blood of bulls" and humankind was not yet carnivorous (Frag. 128) and devouring even themselves (Frags. 136, 137).

Eros and *eris* are not unconnected. Both show a certain struggle to be, a certain striving to be. Hesiod believed there was a good *eris* and a bad *eris*, the first a competitive fostering of productive outcomes, the second only of evil war and battle (*Works and Days*, 11–41). The good *eris* is first born, the bad *eris* second. But is it *eris* alone that can make the difference between the good and the bad, the creative and the destructive?

The intimacy of *eris* and eros is perhaps reflected in Spinoza's *conatus essendi*, which he claims is the essence of each being, its endeavor to be. The gentle Spinoza is recalled by his biographer Colerus as taking delight in setting spider against spider, and watching spiders devour flies in their web, having himself thrown the flies into the web. Spinoza "was so well pleased with the Battel, that he wou'd sometimes break into Laughter." Schopenhauer did not at all like this about Spinoza, for Schopenhauer loved dogs—probably more than humans. We get a whiff of anti-Semitic feeling when he connects Spinoza's hilarity at devouring nature with early chapters of the book of Genesis: people "who are accustomed to purer and worthier doctrines are here overcome by the *foetor judaicus*."[8] Schopenhauer, reminding us of his son, Nietzsche, was a philosopher sensitive to stinks. I take a very different lesson from the "It is good" of Genesis than is to be found in Schopenhauer—or Spinoza. For that matter, if the Will is the blind, violent, relentless striving Schopenhauer claims it to be, he has no basis to scold Spinoza. Striving to be is not easy to disentangle from the strife of being itself. Being itself seems to be strife. This means that it is not only in human societies that we see clash and conflict and war,[9] but in nonhuman nature,

---

[8] Arthur Schopenhauer, *Parerga and Paralipomena*, trans. E. F. J. Payne (Oxford: Oxford University Press, 1974), vol. 1, 73.

[9] Michel Foucault represents an influential contemporary expression of the view: "Isn't power a sort of generalized war which assumes at particular moments the forms of peace and the state? Peace would then be a form of war, and the State a means of waging it." Michel Foucault, *Power/Knowledge: Selected Interviews and Other*

in being itself. "Nature red in tooth and claw" is only a reflection of the ontological law of all being: everything strives to be and has its being in strife. Balance, orders, relativities may come to be from strife, but to be itself is strife.

Enough of this sampling, and to the question: Is such a *conatus essendi* the primitive energy of the "to be"? Is there something more original, before striving, hence something open to something other to strife, and before strife? I argue there is a *passio essendi* more primordial than *conatus essendi*. It follows that there is a love of being that is more primordial than an eros for being. There is a "being given to be" that is prior to striving; indeed striving itself not only presupposes this but it is itself possibilized thereby. If so, there are significant consequences for a peace that is more primordial than *polemos*. You might object: well and good, this being given to be must be acknowledged, but this too is an emergence from more polemical sources—everything given is already the result of an *Ur-streit*, so to say, whatever the terms be in which we formulate this *Ur-streit*, be they ontological, historical, cultural, political, or cognitive, and so on. If this were so, all formations of peace would still be different formations of strife, and hence, in a certain sense, the simulacra of peace. Can we decide if there is an *Ur-streit* at the most elemental level of being, or must we grant something other than this?

It is hard to know how one would decide this question. My surmise is that the question is decided by a philosopher not directly in terms of some extraordinary encounter with the *Ur-streit* or aboriginal peace, but mostly in and though the signs of war and peace given to us in the middle of life, and on the basis of which we glean what is the more ultimate. These signs are not just external tokens we can calculate and weigh this way and that, weigh objectively. The signs are of our own being, in our own being, and in our own participation in being at all. The issue of war and peace can never be a purely objective one, since we are ourselves in question, relative to the meaning of the "to be." Our own "to be" is in question, in its deepest intimacy and the promise of its most extensive self-transcending. In an important respect, we ourselves are the equivocal signs, mixing "yes" and "no," and yet also sifting the "yes" and the "no." Are these equiprimordial in their interplay or is there a relation of priority, even when they are at variance? Here we come to an elemental and

Writings, 1972–1977, ed. C. Gordon, trans. C. Gordon, L. Marshall, J. Mepham, K. Soper (New York: Pantheon Books, 1980), 123.

ultimate question about our own being, with consequences for the being of being, and what the "to be" means in truth.

Our life in the middle shows the mingling, but I think it is very hard to say that being as given comes out of war, since war as such is nihilating rather than creating. If something creative comes, there is more at work in war than war. You might object and invest strife with something of creative striving, and hence of the power to bring something fresh and new into being. True, this can be proposed, but that something new is here possibilized indicates that the striving in question cannot be merely nihilating. Something of more surplus positive power or empowering must be at work, albeit ambiguously, in the striving: an empowering possibilizing that brings to be, that gives form to, that sustains the realization in full of what has been given to be. But what this suggests is something reminiscent of conditions more like those of peace than of war.[10]

If this is true, we are returned to the *passio essendi*, and this as a gift from a surplus empowering source that also communicates the energies of being to us that issue in creative striving. The energy of creative striving is not, as with the fire stolen by Prometheus, a theft from the god. Primally, it is not stolen at all. It is a gift that comes to us in and as the porosity of being. But this porosity is more primordially peace rather than war. War is not the father of all: there is a father/mother more primordial than this father. One might say: War takes for granted being given to be, the primordial gift of being; war may have its deepest roots in forgetfulness of this gift, indeed in refusal of it as gift. To fight for life presupposes being given the gift of life, and the good of this gift.

Interestingly, an immanent consideration of war points in this direction. War, in defense of one's own life or the life of others, shows this *deeper love of life* that is not a condition of war itself.[11] Even wars

---

[10] We can metaphorize war as nothing but the energy of creation, but this is a double-edged metaphor that risks a dangerous falsification of the fuller truth of war. This is something risked by Nietzsche in his hymns to war. One can partially exculpate him from the cruder use of this metaphorics by the Nazis, who did not see anything metaphoric at all. But Nietzsche is not entirely guilt-free here. He dissimulates the energy of war as if it were the higher energy, but this is the prerogative of the peace of creation that passes finitude.

[11] Suffering is not an argument for the evil of being, nor for the ultimacy of war. That we shun it, seek to alleviate it, shows the opposite. (Suffering is not the same as moral evil.) Why alleviate suffering? To preserve life. Why preserve life? Because it is worthy to be preserved, worthy to be affirmed: this again is the good of the "to be" resurrecting itself in the face of threats of life to life itself. See my remarks (at

of aggression or conquest covet the goods of another and usurp their good for one's own. Hence again the wisdom of Aristotle and Aquinas: war for its own sake makes no sense; war is waged for the sake of peace. Both recall us to peace itself as more primordial than war. And there is a peace that is not necessarily for the sake of anything other than itself. We can lose sight of this easily if we take Heraclitus as dictating terms, and if we dominantly foreground the *conatus essendi* to the recession of the *passio essendi*. This, our patience to being, is no mere negative condition, no patience in which we are subjected to a squashing heteronomy, but rather one in which find ourselves released beyond ourselves in a happening as good: the passion of being as good. We are dealing with the love of life, the "to be" as good, that lives us first, before we live it.

I think we can find a rich and ambiguous recognition of this patience to being in some forms of premodern philosophy. In opposition to the agonistic, disputatious view of philosophy, consider the old view of wonder as the beginning of philosophy. As it is famously said in Plato's *Theaetetus*: *thaumazein* is the *pathos* of the philosopher. One notices the *pathos*: the patience of being, the *passio essendi*. Wonder happens to us, strikes us, or comes over us, we do not generate it through our own work. It is not the product of striving or of autonomous self-determining thinking. Far more is it a release of the promise of thought itself. Thinking is first a happening before it shapes itself this way or that. There is something more primordial than the striving to think, and before thought determines itself, or is autonomously for itself. There is the release into mindfulness that is more than any determinate form of thought, over against other forms of thought, and over against being as other to thought.

I speak of this in *Being and the Between* as agapeic astonishment. Astonishment has the bite of happening in it: an otherness is shown or communicated to us, and a celebrating wonder at its sheer being there as given awakens us to it, and indeed awakens mind to itself. I call it agapeic, in that it reveals something of a plenitude: there is a "too-muchness," a certain rich saturation to the thereness. It is not just the indigence of an ignorance that lacks. There is more to what is shown to mindfulness, as well as more to mindfulness, than ignorance. There is a secret communication, or community, between the

---

the end of "Enemies") about Milton's Satan being momentarily disarmed by the beauty of Eve, and being arrested for an interim "stupidly good," and what this entails for a love of good more intimate to hatred than hatred itself.

given otherness of being and mindfulness woken to it, in a delight or love in which it is at home. This again is a happening of the porosity of being: being mindful is a porosity to being other than itself; it is a porosity itself and to itself; it finds itself in a communication with what is other to itself as self-determining. A philosopher who later strives for fidelity to the originating wonder takes pains that this porosity be kept unclogged in his or her thinking.

This view of the beginning of philosophy is closer to what sabbatical being implies and what the meaning of peace betokens. We are opened in agapeic astonishment to what is as given, but ultimately this rich surplus of the given is not outside of our being recipients of communication concerning the "to be" as good. Agapeic astonishment is a primal porosity to being as given, and given as intimately good. Being sabbatical for humans is a keeping in abeyance of the projects of the busybody will, a keeping in abeyance of our striving to grasp things, to be their measure and master. And yet it is not an empty abeyance but a being at the ready, a being available, to the superlative that exceeds us. The abeyance as a readiness is full: full with resting in itself, in being more fully beyond itself, hence more than resting in itself alone, but resting in other-being as giving itself.

This readiness is full with an expectation not amenable to being pinned down just to this or to that specific anticipation. See thus the wonder as a porosity—porosity of mindfulness as a between of passage. Wonder, source of our desire to grasp things in thought, itself puts in abeyance, finds put in abeyance, all thinking that is just grasping. Rather than grasping, it is grasped. The passion of being astonished is prior to the striving of seeking to know: being taken hold of before taking hold; beholden in beholding. In one respect, this porosity might seem to be like thinking about nothing, since it thinks about nothing in particular. It looks like an emptiness. And yet there is a thinking about nothing in particular that is just the *readiness* of thinking to be mindful of what comes, of what comes to show itself. What looks empty is an expectancy of mindfulness that does not have the measure of itself, since it is just the readiness of thought to be in communication with what exceeds the measure of its own thought. This porosity opens expectancy to the pure surprise of the unexpected. As an elemental porosity it is as much full in this readiness as it seems empty in its detachment from fixation on this or that thing.

That is not all that has to be said (*Being and the Between* seeks to address more systematically the different forms of being and mindfulness, both determinate, self-determining, and overdeterminate). Notice now the contrast with more modern ways of emphasizing *doubt* rather than wonder. If I love my wife, I do not doubt her; only when love is dying or dead, do I doubt her or begin to doubt. Doubt comes when the love of being in agapeic astonishment begins to fade or sicken. See Descartes and others: the seed of suspicion toward other-being as such is stirring; and responsively, we do not respond directly to the communication of the "It is good" in the given, but rather seek to secure knowledge by securing self in thought itself, in the *cogito*. Other-being comes to be seen as for me, not for itself. Where then is the "It is good," or even an intimation that this is a deep perplexity for thought itself? Other-being seems more like the equivocal face of an ambiguous thereness before which we stand in a more fearful trepidation, dreading too that the right exclamation before the other-being should be: "It is hostile, it is evil!"

You will demur and say this is too much. You will say: Being is there, there neutrally—good and evil have nothing to do with it. But—I would reply—so-called neutral being quickly becomes being for us; and how we make it for us reflects how we understand the "to be" at all; and if there is nothing good to the "to be," then finally it is nothing of worth outside of us. It is a short step from this worthless-ness for us to its usefulness for us, thence to our exceeding of its worthlessness, and thence finally to the last exclamation: "It is noth-ing for us." Being becomes a matter of serviceable disposability (as I put it in *Ethics and the Between*, chapter 14): as long as it is serviceable, as long as it serves us, we allow it a value; no longer serviceable, no longer serving us, it is disposed of—worthless now, and as nothing. We seem to be on top of it all, but then, even on the polemical view of being, it must come about that we also are destined to be nothing for ourselves. Our being too is serviceable disposability; but what do we serve, and are not we too finally disposable? Seemingly on top of things, we come to lack a genuine other to give meaning to our striv-ing: in being everything, striving too comes to nothing. And in the face of this nothing, as night follows day, the outcry will come: "It is better not to be." For what does everything come to in the end but nothing, for that is all it ever was from the outset.

No doubt there might be many intermediate stages between neu-trality and worthless nothing, and these can keep us busy for a long time. The last exclamation, "It is nothing for us," can take on world-historical form by reconfiguring the ethos of being for an entire epoch. The reconfiguration takes places underground and out of mind. Thoughtful persons will ponder to what extent our immense busyness is a distraction from the fateful question that will finally have its hour: What then the point of it all, what then the good of it all? We make our settlement within a distracted middle, an occupied form of intermediate life that shields itself with great intelligence and ingenuity from the ultimate and the first questions.

Somehow to confront, at last, the possibility that "It is evil" can clear the air of the prudent distraction that engrosses itself in the given without wonder about its why or worth. There is something hyperbolic in the outcry "It is evil." Just as something hyperbolic, the outcry is ontologically shocking in its suggestion of the absence or impossibility of sabbatical being. For this reason we should take very seriously Descartes's hyperbolic thought of the evil genius and its extreme threat. Understood in a certain way, it means the utter loss of the Sabbath of being, and the impossibility of any sabbatical thinking.[12] The very threat posed here not only precipitates in us an uncertain exposure to the precariousness of things, but also a wonder about their preciousness, about what finally is worthy to be affirmed and what sustains its worth. If nothing finally is worthy to be affirmed, we are indeed in nihilism, baptize it as we like with more efficient euphemisms that cushion us from the horror whose hour will come. Worse perhaps: the hour of horror does not come, for we have effectively kept our despair from ourselves, having aborted all sabbatical promises.

One might wonder if human beings are capable of going to the end of this thought—"It is evil"—for surely some threshold to hell must be crossed to bring it to completion. The completion would be utter nihilation. Has any philosophy really gone that far, since any philosopher of which we know speaks of his claim, and hence has lived to tell the tale, and thus is still the beneficiary of being given to be, and its good. Maybe only those who will utterly nihilate themselves (and others), whether in despair or imprecation, are the ex-

---

[12] In an important and mysterious sense, what we often call "knowledge" has some connection with evil, some connection with the "Fall." This cuts us off from the Sabbath of being, and agapeic astonishment. It has to do in some way also with the self-assertion we find flaring up in erotic perplexity, and in the grasping of a curiosity from which the agape of being is absent. It is our *turn away from and toward a different relation to being*: a knowledge that falls into the difference of good and evil, but "outside" reverence for the "It is good." The more we demand a certain kind or way of knowing, the more we make progress in evil.

tremists of the loss of the Sabbath who cross that threshold. I know too that death does not have to be physical, for there are forms of spiritual death: those dead continue to live, even appear to thrive. Honeyed words can be death. The gift of being, while continuing to be given, is being emptied out, hollowed. Living too creates its own counterfeit doubles of living. There is no original as such to these counterfeits, for in counterfeiting nothing, they are themselves nothing. They are negatives of an original, but the original is itself nothing. What life these nothings have is borrowed from the gift of life as given to be.

Making Philosophy Work

Be that as it may, there are shades of darkness between this thought and coming to that threshold. With various degrees of loss, it is understandable why, in this reconfigured milieu of thought, doubt should take on such an importance. In our dwelling in this milieu of being, an air of war, an atmosphere of suspicion and aggression insinuates itself. What is given in wonder and astonishment cannot be completely mastered—there is a constitutive ambiguity, not fully determinable. If we insist on determinability to secure ourselves, inevitably we must turn this "too-muchness" of given being into something else: a something to be overcome, a possible foe. We convince ourselves we need better tools, for tools as extensions of our power are convertible to weapons, and what better tools of knowing might there be than in a new mathematical science. Then we univocalize the equivocal, but in this we risk killing the mystery. Just so the energy of love, with all its ambiguity, is also wounded, if not done away with, if we insist on a mathematical certainty. There is no mathematical measure of love. We need finesse, not geometry. War can call on the strategic uses of finesse but is not itself the more ultimate finesse of the peace it must serve.

The impulse behind this univocalizing is not love. Or it is indeed a love, but more in the form of an eros uprooted from the trace of original plenitude in its own agapeic promise, and given over to a quest for self-completion in terms of our own *conatus essendi*, now seeking to master our own *passio essendi* and making us beings who are not at all given to be but claiming entirely to give itself to itself. With this, there is no true gift of being at all; and no basis for the admiration that exclaims "It is good." Every given is now defined as good in terms of its being my good. In the language I use, astonishment has given way to a perplexity which is not only more erotic than agapeic, but erotic in a mode that refuses the given and hence closes off its own porosity to agapeic promise. We have then a form of self-seeking eros, eros striving to be self, to be itself, which in one direction is massively "subjectified" but which in another direction secretes a project of massive "objectification." For relative to things and processes outside of itself in objective nature, it issues in a form of determinate curiosity in which all enigmas are subject to determinable cognition. If we lose any vision of peace in the beginning, perplexity easily becomes an aggression against the mystery of what is other to us, and curiosity a means by which we assert our determinative cognitions over things. It is an interesting and melancholy thought that science and technology are often spurred on to new discoveries by threats of war or occasions of war. In turn, science and technology make war more efficient and monstrous. Making war more rational means making its nihilating power more and more absolute. This is just another counterfeit doubling of God. Lurking in such technologies is something daimonic, something perhaps Luciferian, even though men with expertise say they proceed only with the best of moral intentions.

Driven by such a doubting perplexity and aggressive curiosity, our minds may well be in bondage to a kind of *pleonexia* in the realm of intellect. For sometimes wanting to acquire more and more knowledge may be a faster and faster way to lose wisdom. We have deserted the space of the deeper peace. Are we not again back with the mourning thought of Plato that *pleonexia* is an intimate source of war? As I said above, we need not necessarily follow through these thoughts to that end, for there are more in-between possibilities. For instance, we can take our sights predominantly from the postures of the workaday week, but without the Sabbath. This reflects one of the dominant configurations of being in modernity, and hence a remark is apposite regarding the connection of work and the modern ideal of philosophy.

My point is not to denigrate work but to ask if the good of work requires something like the amen of the "It is very good," given on the day of sabbatical being. We are inclined to make ourselves the standard of good during the working week, and we say: I work—I am master—I make myself the measure of what is good. At a limit, our being for ourselves, our being given to be for ourselves, turns into itself, and we are tempted to make ourselves the double of God, crowning our self-making with our own amen: I am good, I am very good. Again we court idolatry, for this amen to oneself is a mimicry of the sabbatical Amen. It is to be in a condition of war, and to declare this war to be the true peace, if I claim now to give myself the final peace.

I think of a truer practice of philosophy as the discernment of the false doubles of God and of these counterfeit amens. With Descartes and after, we sense a defect of astonishment, itself turned to doubt, itself sometimes masking an aggressive posture toward being in all its ambiguous mystery. That modern theory often betrays itself predominantly as a philosophy of work gives one to wonder about the loss of those traces of the Sabbath that one can find in the more contemplative orientations of premodern metaphysics. I mean that ancient and medieval *theōria* itself partook of the religious festival, as echoed in the very word *theōria* itself: *theōroi* were those delegates from the city-states whose privilege it was to watch, to enjoy the games themselves: the games themselves were religious games. Playfulness is close to being sabbatical. Thus Plato: "It is the life of peace that everyone should live as much and as well as possible" (*Laws*, 803d 8–10. The best way to spend a life in the highest activity is playing divine games (*Laws*, 803c–e). There should be 365 festival days in the year (*Laws*, 828b).

This higher playfulness is generally treated with contempt by modern philosophy. Again Descartes: let us put away the "useless speculations" of the ancients, and replace them with a new science that is useful, that works for us. If we accept this, our definition of the true becomes ultimately what works for us. This attitude not only is to be found in later, more explicitly pragmatic philosophies, but in more recessive forms underwrites the project of modernity. No longer related to a playful release of *theōria* beyond self, the working knower is the measure of what is, and what is true. I agree: It is true that truth works for us; but this is because truth works for us, not because we make it work as true. The kind of work that sustains the dominion of serviceable disposability is subtended by a secret aggression. We work because we worry. Ontological insecurity today wants to guarantee the day through work, wants to secure the tomorrow — the day after tomorrow. This securing is shadowed by the fear of death. This work is death-bound. We seize the day and more quickly bring on night — even at high noon.

When thinkers like Descartes founded a new science that would work for us, they were sleeping not only to the possible loss of the Sabbath of being but to the need of other *works of love* to rescue us from the nihilism that follows from the ontological war implicit in the loss of the festive thinking of premodern theory. Modern theory might be a working hypothesis; but such a hypothesis is a projection of our thought, which we test over against a supposedly indifferent thereness. It is not a celebration of creation in which we participate. (Celebration may need, for instance, the dark illuminating utterance of the poetic word.) A hypothesis may well be an expression of a secret will-to-power. And all told, is this secret not the kernel? Festive theory is different: a delight in beholding, not an instrumental hypothesis giving us a hold over data. If this delight in beholding was a kind of sovereignty, it was a beholden sovereignty: it released one beyond oneself—into enjoyment of what was before one—into celebrating what was given.

Granted, there is the temptation of that sovereignty to conceive itself a god. There is the danger of the hubris of the philosopher. But is, so to say, a more *benign* hubris possible, more benign than the sovereign servile hubris of modern will-to-power? Nietzsche does not help us see this when he insists that all philosophy masks a will to tyranny (*Human, All Too Human*, §261). Plato, the "monster of pride" (*Gay Science*, §351), will be seen in his own image and likeness: "The lust for tyranny always lurks[,] . . . it was like that with the Greeks: Plato testifies to it in a hundred places, Plato, who knew his peers—and himself" (*Genealogy of Morals*, III, §18). Nietzsche's view seems confirmed when Socrates says (*Philebus*, 28c6–9): "for all the wise [*hoi sophoi*] agree—whereby they really exalt themselves—that mind [*nous*] is king [*basileus*] of heaven and earth. Perhaps they are right." Is this not Socratic self-exaltation? The finesse we need here I think Nietzsche lacks. The point is less self-exaltation as that *nous* is king. A king (*basileus*) need not be a tyrant. Will-to-power as tyrant is not king. Eros can be *eros ouranios* as well as *eros turranos*. And clearly here the wise are under the measure of this *nous* of heaven and earth. You might say: in our being above ourselves, there is a measure above us still. Above Prometheus, a just Jove.

You might still object that the above picture of modern philosophy is all askew, for is not the story one of autonomy, not will-to-power? Such autonomy is our great modern nobility, all the more commendable in being recommended equally for all. This is indeed an edifying discourse, but what is being built up? Sometimes genuine freedom, one cannot deny. But why not sometimes "autonomy" as the moral mask that will-to-power wears in an epoch that still draws on an inheritance in some rapport with the original sabbatical, the original amen—though rapport now takes the predominant form of the un-conditional obligation of the moral law? The "It is good" becomes here, as with Kant, the moral "It is good" of the good will.

While this is not entirely wrong, it is not what is most deeply at issue in sabbatical being, for the meaning of the "It is good" is not just this moral one. In my view, this last already risks a contraction of the "yes," over against the seemingly valueless world of nature. It signals an effort to recuperate what properly is sabbatical, but in moral terms, and recuperate in reaction to the loss of the Sabbath of being in the glory of creation, now vanished in the valueless there-ness of the Newtonian mechanism. I see this at work in Kant's noble moral philosophy, but the issue of sabbatical being is not this. I see a reflection of it also in Kant's *Critique of Judgment* where the human being is the only inherent purpose in a nature devoid of such ends (the last part of this work is not read by many, and certainly not the postmoderns—there Kant is very concerned with the possibility of a theology in an ethical form).

Kant is not a sabbatical thinker but a philosophical rationalist of earnest work. What of his proposals for perpetual peace? We have to work for this, too. The condition of states is like that of individuals before the contract that imposes peace: war of each against all; and peace comes after, if it comes at all. A league of peace is proposed, but this is not sabbatical. Being is not at all sabbatical for Kant. He is famous, or infamous, for saying in his *Perpetual Peace* (First Supple-ment): "The problem of organizing a state, however hard it may seem, can be solved even for a race of devils, if only they are intelli-gent." One feels that such an organized state would be little more than a counterfeit of community: everything would be in order but nothing at all would be in order. The primacy of peace as an ontologi-cal and metaphysical issue seems not even to arise for Kant. As I have already indicated, he is far from unique among philosophers, in this regard. Revealing also are Kant's words to this effect:[13] Aristotle is work but Plato is play; and then Kant goes on to dismiss Plato and praise Aristotle. "The law is that reason acquires its possessions through work." Something of the man is shown in the tone of this dismissal and this praise. One honors the spirit of earnestness that

_____

[13] See "Von einem neuerdings erhobenen vornehmen Ton in der Philosophie," (1796), ed. and trans. Peter Fenves, *Raising the Tone of Philosophy: Late Essays by Im-manuel Kant, Transformative Critique by Jacques Derrida* (Baltimore: Johns Hopkins University Press, 1993).

Kant himself honors, but this spirit also means taking oneself very seriously, too seriously, moralistically. Kant wants to accept nothing he has not earned through his own work. But there is a playfulness that is closer to grace; and Kant is undoubtedly a philosopher of works, not grace.

I find it paradoxical that while the Lutheran tradition stresses grace and not works, so many of the German philosophers, children of Lutheran upbringings, produced philosophies that are utterly grace-less. Again somewhat paradoxically, in Nietzsche, superlative hater of all canting moralisms, and no lover of Christianity, there is a kind of *pagan grace*. One honors this. The philosophers of freedom as rational autonomy purse their lips at the playfulness of grace. I connect these squeezed lips with an inability, or unwillingness, to come to terms with the transcendence of God as beyond autonomy, and with the asymmetrical superiority of the divine—itself expressed biblically in the hyperbolic Amen: "It is very good." But better a pagan "It is good" than those pursed lips.

There is an interesting continuity here between Hegel and Kant. Hegel portrays himself as a great critic of Kant, but when it comes to the idea of thinking as work, they are blood brothers. In fact, one could claim that despite Kant's moral earnestness, it is Hegel who more lethally drives through to completion the notion of thinking as work: the work of the negative. Could one call the work of the negative creative? How could one? Negation presupposes what it negates; and while it brings to determination a modification of what already is, it does not radically bring something new to be. This last might be a definition of creation: the radically bringing to be of a being, originally new in an unprecedented sense. The work of negation might contribute to a process of determination and self-determination: it is not a radical bringing to be. Such negative work cannot have unqualified applicability. If it has a qualified applicability, it is with respect to a becoming, or a self-becoming. But both of these presuppose more primordially the being there of beings: coming to be is prior to becoming; being given to be is more original than self-becoming or self-determination.[14]

---

[14] On the givenness of creation, see my remarks in "Surplus Immediacy: The Defect(ion) of Hegel's Concept," in *Philosophy and Culture: Essays in Honor of Donald Philip Verene*, ed. Glenn Magee (Charlottesville: Philosophy Documentation Center, 2002), 107–27. Hegel tends to reduce immediacy to mere "fact," which then he claims philosophy must raise to the level of self-mediating necessity. He does not

If there is not this prior affirmation of being given to be, and indeed of the goodness and marvel and beauty of this being given to be, the idea of sabbatical thinking makes little sense. As ontologically coming to be is presupposed by becoming, sabbatical thinking is presupposed by thinking as negative work. Hegel has no resources to think this priority. His thinking takes for granted an agonistic, polemical sense of being—perhaps most famously expressed in the master-slave dialectic, as we saw, but not only there. True, Hegel wants to surpass this war or *Kampf zum Tode*, and achieve a reconciled mutuality beyond *Kampf*. Can the "peace" thereby secured be a genuine sabbatical peace? I cannot see how it could be, since neither in the beginning nor in the end is the fuller sense of the amen to being fittingly effective in his way of thinking.

There is no way to transcend war purely in the terms of war itself, no way to transcend *Kampf* in terms of *Kampf* alone, even granting that war might have a kind of dialectical intelligibility. In Hegelian work, and its dialectical *Kampf*, we may well secure a kind of peace, but it will finally be a simulacrum of the great peace. It will be a balance of powers rather than a released love that is beyond itself in community, at peace with the neighbor and itself, with creation and with God. The word "reconciliation" might always be on Hegelian lips, but there are counterfeit reconciliations that look almost exactly like the true thing—but something crucial is missing, and we hesitate to credit the claim. Missing is the "It is good" in the beginning that qualifies all derived development that comes in the second place, and that points beyond self-discordance to an achieved or to-be-achieved peace.

---

fittingly grant the most elemental immediacy: *the givenness of creation*. What is as creation, as being granted, is taken for granted. In truth, what is taken for granted is, in its being granted. This is one reason I speak of a primal *passio essendi*, or ontological patience of being in the given receiving of being at all. This signals an "It is" entirely different to Hegel's mere fact of indigent being. That beings are at all, given to be and not nothing—this is an ultimate immediacy in that without it nothing finite, or nothing within finitude, could mediate its being there at all. For this *being there at all* is presupposed by all such mediations, and all finite intermediations are made possible by it. "Creation" is an immediate ontological intermediation that brings being to be, enabling the finite between to be, and possibilizing its plurivocal promise. Its giving to be is presupposed by all intermediations *within* the *metaxu* of the finite given world. On Hegel and creation more fully, and especially in connection with the Jewish sense of divine transcendence, see *Hegel's God*, chapter 5.

the family and its meal (I mean this not only in a Jewish sense). Fast food overtakes the slower leisure of the family meal. Everything is rushed.

One works and works and works, one throws oneself into this task, that task, one loses oneself in work. These impressive expenditures of our energies often betray our flight from ourselves. We are evasive of life in our relentlessly busy lives. Inevitably, we are alarmed at the emptiness that becomes apparent when we pause. The rush dies down and disquietude is wakened. Work is an anesthesia, but it wears off when we have nothing to do. We make ourselves important by making ourselves useful, but we are on guard against any porosity that exposes us to intimations of mortality, or even a stray delight that might arrest us. Work binds us in a busy bewitchment, but come the time of weariness when I should rest, I cannot sit still, I must be doing something, anything. I cannot delight in things other than myself, or in myself, for I have become a stranger to the porosity of festivity.

The weekend—secular substitute for the Sabbath: I am enjoined to enjoy myself but I am wretched. At loose ends, and suddenly without provocation I am picking a fight with my neighbor. Instead of peace, there is impotence to enjoy the elemental good of the "to be." It is revealing that holidays can prove to be times of violence, exposing the despairs that everyday work keeps secret. This can be at its most drastic in societies where the utilitarian spirit is most revered. If instrumental work is king, there is no king, only servants, though then again there are no servants, for nothing finally is being served. Everything becomes a means to an end, even the Sabbath become the weekend, and there is no intrinsic worth to the work, or indeed to the elemental good of the "to be," nor is there joy in that good, for there is no profit in doing nothing. Even here there will be profit to be made: voilà the leisure industry!—an impossible conjunction of opposites. Not forced labor, but forced leisure! What peace is there in that?

Fortunately, we can be saved by the promise of work, and in it the taste of a different peace can be communicated. Think of works of art: these are creations impossible without something of the artist's exposure to the porosity of being in its original promise. The gift of art is a kind of peace: awakened peace, that is, delight. Schopenhauer, recall, knew something of this peace. Nietzsche, one surmises, despite the posturings against peace, knew more of the delight.

This taste of peace is offered, with ampler broadcast, in what we call the works of love. These works are beyond serviceable disposability and are living reminders of the promise of the "It is good." Of course, there are many different kinds of work, forced labor at one extreme, works of love at the other. The promise of released freedom is at work in all, and never entirely dead. It is brought closer to extinction the closer we move to forced labor. It is the more self-transcending the closer we move to works of love. Most work is somewhere in between. Hegel's dialectic of master and slave suggests there is a freeing and reversal even in forced labor, but, as with all such dialectical accounts, the dominance of the doublet "active/passive" does not have enough finesse for the *passio essendi*, and we cannot discern the subtler releases which transcend this doublet. This is especially true with works that are enacted with some presentiment of a transcendence more ultimate than human self-transcendence. Something of this is communicated in works of love. This is also true of works of art. All ethical work is finally a work of love. This work of love can work in any kind of work, even in forced labor. The work of love transforms all work, frees it into a different dimension. The work of love is sabbatical.

So we are brought through work to the boundary of the religious. One thinks of the peace in the old saying: to work is to pray, *laborare est orare*. We need not work ourselves up on the stage of world-history. Incognito, this is work as creative contribution to the agape of being; work as vocation; work that wills to do as the divine would will. This work is acutely attentive to the thereness of things and others as gifts of the origin. It seeks to mitigate the negation on being, the despite, the "in spite of," involved in much work. It works out an ethics of generosity, freeing human energies toward the goodness of things and others. This work is a communication that renders thanks. It takes time with the perfection of the work. There is time because it is given, and there is not more time because one rushes and finishes the task shoddily. To be grateful for the time given is to make one's consent—in consent to the needed work.

To be able to take time, to take it gratefully, means that one must be at peace with oneself and with being in a manner that exceeds one's own self-determination. One must already live in the gift of peace, or be in the porosity of being that communicates it. One might say then that to live sabbatically would be to *live unweaponed*. The Sunday of life recreates the original porosity between God and human community. In one regard, this might be like a death to the workaday world. And yet there is freer life in this death. There is nothing we can do, nothing we are to do; except to take joy in the gift of being, and to live divine praise. This is to be blessed. Work becomes prayer. Prayer is not now the impotence of work, that is, impotence for which nothing anymore works. Prayer is the empowering apotheosis of powerlessness. In a way, it is at the edge of our power, and indeed a kind of powerlessness; but this is a powerlessness that frees a more ultimate porosity.

To be unweaponed: one will not protect oneself, for there is a radical exposure here, and in this also a suffering, even death of finitude securing itself for itself. One thinks of the exposure of Job. He endured the extremity of suffering, he was a good man, yet he was patient to both evil and God. At the end, his amen is a confession and acceptance of nakedness, and a blessing of this nakedness in his consent to what is hyperbolically beyond his determination—the voice in the whirlwind. Naked I came into being, naked I go out; the Lord gives, the Lord takes; blessed be God forever. This is a sabbatical prayer—a faith in sabbatical being beyond the night of exposure. Sabbatical prayer can come in extreme suffering; in the extremity of the *passio essendi*, beyond the *conatus essendi*.

My sense is that some of the philosophers previously invoked—Descartes, Kant, and Hegel, to name just these—are given to covering over this nakedness. The last especially preaches speculatively against nakedness and every beyond, and the system weaves its conceptual clothes to cover our naked frailties. Being naked is to be unweaponed. Francis of Assisi—homeless, possessionless: but naked and singing and on fire. There is a shame-less peace. Being religious is a being naked. This nakedness cannot be deconstructed. It has no speculative *Aufhebung*. There is no systematic knowing that can cover this nakedness, no deconstruction that can uncover it. And yet the philosopher can discover nakedness; and go out, unhoused and at home.

Is There a Sabbath for Thought? Peace Between Philosophy and Religion

Where does this leave our question: Is there a Sabbath for thought? Is there a peace between philosophy and religion? I mean not only a peace addressed to their difference, but marking something of their familial intimacy. Again you will press the opposite, and protest anew that the practice of philosophical thought is essentially agonistic. We philosophers are concerned with argument: argument is contention, that is, offense and defense, contestation and winning. The stronger argument overcomes the weaker, let the sophists essay to present the weaker as the stronger. The strong shall be first, the weak shall be last. This is war. A powerful image of this: Plato's dramatization of the clash between Socrates and Thrasymachus at the beginning of the *Republic*. This is *eris*, indeed a very violent strife, and not only a war of thoughts but of thinkers facing each other down in the vehement strength of oppugnancy. Why then preach of peace, since this is just what we cannot have here, given the nature of the philosophical agon itself. More, philosophers do not pick fights solely with antagonists. Failing provocation from elsewhere, or incitement, the philosopher picks a *quarrel with himself*. Is not this the very core of philosophy, the quarrel of thinking with itself?

And yet, what is the meaning of disagreement here? Suppose that this quarrel of thinking with itself, rightly noted, is one act in the dialogue of the soul with itself, as Plato defines thought. This dialogue is not only with oneself, as we see clearly from the nature of dialogue itself. Dialogue dramatizes thinking. Dialogue with oneself pluralizes the voices sounded in the immanence of one's own thinking. But there is a pluralization of voices that is not only immanent to one's thinking, since this plurivocity places one's thinking outside of itself in relation to others and to being as other. We see this with the Platonic dialogue, where disagreement clearly cannot be exhausted by the terms of agonistic strife. If we reflect on what disagreement betokens in relation to what it calls forth, namely conversation, sometimes verging on verbal violence, we see that argument moves toward some possible agreement beyond agon. Something of the promise of agreement, and peace, is already given from the outset. This is not only a telos attained at the end but a promise that makes possible the movement itself toward a more explicitly realized peace. I mean that talking and communication are themselves made possible by the promise of a concurrence or concord already at work. The promise stirs even in words at war with each other. The working of a promise is not easy to pin down, but without that promise at work there would be no point to talking. There would be no talking at all, for *talking is itself that promise*. When we talk we are not fighting, though our words be fighting. No agon can be disjoined from the promise of peace. Even if you conceived of an agon that would utterly nihilate the opponent, the peace at stake turns out to be the peace of death, the peace of nothing. But this is to eviscerate the meaning of peace—and indeed of any agon.

The war of words is itself possible only on the basis of a peace promised by the spirit of truthfulness in which agonistic thought, argument itself, participates. Agonistic argument may be eristic, but it cannot be only that. There is always also the eros for truth, and the truthful eros of the philosopher seeking to be true to what is true. The eros of truthfulness reveals a being true beyond eristic contestation. We might connect the agon of philosophy with erotic sovereignty, nevertheless even here a peace-ful playfulness is possible, one that participates in a festivity of being that is agapeic in promise. The impulse to play of agonistic thought need not be antagonistic to peace. Benignity can be at work in playful configurations of polemos. The promise of the sacred is in play. Eros, as we know, is an in-between, a *metaxu*: we do not just lack the truth for which we must fight; we are with the truth, truth is with us possibilizing our seeking of it with its promise (see *Meno*). The seeking is not a mere lack but is endowed with a confidence it cannot explain through itself alone. (In saying "confidence" I draw on the reserves in the words *confides*.) The seeking is made possible, and made possible as con-fident, by the priority of the promise.

This promise is agapeic, I think, for the eros of the philosopher is not just a *penia*. There is, as I suggested, a poverty of philosophy, but this is intimately connected with the porosity of mindfulness itself. The poverty of philosophy is openness to, porosity to the promise of an agapeic peace. If there is a war of words, this is for the sake of the peace of truth. There are truths and a truthfulness that cause one to lose one's peace, of course, but that is not the last word on peace. For this loss of peace is suffered as the unacceptability of a false or counterfeit peace, not as an irreparable strike against peace as such.

Recall the deprivation of peace known by thinkers like Pascal, or the sleeplessness that exceeds the sleep of finitude, and the self-contentments of rationalistic philosophers. Yet there is still a promise of peace more primal than war that endows our hyperbolic seeking, and for the sake of which we fight when the promise of truthfulness is put under risk, or desecrated. We know we must be truthful to this hyperbolic sleeplessness or lack of peace in order merely to be true, to be faithful to the promise of this more original peace. Whether it be the quarrel of thinking with itself, or the dialogue of the soul with itself or with others, it is this peace that solicits guardianship. Offense is defense, but defense of a peace of being that is neither offensive nor defensive, since it is finally agapeic. It comes in a giving beyond both offense and defense. That is, it comes from a goodness that gives the allowance of radical freedom, including the freedom to offend against truthfulness, or to be offensive against goodness. For there are those who tell harsh truths, but they do not tell these truths in reverence for the spirit of truthfulness, but to inflict hurt, to relish the darkness, and to gloat over the discomfiture of more reverent souls. Sometimes the quarrel of thought with what is other to itself can conceal a hatred of the divine as other because it offends the claims of thinking to be absolutely self-determining.

If we have lost finesse for the agape of astonishment, this understanding of an agapeic peace will itself seem offensive. Philosophy will tend predominantly to emphasize its commitment to perplexity, as well as doubt and curiosity. Then we cannot quite see thought as anything other than a contesting and a being contested, or a form of offense or going to war. All of this will be expressed in a high-minded way: war with our own ignorance, or with the deceits of false authority, or with mistaken beliefs, or with the very tradition of philosophy itself, or, at the extreme, an agon with being itself as unintelligible or even hostile to us. Genuine questions can be put in these forms of contestation; but the last contestation itself calls out for contestation. For if we follow this through to the end, we are pointed toward either the loss or denial of the promise of peace, with an accompanying reconfiguration of our entire understanding of what it means to think. Were we to take up residence in this reconfiguration, we would tend to take it as our presupposition or as self-evident, and everything else will be seen in its light. The predilection to think in such terms would take the form of a "postulatory agonism," not unlike what before I called a "postulatory finitism." ("Predilection" is an interestingly odd word in this context, since it refers us to what one favors, or loves: odd, in that what one loves here is not love.)

To contest such a "postulatory agonism"—to contest in the name of the silenced peace—would entail, in my view, an entirely other kind of thinking, which cannot be contained within this reconfiguration itself. Moreover, if this reconfiguration is as extensive as an historical epoch, the task facing a thinker who wants to think otherwise is formidable. If nothing else—and if that promise of peace cannot be entirely lost, short of the loss also of the promise of thinking, and its most primal confidence—we are made to ask: What if we think of the advent of thinking differently? How are we to think of this? Will not what arrives for thought also appear very differently?

Here are some suggestions. If the origins of philosophy intimate a mysterious celebrating peace, and point beyond war to a renewed condition of peace, we will find it hard to trust in such peace if we take our sights exhaustively from agonistic immanence. There can be a kind of immanent peace in the balance of powers and beings, all defined in a network of relations in which none is what it is without the others. This network is also inherently unstable, and given to fall into war. If we dream of peace, we may have to ask if there is something more ultimate or transcendent to this conditional peace of holistic immanence. It seems to me that it is the great figures of religion, more than the philosophers, who call us to a peace more primal than the balance of immanent powers. One thinks of the Buddha, and, in our time, Gandhi. Jesus and Francis call us to a peace absolutely original: his invocation "Peace be with you" carried forward the call of the first peace — as making possible all being; as absolutely transcendent, in respect to being hyperbolic to all the compromised peaces of our finite condition; and yet as intimately immanent and "with" us, incarnated in the very invocation of peace itself. These figures call us to a peace beyond philosophy, but in listening to that call we are made to consider whether philosophical thinking can also participate in sabbatical being.

Some religious people, hostile to philosophy, will reject this as impossible. They will despise philosophy for its threadbare poverty of thought where the ultimate questions are at stake. One mourns that some practices of philosophy justify all too well this rejection. Many philosophers, in turn, may match this rejection by claiming such peace to be incredible. Even if they are not content with the platitudes of professorial badinage (sound ideas must "pass muster," or survive in the "cut and thrust" of argument), they will say that truth demands we remain faithful to the play of war and relative peace in immanence itself. What fidelity is this? And in the name of what is this fidelity made intelligible? Not in terms of finite thought itself, for finite thought justifies itself in terms of this fidelity. The fidelity points to a source of trust very hard to finitize. There is something hyperbolic to this fidelity, its solicitation, its exigencies, and to what it promises were we to remain true. A different way to put the issue would be: Are there wars in immanence that themselves suggest something in excess of immanence, if there is to be any peace at all?

Consider unspeakable evils that seem hyperbolic, mockingly monstrous, to the suggestion of a Sabbath for thought. There are evils that so torture one that, were one to think on them, the mind might well suffer blackout. No possibility of peace would naturally suggest itself, indeed the human spirit might well be hollowed out by a despair we ourselves cannot heal. One finds oneself living posthumously to such evil. The natural peace of the person and its immanent composure is shattered. For instance, Francis of Assisi traveled to the Holy Land to meet the Saracens on a mission of peace that failed, he touchingly tried to persuade to Christianity al-Kamil, sultan of Egypt, and he was shocked at the evils at the siege of Damietta, done by Christians no less than Muslims. It is said he came back a changed man. He was exposed to the monstrous power of war to unleash infernal nihilation, even in those claiming allegiance to the one God of all. Yet at the last, he added to his Canticle of Brother Sun his verse of divine praise honoring sister death.

Such monstrous evil poses a perplexity that seems unanswerable in immanent terms. We are not dealing with a finite problem but a tormenting enigma in the dimension of the hyperbolic. If such hyperbolic evil is to be answered, can it only be answered by good proportionately hyperbolic, that is, disproportionately hyperbolic? This would mean: if there is peace beyond the terms of holistic immanence, it points us to the notion of blessing to counter curse, saving to counter perdition. "Redemption" is a religious name for this hyperbolic peace.

Recall what earlier I said about the different sleeps of finitude. They offer a false or premature peace, which evades the hyperboles of being that wake us to something exceeding the terms of immanent finitude. We sleep in common sense and take things for granted. Philosophy may claim to wake us from this peace by making war on thoughtlessness. Philosophy believes it wakes up from the false peace, but does it give us true peace? Or is it that it falls into a second sleep when it thinks it answers everything in terms of holistic immanence? It falls asleep in its claim to be awake; its being awake is its second false sleep that protects it rationally from the exceeding hyperboles of being.

What of a further awakening? Suppose being religious is the undergoing of this awakening. A great struggle may sometimes be needed to wake beyond the second sleep and counterfeit peace. This third awakening is more truly in the dimension of the hyperbolic, and while it entails the greatest struggle, it exceeds war and struggle in terms of the primal peace and the last peace beyond which there is no surpassing. This is the religious peace that passes all understanding. The further awakening from the sleep of finitude surpasses finitude thus.

Thus to view life sabbatically is not to view it as if there is nothing to be done. If the Sabbath is a holiday of rest, the rest is entirely energizing. It is not a question of going to sleep, but the opposite: a day of being awake. The crucial question is if we can achieve this awakening through our own powers alone. Do we wake ourselves, or are we awakened? If there are different ways of being asleep, there are different awakenings. Suppose philosophy wakes us from everyday sleep—but if thinking is predominantly doubt and work, what then is the awakening? Are we not more likely to wake to what is there, said to be void of any charge of value: wakening not from love and to love, but to being as first indifferently there, and then, in the long run, as hostile to us, and hence over against us, and hence awakening us into the posture of war again? This is tempting if we understand thinking in terms of reason's own autonomous self-determination. What if this awakening is, in fact, a new sleep, a strange sleep that now claims to rationally justify itself as an awakening? How awaken from wakefulness?

I believe the relation between philosophy and being religious is again at issue. Something about being religious awakens us from the sleep of autonomous reason, satisfied with itself. There is no Sabbath for autonomous reason satisfied with itself; for it congratulates itself; it cannot say "It is good." For it is *itself* that is affirmed, not the otherness of creation as good. If there is to be a sabbatical for philosophical thought, it will have to be other than self-determining reason. We will have to consider a heteronomous reason that will grant its own derivation from what it cannot conceptually master, and that it can neither command, for it finds itself in the position of a recipient in relation to this more ultimate origin. "Heteronomous" here need imply no diminution of freedom. To the contrary, what is at stake is more like an elevation, in a sense analogous to the manner in which worship can be said to be an elevation. This is not a self-elevation, but a being raised or released above oneself, through a superior power that communicates from the dimension of height, asymmetrical to horizontal finitude.

This suggestion will also be hard to stomach for philosophy marked by "postulatory finitism," even when it is critical of the pretensions of autonomous reason. We may now have fallen into a new sleep of "postulatory agonism." If a "postulatory agonism" has reconfigured the ethos of the between as a site of strife beyond which there is no appeal; and if this "postulatory agonism" has fallen from mind in its power to frame all mindfulness on this site and about this site; then all our thinking will be mustered along the lines of a struggle of being, and not even the possibility of a more primal peace will arise for thinking. There is indeed a struggle to be, but what restrains us from genuflecting philosophically before this as a surd that is ultimately absurd? I do not see how it helps to claim simply that philosophy must defy that absurdity. Defy in the name of what? The truth of being? But that is supposed to be strife. In terms of intelligibility? But the stability of intelligibility is but the equivocal surface of the unintelligible, the absurdity itself. The good of being? But on the terms of "postulatory agonism" this cannot be ultimate. In the name of itself? But this defiance is itself a concretion of the strife of being in the life of mind. By appealing to the name of its own defiance of absurdity, it only hides its own indirect genuflection to the ultimate absurdity of it all.

Defiant philosophizing is often a deconstructed version of autonomous reason, appearing when reason loses confidence in its own autonomy—but again without any Sabbath. Once more I believe the relation between philosophy and religion is at issue. Something about being religious startles the more naked soul with intimations of a peace that, so to say, is both too low and too high to be even registered on the radar of "postulatory agonism" or "postulatory finitism." One might say a genuflection of reverence is needed, but it is both too low and too high for the defiance of strife that is the obeisance of strife.

Something other is suggested that neither autonomous reason nor defiant philosophizing will find it easy to credit: something like a familial likeness of thinking and praying. Perhaps it is prayer that is the Sabbath of thinking: its fulfillment and the highest lucidity of its peace. Is prayer what happens when thought wakes up to itself, beyond its own work; waking not just to itself, but being awoken to its source and purpose in the ultimate power beyond itself; its release from itself as work; its renewal of mindful porosity to the source(s) of truthfulness; its new nakedness, ever green and ripe; its resurrection to itself as praise of the divine?

Perhaps this is what the peace of sabbatical being and thinking offers: ease more than dis-ease; release beyond oneself to the goodness of creation; release above oneself in presentiment of the first and ultimate God. Far from being "quietist," this release calls forth an ethical-religious service of the other, indeed also of oneself, in the sense implied by the two great commandments: love of God first, and then of one's neighbor as oneself. We are to love ourselves too—the Sabbath is not a day of self-hatred. This service is an agapeic service. This is not the servility of the slaves that Hegel unfairly sees in the Jewish Sabbath. It is not the "being above" of the sovereigns. It is a service beyond servility and sovereignty. It is a service of generosity likened to the generosity spoken at the first in the "It is good." There is the promise of goodness in this first Amen, for it gives a gift with the promise of its own fulfilling good. So in our case, the Amen is a calling: calling for an enactment in a way of life that makes its own endowed good freely available for others.

There is no evasion of the ties of finite life that bind us, for one cannot think of peace without social peace in the most concrete sense: being in community with others, where the commons of a life of the good, or a good life, is enabled. Here there can be counterfeits of peace: for instance, a very efficient order that allows the togetherness of many, but devoid of justice, not to mention love. True social peace cannot be abstracted from the ethical-religious peace of the intimate universal. True peace, in whatever community, is a secret participation in the great Amen.

Holiday Thought

If there is a sabbatical for thought, would it have something to do with holiness—with holiday? A holiday for thought? Thinkers like Wittgenstein would act as if we asked them to suck lemons. Like Kant, they want work from philosophy, not play. Wittgenstein does not like it when language or philosophy "goes on a holiday," for then it seems to do no "work." It does not earn its way. But why is "work" more ultimate than "holiday"? Perhaps Wittgenstein did not know how to take things easy. Is there not an ease infinitely more profound, and rarer than any self-justifying seriousness? Ease, in which the heart is light, and mindfulness sees so lucidly it hardly knows it sees. This being at ease: at home with an unfettered porosity, unknowingly buoyant in the intimate universal. Wittgenstein was uneasy, he wanted to be earnest and to work. But holidays are graced times. Sabbatical being and thought have to do with what comes as a godsend. And is it not right to say that, in a way, philosophy has no work? It is a vocation, not a profession or career path. One might be paid to be a professor; no one pays one to be a philosopher. This vocation is for free.

Sometimes the best thoughts come when one is not *trying* to think. One is at ease, and a thought *strikes one*: it comes to one, as if from nowhere. The arrival of the thought frees one. And yet its *coming* to one strikes one most *intimately*. Was it something like this that Wittgenstein sought: to be beyond the torture of thought, and in a peace that perhaps might allow a different kind of thought to come. Thought coming to one: this is a communication to the *passio essendi*. When one tries too hard to think, the *conatus essendi* has taken over. While much thought can be worked up that way, it is not quite in the same order as those striking communications of thoughts that come to one—as if gifts from the source. Being at peace: a different porosity wherein something comes up in one, passes through one, transforms one, as a kind of medium of truth—like the ultimate porosity of the gifted happening of praying. The amen to being is a godsend confided to thought.

We are not inured to mourning. It is very hard to contemplate peace, to be a peacemaker, when one has been attacked, sometimes unjustly. The fragility of our finite form of being means we are never entirely free from worry about attack. We are afraid to be exposed. Although we are heartened in the intimate universal, we also live in dread. We are never absolutely porous. We do not first *make* peace. Peace *comes* to us. We must not get in the way. We must make way. Peace arrives. From this point of view, God is the only peacemaker. Only God continues to see that "It is good," even when evil makes war on the peace of original creation. God's continual gift of peace is the perpetual re-creation of the world.

Index

Perspectives in
Continental Philosophy Series

John D. Caputo, series editor

1. John D. Caputo, ed., *Deconstruction in a Nutshell: A Conversation with Jacques Derrida.*
2. Michael Strawser, *Both / And: Reading Kierkegaard—From Irony to Edification.*
3. Michael D. Barber, *Ethical Hermeneutics: Rationality in Enrique Dussel's Philosophy of Liberation.*
4. James H. Olthuis, ed., *Knowing* Other-*wise: Philosophy at the Threshold of Spirituality.*
5. James Swindal, *Reflection Revisited: Jürgen Habermas's Discursive Theory of Truth.*
6. Richard Kearney, *Poetics of Imagining: Modern and Postmodern.* Second edition.
7. Thomas W. Busch, *Circulating Being: From Embodiment to Incorporation—Essays on Late Existentialism.*
8. Edith Wyschogrod, *Emmanuel Levinas: The Problem of Ethical Metaphysics.* Second edition.
9. Francis J. Ambrosio, ed., *The Question of Christian Philosophy Today.*
10. Jeffrey Bloechl, ed., *The Face of the Other and the Trace of God: Essays on the Philosophy of Emmanuel Levinas.*
11. Ilse N. Bulhof and Laurens ten Kate, eds., *Flight of the Gods: Philosophical Perspectives on Negative Theology.*
12. Trish Glazebrook, *Heidegger's Philosophy of Science.*
13. Kevin Hart, *The Trespass of the Sign: Deconstruction, Theology, and Philosophy.*

14. Mark C. Taylor, *Journeys to Selfhood: Hegel and Kierkegaard*. Second edition.

15. Dominique Janicaud, Jean-François Courtine, Jean-Louis Chrétien, Michel Henry, Jean-Luc Marion, and Paul Ricœur, *Phenomenology and the "Theological Turn": The French Debate*.

16. Karl Jaspers, *The Question of German Guilt*. Introduction by Joseph W. Koterski, S.J.

17. Jean-Luc Marion, *The Idol and Distance: Five Studies*. Translated with an introduction by Thomas A. Carlson.

18. Jeffrey Dudiak, *The Intrigue of Ethics: A Reading of the Idea of Discourse in the Thought of Emmanuel Levinas*.

19. Robyn Horner, *Rethinking God As Gift: Marion, Derrida, and the Limits of Phenomenology*.

20. Mark Dooley, *The Politics of Exodus: Søren Kierkegaard's Ethics of Responsibility*.

21. Merold Westphal, *Toward a Postmodern Christian Faith: Overcoming Onto-Theology*.

22. Edith Wyschogrod, Jean-Joseph Goux, and Eric Boynton, eds., *The Enigma of Gift and Sacrifice*.

23. Stanislas Breton, *The Word and the Cross*. Translated with an introduction by Jacquelyn Porter.

24. Jean-Luc Marion, *Prolegomena to Charity*. Translated by Stephen E. Lewis.

25. Peter H. Spader, *Scheler's Ethical Personalism: Its Logic, Development, and Promise*.

26. Jean-Louis Chrétien, *The Unforgettable and the Unhoped For*. Translated by Jeffrey Bloechl.

27. Don Cupitt, *Is Nothing Sacred? The Non-Realist Philosophy of Religion: Selected Essays*.

28. Jean-Luc Marion, *In Excess: Studies of Saturated Phenomena*. Translated by Robyn Horner and Vincent Berraud.

29. Phillip Goodchild, *Rethinking Philosophy of Religion: Approaches from Continental Philosophy*.

30. William J. Richardson, S.J., *Heidegger: Through Phenomenology to Thought*.

31. Jeffrey Andrew Barash, *Martin Heidegger and the Problem of Historical Meaning*.

32. Jean-Louis Chrétien, *Hand to Hand: Listening to the Work of Art*. Translated by Stephen E. Lewis.

33. Jean-Louis Chrétien, *The Call and the Response*. Translated with an introduction by Anne Davenport.

34. D. C. Schindler, *Hans Urs von Balthasar and the Dramatic Structure of Truth: A Philosophical Investigation*.

35. Julian Wolfreys, ed., *Thinking Difference: Critics in Conversation*.

36. Allen Scult, *Being Jewish / Reading Heidegger: An Ontological Encounter.*

37. Richard Kearney, *Debates in Continental Philosophy: Conversations with Contemporary Thinkers.*

38. Jennifer Anna Gosetti-Ferencei, *Heidegger, Hölderlin, and the Subject of Poetic Language: Toward a New Poetics of Dasein.*

39. Jolita Pons, *Stealing a Gift: Kierkegaard's Pseudonyms and the Bible.*

40. Jean-Yves Lacoste, *Experience and the Absolute: Disputed Questions on the Humanity of Man.* Translated by Mark Raftery-Skehan.

41. Charles P. Bigger, *Between Chora and the Good: Metaphor's Metaphysical Neighborhood.*

42. Dominique Janicaud, *Phenomenology "Wide Open": After the French Debate.* Translated by Charles N. Cabral.

43. Ian Leask and Eoin Cassidy, eds. *Givenness and God: Questions of Jean-Luc Marion.*

44. Jacques Derrida, *Sovereignties in Question: The Poetics of Paul Celan.* Edited by Thomas Dutoit and Outi Pasanen.